P9-DXM-468

DATE DUE

The Poetic Avant-Garde

The Poetic Avant-Garde

The Groups of Borges, Auden, and Breton

BERET E. STRONG

Northwestern

University Press

Evanston

Illinois

Northwestern University Press
Evanston, Illinois 60208-4210

Copyright © 1997 by Northwestern University Press.
Published 1997. All rights reserved.
Printed in the United States of America
ISBN 0-8101-1508-5 (cloth)
ISBN 0-8101-1509-3 (paper)

Library of Congress Cataloging-in-Publication Data

Strong, Beret E., 1961–
The poetic avant-garde : the groups of Borges, Auden, and Breton /
Beret E. Strong.
p.   cm. — (Avant-garde & modernism studies)
Includes bibliographical references and index.
ISBN 0-8101 -1508-5 (alk. paper). — ISBN 0-8101-1509-3 (pbk. :
alk. paper)
1. Poetry, Modern—20th century—History and criticism.   2. Avant-
garde (Aesthetics)   3. Experimental poetry—History and criticism.
I. Title.   II. Series: Avant-garde and modernism studies.
PN1270.5.S77   1997
809.1′911—dc21   97-18785
                                                                         CIP

Contents

Acknowledgments

Many people helped this book take root and grow into its current form. Robert Scholes sparked my passion for the work of W. H. Auden and helped generate a number of the questions addressed in this book; Edward J. Ahearn and Michel-André Bossy offered valuable insights about ideological criticism and surrealism; and Julio Ortega helped me better understand Jorge Luis Borges. Ana Rosa Rapaport de Genijovich and I spent wonderful afternoons in Buenos Aires discussing the poems of the Argentine vanguardia and translating the early work of Borges and Oliverio Girondo. (Any translation errors, of course, are mine alone.) Ana María Barrenechea and Enrique Pezzoni were generous with their time and ideas, and lent materials not easily found outside the personal libraries of literary Buenos Aires. The librarians of the Facultad de Derecho at the Universidad de Buenos Aires, where a crumbling copy of *Sur* was housed, shared their office for weeks as I read the journal for the first time. Brown University provided financial support during the early years of this project. My students, especially those at Brown and the University of San Francisco, helped me to a better understanding of literary criticism and the institutions that both support and disturb writers and critics.

I thank Liane Strauss, Lucy Rodríguez, Ann Neelon, Peter Allen, Maren Monsen, Jeff Grainger, Jeffry and Barbara Diefendorf, Kare Strong, and Ron Barrineau for their help and support. I would also like to thank Susan Bielstein, Caitlin Wood, Lois Zamora, Betty Waterhouse, Ellen R. Feldman, and Susan Harris for their wonderful editorial assistance. I am grateful to Douglas H. Strong and Kristin Thygeson for their inspiration and encouragement, and to Ruth Lee Thygeson and Gertrude Strong, who taught me the value of good writing.

I dedicate this book to two people. Elizabeth S. Rosenfield, born the same year as Borges, inspired me to love literature and has with her consistently intelligent questions helped me hone arguments and use words with care. The deepest thanks go to my husband, John Tweedy, a critical reader of great skill who helped in every imaginable way from start to finish.

The primary function of poetry, as of all the arts, is to make us more aware of ourselves and the world around us.

—W. H. Auden

I. Elite "Fellowships of Discourse": The Argentine Vanguardia, the Auden Group, and the French Surrealists

Well over a century ago the military origin of the term "avant-garde" gave way to a new meaning, the cutting edge of artistic exploration and innovation. In 1845, Gabriel-Désiré Laverdant wrote in *De la mission de l'art et du rôle des artistes* (On the mission of art and the role of artists) that certain kinds of art are "the forerunner and the revealer" of the human species. Inspired by Romanticism and taking shape in the last decades of the nineteenth century in Continental Europe, the avant-garde has striven to be the agent of dramatic aesthetic and social change. The historical heyday of its groups and their artistic "isms" stretched from early in the twentieth century to the beginning of World War II. Once the province of groups of young artists, in a looser, more individualized form the avant-garde impulse continues to flourish in many parts of the world. Avant-gardism is a creative process rather than a product. Studying its concrete expressions—the product—illuminates the nature of the process, which remains changeable, surprisingly varied, and not entirely knowable.

We in the mainstream are unlikely to encounter the avant-garde's most radical past manifestations. If a group of James Joyces wrote in the eighteenth century alongside Dryden and Pope, it is conceivable that we would have no knowledge of their work today. Some texts by groups historically on the margins of the literary world, such as those by women and cultural, racial, or ethnic "minorities," are being rescued from oblivion, while many others are no longer extant. The situation of the pre–World War II canonized avant-garde is different. Because its movements were peopled with those who, historically speaking, had access to power and who were more likely than many to enter the literary canon—men of the middle and upper classes—the historical avant-garde is a *cas limite* for those studying canonized literature's capacity for social radicalism and aesthetic innovation. As such, its story is an important source of information about canonization and the forces behind it.

This book compares three poetic avant-garde groups active between the world wars: those surrounding Jorge Luis Borges, W. H. Auden, and André Breton. Traditionally, avant-garde writers have had such a tendency to gather together that dictionaries define the avant-garde in the plural. These three groups were composed of poets whose fame has endured and who became members of the historical avant-garde, by which I mean the well-known groups whose "avant-garde" relation to the literary establishment of their time has become part of literary history. This study grew out of my curiosity about the choices avant-garde movements made when their internal, society-altering goals collided with the forces of social and political change that swept through their societies in the 1920s and 1930s. I wondered how radical the avant-garde's goals really were and whether there were limits to its willingness to pursue forms of activism that might jeopardize a group's existence. I found that the interwar poetic avant-garde was both a symptom of art's and the artist's problems and a dynamic search for solutions to those problems; it was both symptom and attempted cure. That the groups discussed here worried about change even as they promoted themselves as its agent struck me as a sticky situation, one whose analysis would reveal the nature of their quests, their deeply held convictions, their limitations, and the inevitable hypocrisies of self-proclaimed seekers of a new order.

This book analyzes the Eurocentric and often surrealism-centric assumptions of major theories of the avant-garde. I reappraise conventional accounts of how these groups were formed and look at how the groups' aesthetic and social agendas and dilemmas played out over time, focusing on the disparity between their radical hopes and actual achievements. The pressures of tradition and the internal drive for consecration drove a wedge between word and deed, aspiration and actual behavior. The role of leaders both within each group and as liaisons between a group and its public is especially important, as this was an era when charismatic authority dominated in politics and the arts. This book also explores the inevitable failure of avant-garde movements to rise to the level of their own expectations, as well as the institutional and individual factors that led to their eventual demise.

One of the historical avant-garde's primary goals was to expand the poet's authority as aesthetic innovator and reconfigurer of the relationship between society and art. In its more radical form, as theorist Peter Bürger points out, the avant-garde hoped to destroy bourgeois society altogether, make poets into social leaders, and reconceive art so that it no longer functioned as a commodity. The avant-garde was caught between contradictory imperatives: a desire to be radically new in some way and a drive, whether weak or strong, to find an audience and to endure. The historical circumstances of the group surrounding Jorge Luis Borges caused its members to choose discursive rebellion and to leave most politically activist forms of rebellion to others, while the groups of W. H. Auden and André Breton were less reluctant to become politically engaged. Movements between the world wars were quick to battle the literary or social status quo, but even the most radical among them stopped short of trying to destroy the things that enabled them to exist. As we will see, not even the Dadaists/surrealists lived up to the wild, often revolutionary desires that drove them. Though the avant-garde's goals tended to be considerably beyond its means, self-extinction was not the aesthetic pleasure avant-garde theorists have made it out to be. A selective conservatism, an aspect of the avant-garde often overlooked in critical accounts of the "radical" avant-garde, was partly responsible for the failure to achieve society-altering goals that could well have brought about the rapid demise of these movements. While the avant-garde's raison d'être, ironically, was the disruption of the status quo, such disruption was strategic and, in spite of the myth of avant-garde "spontaneity" in most things, was often a carefully considered response to the feeling that art and the artist were endangered.

The personal mythologies of individual avant-garde movements have found their way into criticism and theory, where they are often presented as truth. Analysis of the avant-garde's frequent ironic disparities between word and deed shows that critics' excessive willingness to take the avant-garde's language at face value has led many to misapprehend the object of their study. Some perceive radicalism where there is merely a claim to it. Critical assumptions made about the avant-garde are often a product of what we can call the Romantic view of the avant-garde, a reflection of the avant-garde's own passionate habit of self-mythologizing. When critics naturalize the avant-garde's tendency to engage in idealizing group mythologies, they fail to acknowledge fully the complexity of the avant-garde's survival strategies in a world to which it is hostile. This book takes as a premise that no matter what the groups say about themselves, they are more a product of their historical moment and circumstances than of the models from which they may have borrowed.

While a definition of the avant-garde that emphasizes only its most radical—usually Continental—instances is especially relevant to mapping the limits of rebellious action open to writers, alone it does not account for the complex nature of avant-gardism. It does not, for example, explore the need for various forms of conservatism. Given the many contradictions inherent in avant-gardism and the phenomenon's capacity for self-mutation and international migration, it is difficult to arrive at a comprehensive definition of the avant-garde. We may more easily list its traits; it is, for example, "not so much proletarian as proletarianizing" (see Poggioli 1968, 87). The historical avant-garde is well described as a tendency among writers to form communities—fellowships of discourse—from which to explore the possibilities of aesthetic innovation and transfiguring social activism open to writers. I propose a broad definition that captures the avant-garde's unique nature: it is a study in ambivalence and contradictions that inhabits the space between its antibourgeois ideals, its largely traditional roots, and its need to survive. It is useful to see it as an *instrumental* phenomenon: born of a reaction to a set of frustrations, needs, and fears, it is a problem-solving tool for groups of artists.

In order to be considered for this study, poets had to have banded together and presented themselves as a group. It wasn't essential that the poets or their critics identify their group as an avant-garde movement but that the group have an aesthetic and/or social agenda and make use of at least some of the avant-garde's modes of self-expression, among them manifestos or declarations of group purpose; small journals, usually their own; avant-garde "spectacles" or unorthodox attention-getting tactics; book publishing; and interaction with the mainstream press. Certainly this list sounds very traditional today, not a schema to which we would expect a contemporary avant-garde movement to adhere. However, the historical avant-garde was a fairly young phenomenon at the end of World War I. Its main goal was to take the existing relationships among writer, publishing industry, critics, and the public, and deform them at least a little, preferably a lot, so as to promote itself and renovate poetry and preferably the social order as well.

This work provides a road map to a couple of the less-frequented territories visited by the avant-garde impulse, as well as to the most-frequented. I set out to choose three very different groups in order to explore the range of manifestations of avant-gardism in the interwar era: The French Dadaists/surrealists serve as a sort of control group representing the radical (or, otherwise put, the critic's "traditional") avant-garde. The Auden poets were considered avant-garde during the heavily politicized 1930s but for intriguing reasons are no longer considered so. The Argentine vanguardia was a very conservative movement influenced both by Continental movements of the 1920s and by Argentina's rising national literary tradition, yet it continues to bear the "avant-garde" label today. I shall examine the avant-garde as it is manifested in a radical Continental case, an Anglo-American case, and a postcolonial case. The groups of Borges, Auden, and Breton permit a comparison of different national circumstances on two continents and facilitate reevaluation of the main critical and theoretical conceptions of the avant-garde, some of which have become critical truisms.

Numerous groups worthy of comparative inquiry were omitted from this study. Futurism could have been selected as the Continental case, but it played a far weaker role in the theory of the avant-garde than surrealism. The French surrealists are essential to a consideration of critical conceptions of the avant-garde. The Auden poets are somewhat more problematic because there has been so much written about them in recent decades, so little of which identifies them as avant-garde. Though avant-gardism is not frequently associated with the independent, Romantic traditions of Britain, analogues to the behavior and rhetoric of Continental groups are sometimes apparent in British movements. This is the case of the Auden poets, who have the added advantage to the comparatist of being active participants in the European political dramas of the 1930s. The fact that the Auden group was considered avant-garde when it was active but was later not considered so was an invitation to try to find out why the poets have been "declassified." We shall see that the erasure of the label was a reaction to what poets and critics considered an embarrassing failure. The Auden poets, however, merit the avant-garde label more than the Argentine vanguardia, whose claim to membership in the greater avant-garde clan has not to my knowledge been disputed.

I turned to Latin America for my third case in order to learn what happens when the imperatives of Western national and international literary impulses converge. Do they coalesce or collide? In the case of the Argentine poets, there is a striking disparity between word and deed, and between poems and ideological rhetoric. An important reason for choosing the Argentine vanguardia from among other Latin American avant-garde movements was its conservatism. The willingness of critics to apply the avant-garde label to the Argentine vanguardia illustrates the ability of self-consciously constituted groups to fashion their own public identities. If a group insists on wearing borrowed clothes, putting them on backward but repeating often enough "Look at what I'm wearing," those clothes are soon its own, becoming associated with a range of ideas and values to which the group may only partially subscribe. The Argentine vanguardia is an interesting illustration of this sometimes schizophrenic combination of borrowing while asserting independence, and it provides an important contrast to surrealism. Although the movement's rhetoric and group statements suggest that it was derived from Continental models, it was in important ways independent in its platform.

I believe that an exploration of this independence reveals more about avant-gardism than the study of a more obviously "avant-garde," but more obviously derivative movement, such as Creationism, founded by Chilean poet Vicente Huidobro.[1] He and his compatriots would provide an interesting comparison with the surrealists or with the Argentine vanguardia poet Oliverio Girondo, but I found them too heavily influenced by the Continental avant-garde to be as interesting as the Argentine vanguardia, whose responsiveness to *Argentine* circumstances dominated from the movement's inception. Borges's borrowings from the Continent were a weak brew indeed, especially when compared to those of Huidobro. The aesthetically innovative and socially active Peruvian avant-garde poet César Vallejo[2] represents another road not taken. Though Vallejo is a fascinating representative of the radical Latin American avant-garde, he eschewed groups, was sympathetic to the nativist and vehemently anticolonial civil rights movement *indigenismo*[3] and spent much of his life in self-imposed exile in Europe.

High culture has traditionally circulated in elite circles and its writers have often felt isolated from mainstream society. When the patronage system faltered and writers became subject to the demands of the market, such isolation became more problematic, especially for groups alienated from their social and economic class origins. They responded by creating a discursive microcosm even more rarefied than that normally accorded writers and intellectuals. Michel Foucault (1972) argues that "none may enter into discourse on a specific subject unless he has satisfied certain conditions or if he is not, from the outset, qualified to do so" (224–25). The function of "fellowships of discourse" is to "preserve or to reproduce discourse [so it can] circulate within a closed community, according to strict regulations" (Foucault 1972, 225). In order to gain membership in the group of writers permitted to speak, the aspiring poet may need institutional support, a university background, or the right kind of family connections. While members of all three of the avant-garde groups discussed here were from the middle and upper classes, criteria for membership differed considerably. The surrealists had to pledge an absolute devotion to Breton, while the Argentine poets' primary commitment was to a highly metaphorical free verse. While the Auden poets had a vague aesthetic project, the group's class and educational backgrounds were fairly homogeneous. At one time or another, all three groups claimed to want to amend the conditions of entry into literary discourse in order to "democratize" or revolutionize poetry. They did not, however, choose to open their groups in any meaningful way to working-class writers.

Groups of poets differ from individual poets; their work is part of a discursive body bound by a group ideology and a collective project. Creating the group involves a process of minimizing differences and focusing on common ground. Where the individual writer is nearly always the single greatest force in the creation of his or her public persona, a group of poets is as likely to be constituted from the outside—by critics or editors—as it is to make itself into a group. In the case of groups that *intend* to be considered avant-garde, this process often involves a joint declaration of purpose or manifesto that identifies members and enemies. While such groups must have a common purpose—whether renovating poetry, defining the poet's role, or trying to save culture from fascism or the masses—their members do not have to speak the same poetic language. With the help of hindsight, critics sometimes dismantle avant-garde groups on the grounds that their artistic work lacks stylistic coherence. But many avant-garde groups did not aspire to a coherent style. Members often shared certain aesthetic values, such as the privileging of free verse and metaphor, but left much up to the individual poet. Though a doctrine such as that underlying Spanish ultraism involves a number of stylistic dictates, individual Argentine ultraists were idiosyncratic in their application of the formal rules set out by Borges. In the early years of surrealism, poets were allowed to pursue individual style as long as it did not take them far off the path of psychic automatism. Part of the reason they were allowed to pursue individual style, clearly, was that the surrealist movement was slow to acknowledge that style or willful composition had any place in its practice. That the Auden poets permitted themselves even more leeway than the other two groups is a result of the fact that their group was mainly constituted around a sociopolitical—not aesthetic—platform.

What characterizes groups are a common quest and some sort of contact—either personal or through publishing—that result in members being considered a group by nonmembers. Where the surrealists logged many hours together, walking the streets of Paris, engaging in automatist games at their favorite cafés and experimenting with trance states, W. H. Auden, Stephen Spender, and C. Day Lewis, the English poets whose names are most commonly linked by critics, were—according to Spender—never all three in a room together until they met in Venice after World War II. The Auden poets illustrate the power of critical discourse to form groups, even in the absence of meetings, manifestos, and a consistently shared purpose or approach to poetry. Foucault's insistence that discourse creates objects, not the other way around, is borne out by a group that didn't mind the group rubric as long as its members were joined by a common project. Once that project was discarded, the Auden poets felt that their asset—membership in a closed community—had become a liability and so set about dismantling the community. But because discourse once in circulation cannot easily be recalled and modified, they were unable to convince anyone that the group hadn't really existed. Their shifting choices show that participation in a group empowers poets most when they are trying to make a name for themselves. If the project fails or loses its vitality, or if a member achieves sufficient recognition, the group may become a hindrance to the individual poet's development. As a tool that helps recently launched writers become known, the avant-garde group is useful for a limited time only and is then often dismantled as systematically as it was created.

These groups differed considerably in their platforms and even in the degree to which those platforms changed. The Argentine vanguardia had a weak and covert social agenda and an overt but not very innovative aesthetic agenda. In a deep sense, their goal was to maintain the status quo of literary high culture. Both the vanguardia and the Auden poets were conservative about socioeconomic class issues, though the Auden poets had lost a sense of social stability and were compelled to consider alternatives to their tradition as they knew it. Their platform was sociopolitical in a way the Argentines' was not. The surrealists represent an extreme case of the Auden group's experience; for them it was already too late to go back to the old ways. They wanted to make things new, and were willing to consider any means to that end.

The Argentine vanguardia, also known as the Generation of 1922, is an example of a movement whose project was fundamentally constructive. Though influenced by avant-garde movements from France, including futurism and cubism, and sparked by Jorge Luis Borges's importation of Spanish ultraism in 1920, the movement was little concerned with destroying old poetic forms. While its poets rebelled against a few poetic precursors, rejecting rhyme in favor of free verse and eliminating overused words from the modernist vocabulary, its methods and goals were essentially constructive rather than destructive. The movement defied Renato Poggioli's (1968) claim that "every avant-garde movement, in one of its phases at least, aspires to realize what the dadaists called 'the demolition job,' an ideal of the *tabula rasa*" (96). Argentina in the early decades of the twentieth century was forging a national identity and building a national literature. The latter project included the establishment of several literary institutions, state and municipal prizes for writers, a university curriculum, and accompanying mythology and history. Though ambivalence toward the literary market and prestige is typical of the avant-garde in general,[4] this ambivalence meant one thing in Europe and another in Argentina. In the early 1920s in Argentina, for example, prestige had little to do with the number of copies sold. Selling a lot of copies of a book was considered akin to pandering because it meant the audience extended beyond the elite class that traditionally conferred literary authority and value. What most Argentine vanguardia poets, who were from financially well-off families, coveted were the prestige and recognition accorded contributors to high-status publications.

While European intellectuals struggled with their ambivalence about the class system supporting liberalism, Argentina was stunned by the impact on high culture of a massive wave of literate working-class immigrants from Italy and other European countries. Following the precepts of nineteenth-century thinker Domingo Sarmiento, the Argentine cultural elite believed it their duty to protect "civilized" (largely elite European) values from the more populist values of the lower classes. Though most avant-gardes criticize the state, the literary establishment, and the bourgeoisie from which they have sprung, the Argentine vanguardia chose as its project to help preserve literary values dating back to the nineteenth century and to make for itself a place in the national literature. While ambivalent about the consecrated literary publications of its day, the movement was more closely allied with the old guard than with the marginalized and rebellious camp of writers that claimed to write for the working class. One of the clichés of Argentine literary history to come out of the 1920s is the binary opposition *oficialismo* versus vanguardia (Panesi 1985, 13–14). But on the Argentine literary spectrum of the era, these two camps—consecrated high culture and what claimed to be the aesthetically revolutionary fringe (the avant-garde)—were hand in glove. In the much-publicized Boedo versus Florida conflict of the 1920s between social realists with a vaguely leftist orientation (Boedo) and the avant-garde poets (Florida), the avant-garde's "enemy" was not the state or the past; it was a proletarianizing literary group in the present.

The poetry of Borges and other Argentine vanguardia poets is very conservative when compared to the major works of European high modernism. Much of Borges's early poetry contains no technologically modern imagery and expresses a nostalgic view of a premodern Buenos Aires. The abundance of timeless themes—sunsets, dawn, afternoons, the sea— is reminiscent of the pastoral tendencies of the Georgian poets in England. A dissenting voice was Oliverio Girondo, a wealthy Argentine who participated in surrealist and Dadaist events on the Continent and brought the influence of French avant-garde movements and social criticism to the movement. Girondo's radicalism proved too much for the Argentine vanguardia, and he was in many ways marginalized until the 1940s when he took on a paternal role with a young generation of Argentine surrealist poets. The vanguardia was instead dominated by Borges, whose notion of linguistic renovation focused on the substitution of free verse for rhyme and on metaphor as an image-creating device. Far from participating in social rebellion, Borges was in his early days a professed Berkeleyan idealist who focused on discovering or creating *criollismo,* the Argentine cultural essence.

It is interesting that the poets grouped around W. H. Auden in the 1930s are not remembered as avant-garde, though they introduced a new aesthetic into English poetry, had some radical political ideas, allowed themselves to be associated with manifesto-like essays, and tried to combine poetry and social activism. Because they were born into a comparatively conservative political tradition, old-style liberalism, their political views of the mid-1930s are arguably more radical—comparatively speaking—than those of the surrealists. Though over the long haul, critics have been reluctant to associate avant-gardism with the English literary tradition, in the 1930s, a number of critics and poets referred to this handful of writers as an avant-garde movement, accurately describing the group's function at the time. In *The Destructive Element* (1935), Stephen Spender refers to the "'highbrow' literature of young English Communists" as "advance-guard experimental writing imbued with Communist ideology" and cites the *New Signatures* (1932) and *New Country* (1933) anthologies as fitting this description.[5] Malcolm Cowley calls Spender and Auden "merely the vanguard" of the *New Signatures* group. Critic Robin Skelton (1964) refers to the "pontifical" gestures of the "self-appointed leaders" of the "poetic *avant-garde*" in his introduction to *Poetry of the Thirties* (30).

Critics and poets alike agreed that a group had been constituted and a platform advanced. In the context of great cultural crisis and a disturbing division of the English intelligentsia into communist and fascist sympathizers, the Auden poets in the mid-1930s were united by their choice of a leftist solution to the problem of rising Nazism and decaying liberalism. In spite of their stylistic and personal differences, they functioned as a discursive unit, pointing to what was sick in English society and suggesting a largely political cure.

Decades later, however, the consensus was different. Critic Matthew Hodgart writes in 1978, "Auden and his friends and followers were literary conservatives. Their political views and sexual behavior may have looked excessively liberated, but they were really middle-of-the-road, Horace-and-Hardy men at heart."[6] Hodgart is not alone in this view. The borrowing and subsequent rejection of the French term "avant-garde" reflects the instrumental nature of the concept; the label helped give critics and the public a way of conceiving of the Auden poets. But when the label was no longer useful, critics and poets reverted to a more wholly English vocabulary for describing the group. For the Argentines, there was much to gain by borrowing the label, especially given the comparative weakness of their central project, whereas for the Auden poets, already endowed by their educations with considerable cultural authority, there was little long-term incentive.

The Argentine vanguardia's goals—to contribute to the creation of a national literature and to renovate poetic language—pale in comparison to the Auden poets' not-so-secret hope that they could play an important role in preventing another pan-European war. The Auden poets saw poetry as a means of promoting cultural and political change. Avant-garde in their stinging criticism of social and political problems plaguing England, they were forced to consider how high culture would be affected by radical changes in socioeconomic class structure. Publicly expressing ambivalence about their own position within this structure, they argued for communism. In this, they were quite a bit more radical than the Argentine vanguardia poets, who—except for Girondo and Jacobo Fijman—generally avoided the taboo subjects of family, church, state, and sexuality, and whose prose tracts reflect a desire to gain access to the literary establishment's inner circle.

As Robin Skelton (1964) points out, during the 1930s the English poets expended more energy exploring what the poet's function ought to be than fulfilling that function (30). Looking back decades later, Spender recalled the 1930s' belief that an individual's decision—especially a young poet's decision—to take action in the service of personal convictions "could lead to the winning or losing of [the Spanish civil war], could even decide whether or not the Second World War was going to take place" (Spender 1978, 25; qtd. in Kermode 1988, 78). After the Spanish civil war was lost, World War II broke out and Auden wrote a definitive counterstatement: "For poetry makes nothing happen: it survives / . . . A way of happening, a mouth."[7] The Auden poets scattered, abandoning their political activism and the political language in their poetry, and apologizing for their misguided ideas.

In the rush to recant, many of them questioned whether the "Auden poets" had been a group in the first place. Though the voices of critics and literary historians have outweighed those of the poets on the question of whether or not they formed a group, contemporary critics rarely mention that "MacSpaunday"—formed from the beginnings of the names of the core poets, MacNeice, Spender, Auden, and Day Lewis—was avant-garde in character. This is probably partly because by the beginning of World War II being an avant-garde group had become a source of embarrassment to its members. Also, as Poggioli points out, the avant-garde is found less frequently and in weaker forms in England than on the Continent, because "a less rigid classical tradition . . . has made the sense of exception, novelty, and surprise less acute" (Poggioli 1968, 8). The critics of a country without an avant-garde tradition (such as England) tend not to emphasize what can be considered avant-garde, whereas a country prone to cultural imitation of Continental Europe (such as Argentina) may create an avant-garde so conservative in intent and behavior that it hardly merits the label.

The Auden poets were aware that their group was in part constructed by enthusiastic critics and editors, and that similarities of education and background among them as well as the timing and titles of their first books helped create the notion that these were like-minded poets and that they formed a group. The Auden group came along at a moment when literary institutions were under construction. Although English literature was not then nearly so new a concept as Argentine literature was in the 1920s, the post–World War I era in England witnessed the increasing professionalization of writers, the establishment of institutions to support them, the advent of university scholarships in English Studies, and the founding of major bibliographies (Replogle 1986, 22–23). The Auden poets enthusiastically approached the many discursive avenues open to them, acting alternately as poets, critics, journalists, and critics of education. Their project was in fact less revolutionary than critics enamored of the 1930s as the "political decade" suppose. While able to criticize the larger class structure of capitalist society, they had strikingly little ambivalence about the literary market, promoting themselves by all available means. And though they were sometimes guilt-ridden about their many advantages over the proletariat with whom they tried hard to empathize, they did not often express the view that their professional success and its trappings were in any way undeserved.

Auden's poetry provides a window to this ambivalence about the status and role of the poet. Through the use of unreliable speakers, irony, the scrambling of traditional and modern forms, and a striking mixture of vocabularies, Auden of the 1930s acts as a divided poet. Justin Replogle (1986) describes Auden's two voices as poet and anti-poet, the poet battling the ironic mocker (22–23). The mocker undermines the serious voice who would at moments be both prophet and legislator. The gap between the voices also betrays Auden's ambivalence about the value of poetry. His mixed feelings about betraying his serious convictions about poetry and his strong sense of personal irony cause him to take refuge in self-parody and humor. And, as Replogle points out, "what the speakers . . . talk *about* (Freud, Marx, love, cultural sickness . . .) is often less important than what they reveal by *how* they speak. In extreme cases what these poems mean and what their speakers say is completely unlike" (25).

In contrast to the Auden poets' deep ambivalence about individualism, communism, the death of class, and the role of the poet, the French surrealist poets were a relatively unified group with a more clearly outlined ideology and discursive practice. Literary history bears this out in its unwavering characterization of the surrealists as a cohesive avant-garde movement. The discursive history of these poets, though, as demonstrated by André Breton's manifestos and political statements, is one of fracture, Soviet-style purges, and public rancor among member poets. This internal fractiousness does not interfere with the external historicization of the movement because the self-identified surrealist group, whose membership changed significantly from one year to the next, repeatedly drew attention to its own existence as a *group*. The French surrealist poets are a sort of *cas limite* of the historical avant-garde because their rebellion against bourgeois society and its institutions—state, family, and church—was based on violent language and, to a much lesser degree, violent action. While the Auden poets rhetorically attacked such basic institutions of English society as heterosexuality, the public schools, and the class system, they did little to dismantle them. By the 1940s, they reverted to the personal and political conservatism that had characterized them in their Oxford days of the late 1920s. The surrealists, in contrast, remained radicalized largely because the charismatic Breton continued to lead the movement. With their nihilistic Dada roots and history of violence, antirationalism, professed hatred of the bourgeoisie, and hostility to the professionalization of writers, the surrealists attempted to modify the institutional bases of bourgeois art.[8]

The surrealists made an art form of social protest: Stephen Spender compares Louis Aragon's "Front rouge" to Hitler's speeches. The poem's call for the murder of a number of political enemies of the Left caused the French government to arrest Aragon. When *Le paysan de Paris* (The peasant of Paris) was published in 1926, Aragon warned that he would whip any journalist who reviewed it. An intrepid critic published a review in *Les nouvelles littéraires* (Literary news), provoking Aragon to beat him with a cane and throw his typewriter out the window (see Josephson 1962, 228). Though the surrealists sparked public brawls and regularly disrupted performances of important cultural events in violent expressions of protest against high culture, it would be incorrect to imagine they were consistently rebellious. These writers, who were for the most part children of the bourgeoisie—a number of them were once well on their way to medical careers—coveted the prestige accorded writers recognized by the intelligentsia and larger reading public. Following the Dada precedent, they went to great lengths to provoke mainstream culture into responding to them. After the riot of the ill-fated Saint-Pol-Roux banquet in the summer of 1925, members of the mainstream press boycotted the surrealists by refusing to write about their activities. In a world where prestige was linked to the number of column inches on a newspaper page, punishment was meted out in organized institutional silence. Elyette Guiol-Benassaya (1982) notes that the press engaged in selective reception of surrealism, focusing more attention on its scandals than its publications. The surrealists learned early that action was often more effective than words in earning them publicity (11, 56). Breton's open suggestion that writers are entitled to financial support from the society they attack, however, betrays the surrealists' ambivalence about their self-appointed role as destroyers of the upper classes.

The desire for publicity, the accessibility and economics of journals, and traditional cultural elitism caused these avant-garde groups to choose small literary journals as a means of disseminating their writings. As Poggioli (1968) argues, "The triumph of mass journalism is precisely what motivates and justifies the existence of the avant-garde review, which represents a reaction, as natural as it is necessary, to the spread of culture out to (or down to) the vulgar" (23). Because the "masses" were a too insistent, numerous, and unrefined public, the interwar avant-garde was caught between its desire for a large public, its inherent elitism, and its need for some measure of personal expression and privacy. The writer's role was often confusing and ill-defined, a mixture of commitments to public roles and to the individual lyricism whose source is the private life. In the 1927 preface to *Oxford Poetry*, Auden writes, "All genuine poetry is in a sense the formation of private spheres out of public chaos. . . . On the whole it is environment which conditions values, not values which condition environment" (*Oxford Poetry* 1927/1929, v). During the 1930s it became clear that critics had a profound influence over whether a literary work was considered public or private. They chose, for example, to address T. S. Eliot's *The Waste Land* as a poem about social issues and managed to convince Day Lewis that he had written social poetry though he initially had no such intention. Critical perspectives have shifted considerably over time, and are often contingent upon external social and political circumstances. Where there has been a largely static, unchanging reception—as in the case of the Argentine vanguardia—it is partly a reflection of the comparative stability of the years in which the vanguardia was writing and partly a sign of what the movement has meant to Argentine literary culture.

Avant-garde poets are often ambivalent about the role of the poetic "I" and about whether or not a poet should be more concerned with matters private or public. The Auden poets declared themselves for the private life in the late 1920s and early 1930s, reversed their position for several years, then returned with more humility to the earlier position when World

War II broke out. The vanguardia was fairly consistently private in its orientation and conception of its cultural role. On its surface, even the Boedo versus Florida conflict was about writing and writers; its subtext, however, revealed a disturbingly xenophobic social agenda. The surrealists were public in their spectacles and their advertising tactics, and they—like the Auden poets—had a social agenda for a number of years. However, their greatest outpouring of energy was of a more private nature, involving the mental and linguistic processes of individual poets and the dynamics of the surrealist group.

In their poems, these writers experimented with ways of presenting subjectivity. While Auden opted for a divided speaker, the young Borges devoted whole essays to the nonexistence of the self.[9] In the preface to *Fervor de Buenos Aires* (1923), he writes, "Si en las siguientes páginas hay algún verso logrado, perdóneme el lector el atrevimiento de haberlo compuesto yo, antes que él" (Pezzoni 1986, 91). (If in the following pages there is a successful verse, pardon me, reader, the insolence of my having composed it rather than you.) Though Borges was often self-effacing and in his early writings prone to presenting reality as a dream and the self as a mirage, he was in fact obsessed with biography and autobiography throughout his career. He speaks often in the first person and has sapphic moments where his poetic voice alone makes momentous things happen. The surrealist poets are similarly complex in their relationship to the self. Their commitment to psychic automatism effectively privileges subjectivity over objectivity. Their "truth" is the fragmented, dissociative inner voice whose coherence comes mainly from a continuous interior monologue.

Francine Masiello (1986) argues that the tension between public and private can be identified in the two major goals of the avant-garde journal: "El primero, popularizante, se propone introducir al escritor en la sociedad; el segundo, exclusivo y restrictivo, constituye un diálogo entre hombres de talento" (61). (The first, which is popularizing, proposes to introduce the writer to society; the second, exclusive and restrictive, is a dialogue among men of talent.) The "us versus them" logic of the avant-garde encourages the editorial pieces in its journals to clamor loudly for public support in the form of money, publicity, and defense against real or imaginary enemies. At the same time, the coterie spirit of these journals is quite apparent, often contradicting their editors' magnanimous statements of open acceptance policies and avant-garde platforms that claim that all young writers with "new" ideas are welcome to participate. The tension between inclusion and exclusion can often be seen in avant-garde manifestos themselves; the names of the movement's adherents are listed in clear juxtaposition to structures, aesthetics, and writers considered worthy of rejection.

Though they engaged in significantly more collaborative projects than the other two avant-garde groups, the surrealists were quite attached to what Foucault calls "the name of the author," the signature that represents the writer's work as it circulates through society. Of the poets considered here, only Borges ever argued in favor of anonymous composition, though Auden (1964) once wrote, "In theory, the author of a good book should remain anonymous, for it is to his work, not to himself, that admiration is due" (22). On the whole, avant-garde poets have been too attached to the prestige accompanying the signature to loose their writings on the world unsigned. As Borges noted late in life, in Argentina an unsigned work had almost no life at all because of the Argentine public's infatuation with the cachet of the signature. "En Argentine, et dans le monde hispanique en général, l'oeuvre est le plus souvent inférieure à l'homme. . . . Là-bas tout se règle par amitiés et complicités. . . . En Argentine la signature a plus d'importance que le thème traité."[10] (In Argentina and in the Hispanic world in general, the work is most often inferior to the man. . . . There, everything is regulated by friendships and alliances. . . . In Argentina the signature is more important than the theme.)

The radical avant-garde devotes energy to undermining the practice and notion of individual literary production (if not, ultimately, the individual signature).[11] The Dadaists proclaimed that every practitioner was a president of Dada, and a journal called *391* testified to the fact there were 391 such "presidents." Anna Balakian (1947) claims that "there was such a unity of purpose, unity of thought, unity of nihilism among members of the [surrealist] group that it would have been possible to attribute any one writing to any one individual in the clan" (141). But this sounds more like a leftover Dadaist ideal than a fact about the surrealists' literary production. Paradoxically, the surrealists, whose work was clearly marked by the styles of individual authors, had both a democratic ideology promoting collectively produced work and a rigid internal hierarchy headed by Breton, whose titles of "priest" and "pope" are telling honorifics.

That the avant-garde of the interwar period was torn between nationalism and internationalism is most apparent in the Argentine group, which was caught up in national literary and social concerns though it modeled its rhetoric after that of internationalist European movements. Cultural nationalism was a significant influence on Argentine writers, whose conflict developed over a series of decades, becoming acute in the 1950s when Victoria Ocampo's journal *Sur* and Borges were accused of *extranjerismo* (foreignizing) and turning their backs on domestic problems. The Auden poets were not so troubled over this division, being both absorbed by English culture and willing to participate from time to time in life on the Continent. That there was comparatively little nationalist pressure applied to them made their situation easier. The surrealists, on the other hand, were vehemently antinationalist, vocally repudiating France and nationalism in general. Robert Scholes (1989) points out that the "polarity between international and national commitment was a structuring element of the modernist dialectic for several decades, ultimately being rewritten as a battle between socialism and fascism" (36). These poles were not so far apart after all; indeed, the dogmas often overlapped and left-leaning poets —including Auden—were startled to find themselves flirting with fascist ideas. Nor is the dichotomy between aestheticism and politics so polarized as it often appears. Scholes (1989) notes that fascism could function as an "aesthetically organized secular religion," a "religion of high modernist art" (31). When the Auden poets' ideology collapsed, so did the thing known as the "Auden poets." So inevitably have all avant-garde groups.

Though the avant-garde now encompasses movements from many parts of the world, the chief theoretical locus remains the developed West, especially Continental Europe, and most especially Paris. The premises and hypotheses of important theories of the avant-garde—especially Peter Bürger's *Theory of the Avant-Garde* and Renato Poggioli's *The Theory of the Avant-Garde*—are based almost exclusively on movements that arose on the European continent. Insofar as their works are intended to describe what is now a global phenomenon, Eurocentric overgeneralizations abound. Bürger acknowledges that the surrealists provide the basis for his theory. In the "Advertencia" (Notice) in the Spanish edition of his book, *Teoría de la vanguardia,* he writes,

> El presente trabajo proviene de mi libro sobre el surrealismo. Para la presentación de cualquier análisis particular me remito a él de manera global. . . . Los ejemplos de literatura y artes plásticas no se ofrecen como interpretaciones histórico-sociológicas de obras concretas, sino como ilustración de una teoría. (Bürger 1987, 31)

> (The present work derives from my book on surrealism. For the presentation of particular analyses I refer to it in a global manner. . . . The

literary and artistic examples are not offered as historico-sociologic interpretations of specific works, but as illustrations of a theory.)

This "Notice" does not appear in the English edition, which was published in 1984, three years before the Spanish edition. Elsewhere Bürger makes the important point that the avant-garde is very concerned with the status of art and the artist, and their function in society. Given that Bürger's theory focuses on the institutional underpinnings of art, it is strange indeed that he doesn't make allowances for the social, economic, and historical differences among nations, especially as many of his ideas are relevant to the non-Continental avant-garde.

While Poggioli's (1968) book takes in more instances of the avant-garde—mainly Continental examples—systematic exaggerations found in his account reflect the avant-garde's desires more accurately than its actual choices. He argues, for example, that "the avant-garde faithfully . . . [displays] its own antagonism . . . by a polemical jargon full of picturesque violence, sparing neither person nor thing, made up more of gestures and insults than of articulate discourse" (36–37). He overstates the facts about even the most radically nihilistic movement of the canonical avant-garde, Dadaism.

The avant-garde is generally conceived as a function of the modern, especially in older Western nations with strict classical traditions. Massimo Bontempelli argues that avant-garde art is "an exclusively modern discovery, born only when art began to contemplate itself from a historical viewpoint" (qtd. in Poggioli 1968, 14). Much of the canonized avant-garde finds its roots in the Romantic impulse and requires some sort of orthodoxy as a backdrop against which it can define itself. The orthodoxy need not be a classical or neoclassical tradition; as we have seen, it may be of another nature, including a colonial legacy. Very frequently, avant-garde movements are considered in terms of the standard established by surrealism, and contributed to by futurism, Dadaism, cubism, and other European artistic -isms of the early twentieth century. Poggioli (1968) notes that

Anglo-American criticism often uses these terms [vanguard and avant-garde] with primary reference to French art and literature, or to its influence and reflections beyond French borders, as if avant-garde art was an international manifestation only in an indirect and mediated way; more specifically, as if it were a continental and extracontinental extension of certain aspects of the French intelligence—a real, true case of spiritual Gallicism. (8)

He identifies "the meager fortune of the term and concept within cultures like the American or English; there the formula is either ignored or used in unstable variants, sometimes the French 'avant-garde,' sometimes the English 'vanguard.' Lexicographical uncertainty is added to a patent sense of semantic inadequacy" (7). A non-Western avant-garde might once have been considered by Eurocentric critics to be an oxymoron. Western countries with colonial pasts are often considered either to lack the avant-garde impulse altogether or to have it appear sporadically and in a weak, derivative form. Poggioli sees Latin American avant-garde movements as weak and heavily derived from "spiritual Gallicism." It is true that avant-garde groups may not stand out so starkly—may not have become a convention—in countries with a weak or no classical tradition, but it is also true that each avant-garde movement is heavily influenced by its national circumstances.

Today the term "avant-garde" is sometimes so broadly construed as to mean anything that is shockingly or even surprisingly new in content or form. Artists' obvious desire to shock, rather than to innovate artistically or renovate politically, may cause critics and artists to apply the label. Theorists sometimes see avant-gardism where it is not. Poggioli, for example, calls the *Nouvelle Revue Française* "the organ of the avant-gardes between the two wars" and identifies the *Revista de Occidente* as having an analogous, if less powerful, role. Similarly, he calls Argentina's *Sur,* established in 1931, an organ of the avant-garde (22–23). The fact is that *Sur* is patently anthological and aesthetically and politically moderate in impulse, incorporating both foreign and Argentine writers into its early hodgepodge of essays. The *Nouvelle Revue Française* and the *Revista de Occidente* published many important young writers, but they were not strictly speaking organs of the avant-garde. Nor were their editors, André Gide and José Ortega y Gasset, avant-garde in outlook. Poggioli too nearly approaches the avant-garde's self-idealizing view of itself in his discussion of its journals, which, he says, function "as an independent and isolated military unity, completely sharp and detached from the public, quick to act, not only to explore but also to battle, conquer, and adventure" (23). Avant-garde journals, especially those of movements active between the world wars, did not operate as "isolated" units, nor were they able to detach themselves from the public. Because they defined themselves in opposition to what already existed, their insistence that they arose almost ex nihilo is flawed. In their own self-conception, they were independent and ahistorical, largely free of the influence of literary ancestors. This is their myth of self, but their literary incarnations were, as we will see, more variously and deeply rooted than such a myth would suggest.

Fairly often, the label "avant-garde" has been applied to writers and artists, especially the young, who have taken it and made it theirs. This implies a high degree of self-consciousness and historical awareness. Avant-garde gestures, however, do not require this degree of self-consciousness; they can be a spontaneous response to a set of frustrating circumstances. To ask whether a group can be avant-garde when it has no knowledge of the historical phenomenon known as the avant-garde is to ask a Eurocentric question. It is ridiculous to suggest, as this question does, that artists can't rebel against their circumstances without reiterating the post-Romantic European model. They can and do; their work, however, is generally historicized along other lines. As for the historical avant-garde movements in the West, their visibility is due in large measure to the high degree of international literary self-consciousness of the early twentieth century. The modernist spirit was as international as it was flamboyant. The sense that poetic language needed renovation was shared, as was unease about the poet's perceived loss of power in the modern era.

A conservative view of the avant-garde holds that it is merely the cutting edge of the modern, an extreme form of modernism that will inevitably be absorbed into its main body (see Karl 1985, 13). In this view, the avant-garde is in constant danger of extinction, either because modernism catches up with it and absorbs it, causing it to lose its adversarial life force, or because it is too radical to find a discursive or institutional site from which to speak.[12] This avant-garde is a special case of modernism's retreat from an undesirable social context into extreme forms of aestheticism. A more radical view holds that the avant-garde *attacks* modernism's retreat into art for art's sake. Instead of trying to circumvent the problems of writers who lack a supportive audience, the culturally alienated avant-garde politicizes them by making public its confusion and rage. Criticizing the social through the aesthetic is a traditional tactic, one in which all three groups studied here engaged. Only two of them — the surrealists and the Auden poets — went so far as to experiment with social action.

In his surrealism-inspired book, Bürger argues that the avant-garde has the rare ability to criticize the conditions of its own production.[13] It functions not to organize the past but to force the relationships among literature, institutions, the market, and the reading public to reveal themselves. Where the mainstream literary establishment naturalizes relationships among author, critic, text, and market, the avant-garde points out the artifice of this tendency by self-consciously creating its own history—replete with exposed power dynamics—and loudly criticizing society and the literary tradition. In this more political view, the avant-garde is not so much the front runner of modernism (or any other literary tendency) as its enemy, at least insofar as it attacks the hand that feeds it.

Terry Eagleton (1990) argues that modernist literature's almost impossible goal and source of internal conflict is the achievement of its own autonomy and integrity in spite of the fact that it is a commodity in bourgeois society. He locates the "inscription of its own material conditions" on the work of art's "interior." Given this untenable situation, Eagleton continues, "It would seem that art must now either abolish itself entirely—the audacious strategy of the avant-garde—or hover indecisively between life and death, subsuming its own impossibility into itself" (349). But it is not a question of avant-garde versus non–avant-garde; what Eagleton is in fact describing is the radical avant-garde of the Dadaists versus more moderate avant-garde movements. All three of the groups discussed in these pages chose survival over extinction. An avant-garde movement that has become part of the literary canon has, of course, long since lost its initial, oppositional status, though surrealist tactics still have a certain freshness. Eagleton (1990) sees the radical mode as an unusual stance, one that rarely succeeds, given the paradox that "art's autonomy is a form of reification, reproducing what it resists." Avant-garde art needs some sort of ground on which to locate its innovative figurations if a lack of referentiality and an excess of chaos are not to result in meaninglessness (351, 354).

Frank Kermode (1988) argues that literary history tries to make "a usable past, a past which is not simply past but also always new. The object of all such thinking about the canonical monuments, then, is to make them *modern*" (116). The avant-garde, though, often tries to make itself new without reference to anything older than the generation that precedes it. The immediate ancestor is generally treated with great scorn. There are thus two kinds of modernism, one that "makes new" the past and another intent on destroying that past. The Argentine *vanguardia* belongs to the former type, the French surrealists to the latter, though neither approaches its goal with the firmness of purpose it claims to have. "Delusion," argues Eagleton (1990), "is art's very mode of existence" (352). Frederick Karl (1985) points to the avant-garde's myth of its own history: "Modernists in nearly all their innovative phases view themselves not as part of a tradition but as ahistorical. . . . The avant-garde, especially, is based on this assumption: to move so far outside the mainstream that historical development no longer applies" (xii).

The avant-garde likes to think itself beyond the "anxiety of influence," Harold Bloom's term for the writer's fear that there is no essential creative work left to perform. Poets then misread their predecessors, writes Bloom (1973), in order "to clear imaginative space for themselves" (5). Avant-garde poets may be spurred more by this fear than other poets, but they take pains not to admit it. Poggioli (1968) quotes Apollinaire as saying, "You can't lug the corpse of your father all over the place" (35). The fact is that psychologically and aesthetically speaking most writers do just that, though the radical avant-garde prefers to dismember the father and carry him around in pieces. Each of the groups I shall discuss showed abundant signs of rhetorical and thematic borrowings from earlier generations of poets.

Poggioli (1968) posits a life cycle for the avant-garde that focuses on four "moments" or phases: enthusiastic activism, antagonism, a transcendental antagonism he calls "nihilism," and agonism or self-ruin. They are meant to describe the psychology of the avant-garde. Looked at as a cycle, these four moments describe exceptionally well the rise and fall of Dadaism, though one would have to note that the Dadaists' activism embraced agonism *and* nihilism; theirs was an activist nihilism. In fact, as Poggioli points out, these "moments" create the dialectic of an avant-garde movement. That all avant-gardes have constructive passions and antagonisms is doubtless true, but the cases studied here suggest that Poggioli's model does not pertain to all movements, that nihilism is not, in fact, an inevitable outgrowth of the basic oppositions that structure the avant-garde (25–26). Its antagonisms, after all, sometimes *helped* the historical avant-garde to achieve its goals, many of which were far from nihilistic, as I have already observed. Tensions within a group of writers and tensions between the group and the society in which it exists are the motors that drive the avant-garde. Sometimes a movement "takes shape and agitates for no other end than its own self, out of the sheer joy of dynamism, a taste for action." More often, continues Poggioli, a movement "is constituted primarily to obtain a positive result, for a concrete end" (25).

The French term avant-garde is by nature activist, a marching toward. Poggioli correctly emphasizes that no work is completely avant-garde because every work necessarily relies on existing values. He defines avant-garde art as that which "creates value not previously existent" (163). This definition, while useful, is too broad in that it includes all important works of art to some degree and leaves us struggling to identify the uniqueness of the avant-garde. Helio Piñón asks whether the avant-garde is a critical attitude or a concrete artistic manifestation. Is it, he wonders, something alien to art that acts through art or is it a point of view in art that denounces social pathology? (qtd. in Bürger 1987, 6–7). Of the movements studied here, only the French surrealists fit Denis Hollier's (1988) definition of the avant-garde as "an experiment in transforming social life into art" (xiv).

Bürger's definition of the modernist avant-garde as art criticizing the social through a high degree of aestheticism makes an important statement about the nature of modernism in general. However, the definition neither applies to all instances of the avant-garde nor takes into account the important social behavior that often accompanies this aestheticism. Only after much struggle does the modernist avant-garde come to view aestheticism as the proper vehicle for its goals. By the time—or perhaps because—the Auden poets reached such a consensus, their movement died off. Similarly, it is problematic to identify the avant-garde solely with art that exposes the logic and ideologies of bourgeois art, such as the notions of the organic whole, individual production and reception, and so on. A model of avant-gardism based on a semiotics of fragmentation comes dangerously close to associating the avant-garde with a single modernist or postmodernist style. Such a definition can be applied only inconsistently, to Oliverio Girondo but not to Jorge Luis Borges, to André Breton but less well to Paul Eluard. Bürger (1984) defines the avant-garde as the instance of art criticizing not only itself but the institutional context that permits it to exist (20–23). While all of the movements studied here engaged in self-criticism, only the Dadaists/surrealists devoted significant energy to questioning and changing the relationship between bourgeois art and society. The Auden poets tried to make this gesture, but their discussions more closely resemble theoretical abstractions than a program for change. Both groups did, however, criticize their institutional contexts; only the Argentine vanguardia, as a matter of unstated policy, largely avoided such criticism.

While Poggioli acknowledges that individualism sometimes characterizes avant-gardism, Bürger (1984) argues that the avant-garde denies the concepts of individual production and of "autonomous" art, that is, of art separate from society (53). Bürger's model best describes the "pure" Continental avant-garde and as such is less applicable to the Argentine movement or the Auden poets. Even so, it is inaccurate: though the surrealists took steps to deny the notion of individual literary practice, they ended up falling back into conventional choices regarding the individual signature (which, ironically, was especially dear to their manifesto-writing leader, André Breton). Because the historical avant-garde is itself a product of the bourgeoisie and because it cannot escape the influence of its environment and history, a view of the avant-garde as constitutionally antibourgeois is misleading.

In the hierarchy of the avant-garde's priorities, both aesthetics and politics sometimes took a back seat to issues of survival. For the consecration-oriented Argentines, who did not want to destroy a national literature still in its formative period, an aesthetic revolution worthy of the label was an undesirable choice even though the avant-garde rubric conferred much-desired European authority. While the Auden poets claimed that their society was desperately in need of social revolution, they did not fully give their hearts, let alone their lives, to the cause. What these poets really desired is not always easy to determine, though there are abundant hints. As Auden (1977) wrote in 1939, "I have never yet met a Left-Wing intellectual for whom the real appeal of Communism did not lie in its romantic promise that with the triumph of Communism the State shall wither away" (405). The surrealists, whose revolutionary impulse ran deeper, generally stopped short of radical social activism and terrorism, allowing their inconsistently pursued crusade to be mainly one of words. Having participated in Dada's self-extermination mission, the surrealists took its experience to heart.

Expanding the role of the poet was a goal shared by all three groups. Each sought to annex foreign discursive territory and to help its society overcome a variety of what it perceived to be threats to emotional, psychological, and physical well-being. The Argentine poets were formally innovative, but were unwilling to speak openly about their role as defenders of Argentina's high cultural tradition, perhaps because to do so was to deconstruct their own theoretical texts. The Auden poets concluded in the late 1930s that the poet's proper relationship to political concerns was to maintain a healthy distance from them and heed Julien Benda's warnings in *La trahison des clercs* (The treason of the intellectuals). Benda (1969) laments the role of intellectuals in theorizing what he terms political hatreds, specifically hatreds of race (he offers as an example anti-Semitism), class (antiproletarianism), party (antipopulism), and nation against nation. "Our age is indeed the age of the *intellectual organization of political hatreds*" (26–27). In the late 1920s, Benda argued for the return to what he saw as the intellectual's traditional abstention from political passions.

Distressing fluctuations of meaning during the interwar period introduced different sorts of relativism in the meanings of words such as "revolutionary," "literature," and "morality." The movements themselves were very much in flux, providing the grounds for a theoretical model of the avant-garde based on its flexibility, especially the tension between seeking effective expressions of rebellion and seeking means of self-consecration. At times, aesthetic concerns were less important than the political issues on each group's agenda. The Argentine vanguardia managed to combine aesthetic and political goals largely because its politics were so conservative. It sought to preserve the purity of Spanish, to check the rise of popular literature and, it seems, to check even the flow of immigrants into the country. The Auden poets found their aesthetics inadequate to achieving political goals and their brief experiment with politicized poetry and activism proved no more successful. Only for the surrealists, who failed in their political projects and nearly destroyed their group by experimenting with totalitarian tactics, did aesthetic concerns prove enduring and redemptive.

The period between the world wars was rife with fear, especially the fear that extinction loomed in the future. Poggioli (1968) claims that the artist during this period was sometimes drawn by the attraction to anarchy into "a morbid condition of mystical ecstasy, which prevents the avant-garde artist from realizing that he would have neither the reason nor the chance to exist in a communist society" (100). This is the equivalent of arguing—mistakenly and I think somewhat patronizingly—that the avant-garde is not rational. The Auden poets were forced to think this particular dilemma over carefully, and they publicly admitted that the prospect of a communist England made them very nervous. The Argentine vanguardia chose to reject communism as having little to do with their prosperous national reality. And the surrealists, as is well known, came to blows with one another in 1929 about whether to privilege communism over the aesthetic and psychological agenda of the 1924 *Manifeste du surréalisme* (First manifesto of surrealism).

While self-interest and self-preservation are instincts common to all institutions, to render these instincts invisible or make them seem "natural" is a political act. In late nineteenth-century Europe, with the rise of a massive literate public demanding new reading materials—especially tabloid journalism and realist novels—writers struggled to adjust to changing relationships among themselves, their support systems, and the public. Bürger (1984) argues that art for art's sake was a response in "developed bourgeois society" to art's progressive loss of social function (32). Its message was that art need serve no interests other than its own: not the needs of the reading public, the society at large, or the market. The historical avant-garde takes this defensiveness a step farther in its attack on literary ancestors, society, and—in the case of the radical avant-garde—the institutional forces behind literature itself.

The surrealists initially imagined an even more ambitious role for the poet than did the Auden poets. However, they were quickly mired in the same aesthetics-versus-politics debate. Breton, who intended not only to save Western civilization from destruction but also radically to alter the inner workings of human perception and thus the world order, ultimately came down on the side of aesthetics and Freud. Given that he realized before 1929 that the revolution proposed in the *Manifeste du surréalisme* had in important ways failed in its infancy, this was a conservative, if hopeful, choice. His role as charismatic leader led him to risk destroying the movement, though it was a role he was never willing to give up. A major lesson of these three movements is that it is extremely difficult to change the course of a nation, let alone the world, and that the rebellious movement is most at risk of destroying itself if it breaks too fully with the institutional context against which it reacts. In pointing out in the chapters that follow how difficult it was for avant-garde groups to attain their goals, it is not my intention to discredit them; rather I shall show how impossibly ambitious they were given the political volatility of their era and the inherent conservatism of the literary institution.

The avant-garde takes its most extreme forms at moments of cultural and political crisis. Dadaism, the most radical canonized literary and artistic avant-garde movement of this century, began in Zurich in 1916 as an anguished response to World War I, which demolished essential cultural values, accelerated the failure of political liberalism, and killed off a generation of young men.[14] A movement of nearly unremitting anarchism and nihilism, Dadaism clearly also represents the most radical canonical instance of an avant-garde critique of society's relationship to art. One of its defining characteristics is a deep hatred of the bourgeois status of art, a hatred that led the movement to try to produce anti-art. Eagleton (1990) may have the Dadaists in mind when he discusses art that tries to reinvent itself as anti-art:

There would seem only one route left open, and that is an art which rejects the aesthetic. An art against itself, which confesses the impossibility of art. . . . An art, in short, which will undo all this depressing history, which will go right back even before the beginning, before the dawning of the whole category of the aesthetic, and seek to override in its own way that moment at the birth of modernity when the cognitive, the ethico-political and libidinal-aesthetic became uncoupled from one another. This time, however, it will seek to do it not in the manner of the radical aestheticizers, by the aesthetic colonizing of these other two regions, but by folding the aesthetic into the other two systems. . . . This is the revolutionary avant garde. (370)

Whether Dadaism's mission was to integrate poetry and sociopolitical activism is arguable, but its fate illustrates the riskiness of achieving prestige on a platform of pure destruction. Once everything, including the movement itself, had been leveled, there was no convincing raison d'être: Dada's mission had been accomplished and it was too late to rewrite the agenda.

Eagleton's (1990) other, more positive incarnation of avant-gardism opts for different strategies of social rebellion. This avant-garde believes that if, for example, avant-garde paintings are used to decorate banks, "that means only one thing: not that you were not iconoclastic or experimental enough, but that either your art was not deeply enough rooted in a revolutionary political movement, or it was, but that this mass movement failed. How idealist to imagine that *art,* all by itself, could resist incorporation [by the ruling order]!" (372).

The surest key to avoiding such incorporation, of course, is not to leave any artifacts; instead, one can create defiant public spectacles or make art out of garbage—though even these tactics do not always work. Most avant-garde movements, however, do want to create artifacts, and insofar as twentieth-century poets seek audiences through published texts, the anti-art option has unpleasant limitations. Poggioli (1968) refers to "that predestined unpopularity which avant-garde followers, light-heartedly and proudly, accept" (39). He also argues that a deep masochism (or martyrdom, depending on your point of view) runs through much avant-gardism. "This immolation of the self to the art of the future must be understood not only as an anonymous and collective sacrifice, but also as the self-immolation of the isolated creative personality" (67–68). But he is wrong about the canonical avant-garde that is his subject; it is neither anonymous nor easily inclined toward self-immolation. As his exchanges with Breton show, not even Dadaist leader Tristan Tzara went gentle into that good night. Elsewhere Poggioli acknowledges that in its "day-to-day reality . . . even the avant-garde has to live and work in the present, accept compromises and adjustments, reconcile itself with the official culture of the times, and collaborate with at least some part of the culture" (79).

As the Argentine vanguardia illustrates, the avant-garde's platform may be aesthetically radical given the context from which it emerges, yet at the same time socially conservative. In the case of more radical movements such as Dadaism and surrealism, the socioeconomic class system may come under fire. Because the literary avant-garde—which until recently was made up primarily of middle- and upper-class writers—depends on the same institutional support as the main body of high culture, such attacks are risky. As the avant-garde warms to the task of criticizing the literary establishment, members of that establishment, whether critics or journalists, increasingly return the favor, pointing out the inevitable hypocrisies of economically privileged poets on the warpath. This historical antagonism to the bourgeoisie and to the status of art in bourgeois society (Bürger 1984, 49) is an ironic yet frequent instance of the avant-garde biting its own tail. But while avant-garde writers may be openly ambivalent toward the state, the market, and the trappings of literary prestige, their sometimes hypocritical protests don't often involve abdicating or threatening their positions of privilege.[15] After all, if the avant-garde has no voice or position from which to speak, it fails. (Or, in the quirky logic of the nihilistic avant-garde, it succeeds.)

Walter Benjamin identifies this paradoxic tension between self-preservation and the call for revolution in the early decades of the twentieth century: "the bourgeois apparatus of production and publication can assimilate astonishing quantities of revolutionary themes, indeed, can propagate them without calling its own existence, and the existence of the class that owns it, seriously into question."[16] The avant-garde's strategies of rebellion betray a need to counter rebellious or other self-destructive gestures with acts designed to avoid causing a movement to self-destruct. Its tendency to locate and strain against the line that divides survival from self-destruction shows that literature that strays too far beyond the limits of the regime of cultural truth and fair-dealing risks self-annihilation, as the Dadaist experience shows. Many avant-garde movements betray their fear of this sort of fate through the choice of radical rhetoric to promote a tame rebellion. In the 1920s the Argentine vanguardia went to the extreme of using the rhetoric of political revolution to argue for free verse instead of rhyme.

Threats perceived to jeopardize culture or civilization in its entirety necessarily threaten the avant-garde's sense of existence, thus putting to the severest test its commitment to oppose mainstream and consecrated high culture. The period between the two world wars was such a time, providing a testing ground for how the historical avant-garde reacted to threats to national sovereignty, the social class system, and literature. Would the radical avant-garde, for example, continue to reject a tradition-based canon in danger of being dismantled if fascist regimes controlled Europe? Would bourgeois writers oppose capitalism if they had the power to create a communist Europe? Under a noncapitalist regime, after all, the avant-garde would have to find a different raison d'être and in fact would not survive as originally conceived. The avant-garde's answer to these questions was, as I've suggested, often conservative. A new cultural regime was wanted, but not at the expense of the avant-garde's existence. Art, for most avant-garde movements, is in moments of political and cultural crisis separate from and more important than politics.

In *The Great War and Modern Memory*, Paul Fussell (1975) writes that the twentieth century's inclination toward "gross dichotomizing" in its thinking grew out of the polarization of warring nations and the us-versus-them mythologization of World War I. The "versus habit" (79), as Fussell calls it, finds its most durable metaphor in the dichotomy of civilization and barbarism. Each side feels itself to be normal and natural, threatened by a grotesque, irrational, and barbarous enemy. The avant-garde, ambivalent about its place in culture, is also based on the "versus habit," especially on variations of the civilization-barbarism dichotomy. Spender (1937), for example, expresses this opposition bluntly in *Forward from Liberalism:* "Communism is the struggle to inspire the standards of our civilization with the political will not only to survive the attacks of barbarism growing up in our midst, but also to go forward and create a more extensive civilization which will grow from the roots of a classless society" (15).

Argentine critic Beatriz Sarlo defines the avant-garde's structuring dichotomy as "aesthetic rupture" that

> *reacciona contra* el sistema de consagración, las jerarquías culturales y la mercantilización del arte, . . . [e incluye] la existencia de un público al

que la vanguardia divide, y los mecanismos de un mercado frente al que la vanguardia experimenta, al mismo tiempo, náusea y fascinación. (in Barrenechea, Jitrik, Rest, et al. 1981, 73–74; my emphasis)

(*reacts against* the system of consecration, cultural hierarchies, and the commercialization of art, . . . [and that includes] the existence of a public over which the avant-garde is divided, and the mechanisms of a market in reaction to which the vanguardia simultaneously experiences nausea and fascination.)

The attraction to binary thinking causes the avant-garde to be caught between opposing choices. In *El texto y sus voces* (The text and its voices), Argentine critic Enrique Pezzoni (1986) identifies the ambivalence that makes the avant-garde's behavior appear to outsiders to be confused and contradictory. Impulses toward *ruptura* (rupture, rebellion, and change) and *decoro* (consecration, acceptance, propriety) are simultaneously at work. "Ruptura" is the avant-garde's rebellious impulse to initiate change, while "decoro" is the desire for prestige and a conservative instinct of self-preservation (13–14). Pezzoni argues that this tension is the operating principle of the avant-garde and that it inevitably causes its demise. He calls the victory of civilized "decoro" over barbarous "ruptura" the moment of "neutralization," when "*la vanguardia* se hace *guardia y guarida:* defensa empecinada de un territorio ya conquistado donde el rebelde adquiere la prepotencia del tirano" (13) ("*the avant-garde* makes itself into *guard and hideout:* stubborn defense of already conquered territory, where the rebel takes on the tyrant's arrogance"). In other words, once the avant-garde has taken over enough cultural turf, obtaining the power it covets, it frequently turns its energies to protecting its gains. This is accomplished by a variety of means: rejecting or revising the new aesthetic in favor of something even newer (as the surrealists did), stumping for the group even as it changes (as Breton did), rejecting the notion of the group (as some of the Argentines did), and pursuing individual fame (a path the Argentines and the Auden poets chose).

Critics of earlier decades reveal themselves to be influenced by the avant-garde's binary logic. Dadaism's metamorphosis into surrealism, for example, is variously described as being an absolute reversal—from a destructive to a constructive project—and as merely two phases of the same project.[17] The truth probably lies between these two views. Poggioli's (1968) theory of the avant-garde also takes as its basis binary logic, its agonistic and nihilistic "moments" combining to form a sadomasochistic dialectic (68). He identifies the activist and antagonistic "moments" as the ones that "establish the method and ends of action," and the agonistic and nihilistic as having an "absolute irrationality." Together the two pairs create "the *dialectic of movements*" (26–27). Poggioli's pessimistic and schematic vision of the avant-garde's trajectory toward self-destruction suggests Pezzoni's view of *decoro* overcoming *ruptura*. Poggioli writes, "Each specific avant-garde is destined to last only a morning. When a specific avant-garde which has had its day insists on repeating the promises it cannot now keep, it transforms itself without further ado into its own opposite. Then, as happened with futurism, the movement becomes an academy" (223). The avant-garde's military origin resonates, in Pezzoni's (1986) words, as "transgresiones normalizadas por el prestigio" (transgressions normalized by prestige) (16).

Carlos Altamirano and Beatriz Sarlo (1980) argue convincingly that the avant-garde exists by denying the legitimacy of consecrated literary culture (130). It defines itself in opposition to this culture, the literary past, and the society that marginalizes it for being avant-garde. When it lacks an "opposing dialectic" (Pezzoni 1986, 27), the avant-garde must either become consecrated, entering the canon, or fade away. In the Argentine case, "la mezcla de fascinación y desdén por el prestigio y el mercado" (Pezzoni 1986, 68) (the mixture of fascination and disdain for prestige and the market) was never resolved. Though a binary division between forging a new aesthetics and making money existed, the former considered civilized and the latter barbarous, the Argentine poets went to great lengths to develop a reading public and obtain maximum exposure for their many journals and books. Though often characterized as ahistorical or antihistorical, the avant-garde is in fact unusually self-conscious about its role in the history of art and literature, often exhibiting in its journals a compulsive need to historicize itself. Telling the same story over and over again, whether of the group's platform or history, leads to greater attention from critics outside the movement and makes the road to consecration and canonization shorter. The surrealists claimed to scorn the public and the market, but they issued more public announcements—in the form of appeals and declarations—than the vanguardia and the Auden poets combined.

Binarisms also provide a convenient tool for differentiating among and classifying ideas. Where fundamental oppositions are found—especially the split between good and evil—relations of power are at work performing their sacred value-creating duties. The avant-garde's dependence on defining itself through its opposition to real or imagined enemies some-times leads it to create "straw man" opponents. The Argentine vanguardia, for example, did much to promote the famous Boedo versus Florida conflict, which lasted from 1924 until 1927 and which Borges later said was an invention of critics. While this conflict was initiated and to an important degree sustained by the participants themselves, some oppositions are more completely the products of critics. Critics have sometimes opposed the aesthetically oriented "Bright Young People" and the "Political Activists" in England, though the former were a 1920s generation and the latter belonged to the 1930s. Such choices certainly contributed to the aesthetics-versus-politics opposition so important to high modernism (see Hynes 1972, 27). While the Argentine vanguardia and the Auden poets located the "enemy" in the world outside their group, surrealism—largely because of Breton's demand that participants obey his directives—as often as not found the enemy to be within its own ranks. Similarly, while members of the vanguardia and the Auden poets were essentially free to dissent, recalcitrant surrealists were often expelled posthaste from the movement.

Examined together, these three very different groups show the avant-garde to be an elastic phenomenon, capable of adapting to a variety of historical circumstances. Avant-garde movements proved useful to young poets searching for recognition, providing an arena where they could struggle with issues of literary ancestry, the canon, and whether to gain membership in it or find recognition and claim an audience outside it. The goals of groups varied with their national circumstances, and they used the tools most readily available to them. Though Breton proposed psychic freedom as the key to a new world, he borrowed the repressive ideology and tactics of fascism. In Argentina, where a period of prosperous liberalism was still being enjoyed, the goals were modest; the vanguardia was more of an experiment in aesthetics and polemics than it was a serious quest for change. In Auden's 1930s, the goals evolved as the political landscape changed; here especially the avant-garde showed itself to be flexible, mutating and attaining new forms from one year to the next.

The values of critics metamorphose as well. In the case of the Auden poets, a generation of critics built a group only to have its successors tear it down, and generations after that continue to argue about which was the better choice. This cyclical process happens again and again in literary history: William H. Pritchard, for example, in a 1988 review of Frank Kermode's *History and Value*, helps rebut Kermode's case for promoting the "undervalued" Auden poets. Pritchard likes best Kermode's emphasis of the poets' "mixed feelings" about their choices and their clear ambivalence about supporting a revolutionary cause. The myth to be undermined here, in Kermode's words, is that of "the half-hearted, the gullible, the gutless Thirties poets." A bit facetiously, Pritchard (1988) addresses his *New York Times* readers as "we prisoners of the myth" and goes on to rebut Kermode by arguing that Auden's work is already highly valued and that Spender and Day Lewis don't deserve any more fame than they've already got (14–15). The cycles of constructing and dismantling, and valuing and devaluing, suggest that literary value and meaning are perhaps too often forced to adapt to the changing agendas of critics. If this state of affairs is inevitable and in some ways useful—and I believe it is—then a self-conscious, self-interrogating criticism is needed.

It is difficult to imagine a literary work, commentary, or history that lacks an interest in its own fate. Obsessed with creating their own myths and histories, avant-garde writers were apt to take poems already in circulation and try to suppress or edit them. Auden and Borges were much more prone than Breton to be public about their desire to erase statements they had made but come to disagree with, and their assumption that they controlled their discourse put them at odds with critics and literary historians who felt that a text once published belonged to the public domain. Auden changed his mind many times. In the foreword to B. C. Bloomfield's bibliography, for example, he tells the now famous story of how he handled the poem "September 1, 1939":

> Rereading [it] . . . after it had been published, I came to the line "We must love one another or die," and said to myself: "That's a damned lie! We must die anyway." So in the next edition, I altered it to, "We must love one another and die." This didn't seem to do either, so I cut the stanza. Still no good. The whole poem, I realized, was infected with an incurable dishonesty. (qtd. in Bloom 1986, 170)

Critics often overruled Auden's choices and in some cases made early drafts of poems the official texts. Edward Mendelson's compilation of texts for *The English Auden* is full of judgment calls, some of which Auden would certainly have disliked. Mendelson explains these choices:

> I have used the text in the form it reached at the end of 1939. . . . I have incorporated corrections and changes Auden made in friends' copies, and have occasionally amended according to manuscript readings. . . .

When a poem made its way into one of the plays I have not felt bound to use the latest version, which was often as much the product of stage necessities as of literary ones. . . . In a few places in *The Orators,* and once in a "Letter to Lord Byron," I have restored manuscript readings changed in the printed editions to avoid libel, obscenity or discourtesy. . . . I have not . . . interfered with the punctuation of . . . printed texts except to replace full stops or semi-colons with colons where the sense clearly demands them, and to make a few other changes. . . . I have corrected Auden's miscopied quotations from books under review. (Auden 1977, xxi–xxii)

The struggle between authors, critics, and historians provides a window to the fierce competition for power among those who produce literary meaning and control intellectual property.[18]

Literary meaning is very much a function of context partly because we are forced to read texts written in other eras in light of our own historical moment. Every text, especially those that comment on other texts, should pose the question: What is at stake in this act of valuation or interpretation? An avant-garde group poses that question when it asks of itself the impossible: that it rebel in ways that threaten its constructive projects, its future status, and even its existence as a movement. The crooked line traced between avant-garde values and behavior reflects the critics' own ambivalent, contradictory behavior with respect to the rhetoric of a democratic canon and the intellectual's traditionally elitist role as guardian of the canon's gates.

Critics' naturalization of avant-garde myths of self apologizes for and neutralizes the avant-garde's behavior, though the avant-garde is not committed to behavioral consistency or to the standards of objectivity and fairness of the critical community. Naturalization also obscures the uncomfortable problems of professional survival, internal stability, power, authority, and public recognition shared by writers and critics. Both groups consider questions of canonicity vital. Literary humanists have a lesson to learn from the avant-garde: there is little that is "natural" in the world of discourse, including in the practice of literary critics.

While the avant-garde nakedly displays its drive for power and authority, criticism today is divided over whether authority should reside mainly with writers or with critics. Because the avant-garde tends to expose its strategies and needs, it can be used as a mirror for critics who want to investigate the goals and needs that drive critical practice. Examination of early reception and of shifting patterns of reception—inconsistent standards applied to poets of the same group, a dramatic about-face of critical reaction to a given poet or group—shows that criticism has its own internal politics, myths, and blind spots.

Author of the term "the hermeneutics of suspicion," Charles Altieri is wary of the critic who emphasizes politics and ideology, as I do here. "It is a mistake," he argues, "to read cultural history only as a tawdry melodrama of interest pursued and ideologies produced" (qtd. in Harris 1991, 118). A critical approach that examines one facet of a text to the exclusion of others is reductive, but when critics discuss only the aesthetics of a text, their view is not usually labeled "tawdry." It is important to strike a balance between theories that privilege the text's inner workings, and theories and criticism that examine the relationship between the text and the world. Northrop Frye (1971) argues that criticism, by nature, has two aspects, one oriented toward literature's own structure and the other oriented toward its social environment. He warns against the "centrifugal" and "centripetal" fallacies, where critical meaning depends on social determinism and on the critic's own values, respectively (25, 32–33).

I adopt as a premise that the practice of criticism is as self-interested as the avant-garde's quest for freedom and power. As Paul Bové (1986) argues, "critical practice is always situated and occasional, that is, positioned within sets of discursive and institutional formations that are parts of larger constellations of cultural and political power" (239). Because truth and value are culturally relative and often act in the service of a dominant cultural or socioeconomic class, the literary tradition and canon are not necessarily more "natural" than the ruling class's right to power. The institutions that produce and protect literature have reasons not to threaten the forces that create, evaluate, and disseminate literary value. The products of the cultural (and often economic) elite are often disseminated as the product of native talent, as something disinterested and innately valuable. Humanism, argues Paul Bové (1986), "except in its most oppositional forms, refuses to pose the question of power except to deny it" (xvi). Its "production of an image of 'tradition'" is "always a necessary tool for the elite to go on 'guiding' the species (or nation or race or class) toward perfection" (Bové 1986, 256).

Truth as propounded by the ideologies of political liberalism and literary humanism often appears to represent equal opportunity, progress, and freedom. In *The Revolt of the Masses* (1932) José Ortega y Gasset defined nineteenth-century liberalism as "the supreme form of generosity; it is the right which the majority concedes to minorities and hence it is the noblest cry that has ever resounded in this planet. It announces the determination to share existence with the enemy [the masses of mankind]; more than that, with an enemy which is weak" (qtd. in Aney 1954, 11).

In a similar vein, Willson H. Coates and Hayden V. White (1970) argue that humanism "has stood for political and judicial equity, the indispensability of open discourse, and the healing mission of fair dealing" (448). By the early twentieth century, Zygmunt Bauman (1987) points out, the word "intellectuals" was "addressed to a motley collection of novelists, poets, artists, journalists, scientists and other public figures who felt it their moral responsibility, and their collective right, to interfere directly with the political process" (1). Troubled by the trend toward increasing professional specialization, intellectuals opted for a label that permitted them to function as a united front. "The concept of the intellectuals was coined as a rallying call, and as an attempt to resuscitate the unfulfilled claims of the past," writes Bauman. "Ostensibly, it referred to qualities its intended recipient already possessed; in fact it connoted motives and actions wished for the future" (23). Preoccupied with "truth, judgement and taste" (Bauman 1987, 2), the self-acknowledged role of the intellectual and of many of the poets in the 1920s and 1930s was that of legislator or prophet. Day Lewis (1942), the Auden group poet, made this role clear: "Circumstances may force the poet unwillingly to take up the position of prophet" (14–15).

The role of the critic generally is to evaluate and analyze, and to maintain the critic's cultural authority. As Frank Kermode (1985) argues, "Since we have no experience of a venerable text that ensures its own perpetuity, we may reasonably say that the medium in which it survives is commentary." Kermode points out that the success of an interpretive argument is "not to be measured by the survival of the comment but by the survival of its object" (36, 37). In England of the 1930s, where cultural authority was at a low ebb, critics were especially concerned with the creation of literary value. This attitude seems to have infected the other side of the Atlantic as well. In 1941, Randall Jarrell concluded a discussion of Auden's post-1930s changes with an apology for not creating enough value: "I feel embarrassed at having furnished . . . so much Analysis and so little Appreciation. But analyses, even unkind analyses of faults, are one way of showing appreciation."[19]

Critics today do not often publish essays whose main focus is the creation of value.[20] Barbara Herrnstein Smith (1988) puts it bluntly, "Evaluative criticism remains intellectually suspect." These days the critical quest has a different aim—interpretation—the focus of which is meaning. Value, argues Smith, "is radically contingent, . . . an effect of multiple, continuously changing . . . variables, . . . the product of . . . an *economic system*" (23, 30). The value of discourse, according to Michel Foucault (1972), is greatly affected by its capacity for circulation, transformation, and exchange. A book, like a statement, "defines, in what precedes it, its own filiation, redefines what makes it possible or necessary, excludes what cannot be compatible with it" (124). Once written, it may be published, sold, reviewed, amended, excerpted, reprinted, canonized, forgotten, or burned.[21] Meaning, as we shall see in these case studies, is very much a function of historical context.

European avant-garde movements of the interwar period struggled to overcome their attachment to individual expression and privilege, but could not help revealing that poetry for them was a kind of secular scripture.[22] Literary scholarship's relationship to textuality similarly propels the hermeneutic enterprise; we tend to believe that textual interpretation is required in order to lay bare hidden meanings. Poets of the historical avant-garde showed signs of believing in the arbitrariness of the linguistic sign, but were in fact more closely allied with the priesthood of poetry than with modern semiotics. Critics are caught in a conflict between their facility for deconstructing value and meaning and their need to validate their role as guardians of cultural treasure. Bové warns that many "humanistic visions . . . fail . . . because they do not research the institutional and discursive conditions of their own work."[23]

A debate continues about the propriety or impropriety of revisionist historiography. The Auden group's painful experiences during the 1930s (their project of making the poet into a sort of visionary social leader was an embarrassing failure) prove that value is a mutable and often fragile quality. Critics who believe that value inheres in literary texts are perhaps most comfortable with the critic's appropriation of new roles. Those who fear that critics can damage the standing of texts whose social dynamics the critics find offensive are more likely to see in such practice a "hermeneutics of suspicion." F. R. Leavis, for example, blamed critics for catapulting the young Auden too quickly into fame and thus not forcing him to mature in ways Leavis thought he should. Criticism is nearly always purposeful and strategic, even when it does not acknowledge what is at stake in its values, preferences, and conflicts.

A goal of criticism should be a greater awareness of and an effort to change the often unequal power dynamics that govern humanism's vision of egalitarianism and objectivity. Such a criticism assists literary human- ism to rise to the level of its own values in a more reasoned and honest way than in the past. To this end, it is possible to consider the avant-garde experience a metaphor for contemporary academia, where the internal requirements for membership are sometimes rigid and the quest for ex- ternal influence strong. This book will, I hope, contribute to forging a criticism that better resists polarized views, distorting myths, inadequate acknowledgement of bias, and the erasure of a shared and necessary quest for power.

The Argentine Vanguardia

2. The Radical Conservatism of the Journals and Manifestos of the Argentine Vanguardia

In the 1920s Buenos Aires was like a European city that by some bit of bad luck had found itself on the wrong side of the Atlantic. European influence was not new: by 1914, almost a third of the population was foreign-born, including an especially high percentage of men over age twenty (Leland 1986, 6). The golden days of the ruling oligarchy's "liberal authoritarianism" (Matamoro 1975, 114–15) were coming to an end as Argentines struggled with the rise of populism and the xenophobic nationalism of those reacting against it. Because foreign influences were so strong, the nation had to make a special effort to remain aware of its colonial roots. *Hispanismo,* or Spanish heritage, became a positive value in the quest for Argentine identity. Intellectuals opposed spiritualism to the more "Anglo-Saxon" values of commercialism and materialism (Rock 1987, 273), valuing highly writers who claimed total independence from market influences. For writers who came of age when Argentina was torn between the pressures of international cultural exchange and an urgent need to assert national identity, the conflict between the domestic and the foreign was divisive and confusing. The young polyglot Jorge Luis Borges spent World War I in Switzerland and in 1921 brought the avant-garde ideology of ultraism from Spain, yet many of his early poems and essays aim to evoke or describe the elusive national essence known as *argentinidad.* Like other poets who became members of the vanguardia, Borges had contradictory loyalties to both sides of the decade's binary division between European cosmopolitanism, characterized by Domingo Sarmiento's "civilization," and the innate "barbarism" of argentinidad based on violent folk heroes and the sprawling pampas.

Given the constructed nature of literary groups, it should come as no surprise that the Argentine vanguardia was not one group, but several groups whose ideas shifted with the changing projects of a series of small literary journals. Their memberships changed as fast as did the journals' names; the poets of the 1920s were at different times called the ultraists, the Generation of 1922, the Generation of 1927, Florida, the martinfier-ristas and, of course, the vanguardia. Their work was labeled "la nueva sensibilidad," "metaforismo," and "imagenismo" ("the new sensibility," "metaphorism," and "imagism") (Running 1981, 31). If, during the 1920s, they were a kaleidoscopic assortment of signatures, labels, projects, and individual talents, contemporary critics are generally comfortable referring to them as the vanguardia without examining whether theirs was a coherent movement.

In significant ways, the Argentine vanguardia was avant-garde in name only, capitalizing on a Continental European concept appropriate to an entirely different set of social and cultural circumstances. Far from rebelling against the status quo of the literary establishment, it helped strengthen that establishment. The avant-garde's project—apart from popularizing free verse and the metaphor—had little apparent innovative content. By attempting to expose a timeless national identity[1] thought to be buried under the collective weight of several million immigrants, Borges and his peers were—theoretically at least—excavating the past, not creating something new.

When Borges imported ultraism from Spain, he was on his way to becoming the de facto leader of what became the vanguardia. "Imported" may be too strong a word, however; Spanish ultraism was vaguely defined and its tenets not markedly different from statements made by the vanguardia's powerful predecessor, Leopoldo Lugones. In the prologue to his most influential book, *Lunario sentimental* (Sentimental moonscape) (1909), Lugones (1961) states that "hallar imágenes nuevas y hermosas, expresándolas con claridad y concisión, es enriquecer el idioma, renovándolo a la vez" (7) (to discover new and beautiful images, expressing them with clarity and concision, is to enrich and renovate the language). Lugones's vague quest for novelty and renovation is little different from that expressed in ultraism's even less specific 1919 Spanish manifesto: "Our motto will be 'Ultra.' . . . And in our credo all tendencies will fit, without discrimination, as long as they express a craving for what is new. Later, these tendencies will attain their nucleus and will be defined." [2]

Borges clearly felt the need to offer a more specific agenda. The first ultraist manifesto to appear in Buenos Aires was a broadside, *Prisma* (Prism), pasted on walls on several streets of the Barrio Norte and Palermo districts of Buenos Aires in December 1921 and March 1922. Poets and writers quickly referred to *Prisma* as a journal, though it could equally well have been thought an isolated expression of a handful of unknown writers. Although my point of view is Eurocentric, I have called its statement of purpose a manifesto because it introduces ultraism in the manner of European manifestos. I believe that *Prisma* would not have taken the form it did nor have a statement of purpose had it not been for the influence of Continental movements on the very young Borges. The distribution of *Prisma* represents a significant break with convention, a gesture toward democratizing access to high literary culture. While Avenida Santa Fe and Callao, two of the streets targeted, were not so elegant as downtown Florida, they reflect the choice of a middle- and upper-class audience. In spite of this choice, the manifesto was a rebellious gesture, and the aristocratic editor of *Sur,* Victoria Ocampo, later likened its mode of distribution to that of "un vulgaire avis" (a vulgar advertisement). [3]

Prisma's use of anticommercial language in an aesthetic platform is a striking sign of avant-garde ambivalence toward the marketplace. The manifesto begins, "Nosotros los ultraistas en esta época de merca-chifles . . ." (We the ultraists in this era of cheap merchants . . .) [4] and goes on to reject those who "sell" words, "traficando con flacas nonerías i trampas antiquísimas" (trafficking in weak remarks and very old tricks). It clearly rejects Rubén Darío and the modernists, but the commercial language is not relevant to them because they were hardly in a position to "traffic" in anything. Such language betrays ambivalence about the commercialization and democratization of literature in an age of mass literacy. The attack on the modernists is informed by fear of the effect of huge waves of literate lower- and middle-class immigrants on the status of poetry. The two kinds of ambivalence—about Darío's language and about the Argentine reading public—are conflated as fear of the socially new spurs production of the aesthetically new (Pérez 1986, 141). The manifesto defines ultraism's goal as the discovery of unsuspected facets of the world. These facets, it claims, will be unveiled through the use of poetry's "elemento primordial: la metáfora" (primordial element: the metaphor).

The budding avant-garde's statement of purpose reflects a desire for consecration and acceptance into the high cultural canon. Its authorship has been disputed; the statement is signed by Borges, his cousin Guillermo Juan, Eduardo González Lanuza, and Guillermo de Torre. De Torre later complained that the manifesto came ultimately to be attributed only to Borges. María Luisa Bastos, on the other hand, reports a different set of signatures for the founding group, omitting de Torre and including Norah Lange. Córdova Iturburu fails to mention de Torre as a collaborator on *Prisma,* naming instead Borges's sister (de Torre's future wife) Norah and Francisco Piñero.[5] The problem of identifying the owners of this intellectual property reflects the degree to which membership in groups can make or break careers.

The month *Prisma* appeared, Borges published a manifesto on ultraism in *Nosotros* (Us), the main journal then representing consecrated literary culture. The choice of publication was influenced by the fact that *Nosotros* was one of the few journals publishing critical essays about poetry. According to early critic Nestor Ibarra, poetry, like the rest of literature and art, was "el más . . . accesorio aspecto de la vida del país. . . . [Y] fuera del grupo cerrado de colaboradores de *La Nación,* la . . . revista *Nosotros* era . . . el único lugar en que se hablaba de literatura con alguna insistencia" (Ibarra 1930, 15–16). (the most . . . accessory aspect of national life. . . . And outside the closed group of contributors to [the newspaper] *La Nación,* the . . . journal *Nosotros* was . . . the only place where literature was spoken of with some insistence"). As the *Nosotros* group derived from the provincial aristocracy, Borges's choice represents a surprising debut for an avant-garde that claimed to be opposed to the literary establishment. John King reveals the confusion that often arises in historical accounts of the movement when he writes: "*Nosotros* became a cultural institution in Buenos Aires, and established a tradition of letters that the avant-garde movements of the 1920s would react against" (King 1986, 14).

There is a discrepancy between the group's stated intent and its behavior; what King writes is both true and not true. Argentine literary culture had an ambivalent relationship to Continental avant-garde movements, and involvement with them was limited largely to the somewhat contradictory choice of reprinting their texts and publishing essays about the excesses of avant-garde ideology and practice. Peruvian poet César Vallejo's "Autopsia de superrealismo" (Autopsy of surrealism), for example, published in *Nosotros* in 1929, announces the death of French surrealism with the comment that there was nothing constructive about it, that its theory was pompous and its ideas unoriginal. It was, according to Vallejo, heavily engaged in "juegos de salón" (salon games).[6] Journals were also sometimes inconsistent in their choices. Though *Nosotros* published various ultraist poems, chief editor Roberto F. Giusti publicly announced his scorn for the way *Prisma* was distributed. Giusti later wrote,

> ¿Qué significa fijar revistas murales, como me dicen que van a hacer algunos jóvenes de Montevideo, a imitación de lo que hicieron algunos de Buenos Aires, supongo a imitación de algunos de París? ¿Pretender hacer arte para el pueblo? . . . ¿Pero eso es literatura? ¡Puah![7]

> (What does it mean to post wall journals, as they tell me some of the young people of Montevideo are going to do in imitation of what some have done in Buenos Aires, I suppose in imitation of some in Paris? To try to make art for the people? . . . But this is literature? Bah!)

Borges later engaged in criticism of his own, calling *Prisma* a poster that not even the walls read.

Borges's *Nosotros* manifesto does not repudiate Lugones or the generation that immediately precedes the vanguardia. Instead, Borges rejects the language of the modernist poets, known as the Generation of 1898, as the "monederos falsos" and "oxidadas figuras mitológicas" ("counterfeit coins" and "rusty mythological figures") of Darío. In other words, he attacks the generation of his literary grandfathers, yet admires his literary fathers. A more radical movement, in an effort to be wholly new, would reject both. Borges describes modernism as a body that is now a skeleton, identifying its flaws as worn-out images, bad rhetoric, and anecdotism. He identifies a new and better poetics but he chooses to name names rather than present a theory of ultraism. He lists more than twenty Argentine ultraists and a handful of foreign poets he claims are ultraists, such as Vicente Huidobro, José Ortega y Gasset, and Ramón Gómez de la Serna. Ultraism's purpose, he says, is to respond to the problem of the declining prestige of poetry in Argentina.[8] Though the manifesto contains more advertising for ultraism than it does ultraist ideas, Borges makes a point of defining traditional subjectivity, arguing that ultraism concerns itself with the "meta primicial de toda poesía, esto es, a la transmutación de la realidad palpable del mundo en realidad interior y emocional" (first goal of all poetry, that is, the transmutation of the palpable reality of the world into inner, emotional reality). The proponent of the "newest aesthetic" does not seem concerned that the aesthetic is actually quite classical. Though formally innovative in its use of free verse, Ernesto López-Parra's "Casa vacía" (Empty house)—offered by Borges as an illustration of ultraism—is strikingly traditional and pre-modernist in its subject matter:

> Toda la casa está llena de ausencia
> la teleraña del recuerdo
> pende de todos los techos.
>
> . . . .
>
> En el reloj parado
> se suicidaron los minutos.
>
> (The entire house is filled with absence
> the spiderweb of memory
> hangs from all of the ceilings.
>
> . . . .
>
> In the stopped clock
> the minutes commit suicide.)

The opening lines of Darío's "Pensamientos de otoño" (Autumn thoughts), written years before ultraism was conceived of, provide a contrasting nostalgia:

> Huye el año a su término
> como arroyo que pasa,
> llevando del Poniente
> luz fugitiva y pálida.
>   (Darío 1956, 40)
>
> (The year hurries to its end
> like a brook passing,
> raising from the West Wind
> fugitive and pale light.)

While both poems foresake rhyme and share a common theme of the inexorable passage of time, López-Parra's personified minutes committing suicide are intentionally startling. Darío's lines are slightly more regular than those of López-Parra, but they are rhythmically similar. Thematically, ultraism is often little different from earlier Argentine poetry, but it is formally quite similar to surrealism in its use of metaphor. And while ultraism's metaphors are more conventional than those of surrealism, their common roots are unmistakable.

Borges's manifesto informs the elite literary community about ultraism through a list of rules, which include the "reducción de la lírica a su elemento primordial: la metáfora" (reduction of the lyric to its primordial element: the metaphor), the synthesis of two or more images, and the avoidance of useless adjectives, obscurity, ornamentalism, and confessionalism. In an article published earlier that year in Madrid, Borges selected metaphor and rhythm as the two essential means to expose "la *sensación* en sí" (*sensation* in itself) and "la emoción desnuda" (naked emotion). He described metaphor as the shortest line between two spiritual points (Borges 1921a, 41). Because this list of rules serves best to instruct those interested in becoming ultraists, Borges appears to address a community of fellow poets. This community speaks from the streets of the microcenter of the city; it is cosmopolitan, is from the middle and upper-middle classes, and is not university based. Its members trade on youth, the authority of borrowed European forms, and a willingness to attack popular literature and the market and audience that support it. Their tools are innovative diction, emphasis on specific rhetorical tropes, and new modes of distribution; their object is the renovation of poetic language and the acquisition of a significant role in contemporary poetry and high cultural life.

In 1925, two years after he arrived for what proved to be his permanent installation in Europe, the Peruvian poet Vallejo published in Lima an essay entitled "Contra el secreto profesional" (Against the professional secret), which accuses the current generation of Latin American poets of being as "rhetorical" and lacking in "spiritual honesty" as its predecessors. He goes on to describe in detail seven characteristics of the new Latin American poetry, labeling each a "Postulado europeo" (European postulate) and identifying its Continental origin. For "that José [*sic*] Luis Borges," he reserves special scorn, mocking the title of Borges's first book, *Fervor de Buenos Aires,* when he describes him as exercizing "un fervor bonaerense . . . falso y epidérmico" (a false and superficial Buenos Aires fervor). Vallejo sees his generation as quintessentially hypocritical, following "los mismos métodos de plagio y de retórica" (the same methods of plagiarism and rhetoric) as the generations it claims to reject (Verani 1990, 192–94).

As political texts, Masiello (1986) argues, Argentine literary manifestos condemn the views and ideas of others; as literary texts, they exalt the individual writer; and as prefatory statements to new journals, they have an anthological function that aims primarily to unify divergent tendencies (67). That Argentina did not have a tradition of manifestos before ultraism perhaps explains why Borges's first effort was somewhat vague. The aesthetic platform of the vanguardia, as Vallejo points out, is not significantly different from that of the modernists or even from that of Lugones. It contains little social rebellion and its constructive project furthers the goals and ideology of modernism. Argentine modernism's goals, writes King (1986), were

> the separateness of poetry from its social context and the need to extend and perfect the craft of literature. It was, of course, a revolt within a system: for all its rejection of bourgeois positivist values, it relied on the patronage of the oligarchy, especially that of the great newspapers such as *La Nación,* in which the writers worked as journalists. (10)

Like the modernists before them, the vanguardia poets wanted to force the newly developing literary tradition to allow qualified members of the middle classes to join the cultural elite. And in keeping with the Generation of 1880 and Sarmiento's call to ward off barbarism, they joined forces with the cultural elite to try to exclude immigrants, the economically disadvantaged, and writers with a social agenda. Theirs was thus an extremely selective democratization of the canon. That the ultraist project was quite conservative can be attributed in part to the facts that Argentine literature was a young literature and that Argentina enjoyed economic good fortune during the 1920s, which Carlos Mastronardi described as the last decade of "happy men." He recalls a country very different from postwar Europe: "In spite of the World War, the generation to which I belong knew a world which was still stable. Only later did the cement of that moral and spiritual universe crumble" (qtd. in Leland 1986, xv). Ultraism's conservatism can also be attributed to the fact that Argentine society was heavily influenced by an influx of fortune-seeking immigrants who threatened to change permanently both political life and the values of literary culture.

While the journal *Proa* (Prow) bears the signatures of important vanguardia poets, its content falls far short of the promises of the movement's rebellious rhetoric. The more vibrant *Martín Fierro* is riddled with contradictions between the radical ideology of the international avant-garde and its own more conservative agenda. It is caught between a tendency toward ancestor worship and reliance on mentors, and the need to be independent, influence free, and shockingly new. National literary organizations and the state are alternately friend and enemy: conforming to the demands of the literary market might threaten a journal's literary quality; yet such conformity was essential to *Martín Fierro*'s survival. The Auden poets and the surrealists, in contrast, had a greater desire to be popular, though they might not have described it that way. Though they did not take the necessary steps, they sporadically wanted to communicate their message to a large public. Similarly, the vanguardia's journals are a study in ambivalence; although this avant-garde spoke in a radical tongue, it generally abided by conservative rules.

The poets of the 1920s wanted to be both modern and Argentine.[9] The goals were in many ways antithetical, and Borges's erratic path through the decade marks his aborted attempts to synthesize the two. The desire to find a poetics independent of Europe and the Argentine modernists led him to create his own brand of linguistic argentinidad and to choose overtly traditional poetic values. His nostalgic representations of a premodern Buenos Aires are not surprising in a country engaged in "founding" a national literature, though they are surprising for an avant-garde leader. Between 1900 and 1930, writers and critics were also faced with the task of making a newly constructed tradition look well established. During the years when the young canon opened to include books about barbarism, such as José Hernández's *Martín Fierro* (not to be confused with the vanguardia journal by the same name), the background of the Argentine writer was shifting. Whereas the writer of the Generation of 1880 was likely to be an aristocrat who wrote avocationally, the writer in 1920 was more likely to be middle class, an aspiring literary professional, and the son or grandson of an immigrant. In between, Rubén Darío's Generation of 1898 was torn between the needs of a burgeoning literate middle class and the state's need for a national literary tradition. Darío complained in *La Nación* that at the turn of the century only the very rich could publish books. However, Italian immigrants and lower-middle-class writers were for the first time represented in major publications; middle-class women began to publish. In 1903, the budding class of bourgeois writers, which had great disdain for what they saw as the bought discursive privileges of their predecessors, called a writers' strike. Even so, many denied any interest in the market, claiming to be motivated only by aesthetic values. This contradiction between stated position and actual behavior became a hallmark of the modernist movement (Viñas 1971, 43–44; 1965, 45).

Early in the century, a bartered compromise was struck: the state would protect the writer and the writer would affirm a state-sanctioned national literature. Through national prizes, authorized by law in 1913, the government assumed the role of institutional literary patron. A specifically Argentine literary curriculum was established in 1912 at the Universidad de Buenos Aires, and in 1915 the Biblioteca Argentina was established to help canonize the official version of Argentine literature. By 1920, the Argentine writer was thoroughly entrenched in the role of cultural interpreter and builder of "la ideología estatal" (state ideology) (Masiello 1968, 34). The vanguardia, however, claimed independence, though its role in creating the national literature and protecting the Spanish language from corruption allied it strongly with oligarchic predecessors. The journal *Martín Fierro* (1924–27),[10] for example, explicitly rejected past masters, only to display reverence for them.[11] Not even the name was new; *Martín Fierro,* José Hernández's famous narrative poem about a gaucho, appeared in 1872. Both *Martín Fierro* and *Proa* made brief appearances after World War I. The three numbers of the first *Martín Fierro* appeared in 1919 and the three numbers of the first *Proa,* all six pages of each issue, appeared in 1922, according to Borges. The journals referred to here are both then "second series," though there will be no further reference to that fact. It is noteworthy that names of old, aborted journals were recycled by a movement obsessed with the new. The journal hid its quest for the power available to consecrated writers behind avant-garde rhetoric while making choices that guaranteed it wouldn't alienate the literary establishment.

Ironically, in many contemporary histories of Argentine literature of the 1920s, the vanguardia was the literary establishment insofar as it was the most important and often discussed literary movement of the decade. Paul Bové's argument that literary humanism naturalizes and refuses to speak openly about power is illustrated by the movement's willingness to ride on the coattails of European avant-gardism—capitalizing on the prestige accorded Continental culture in Argentina—while failing to produce truly avant-garde goods.

The Boedo-Florida conflict between the prose-writing social realists and the vanguardia poets was in part a class war disguised as a literary polemic. Even before the conflict was created, Florida displayed hostility toward the lower classes. In the first issue of *Martín Fierro,* Evar Méndez calls Darío a "plebeian poet." Referring to one of Darío's most famous works, he writes, "Allá por la calle Boedo, lejano rincón . . . ve la luz una popularísima edición de las 'Prosas Profanas,' en vulgar papel de diario, 32 páginas."[12] (There in Boedo Street, distant corner . . . the extremely common edition of "Profane Prose" saw the light of day, on vulgar newspaper paper, 32 pages.) Méndez attacks Darío for allowing the masses to have access to poetic riches. "Indefectíblemente se llega a las multitudes, fatalmente la plebe iletrada se adueña del tesoro mental y rítmico" (*Revista Martín Fierro* 1969, 19). (Unfailingly it gets to the masses, inexorably the illiterate rabble takes possession of the mental and rhythmic treasure.) As most residents of Buenos Aires or *porteños* were literate at this time, the charge of illiteracy was unfounded. The rejection of Darío reveals the vanguardia's tendency to define itself as a socioeconomic elite, though it is more accurately a self-appointed cultural elite. In a satirical poem published soon thereafter, Héctor Castillo hints at the hero worship typical of this era:

> ¡Tú conociste esas veladas, Rubén Darío,
> maestro de todos, padre mío!
>
> · · · · · · · · ·
>
> y en nuestras imaginaciones adolescentes
> surgía tu figura divinamente humana:
> veíamos tu sombra en la mesa lejana,
> indiferente a nuestras miradas reverentes.[13]

> (You knew those night meetings, Rubén Darío,
> master of all, my father!
>
> · · · · · · · ·
>
> and in our adolescent imaginations
> your divinely human form arose:
> we saw your shadow on the distant table,
> indifferent to our reverent gaze.)

Where a more recent poetic forefather, Leopoldo Lugones, is concerned, this ambivalence about whether to reject or admire takes more extreme forms. Though the vanguardia rebels against Lugones, his approval of the manifesto published in number 4 of *Martín Fierro* was solicited and obtained (*Revista Martín Fierro* 1969, 10). The martinfierristas, argued vanguardia poet Leopoldo Marechal, were motivated by "un deseo de modificar las cosas y entrar en la literatura argentina, [y] como no nos dejaban entrar por la puerta, entrar por la ventana o por la claraboya" (Viñas 1971, 43–44) (a desire to modify things and enter into Argentine literature, [and] as they didn't allow us to come in through the door, to enter through the window or the skylight). The means of entry may have been unorthodox, but the goal—consecration—was not.

Martín Fierro's manifesto, written but not signed by Oliverio Girondo, begins in standard Continental avant-garde fashion. A call for poetic renewal is prefaced by a rejection of the institutional consecration of literature and of the state's ideological projects.[14] This anti-institutional posturing and the overt rejection of intellectual nationalism are belied by the presence in the same issue of an unsigned article on municipal literary prizes. Far from rejecting the state's role in promoting intellectual nationalism, *Martín Fierro* complains merely that the city judges have bad taste and should be replaced by an independent body under the Minister of Public Instruction.

Nearly all of the manifesto's paragraphs begin with "MARTÍN FIERRO" as the speaking subject: an unidentified but clearly elite "we" with which the reader is encouraged to ally him- or herself. Membership in this exclusive group is made to sound available to all because the journal intends "salir a la calle a vivirla . . . con sus nervios y con su mentalidad de hoy" (*Revista Martín Fierro* 1969, 26) (to go out into the street to live . . . with its nerves and mentality of today). But the streets are not necessarily where *Martín Fierro* wants to be. Its tastes are modern and upscale: it prefers a "modern transatlantic liner" to a "Renaissance palace." It believes in the importance of the American intellect "severed from all umbilical cords," but warns that "we" should not forget that "todas la mañanas nos servimos de un dentífrico sueco, de unas toallas de Francia y de un jabón inglés" (*Revista Martín Fierro* 1969, 27) (every morning we use Swiss toothpaste, French towels and English soap). *Martín Fierro* borrows freely from European modernist and avant-garde movements, publishing articles on everything from atonal music to Le Corbusier's architecture.

As one critic puts it, Spanish ultraism is the product of "indiscriminate and eclectic borrowings" from other European avant-garde tendencies (Running 1981, 1). Though it is also nationalistic, the Argentine vanguardia is in many ways derivative—the one quality to which no avant-garde will admit. Surrealism is more original in conception, perhaps because it feels free to be antinational. The Auden poets are a hybrid, being more original than derivative, and more gently nationalist than antinationalist. Theirs is a nationalism of default: their revolutionary impulse does not really extend to a vision of a unified world, but to the England of the future.

Martín Fierro claims in its manifesto to have "fe en nuestra fonética, en nuestra visión, en nuestros modales, en nuestro oído" (*Revista Martín Fierro* 1969, 27) (faith in our phonetics, in our vision, in our behavior, in our hearing). But whose phonetics are referred to here? As Beatriz Sarlo points out, the journal refers frequently to popular literature and the immigrant population's "deformities of pronunciation." Its valuing of "linguistic purity" is tied to an ideology of racial purity: bilingualism acquired through education and travel by the upper classes is valued highly, while the natural bilingualism of immigrants and their children is considered a corruption of the Spanish language. The condescending editorial bias of *Martín Fierro*'s "Suplemento explicativo de nuestro 'Manifiesto'" is directed against social realists, Italian immigrants, and the Argentine provinces: "Todos somos argentinos sin esfuerzo, porque no tenemos que disimular ninguna 'pronunzia' exótica." (We are all effortlessly Argentine because we don't have to hide any exotic "pronunziation.") [15]

Roberto Mariani opens the Boedo-Florida conflict by attacking *Martín Fierro* for appropriating the title of a book widely recognized as the symbol of criollismo. He accuses the martinfierristas of being antinational, of having too much admiration for "mediocre" European writers, and of displaying a "scandalous" respect for Lugones, a known fascist sympathizer. *Martín Fierro* responds by claiming to be concerned only with the literary and thus to consider Lugones's politics irrelevant.[16] It opposes "true" art to the literary market, making the sort of arguments soon to be publicized through Benda's *La trahison des clercs* (1927): "*Nuestra* redacción está compuesta por jóvenes con verdadera y honrada vocación artística, ajenos por completo a cualquier afán de lucro que pueda desviar*los* de *su* camino" (*Revista Martín Fierro* 1969, 55; my emphasis). (*Our* editorial staff is composed of young people with true and honorable artistic vocation, completely free of any eagerness for money that could make *them* swerve from *their* path.) Though *Martín Fierro* uses the first-person plural freely, here is a midsentence retreat to the third person, making the statement appear more factual than subjective. Indeed, the second half of this sentence is sometimes quoted out of context and accepted at face value by critics.

The debate between Boedo and Florida is quickly cast in binarisms. Boedo calls itself the extreme left and Florida suggests that Boedo is right-wing and fascistic,[17] though left and right denominations have little meaning at this time in Argentine history. Each side caricatures the other: Florida portrays Boedo as uncultured and uncouth market-oriented naturalists. Boedo depicts Florida as so infatuated with antirepresentational "pure art" that portraits, landscape, characters, ideas, and feelings are all at risk of being abandoned.[18] This vision, which makes Florida appear more avant-garde than it in fact is, may explain Florida's interest in participating in a rather trumped-up polemic. The labels "Boedo" and "Florida" were not applied to the conflict until August 1925, more than a year after what was historicized as the opening salvo. The vanguardia was the first to label its opponent. Given the number of labels used to identify the vanguardia poets, we can conclude that generation-naming and conflict-naming accelerated the historicization process and thus functioned as acts of consecration in the 1920s.

While the struggle over the relationship between literature and the market is real, the Boedo-Florida conflict was in important ways faked by groups that weren't in competition for the same readers, preferred different genres, and had little need even of communicating with each other. Boedo's limited poetic oeuvre is formally and thematically different from Florida's. Compare the rhymed opening stanza of Boedan Celedonio Flores's "La muerte de la bacana" (Death of the wild woman):

> Ya no se oyen cantos en la linda pieza
> donde en otros tiempos la paica reinó,
> hoy flota un ambiente como de tristeza
>   o de qué sé yo.
> (Aguirre 1979, 1:158)

> (Songs are no longer heard in the pretty room
> where in another time the young girl reigned,
> today there's an ambiance of sadness
>   or of what I cannot say.)

with the beginning of Oliverio Girondo's "Insomnio" (Insomnia), also published in 1922:

> ¿Será mío este brazo que está bajo la almohada?
> Las ideas me duelen como muelas cariadas.
> Los minutos remachan sus clavos en mi sien.
> Una inquietud sin causa me ilumina los ojos
> y a través de mis párpados pasa un absurdo "film."
> (Aguirre 1979, 1:125)

> (Is it mine, this arm beneath the pillow?
> Ideas hurt me like rotten molars.
> The minutes hammer their nails into my forehead.
> An inexplicable uneasiness illuminates my eyes
> and through my eyelids an absurd "film" plays.)

The vanguardia would consider the vague emotion in Flores's quatrain maudlin and the rhyme a sign of weakness. Girondo's poem is reminiscent of surrealism in the alienated wonder of the speaker toward parts of his body and the metaphoric linkage of this body with thoughts, feelings, and sensory experience. Boedan poetry, in contrast, tends toward bathos, traditional form, and lower-class themes. While their literary orientations are different, Boedo and Florida are, however, competing for recognition by official culture. Their conflict reveals the vanguardia's painful obsession with market success and its fear that the lower classes will dominate literary culture. To this end, *Martín Fierro* accuses Boedo of crude realism involving "masturbación, prostitución, placas sifilíticas, piojos"[19] (masturbation, prostitution, syphilitic scabs, lice). *Martín Fierro* views its mission as the education of the barbarous, Boedans and others included: "Dos años y pico . . . son muy poca cosa para conseguir acortar las orejas de los burros y transformar le mentalidad de millares de cretinos."[20] ("The little over two years [that *Martín Fierro* has existed] . . . is a very short time for managing to shorten the ears of the asses and transform the mentality of thousands of cretins.")

It is easy to infer from the language of the two groups that the Floridians are upper class and the Boedans working class. In fact, both were largely middle class, though the Floridians were generally better off. Both sides went to great lengths to emphasize the differences between them. In a formula that prefigures surrealism's increasing political involvement in the late 1920s, Boedan Leónidas Barletta sums up the differences as "Art for the Revolution" versus "The Revolution for Art" (qtd. in Leland 1986, 39). The bracketing of these labels is appropriate because the vanguardia was politically conservative and aesthetically innovative, while the Boedans, only vaguely leftist, emphasized a commitment to social realism. To confuse things further, the vanguardia liked to bandy about the adjective "revolutionary" to describe its own activities. Both groups were committed to identifying and producing models of argentinidad and to canonical consecration. Their rhetoric is similar and their missions vague. As binarisms go, the Boedo-Florida conflict is one of the weakest—yet paradoxically most famous—to structure the literary history of this period.

Choosing Boedo as an opponent enabled Florida to attack the market, the popular audience, and Boedo's "novela semanal" (weekly novel).

Sabemos, sí, de la existencia de una subliteratura, que alimenta la voracidad inescrupulosa de empresas comerciales creadas con el objeto de satisfacer los bajos gustos de un público semianalfabeto.[21]

(We know, yes, of the existence of a subliterature that feeds the unscrupulous appetites of commercial enterprises created to satisfy the lowly tastes of a semiliterate public.)

Criticism flew in both directions. As the Boedan journal *Los Pensa-dores* wrote, "¿Quién entiende lo que dice *Martín Fierro? Proa.* ¿Y lo que dice *Proa?* Lo entiende *Martín Fierro.*" [22] (Who understands what *Martín Fierro* says? *Proa.* And what *Proa* says? *Martín Fierro.*)

While there are dozens of critical accounts of the Boedo-Florida con-flict, most reflect Florida's point of view. Emir Rodríguez Monegal (1978) adopts a militantly pro-Florida stance and distorts the political spectrum of the period. He alludes to Boedo: "The publicity stunt was part of a determined effort by some writers more or less connected with the emerging Communist Party to gain control of or destroy the avant-garde movement" (192). María Raquel Llagostera's (1987) introduction to the an-thology *Boedo y Florida* reflects the unequal status of the two groups. The discussion of Florida precedes that of Boedo and is nearly twice as long (i–viii). And in a contemporary collection of journal reproductions, *Nosotros, Proa, Martín Fierro,* and *Inicial* are represented and Boedo's important journals are not. The title of one of the few histories told from Boedo's per-spective, Barletta's *Boedo y Florida: una versión distinta,* identifies itself as an "unofficial history" and hints at the plethora of opposing official histo-ries. That Boedan Barletta was born in Barrio Norte, one of Buenos Aires's fanciest districts, illustrates the danger of making socioeconomic distinc-tions between the groups. Barletta's argument is much like that of leftist critics such as Blas Matamoro and David Viñas. Its thesis is that the upper classes established journals, publishing houses, and literary organizations in order to ensure that their literary paternalism would survive changing social conditions and the democratization of culture. Barletta argues that Boedo was humanistic in the broadest sense, especially in its desire to have art address the concerns of all people, not just the privileged minorities. In his view, Florida's main goal was to stop popular consciousness from being awakened to social inequities. Given that Florida's work did not reach the popular audience and that Florida actually helped publicize Boedo, this argument seems specious. In fact, Boedo and Florida were so similar in important ways that a number of writers—among them, Nicolás Olivari, César Tiempo, and Enrique and Raúl González Tuñón—belonged to both groups.

In a 1927 *Nosotros* article, Borges rejected the idea of Boedo and Florida, which he continued for the rest of his life to ridicule as a boyish prank and an invention of the critics. Late in life, Borges told an interviewer that neither Boedo nor Florida existed and that Roberto Mariani and Ernesto

Palacio were responsible for a sham conflict based on imitating the literary meetings of Paris. He further claimed that he had asked to be in Boedo, but that the "organizers" told him he'd already been assigned to Florida (see Vázquez 1984, 306–7). He did not take these stands, however, until the conflict had died of its own accord and long since ceased to be a useful publicity tool for the vanguardia. Much as avant-garde groups are sometimes dismantled when no longer useful, so their enemies are abandoned and devalued when they have outlived their purpose. By the time Borges undermined the polemic, Argentine critics had made an investment in historicizing Boedo-Florida that he was powerless to destroy.[23]

That *Martín Fierro* had done its best to ensure that the conflict would not be soon forgotten reflects a central contradiction of avant-garde movements. While tending toward the ahistorical and even antihistorical in their rejection of literary influence, they are often obsessed with historicizing themselves. This obsession is part of the avant-garde's suicide watch: the vast majority of movements seek to present themselves in a memorable and lasting way. In retrospect, Florida's taking up the gauntlet with Boedo served mainly to publicize both groups and to allow Florida—which by its borrowed avant-garde nature had to have enemies—to choose a low-risk opponent. Though often considered the irrational and ephemeral fringe of literature, the avant-garde makes choices that promote its power, integrity, and survival. Attacking the state or high culture would have been suicidal in the context of a barely formed literary culture. Attacking the social realists, on the other hand, gained the vanguardia the approval of consecrated cultural authorities and facilitated the movement's canonization.

Like Boedo and Florida, which emphasized weak points of opposition (such as the poets' backgrounds) and slighted strong ones (such as difference of genre and audience) *Martín Fierro* frequently contradicted its stated values and goals. An article "¿Quién es '*Martín Fierro*'?" opens with a barrage of insults about the ignorance and bad faith of literature's "bajo fondo" (lowest depths), a promise that "our cretins" will receive no more explanations of *Martín Fierro*'s mission, and a bullying statement that the journal will cease publication "quando llegue el momento en que nos desagrade seguir publicándolo"[24] (when the moment arrives when it displeases us to keep publishing it). The editors go on to reiterate the journal's platform and list the names of its active membership and famous contributors. The latter group includes Federico García Lorca, Guillaume Apollinaire, Rainer Maria Rilke, Paul Eluard, and Pablo Neruda. Within six months of publishing a manifesto where all readers are encouraged to participate in the pronoun "we," the imaginary reader becomes the hostile Boedan and the editorial "we" is restrictive.

This mini-manifesto is only one of several to appear during the journal's short life. In mid-1925, two thousand copies of a flyer announce that *Martín Fierro* has twenty thousand "truly intellectual" readers, an unusually high number for an avant-garde journal. But even the flyer contains a defensive note: "'MARTÍN FIERRO' necesita su protección" ("MARTÍN FIERRO" needs your protection). It is hard to imagine what enemy could be threatening it, given that its readership vastly surpasses that of *Nosotros* and that, as enemies go, Boedo is something of a straw man. Bastos reports that twenty thousand copies were printed of number 18 of *Martín Fierro;* Iturburu concurs. Jorge B. Rivera, on the other hand, reports a printing of seven thousand copies and a readership of between twenty and thirty thousand (Bastos 1974, 37; Iturburu 1962, 25; Rivera 1985, 377). *Nosotros,* in contrast, published approximately one thousand copies per issue. *Martín Fierro*'s tabloid format, price, and use of color, photographs, and humor can be read as overtures toward the popular market. Ironically, the success of its marketing and self-promoting strategies may have increased the journal's editorial wrath toward Boedo.

In its last number, *Martín Fierro* claims to be the only "tribuna libre" (open platform) in the Americas or Europe.[25] The journal's democratic self-image is not new in Argentine high culture. *Nosotros*'s "Nuestro programa" (Our program) states, "La revista es de todos, culta y autorizada tribuna en donde se han encontrado los hombres de las más varias edades, tendencias y credos, y donde no flamea ni ha flameado otra bandera que no sea la de la libertad."[26] (The journal is for everyone, a cultured and authorized forum where men of the most varied ages, tendencies and creeds have met, and where there neither flutters nor has fluttered a banner that isn't the banner of freedom.") This statement, however, is oxymoronic: given the elitism of cultural authority, the journal can't simultaneously be "de todos" (for everyone) and a "culta y autorizada tribuna" (cultured and authorized forum).

Literature, *Martín Fierro* argues, is not what pleases the masses. In its last issue, the journal reviews its own history and ideological positions by citing statements from numbers 2, 3, 4, 5–6, 7, 16, and 17, and reiterates a commitment to absolute apoliticism,[27] though there is evidence that the journal folded for specifically political reasons. The most common explanation of its November 1927 demise involves party politics of the sort to which the journal was most opposed. Electoral politics were considered the worst kind of politics because they were associated with rampant corruption. (Politics more broadly construed were less offensive. This distinction becomes clearer in the 1930s journal *Sur*, where electoral politics were shunned and international political issues embraced.) One group of martinfierristas wanted the journal to support Hipólito Irigoyen of the Radical Party for the Argentine presidency and another did not. According to Girondo, the ensuing impasse caused Evar Méndez to shut down the journal. That the editor alone—a man older and more experienced than many of the contributors—may have shut it down suggests that the vanguardia's most vital organ of expression did not in fact altogether belong to them. Like earlier generations of poets, they depended on sources of money and influence whose power was greater than their own and that they could not control (Schwartz 1987, 126; see also Altamirano and Sarlo 1980, 169).

Martín Fierro's rebellion against the bourgeoisie was weak compared to that of European avant-garde movements. As Sarlo puts it, "*Martín Fierro* difunde las vanguardias europeas menos radicales y sus elecciones tienen que ver también con los límites de su crítica al filisteísmo burgués: crítica estética que deja intactas la hipocresía moral, la represión sexual e ideológica" (in Barrenechea, Jitrik, Rest, et al. 1981, 84). (*Martín Fierro* disseminates the least radical European avant-garde movements and its choices also have to do with the limits of its criticism of bourgeois philistinism: aesthetic criticism that leaves moral hypocrisy and sexual and ideological repression intact.)

Nor was the vanguardia wholly a product of the young and the new. Macedonio Fernández, critic and literary elder statesman, strongly influenced the martinfierristas, and Ricardo Güiraldes and Evar Méndez— both years older than Borges—helped get *Martín Fierro* off the ground at the instigation of publisher Samuel Glusberg. The fact that older writers were mentors for younger writers and helped lead the movement conflicts with the vanguardia's definition of itself as wholly young. The 1923 *Nosotros* survey of the new literary generation specifically defines its target group as those under thirty years old.[28] Girondo, who traveled to several countries promoting the *vanguardia,* turned thirty very early in the 1920s. It is problematic to suggest—as many critics nevertheless do—that *Martín Fierro* was a product of youthful spontaneity. I suspect that this view is often accepted partly because the vanguardia reiterated it so many times. Like the English *New Signatures, Proa* and *Martín Fierro* were the products of enterprising editors and fame-seeking poets, not simply the spontaneous expression of young people motivated by a common goal. *Prisma* fits most closely the vanguardia's idea of itself as a spontaneous, natural, and irrepressible force. But the more Continental *Prisma,* it should be remembered, was one page long and survived for only two numbers.

The 1924 platform of *Proa* (1924–25) is based on a rhetoric of diversity and the spiritual compatibility of four personally and politically different writers.[29] As Borges later recounted *Proa*'s founding, Alfredo Brandán Caraffa told Borges he had been talking with Pablo Rojas Paz and Ricardo Güiraldes and that they wanted Borges's help in starting a new journal. The flattered Borges ended up in a hotel room with the equally flattered Güiraldes and Rojas Paz, to whom Brandán Caraffa had told the same story. Each contributed fifty pesos toward paying for the journal's first number (Ferrari 1985, 106–7). Borges later claimed that the four founders discovered only "little by little" one another's politics. Borges describes himself as an anarchist and individualist and Brandán Caraffa as a member of the Radical Party. González Lanuza, also important to the journal, was a "pacifistic communist." Leland hints that Brandán Caraffa was a budding fascist in the 1920s. An article Brandán Caraffa published in *Inicial* identifies as "forces of light" things Italo-French, Catholic, and antidemocratic, and labels "forces of darkness" things communist, Jewish, puritan, and capitalist.[30] Recalling the 1920s several decades later, Borges erases the political fervor of the era when he says that the reason the poets learned only gradually of one another's politics was that "en aquel tiempo la pasión política no existía" (Vázquez 1984, 254) (at that time political passion didn't exist).

Proa's upbeat manifesto argues that literary youth have a collective duty to take advantage of a moment of cultural flowering and spiritual growth in Argentina. But the proposed synthesis of diverse strands of Latin American and European literature, to be achieved in part through the itinerant Girondo's pan-Latin American public relations work, resulted in an anthological journal inconsistent with the premises of avant-gardism. The journal's stated project is the creation and dissemination of high culture in Argentina, not avant-garde innovation. It also emphasizes the commodification of literature: "La alta cultura que hasta hoy había sido patrimonio exclusivo de Europa y de los pocos americanos que habían bebido en ella, empieza a trasuntarse en forma milagrosa, como producto esencial de nuestra civilización."[31] (The high culture that until today had been the exclusive patrimony of Europe and of the few Americans that had drunk its waters, begins to translate itself miraculously into an essential product of our civilization.)

Proa's manifesto makes the hardly credible choice of identifying World War I as the Argentine vanguardia's catalyst. If this inconsistency can be ascribed to too-direct borrowing from European models, other choices are more mysterious. The manifesto, for example, cites approvingly such figures as Diderot, Machiavelli, Faust, and God, and the journal goes on to promote openly the professionalization of the writer, celebrating and selling itself through the approval of the cultural elite: "Poco a poco las clases cultas comprendieron la magnitud del fenómeno y después de observarnos de lejos con curiosidad mezclada de duda, nos dieron su sanción más amplia."[32] (Little by little the cultured classes understood the magnitude of the phenomenon and, after observing us from afar with curiosity mixed with doubt, gave us their fullest approval.) In avant-garde terms, then, *Proa*'s manifesto is largely an antimanifesto. To place this in a Continental perspective, André Breton threw writers out of the surrealist movement for subscribing to considerably milder consecration-oriented points of view. The vanguardia's journals were important to the movement. Without them, there was no consistently available means of communicating with the public. The surrealists needed theirs as well, and were more adept at creating new ones when the old ones faded in importance or failed to meet current needs. The Auden poets, thoroughly traditional in their self-promotion strategies, hardly needed journals at all.

Martín Fierro and *Proa* participated in a successful commercial project that enabled the vanguardia to publish its most important works independently of the mainstream market. In 1924, vanguardia "elders" Girondo, Méndez, and Güiraldes founded an avant-garde publishing house. Editorial Proa offered a modified version of the author-paid edition by which the vast majority of books were published in Argentina at the turn of the century. The goal of its fellow press, Editorial Martín Fierro, was much grander than the small editions would allow: "Desearíamos llevar a la gran masa de público la obra de los martinfierristas, producción de índole popular, propaganda de ideas nuevas."[33] (We want to carry to the great public masses the work of the martinfierristas, a popular sort of product, propaganda of new ideas.) In spite of this rhetoric, the establishment of the press is a sign of rebellion against the popular market and an illustration of the movement's willingness to buy its way into the book market.[34]

Proa's only complaint about *La Nación*'s 1924 article "Los poetas jovenes" (The young poets) is that the all-inclusive title was not followed by an all-inclusive treatment of such poets. Its editors and poets do not object to *La Nación*'s role as consecrator of young poets so long as certain names aren't overlooked. *Proa* also speaks in favor of the newly founded, elite Sociedad Amigos del Arte, which it describes as an organization "formada por lo selecto de nuestras clases dirigentes"[35] (formed by the elite of our ruling classes) to create an environment where true artists can produce "la obra perdurable" (lasting works).

In the first issue of *Proa*, Borges rejects ultraism, using the past tense to show that he considers the movement and its aesthetic to be dead. Even the rejection of Darío and praise for the metaphor are recounted in past tense. Borges discounts *Prisma* as the "primera, única e ineficaz revista mural" (first, unique and ineffective wall journal).[36] If we believe him, we are clearly already in another era, that of the post–avant-garde.

But the poetry published in *Proa* is typically ultraist and the journal makes no effort to reconcile the conflicting stances. Raúl González Tuñón's "Humo" (Smoke), for example, is riddled with metaphors such as: "Tu violín está enfermo de parálisis; / se ahorcan los sonidos." (Your violin is ill from paralysis; / the sounds hang themselves.) In "Poemas solitarias," Güiraldes's theme is rural and antimodern:

> He puesto mis labios en los de la vida:
> Náusea.
>
> .   .   .
>
> Recuerdos:
> ¡Qué blancos eran los muros de las casas, que heróicos los hombres!
> .   .   .   .
> El toro con sus guampas rompía viento como los mástiles.
> Y todo era más abierto.
>
> (I have put my lips to those of life:
> Nausea.
>
> .   .   .
>
> Memories:
> How white the walls of the houses, how heroic the men!
> .   .   .   .
> The bull cut the wind with horns like masts.
> And everything was more open.)

There are several signs of ultraism in these lines: a Borgesian rejection of the urban, personification, free verse, and the fusion of different elements (here, land and sea) in a single metaphor. "Metaforismo" is an apt description of this aesthetic and there is comparatively little thematic innovation. For all of its "newest aesthetic" rhetoric, ultraism is well represented by such nostalgic poems.

Proa's lack of coherent platform and enemies make it tend toward random anthologization, conservative articles, and anti–avant-gardism. De Torre, for example, dismisses surrealism by arguing that it would destroy all normal intellectual interaction. Nevertheless, *Proa* risks being overrun by French values. In number 8, there are as many advertisements for literary journals from Paris alone as from all of Latin America. The issue opens with a congratulatory message from Valéry Larbaud translated from the French. Larbaud cannot keep Europe out of the picture, nor indeed can *Proa* see itself except through European eyes: "De aquí en adelante, el escritor hispano-americano no será un europeo desterrado en un país hostil cuyos habitantes lo miran con desconfianza y desdén."[37] (From here on, the Spanish-American writer will no longer be a displaced European in a hostile country whose inhabitants look at him with mistrust and disdain.) Because the search for the new was so important to the Argentine vanguardia and because *Nosotros* had already published many European texts, Borges resorted in *Proa* to the novelty of first translations with a page from Joyce's *Ulysses*. "Soy el primer aventurero hispánico que ha arribado al libro de Joyce: país enmarañado y montaraz."[38] (I am the first Hispanic adventurer to put into port at Joyce's book: muddled, primitive country.) His choice is noteworthy, partly because—as Borges mentions—many members of the cultural elite cannot read English, though nearly all read French (Ferrari 1985, 103). Borges admits he hasn't finished reading *Ulysses*, a "critic's" book that will be better understood a decade hence. His translation of the last page appropriates the Irish epic for the use of the Río Plata region by using the "vos" form and changing "James" to "Jaime" in the final signature.

Borges's strategies here present the Argentine vanguardia as a pioneering explorer of European culture, but the vanguardia was neither a first explorer of European letters nor did it expand significantly the range of issues addressed by journals of *Proa*'s type. Furthermore, such experiments did not help *Proa* survive. A 1925 letter from Güiraldes to Larbaud describes disloyal collaborators and an indifferent public (Güiraldes 1962, 767). *Proa* exemplifies the avant-garde journal that skips the *ruptura* stage, moves directly to *decoro,* and fails quickly. But why is the journal that failed to create a life-sustaining conflict consistently labeled avant-garde? The answer has much to do with the dominant role accorded the author in Argentine culture: *Proa* is short on avant-garde ideology, but it has all the right signatures. For the surrealists, in contrast, what is said is in many instances more important than who says it, except in the context of surrealism's internal power struggle.

In 1927, Evar Méndez describes the Argentine vanguardia as a sort of anti–avant-garde having "nada de anarquismo, confusión, nihilismo. . . . Ninguna locura, ninguna desmedida fantasía, nada de dadaísmo o anti-literatura disolvente, ni siquiera dejar hablar del subconsciente" (Méndez 1927, 18) (nothing of anarchism, confusion, nihilism. . . . No madness, no excessive fantasy, no dadaism or dissolving anti-literature, not even a mention of the subconscious). The poets, he argues, are revolutionary in comparison with those who follow the laws of rhetoric books. But we have seen that the vanguardia poets are only relatively and contextually revolutionary. Their revolution is aesthetic, but as their goal is to produce the purest, most classical free verse possible, it is a modest revolution. In his essay "Doce poetas nuevos" (Twelve new poets), Méndez (1927) renames them the "poets of 1927," rehistoricizing the Generation of 1922. His title refers to "new poets" as though he were the first to discover them. This example of the redundant renaming of a group may have been intended to modify public opinion, to revise the group into a "conservative" group or to renew it in some other way (15–16).

Ultraism's form is modern, though its subjects are often premodern. Borges and Girondo represent the opposing discursive boundaries of the Argentine vanguardia; other members of the group fall eclectically between them. Ricardo Molinari and Francisco Luís Bernárdez are formally conservative. González Lanuza and Norah Lange, the movement's only woman, come closest to following the formal dictates of ultraism, though Lange breaks the rules by writing romantic poetry. González Lanuza's ultraist "La vaca" (The cow) is as pastoral as a poem by a Georgian on a country holiday:

> La vaca es una pausa sobre el campo
> está ruminando siglos.
> Cuando los mediodías triscan sobre los prados
> en una blanda lentitud de ensueño,
> se duermen en sus ojos los ocasos.[39]

(The cow is a pause over the countryside
it is ruminating centuries.
When the middays romp over the fields
in a soft, dreamy slowness
the sunsets sleep in her eyes.)

Traditional diction and themes are paired with ultraist rhetorical tricks
such as the making of verbs into nouns ("La vaca es una pausa"), intran-
sitive into transitive verbs ("está ruminando siglos"), and the animation of
the inanimate ("se duermen . . . los ocasos").

Jacobo Fijman stands out among the vanguardia poets for his willingness to criticize society. In a gesture uncharacteristic of the group, he
attacks his own participation in the mythology of the cultural elite:

> Me ha liberado de los cuatro puntos cardinales,
> Y del bien y del mal;
> De mi ciencia de biblioteca,
> De mis pequeños sueños de orangután civilizado.[40]

> (I have freed myself from the four cardinal points,
> And from good and evil;
> From my library science,
> From my little civilized orangutan dreams.)

This direct criticism of Argentine intellectualism is not reprinted in the
major vanguardia anthologies nor is Fijman more than briefly mentioned
in the more important historical accounts of the movement. He was marginalized for a number of reasons: he was an immigrant Jew who converted
to Catholicism and his poems were sometimes thematically rebellious. His
relationship to the irrational and madness and his experiments with form
pushed him, like Girondo, to the margins of the movement.[41]

When a group's poetry is as eclectic as that of the Argentine vanguardia or resembles the work of its predecessors as closely as theirs does, it
is difficult to argue convincingly that formal innovation is its true raison
d'être. The following lines call into question the poetic uniqueness of the
vanguardia. Which poet, for example, wrote "La noche nueva es como
un ala sobre tus azoteas" (The new night is like a wing over your flat
roofs)? Which "Sobre la O vocativa de las bocas abiertas" (Over the vocative O of the open mouths)? Or "el jazz-band de los ángeles / toque el
fox-trot del juicio final" (the jazz-band of the angels / plays the foxtrot of

the final judgment)? "El mar . . . / refleja la lámina de un cielo de cinc" ("The sea . . . / reflects the metal of a zinc sky)? "En la red de su ingenio caían las metáforas" (Into the web of his genius metaphors fell)? Which is by Florida, which Boedo, which Darío, which Lugones? Do these lines — written by poets of three poetic generations and a variety of orientations — differ in fundamental ways? The first is from Borges's poem "Montevideo," the second is from Lugones's *Los fuegos artificiales* (The artificial fires), the third González Lanuza's "Apócalipsis" (Apocalypse), and the fourth Darío's "Sinfonía en gris mayor" (Symphony in gray major). The last is Boedan poet Gustavo Angel Riccio's elegy to "Claudio G. Amoroso." The line cited from it, however, is not representative of Boedan poetry, which tended to be rhymed and to treat social themes.[42] What's interesting about these lines is that the Boedan speaks of metaphors while pre-ultraists Darío and Lugones produce perfect ultraist-style metaphors of their own. Though the vanguardia's poetry was not so different from that of ancestors or enemies as the poets or critics have wanted to believe, what distinguishes it is the *sustained* use of innovative, grammar-transforming metaphor.

Critics of the Argentine vanguardia have tended to adopt the *vanguardia's* myth of itself—as expressed in *Martín Fierro* and the early ultra manifestos—in spite of the movement's many contradictory behaviors. Masiello (1986) writes:

> Los jóvenes escritores argentinos de los años veinte se adjudicaron el rol de líderes de la cultura. Reconstruyeron los problemas artísticos en un estilo *rádicalmente agresivo y siempre estuvieron prontos para repudiar los esfuerzos de los poetas consagrados que los procedieron.* (27; my emphasis)
>
> (The young Argentine writers of the twenties appropriated the role of cultural leaders. They reconstructed their artistic problems in a *radically aggressive style and were always quick to repudiate the forces of the consecrated poets who preceded them.*)

In overstating her case, Masiello sounds a bit like the vanguardia itself. What is at stake in believing the negatively charged rhetoric of a group dedicated to positive, constructive projects? Clearly the vanguardia used persuasive, sometimes propagandistic language in an effort to make its audience believe its arguments. Official histories have over the years privileged written self-portraits over behavior contradicting those self-portraits.[43] Masiello's failure to acknowledge here that the martinfierristas often idolized their consecrated predecessors shows that intelligent critics can be seduced by a group's rhetorical self-image. This privileging of rhetoric over behavior is especially interesting in the case of the surrealists, whose behavior, designed to *épater les bourgeois,* was so integral to their project that conscientious critics must take it into consideration in order to understand the movement. In fact, however, many critics of surrealism have avoided analyzing the poets' behavior where it contradicts the ideology advanced in Breton's two *Manifestes.* Literary history tends to exist as a lineage of texts—texts that refer to other texts and that do not necessarily consider fully the role of nondiscursive behavior.

As we have seen, the martinfierristas moved eagerly to participate in a polemic that forced them to contradict themselves and to deviate from the most basic tenets of European avant-gardism. It appears that Florida felt it had to combine the language of traditional values with avant-garde rhetoric if it was to survive. Indeed, there is no reason to believe that a more radical movement could have survived in high cultural circles at this time. And because, as Kermode argues, literature survives in large measure through the agency of commentary, rapid historicization of memorable ideas and oppositions is necessary. The avant-garde tends to find the limit of the possible for its time and place. Because of its lack of sustaining internal tension, this instance of it dissolved soon after *Martín Fierro* folded and its poets then embarked on different paths. The Auden poets had ample raw material with which to sustain themselves, but decided late in the 1930s that they had failed in their mission. The surrealists, who had the most radical mission of all, reconstituted themselves and, in a progressively weaker form, kept going.

Vanguardia poet Bernárdez, like Auden, became more religious and wrote formally traditional poetry. Marechal followed a similar—though more nationalistic—path. A couple of poets became communists and several, including Borges and Girondo, ended up in the pages of *Sur.* Because suppressed differences among poets later surfaced, their early separation had the salutary effect of helping preserve the idea of a unified movement. The diverse group of writers obtained access to high cultural circles by using the avant-garde as a launching pad for their careers and disbanding when they had gained enough status individually. The surrealists, in contrast, were less concerned with individual careers; for them, the group and its mission mattered most.

Examined in its conservative historical context, the Argentine vanguardia *was* radical. If anything, however, it did the opposite of its stated intention. Instead of protecting official culture from the market, it became the first generation of writers to enter fully into that market and to appropriate space in it through journals and publishing houses. If *Martín Fierro*'s epithets about Boedo are read as an index of its editors' feelings about the market, the transition was a painful one involving fear of lost literary quality and status. Florida may have felt that if it did not become more like Boedo, it would have no audience. Even the martinfierristas understood that *Proa*'s shipwreck was a failure to appeal to any sort of audience, popular or elite. Indeed, *Martín Fierro*'s aggression toward Boedo was stimulated partly by the schizophrenia of its own choices. The avant-garde protests most vocally what it perceives as threats to its status and independence. Unlike more conservative movements, it tends to make public inner conflicts and areas of ambivalence, exposing its psychic wounds. As *Martín Fierro* reveals, the more painful the choice, the shriller the cry of distress. The tendency of official histories to reiterate the avant-garde's myth of itself suggests that critics and historians share a stake in keeping under wraps the ambivalences inherent in high culture's gestures of self-preservation.

3. Borges and Girondo:
Who Led the Vanguardia?

In the 1920s, the Argentine vanguardia valued Borges's lyric poems more highly than Girondo's prose poems. Aside from their mutual commitment to the use of metaphor and to a couple of new literary journals, the two poets had little in common. In important ways Borges was as conservative and traditional as Girondo was radical and avant-garde. That Borges's early work was at that time more highly valued than Girondo's is partly because of the literary establishment's conservatism and the vanguardia's unwillingness to risk upsetting that establishment. Where Girondo was critical of the wealthy, state institutions, the Catholic Church, and the sexual mores of his day, Borges avoided topical issues. He changed course several times in his early years, while Girondo—like Breton—remained committed to the philosophy of the vanguardia. Though both were products of the same cultural atmosphere and had experienced European avant-gardism firsthand, they grew farther and farther apart over the decades. Girondo produced his most radical book, *En la masmédula* (In the uttermarrow, 1954) at a time when Borges was fast becoming a literary and political conservative.

In recent years, critics have echoed the values of the vanguardia by privileging Borges—who helped promote Argentine literature's image of itself as serious and traditional—over Girondo, who mocked and rebelled against this notion of the national literature. Moreover, their treatments of Girondo emphasize his role as the enfant terrible of the vanguardia; he becomes a colorful illustration of avant-garde outrageousness. That he is the *only* such illustration often goes unmentioned. Ironically, Girondo legitimates the vanguardia's status as an avant-garde, while Borges legitimates a decidedly un–avant-garde national literature-in-formation. Through the repetitive action of generations of critical texts, the vanguardia has in many ways become synonymous with Borges, whose poetry and essays stand in an ironically antithetical relationship to the movement's rhetoric. Umberto Eco (1983) writes, "It is not the ability to speak that establishes power, it is the ability to speak to the extent that this ability becomes rigid in an order, a system of rules, the given language" (240–41). The official critical myth also emphasizes the Boedo-Florida conflict and fails to examine with care the differences between the movement's two leaders. Coupled with the rigidity of the movement's reiterated myth-of-self, these critical choices distort the history of the vanguardia.

The literary establishment's attention to Borges during the 1920s and 1930s is consistent with its promotion of projects of cultural nationalism, such as the consolidation of a canon and the building of national literary institutions. To put it bluntly, Borges was a better instrument of cultural propaganda than Girondo, who consequently received less credit for his important role in the movement. The many differences between the poets should present a challenge to critics who start from the erroneous premise that the vanguardia's work was poetically and theoretically consistent. I suspect, though, that an important reason why critics have elided the contrasts between Girondo and Borges is that such an analysis would contribute to the dismantling of the official myth of a unified avant-garde.

Because Borges's oeuvre has been internationally acclaimed while Girondo is known primarily to literary Hispanists, there has also been a tendency in recent years to emphasize Borges in these histories. But as early as 1930 Borges was historicized as the official vanguardia leader, even though having a conservative leader runs afoul of avant-garde ideology. The privileging of Borges over Girondo in later years was increasingly influenced by questions of value and Borges's international fame. Fame, of course, builds on fame. But while Borges was certainly the superior writer when he turned his hand to fiction, Girondo's early poetry is significantly more interesting and innovative than Borges's from an avant-garde point of view. Neither poet produces during these early years an especially memorable body of poetry; Borges evokes a subtle and appealing lyricism, but Girondo's work would have the greater impact on later generations of Argentine poets. Girondo is perhaps the less fortunately born in the sense that he is less suited to his place of birth and would have done better had he been born in Europe. As it is, he turns to Europe for inspiration and support. Similarly, Stephen Spender, C. Day Lewis, and Robert Desnos were not altogether well suited to the circumstances in which they found themselves. Inevitably, some avant-garde poets are miscast in their roles.

In its historical series on the vanguardia, the Centro Editor de América Latina devotes most of two essays to the movement's official history, especially martinfierrismo and the Boedo-Florida conflict. Girondo and Borges are treated separately from each other. When the poets are mentioned together, the emphasis is usually on finding some degree of commonality. About their first books, Carlos Mastronardi (1980/1986) writes: "Se trata de obras nada semejantes entre sí, pero que responden con pareja eficacia a las apetencias de remozamiento que . . . empieza[n] a manifestarse con creciente intensidad" (1). (The works have nothing in common but they respond equally effectively to the appetite for rejuvenation that . . . is beginning to show itself with increasing intensity.) Masiello makes much the same gesture, but treats their poetry separately.[1] Leland (1986) points to the poets' shared "concern for the resonances of the image" without mentioning the differences between them (36). Sarlo Sabajanes emphasizes the diversity of the vanguardia group, only to make her own gesture of erasure of their differences:

> Se ha hablado mucho de la falta de coherencia interna del grupo que hizo la revista *Martín Fierro*. . . . Lo cierto es que . . . el martinfierrismo trasciende a *Martín Fierro,* supera las fronteras, existentes pero invariablemente laxas, de la revista y se conforma en signo constituyente de un grupo coetáneo y generacional.[2]

> (Much has been said about the lack of internal coherence of the group behind the journal *Martín Fierro*. . . . What is certain is that . . . martinfierrismo transcends *Martín Fierro,* overcomes the existing but invariably lax borders of the journal, and becomes the constituent sign of a contemporary and generational group.)

A number of histories of the movement—such as Iturburu's *La revolución martinfierrista,* María Raquel Llagostera's prologue to the anthology *Boedo y Florida,* and Teodosio Fernández's (1987) *La poesía hispánoamericana en el siglo XX* (28–33)—follow the pattern of discussing the vanguardia's central polemic—Boedo versus Florida—without examining the differences dividing the leading vanguardia poets themselves.

Compared to Borges and Girondo, the central Auden poets were quite similar, though when they disbanded at the end of the 1930s, a clamor of voices—including those of the poets themselves—argued that the poets had never had much in common. This refutation was based on hindsight and a collective sense of a failed mission. But the Argentine vanguardia has been historicized as a successful and important movement, which it in fact was. It seems odd that the vanguardia's cohesiveness and integrity have gone unchallenged except by a handful of critics such as Beatriz Sarlo. Given the institutional drive to divide literary history into movements, undermining the vanguardia's integrity would force a revision of Argentine literary history as written. All historical revisionism involves a loss of previously accepted meaning, which can in turn threaten the institutional ideology that erected the history in the first place.

The differences between Borges and Girondo suggest that poetic and personal differences are often less important than the company poets keep and the publications in which their signatures appear. Borges's choice of journals, for example, largely accounts for why he was identified with Florida instead of Boedo. Had he made different publishing choices and had different friends, he might have been able to write the same poems and publish some of them in Boedo's journals.[3] In an important sense, however, Borges was destined for Florida long before the conflict between the groups arose. He had laid the groundwork for an aesthetics-realism opposition when he brought ultraism to Buenos Aires and helped gather together a new generation of aesthetics-oriented writers. Borges was allied with Florida for reasons extending beyond his texts to the social circumstances of his life. And though avant-garde movements like to believe that their every new move is made with the freshness of total autonomy, Borges in 1924 was already largely determined by the Borges of 1921 who helped create *Prisma* and whose family was socially connected to the cultural elite.

When it came to marketing and self-promotion, the young Borges was a traditionalist. If the primary journal of the vanguardia, *Martín Fierro*, occasionally lapsed into the taboo rhetoric of popular advertising, its leading poet did not. Borges paid three hundred pesos to publish three hundred copies of *Fervor de Buenos Aires* (Fervor of Buenos Aires) (1923) and refused to promote it for the public. Though he later wrote, "I never thought of sending copies to the booksellers or out for review" (Alazraki 1987, 34), he devised a publicity strategy aimed directly at important literary figures. He talked *Nosotros* editor Alfredo Bianchi into slipping copies of the book into the coat pockets of the journal's visitors and staff (Alazraki 1987, 34). When he returned from Europe a year later, Borges found he had a reputation as a poet. He describes this first book as "essentially romantic," a reflection of his desire to write "poems beyond the here and now, free of local color and contemporary circumstances" (Alazraki 1987, 84–85). The antithesis of the early Auden, pylon poet and lover of modernity and machinery, Borges here empties the city streets that Darío filled with people some twenty years earlier.[4]

The effect of Borges's unwillingness to participate in modern marketing techniques is mitigated by his prolific output of literary and theoretical texts during the 1920s and his willingness — shared by Breton — to publish and republish his early essays. Most of the essays in *El tamaño de mi esperanza* (The dimension of my hope) (1926), for example, had already appeared in *La Prensa, Nosotros, Inicial, Proa,* and *Valoraciones.* Borges participated simultaneously in mainstream and avant-garde publishing. In comparison, the Auden poets published more in the mainstream, while the surrealists stuck more closely to their own publications. All three groups, however, published books with major presses and wrote from time to time for major journals. Their postures vis-à-vis the market were different, however. Where Borges appears to have been reluctant, the Auden poets were unabashed in their self-promotion. The surrealists were most inventive in their strategies; they wanted both to insult the market and to make it do their bidding.

Like the martinfierristas, Borges tended to say one thing and do another when it came to getting his work into print. To *Nosotros*'s 1923 survey of the new literary generation, Borges gave antimodern responses. Asked his age, he responds "Ya he cansado veintidós años." (I've already exhausted twenty-two years.) He professes a commitment to ultraism, classical syntax, and sentences "complejas como ejércitos" (as complex as armies). About older literary masters he admires, he says: "Mis entusiasmos son ortodoxos. Entre los santos de mi devoción cuento a Capdevila, a Banchs, y señaladamente a nuestro Quevedo, Lugones."[5] (My enthusiasms are orthodox. Among the saints of my devotion I count Capdevila, Banchs, and most of all, our Quevedo, Lugones.) To admire postmodern poets — the nearest literary ancestor — is not only anti–avant-garde behavior, but is also a less self-differentiating choice than most young poets tend to make.

A number of critics have accepted uncritically Borges's canonization choices, echoing and reinforcing his opinions. José Miguel Oviedo's comments reflect Borges's changing point of view. Of Borges's first three books of poems, he writes:

With them, Borges wanted to create a new poetic tradition, specifically Argentine, which . . . was a *challenge to tradition* and the Hispanic legacy, a *gesture of radical independence.* The argentinisms and neologisms of his early poetry (which have been erased or revised in later editions) were a *defiant sign of his literary stance of that decade.* (in Cortínez 1986, 124–25; my emphasis)

Only in his earliest essays did Borges make such claims, though Oviedo —echoing the early manifesto-writing Borges—represents him as having succeeded at them. Borges was no revolutionary, and in later life he disagreed with Oviedo's point of view: "I can now only regret my early ultraist excesses. After nearly half a century, I find myself still striving to live down that awkward period of my life" (Alazraki 1987, 35). If Oviedo were to consider fully Borges's admissions of debt to older poets and how his attitude toward his early work changed, he would find it difficult to call the poetry a product of "radical independence." Borges realized that his early claims were exaggerated, for though he distinguished himself through the use of argentinisms and neologisms, he brought neither device to Argentine literature. It is widely known that modernist poets invented criollo and Greek- and Latin-based neologisms. "Luna ciudadana" (Citizen moon) shows that by 1909 Lugones had set the standard for linguistic exploration: "Mientras cruza el tranvía una pobre comarca / De suburbio y de vagas chimeneas . . . / *Fulano,* en versátil aerostación de ideas, / Alivia su consuetudinario / Itinerario" (Lugones 1961, 110). (While the streetcar crosses a poor area / Of suburbs and vague chimneys . . . / *John Doe,* in a versatile air station of ideas, / Lightens his usual / Itinerary.)

Critics have supported Borges's efforts to remove the bulk of his early work from the Borges canon. The international literary community's portrait of "Borges" is that of a great short story writer and mediocre poet of conservative political and traditional literary values. Most of the time "Borges" is the older fiction-writing Borges, the one who became known in Europe and North America only after he shared the Formentor Prize with Samuel Beckett in 1961. This Borges is a product consumed on northern soil whose literary works date mainly from stories written in the late 1930s, 1940s, and 1950s, and whose philosophical point of view is generally taken from *Otras inquisiciones* (1952) and interviews conducted late in life. In his biography of Borges, Emir Rodríguez Monegal has contributed to the notion that the early Borges was somehow not the real article by calling him "Georgie" for the first three decades of his life. In 1930, "Georgie" magically turned into "Borges," though we are never told how he finally earned the right to wear the long pants of the adult writer.[6] Borges's abundant output in the early years is not unusual among important avant-garde figures. Auden, Spender, and Day Lewis were prolific poets, essayists, critics, and journalists, and Breton and Aragon each published several important texts in their early years. Though militantly avant-garde writers such as Breton were vociferous in their opposition to the professionalization of writers, such voluminous output certainly suggests that Breton *was* a professional writer. Flooding a literary market he claimed to disdain is a contradictory choice. It is the Dada paradox all over again: How does a movement create the public it needs to sustain itself without pursuing traditional avenues of self-promotion and consecration? No movement has satisfactorily solved this problem that provided the raw material for many of surrealism's fiercest in-house battles.

The secondary erasures of critics—where they devalorize what Borges removed from his canon or did not allow to remain in general circulation—mask the poet's sometimes violent means of exercising power over the canonization process. Borges later explained that he suppressed a lot of work because he felt he had been carelessly prolific:

> This period, from 1921 to 1929, was one of great activity, but much of it was perhaps reckless and even pointless. I wrote and published no less than seven books—four of them essays and three of them verse. I also founded three magazines and contributed with fair frequency to nearly a dozen other periodicals. . . . Three of the four essay collections—whose names are best forgotten—I have never allowed to be reprinted. (Alazraki 1987, 37–38)

Auden edited his work heavily and experimented with ordering his poems in ways that disturbed the chronology of their composition. Breton, too, revised himself, but he did not try to outmuscle the predilections of critics the way the other two did. Instead, he merely added a new text amending or adjusting his previous point of view to his extremely long list of publications. He was less focused on what his body of work would look like posthumously and more on what he wanted to say at a given moment. He exemplifies the radical avant-garde's obsession with the present.

Critics have by and large opted to reinforce Borges's choices by assessing the early poetry and essays as less valuable than the later fiction and by opting not to write about them much. In fact, the early work is considerably less valuable in that it is less universal and less interesting than the later work. But it is also important to note that the excision of some of it from his canon served Borges's desire to present a consistent face to the world. In contrast, Auden's carefully considered revisions were often overruled by critics who rejected editorial changes he made on his 1930s poems after the decade was over. There were two Audens, a number of critics argued, and the later one was inferior to the "social poet." This divided Auden became a convenience to those who wanted to treat "the early Auden" separately.

Borges's case is the other side of the coin. Where a rupture in a poet's work is difficult to deal with—as in the case of Auden in 1940 and Borges's Spanish ultraism days—critics have been surprisingly willing to opt for the cleaver. While the juvenalia of many writers is less interesting than more mature work, Borges, the object of hundreds of critical works, is no ordinary writer. Auden's juvenalia has received abundant attention, Borges's very little. Graciela Palau de Nemes has labeled Borges's early history—a history he largely rejected—"prehistory."[7] De Torre's article "Para la prehistoria ultraísta de Borges" (For Borges's ultraist prehistory) includes a discussion of *Prisma*'s 1921 debut, thus suggesting that Borgesian "history" began in 1922 or 1923.[8] In the face of lesser deviations, such as Borges the erratic vanguardia leader, critics sometimes go to considerable lengths to sew up the holes and inconsistencies in their portrait of the writer.

I am not aware of a work that plumbs the ideological implications of Borges's suppression of his early work, though Borges's own critique is interesting. He condemns for their excesses *Inquisiciones* (Inquisitions) (1925), *El tamaño de mi esperanza* (1926), and *El idioma de los argentinos* (The language of the Argentines) (1928), and claims to have written and destroyed three books before he published *Fervor de Buenos Aires. Los naipes del tahúr* (Tarot cards) he describes as literary and political essays. Another early work was approximately twenty free-verse poems "in praise of the Russian Revolution, the brotherhood of man, and pacifism. . . . This book I destroyed in Spain on the eve of our departure" (Alazraki 1987, 33). In his "Autobiographical Essay," however, Borges says he destroyed the book of poems because he failed to find a publisher for it (Rodríguez Monegal 1978, 165). Borges describes his early experiences with literary journals in an agentless way that absolves him of responsibility for seeking a publisher: "Three or four of [the poems] *found their way* into magazines—'Bolshevik Epic,' 'Trenches,' 'Russia'" (Alazraki 1987, 33; my emphasis). About one of the books of essays he did publish, Borges writes,

I was doing my best to write Latin in Spanish, and the book collapses under the sheer weight of its involutions and sententious judgments. The next of these failures was a kind of reaction. I went to the other extreme—I tried to be as Argentine as I could. I got hold of Segovia's dictionary of Argentinisms and worked in so many local words that many of my countrymen could hardly understand it. (Alazraki 1987, 38)

Borges's early ultraist poems are tinged with political and erotic language, language he later avoided in his work. The early work should be studied because its suppression raises the question, What is the critic's stake in starting a history well after that history has begun? Here the problem is an anomalous stage of Borges's development, one that doesn't fit the impersonal, nostalgic, Berkeleyan poetry he later writes. Like Auden, Borges often revised his discursive persona and creative work. Unfortunately, he and critics have erased too well some of the contradictions that characterize his first decade in the public eye. Of Borges's transition from ultraist poet to fiction writer in the early 1930s, Rodríguez Monegal offers such comments as "subtly, ironically, through his example, [Alfonso] Reyes would lead Georgie away from the baroque and teach him how to write the best Spanish prose of the century." But this statement is too simple an explanation of the transition (Rodriguez Monegal 1978, 213). Assigning an end date to ultraism presents yet another problem, for while ultraist poets continued to publish ultraist poems in the late 1920s, Borges became the single most powerful force in the dating of the movement. De Torre claims the movement was over in the spring of 1922, while Robert A. Ortelli argues that it was thriving in 1923, a proof being the publication of Borges's *Fervor de Buenos Aires* (Bastos 1974, 76). This illustrates the critic's tendency to identify movements with their leaders.

In rejecting poetic predecessors, the ultraists most often emphasized their objection to rhyme and to worn-out metaphors. In his early essays, Borges expresses some disdain for Lugones, the champion of rhyme, though he acknowledges him in the *Nosotros* survey as an important influence on the vanguardia. In *Leopoldo Lugones,* published decades later, Borges insists: "I affirm that the work of the 'Martín Fierro' and 'Proa' poets . . . is absolutely prefigured in a few pages of the *Lunario*" (qtd. in Running 1981, 149). In his eighties, Borges comments, "Todos—en aquel tiempo—no sólo lo imitábamos sino que hubiéramos querido ser Lugones" (Ferrari 1985, 210). (All of us—at that time—not only imitated him but would have liked to be Lugones.) Such inconsistencies help explain why Borges wanted to suppress his essays. The essays reveal, for example, that Borges, a determined writer of free verse, chose a critical battle—the rejection of rhyme as an important aspect of ultraist poetics—that he as a *poet* had already settled. Though heavily influenced by Lugones, Borges was even more influenced by Walt Whitman, at least on the question of free verse versus rhyme. Why then did he expend so much energy on an issue he had resolved for himself? Was it to defend the vanguardia movement's rebellion of choice[9] or, like *Martín Fierro,* to engage in avant-garde–style battles for the sake of creating polemics and attracting publicity? This is the kind of question that should be asked if we are to understand what is at stake in his selective canonical suppressions. We might come to view certain strategic choices as the erasure of embarrassing experiments with the power of trumped-up polemics.

Such polemics contrast with the traditional values the young Borges expressed about poetry: "El ultraísmo no es quizá otra cosa que la espléndida síntesis de la literatura antigua."[10] (Ultraism is perhaps nothing other than the splendid synthesis of ancient literature.) In fact, his earliest published poems, even those with topical references, are undeniably antimodern. "Guardia roja" (Red Guard) appears to be about the Russian Revolution but, except for the title, it could describe a number of premodern wars:

> El viento es la bandera que se enreda en las lanzas
> La estepa es una inútil copia del alma
> De las colas de los caballos cuelga el villorio encendido
> y la estepa rendida
> no acaba de morirse
> Durante los combates
> el milagro terrible del dolor estiró los instantes
> ya grita el sol
> Por el espacio trepan hordas de luces
> En la ciudad lejana
> donde los mediodías tañen los tensos viaductos
> y de las cruces pende el Nazareno
> como un cartel sobre los mundos
> se embozarán los hombres
> en los cuerpos desnudos.[11]

> (The wind is the flag which tangles in the lances
> The steppe is a useless copy of the soul

From the horses' tails hangs the burning jerkwater town
and the conquered steppe
does not finish dying
During the battles
the terrible miracle of pain stretched the moments
the sun already screams
Through space hordes of lights climb
In the distant city
where the middays strum the tense viaducts
and the Nazarene hangs from the crosses
like a handbill over the worlds
men will cover themselves
in naked corpses.) [12]

In contrast to early surrealism's valorization of the metaphor whose tenor and vehicle form the most striking and unlikely pair, ultraist metaphors tend to link the spiritual and the human with the physical, non-human world. Here the sun screams, human pain and the middays play the viaducts like a musical instrument, and the landscape mirrors the soul. There is no modern diction here; only a lack of punctuation and insistent assonance assert the poem's modernity. Senses are mixed up; the sun, usually represented by visual or tactile imagery, is here anthropomorphized into a screaming, dying soldier. The oxymoron, a quintessentially Borgesian trope, is represented by the "terrible miracle" of pain. The perspective is that of a human survivor, the distant village hanging from the tail of a running horse. There is Girondian hyperbole—men up to their eyes in corpses—and irreverence, Christ hanging like the poster for a local show. Both tendencies will be muted in poems Borges writes a mere handful of years later.

Like Whitman, Borges has a very personal relationship to poetry and often invokes the first person. In "Himno del mar" (Sea hymn), published in Spain, he sounds like Whitman:

Oh mar! oh mito! oh sol! oh largo lecho!
Y sé por qué te amo. Sé que somos muy viejos,
Que ambos nos conocemos desde siglos.
Sé que en tus aguas venerandas y rientes ardió la aurora de la Vida.
(En la ceniza de una tarde terciaria vibré por primera vez en tu seno)
(Meneses 1978, 58)

(O sea! O myth! O sun! O long seabed!

And I know why I love you. I know we are very old,

That we have known each other for centuries.

I know that in your venerable and laughing waters burned the dawn of
Life.

(In the ash of a terciary afternoon I vibrated for the first time in your
bosom)

The poem prefigures the Borges who at age twenty-five will write:
"Creo que no veré, ni realizaré cosas nuevas" (I believe I will neither see
nor accomplish new things).[13] This Borges looks into the past for timeless sources of poetry. Nestor Ibarra (1930) — not insignificantly a Borges
scholar — argued in 1930, "Lo moderno no ha arraigado, no ha podido ar-
raigar en la Argentina" (126). (The modern has not taken root, has not
been able to take root in Argentina.) Girondo (1987) the rebel of the
vanguardia, contradicts Ibarra's assessment. "Biarritz," from *Veinte poemas
para ser leídos en el tranvía* (Twenty poems to be read on the streetcar)
(1922), contains the following undeniably modern fragments:

Automóviles afónicos. Escaparates constelados de estrellas falsas. Muje-
res que van a perder sus sonrisas al bacará.

Cuando la puerta se entreabre, entra un pedazo de "foxtrot." (21)

(Hoarse automobiles. Shop windows constelled of false stars. Women
who will lose their smiles at baccarat.

When the door opens, a piece of "foxtrot" comes in.)

While Girondo shares many of Borges's devices, his subject and diction create a portrait of modern urban decadence. He uses a form of
telegraphese more commonly found in European poetry and his speaker
avoids personal pathos and moral judgments. Because of the differences
between Girondo and Borges and the analogous gap between the vanguardia's rhetoric and behavior, descriptions of the movement diverge widely.
Critics who take at face value the vanguardia's statements tend to see radical innovation while others emphasize its (that is, Borges's) conservatism.
Ultraism, according to Ibarra (1930), is a purely rhetorical school characterized by vagueness, temporal and spatial dimensions, a lack of argument, and idealism (104). But this description pertains to *Borges's* poetry,
not to that of other ultraist poets, and certainly not to Girondo's prose

poems. Rodríguez Monegal (1978) points out that Ibarra's work, while ostensibly about the ultraist movement, is really the first book-length treatment of Borges. As such, it conflates Borges and the vanguardia (239).

Borges was interested in German Expressionism, English poetry, and the comparatively tame experiments of ultraism, while Girondo participated in early Dadaist and surrealist *spectacles* in Paris. In poetry, Borges privileges the traditional; Girondo, the modern. Though he seeks a timeless national essence, however, Borges fails to escape the modern. "Jactancia de quietud" (Boasting of stillness) creates an "I"-"them" opposition where "they" are time pressed, market oriented, and modern. The speaker, in contrast, is a philosophical Whitmanesque Everyman who inhabits the countryside.

> Seguro de mi vida y de mi muerte, miro los ambiciosos y quisiera entenderlos.
> Su día es ávido como un lazo en el aire.
> Su noche es tregua de la ira en la espada, pronta en acometer.
> Hablan de humanidad.
> Mi humanidad está en sentir que somos voces de una misma penuria.
>
> .   .   .   .
>
> Mi nombre es alguien y cualquiera.
> Su verso es un requirimiento de ajena admiración.
> Yo solicito de mi verso que no me contradiga, y es mucho.
>
> .   .   .   .
>
> Paso con lentitud, como quien viene de tan lejos que no espera llegar.[14]

> (Sure of my life and death, I look at the ambitious and would like to understand them.
> Their day is avid like a lasso in the air.
> Their night is a respite from the sword's ire, ready to attack.
> They speak of humanity.
> My humanity is in feeling that we are voices of a shared poverty.
>
> .   .   .   .
>
> My name is anyone and whoever.
> Their verse is a necessity of alien admiration.
> I ask of my verse that it not contradict me, and that is a lot.
>
> .   .   .   .
>
> I pass slowly, like one who comes from so far he has no hope of arriving.)

The voice of this poem is surprisingly mature for a poet in his mid-twenties. Rural, timeless, and in many ways transpersonal, the poem nevertheless bears the marks of avant-garde ideology. The "other" is portrayed as ambitious, hurried, perhaps insincere ("they" speak of humanity, but what have they said?). Most important, "they" are *poets*. The "alien admiration" that supports their verse might well be the plebeian tastes of a market supported by recent immigrants. Though gentleness replaces *Martín Fierro*–like rhetoric, the poem features an opponent against whom the speaker defines himself. For all of Borges's attempts to be timeless, we are still in the 1920s, one of Argentine literature's more binary decades.

One of Girondo's many "membretes" or memoranda, published only two years later, offers a very different view of argentinidad and nationalism:

¿Estupidez? ¿Ingenuidad? ¿Política? . . . "Seamos argentinos"—gritan algunos. . . . —Sin advertir la confusión que implica ese imperativo, sin reparar que la nacionalidad es algo tan fatal como la conformación de nuestro esqueleto.[15]

(Stupidity? Ingenuousness? Politics? . . . "Let's be Argentines"—some shout. . . . Without understanding the confusion this imperative implies, without noticing that nationality is something as inevitable as the shape of our skeletons.)

Responding to a 1924 *Martín Fierro* survey on whether a specifically Argentine sensibility and mentality exist, Girondo answers yes, but he states that he sees no reason why writers should have to prove the existence of argentinidad by displaying it in their work.[16] This attitude places Girondo at the margins of the vanguardia's projects of cultural nationalism. Early efforts to place him at its center failed. One such effort, an unsigned essay in *Martín Fierro*, makes the weak argument that Girondo brings a new sort of criollismo to Argentine literature: "algo de franqueza gaucha mezclada con rudeza y desplante indígena"[17] (something of the gaucho's frankness mixed with indigenous coarseness and arrogance). Though much of *Veinte poemas* and all of *Calcomanías* were written in Europe and Girondo was apparently unconcerned about being labeled *extranjerizante*, his editors are still apologizing for him. In the prologue to *Veinte poemas para ser leídos en el tranvía, Calcomanías, Espantapájaros* (Twenty poems to be read on the streetcar, Decals, Scarecrow) (1987), Rodolfo Alonso argues that Girondo is "no menos nacional por más universal" (Girondo 1987, 1) (no less national for being more universal). This argument was hard to make in the 1920s, when the national and the universal were one of the era's major binary divisions. The fact that it was still being made in the 1980s reflects the strongly held Argentine belief that the nation's writers should concern themselves with national reality.

Girondo and Borges represent two views of cultural nationalism in the 1920s. Girondo believed that—being Argentines—it was impossible not to produce Argentine literature, while Borges felt a literary text was national only if its contents dealt with national themes and motifs (Borges 1974, 48, 57; Girondo 1987, 10). Borges later rejected his early view and the change of heart caused him to discard a number of his early poems. In an interview conducted when he was eighty-five, Borges says of *Luna de enfrente* (Moon across the way): "Cometí un error capital, que fue el de 'hacerme' el argentino" (Vázquez 1984, 51). (I committed a capital error, which was to 'make myself' Argentine.) Borges made Buenos Aires the focus of his early poetry. "Las calles" opens with "Las calles de Buenos Aires / ya son mi entraña."[18] (The streets of Buenos Aires / are already my innermost self.) Many of *Fervor*'s poems are set in Buenos Aires: in the rich man's cemetery Recoleta, in the *arrabales* or suburbs, and at the Plaza San Martín. Borges (1974) imagines his own death in Buenos Aires, calling Recoleta "el lugar de mi ceniza" (18) (the site of my ashes). In the spirit of linguistic nationalism, Borges fashions a new spelling from Argentine dialect. In "Atardeceres" (Dusks) he omits the final "d" from "oscuridad" and in "Calle con almacén rosado" (Street with a pink store), he uses the "vos" form. Early essays betray an even more insistent commitment to his version of criollo spelling. In contrast, Girondo's nationalist gestures are much milder. In the 1922 prologue to *Veinte poemas,* he argues the importance of having faith in "our phonetics," only to undermine himself by saying that these phonetics are perhaps "badly educated."

If in the 1920s Borges is a Berkeleyan idealist, in later life he modifies his stand, making a statement in *Otras inquisiciones* that critics have taken to mean that he was a realist: "El mundo, desgraciadamente, es real; yo, desgraciadamente, soy Borges." (Borges 1974, 771). (The world, alas, is real; I, alas, am Borges.) But the early poem "Amanecer" (Dawn) describes daybreak as a threat to all life because, as Berkeley argued, if things exist only because they are perceived, there is little to guarantee the existence of the world when everyone sleeps. The poem's speaker, one of the few nocturnal *flâneurs* or street wanderers who keep the city alive each night, philosophizes about his experience:

> reviví la tremenda conjetura
> de Schopenhauer y de Berkeley
> que declara que el mundo
> es una actividad de la mente,
> un sueño de las almas,
> sin base ni propósito ni volumen.
> (Borges 1974, 38)

> (I felt again that tremendous conjecture
> of Schopenhauer and Berkeley
> which declares the world
> an activity of the mind,
> a dream of souls,
> without foundation or purpose or volume.)
> (trans. di Giovanni; Borges 1985, 25)

This excerpt, however, is not what Borges wrote in the early 1920s. It is the official version disseminated by translators to the English-speaking world and it is the edited version found in his *Obras completas* (Complete works). Borges originally wrote:

> realicé la tremenda conjetura
> de Schopenhauer y de Berkeley
> que arbitra ser la vida
> un ejercicio pertinaz de la mente,
> un populoso ensueño colectivo
> sin basamento ni finalidad ni volumen.
> (Borges 1923a, n.p.)

> (I fulfilled the tremendous conjecture
> of Schopenhauer and of Berkeley
> that contrives to make life
> a tenacious exercise of the mind
> a populous collective dream
> with neither foundation nor finality nor volume.)

The differences between this and the later version are small but important. The early language is more erudite and therefore less accessible to some readers. The speaker is more arrogant about his experience—instead of merely reliving ("reviví") the idealist conjecture, he has caused it to happen or fulfilled it ("realicé"). The agent or speaker has a more active role and through the force of will and effort has saved the city almost single-handedly. Borges frequently explores the power of the poetic speaker. In the *Nosotros* ultraism manifesto, he argues that ultraism supports "la meta principal de toda poesía, esto es, a la transmutación de la realidad palpable del mundo en realidad interior y emocional"[19] (the principal goal of all poetry, which is the transmutation of the palpable reality of the world into inner, emotional reality). In *Fervor*'s "Caminata" (Long walk), the speaker makes an even clearer statement about the power of a solitary night walker to keep the world alive in an idealist's world: "Yo soy el único espectador de esta calle, / si dejara de verla se moriría" (Borges 1923a, n.p.) (I am the only observer of this street, / if I stopped looking at it, it would die.)

Borges, who admired and tried to emulate what he perceived as the intellectual humility of Macedonio Fernández, later did his best to erase some of these early quasi-autobiographical traces. In the 1969 revision of the prologue to *Fervor*, notes Pezzoni, Borges deletes a reference to himself as a "desconfiado y fervoroso escribidor" (fervorous and mistrustful writer). He is trying to cut the early Borges down to size.[20] Borges's early conception of the self is erratic. In "La nadería de la personalidad" (The nothingness of the personality), published in 1925, he agrees with Schopenhauer: "El yo no existe" (The self doesn't exist) and argues that the personality is a dream or illusion. A year later, he writes, "Toda literatura es autobiográfica, finalmente." (All literature is ultimately autobiographical.) Literature may be imaginary, archetypal, or personal, he writes, adding "Yo solicito el último." (I seek the last [of the three].)[21]

In early essays, Borges views the subject as a linguistic—but not transcendentally powerful—entity. He writes (1928) "El ser no es categoría poética ni metafísica, es gramatical" (126). (The self is neither a poetic nor a metaphysical category—it is grammatical.) This view is not borne out by his poetry, however, where speakers often function as interpreters of a world they create through metaphor. In "Singladura" (Day's run),

El mar es una espada innumerable y una plenitud de pobreza.

. . . .

El mar es solitario como un ciego.
El mar es un huraño lenguaje que yo no alcanzo a descifrar.

. . . .

En la cubierta, quietamente, yo comparto la tarde con mi hermana
como un trozo de pan.[22]

(The sea is a countless sword and a plenitude of poverty.

. . . .

The sea is as solitary as a blind man.
The sea is an unsociable language I cannot manage to decipher.

.   .   .   .

On deck, quietly, I share the afternoon with my sister like a piece
of bread.)

Though the speaker calls attention to the failure of his meaning-making
activities, he is nevertheless interpreting the sea through the lens of
Borges's experience—a father going blind for congenital reasons, lunch
with Norah, the habit of making text out of world. His litanic attempts
to evoke the sea suggest that the poet triumphs over his subject, even as a
diagnostician of its mystery.

Where Borges constructs the world, Girondo tears it—both subjects
and objects—apart. A clear illustration of the subject's instability can be
found in *Espantapájaros* (Scarecrow) (1932):

Yo no tengo una personalidad; yo soy un cocktail, un
conglomerado, una manifestación de personalidades.
En mí, la personalidad es una especie de forunculosis
anímica en estado crónico de erupción; no pasa media
hora sin que me nazca una nueva personalidad.

(Girondo 1987, 66)

(I don't have a personality; I am a cocktail, a
conglomerate, a manifestation of personalities.
In me, personality is a sort of psychic boil in a
chronic state of eruption; not half an hour goes by
without a new personality being born.)

Girondo and Borges share a love of the first person and its power. But
Borges uses the spiritual power of the self to make things poetic, while
Girondo makes poetry by destroying and dismembering synecdochally the
world around him and the poetic subjects who people it. Borges's "Otra
vez la metáfora" (Once again the metaphor) contains the following statement: "Las cosas (pienso) no son intrínsecamente poéticas; para ascender-
las a poesía es preciso que las vinculemos a nuestro vivir, que nos acostum-
bremos a pensarlas con devoción" (Borges 1928, 56). (Things [I think] are
not intrinsically poetic; to raise them to the level of poetry we must link
them to our lives, so that we become accustomed to thinking of them with
devotion.) Borges's project is thus antithetical to that of Girondo, who,
Masiello (1986) argues,

produce un sujeto violento, que viaja a través de la moderna civilización. Agresivo y descaradamente fuerte, su sujeto lírico es el terrorista máximo de la vanguardia, que proclama su poder por los abundantes lugares e imágenes que se atreve a poseer y destrozar. (114)

(produces a violent subject who travels through modern civilization. Aggressive and impudently strong, his lyrical subject is the greatest terrorist of the avant-garde, proclaiming his power through an abundance of places and images he dares to possess and destroy.)

While in *Inquisiciones* (1925), Borges offers a detailed discussion of types of metaphors, by 1928 he argues that the poet should *not* focus on creating new metaphors.[23] And whereas he began the decade rejecting the anecdotal in poetry, he ends it arguing that poetry should be anecdotal and that abstractions are unpoetic (Borges 1928, 127). The poem "Arrabal" (Suburb) reflects this evolution, changing markedly between 1921 and 1943. In the early version, Buenos Aires is a text created by the speaker:

> . . . y sentí *Buenos Aires*
> y literaturicé en la hondura del alma
> la viacrucis inmóvil
> de la calle sufrida
> y el caserío sosegado [24]

> (. . . and I felt *Buenos Aires*
> and made literature in the depths of the soul
> from the immobile crossroads
> of the suffering street
> and the quiet hamlet)

In any hands but these, the man-as-city device would be unmistakably modern. But as we have seen, Borges specializes in the paradox of modern urban atavism. In the 1943 version—which became the standard version of the *Obras completas*—Buenos Aires has metamorphosed from *text* to *world*. The speaker's role has thus changed substantially. No longer is the poet making literature of the city or creating the city in and through language. Instead, there is a simple, personal statement of belonging to a place:

> . . . y sentí *Buenos Aires*
> Esta ciudad que yo creí mi pasado
> es mi porvenir, mi presente;

los años que he vivido en Europa son ilusorios,
yo estaba siempre (y estaré) en Buenos Aires.

(Borges 1974, 32)

(. . . and I felt *Buenos Aires*
This city that I believed to be my past
is my future, my present;
the years I have lived in Europe are illusory,
I always was (and will be) in Buenos Aires.)

Whereas for Borges the city is often closely identified with the poetic subject, Girondo consistently objectifies and makes it alien. In *Veinte poemas'* "Verona," for example, Girondo has a statue of the Virgin menstruate into a fountain:

La Virgen, sentada en una fuente, como sobre un "bidé," derrama un agua enrojecida por las bombitas de luz eléctrica que le han puesto en los pies.[25] (The Virgin, seated in a fountain as over a "bidet," leaks water reddened by the electic lamps they have put at her feet.)

Unlike Borges, Girondo (1987) makes baldly contemporary references. In "Croquis de arena" (Sketch in the sand), photographers sell the bodies of bathing women for eighty centavos apiece (14). Like the French symbolists who were one of his most important influences, Girondo enjoys shocking the conventional reader. In "Milonga," the dancers are crudely sexualized:

El bandoneón . . . imanta los pezones, los pubis y la punta de los
   zapatos.
Machos que se quiebran en un corte ritual, la cabeza hundida entre los
   hombros, la jeta hinchada de palabras soeces.
Hembras con las ancas nerviosas, un poquitito de espuma en las axilas,
   y los ojos demasiado aceitados.
De pronto se oye un fracaso de cristales. Las mesas dan un corcovo
   y pegan quatro patadas en el aire.

(Girondo 1987, 91)

(The accordion . . . magnetizes nipples, groins and shoetips.
Males who break in ritual twist and jerk, their heads sunk between
   their shoulders, their mugs swollen with vile words.
Females with nervous rumps, a little sweat in their armpits and overly
   greasy eyes.

Soon the noise of breaking glass is heard. The tables hump and buck, kicking their four legs into the air.)

Whereas Borges renders the world sacred, Girondo, consistent with the Continental avant-garde, attacks cultural icons and institutions, here eliding the difference between people and furniture as both metamorphose into barnyard animals. Breton would have approved: Girondo personifies the inanimate, dehumanizes the animate, profanes the sacred, works to defy expectation, and turns the world upside down. Carnivalesque in the Bakhtinian sense, he overwhelms even Borges. In a 1925 review of *Calcomanías*, Borges applauds Girondo's work in a qualified way: "Es innegable que la eficacia de Girondo me asusta. . . . Girondo es un violento. Mira largamente las cosas. . . . Luego las estruja." [26] (It is undeniable that Girondo's effectiveness scares me. . . . Girondo is a violent person. He looks generously at things. . . . Then he crushes them.) J. Schwartz (1979) calls the anthropomorphization of things and the "cosificación" (thingification) of people in Girondo's poetry a "fusion of differences" (192–94). Girondo's modern city collapses the division between subject and object, revealing the alienation and sterility that result from a loss of individuality and separateness. Like Eliot, he indicts modernity even as he modernizes literary form.

The prologues to their first books illustrate well the differences between Borges, an exemplar of Argentine cultural identity, and Girondo, an affront to it. Borges is earnest, self-important, and serious. His project is the nationalization of Buenos Aires: "He rechazado los vehementes reclamos de quienes en Buenos Aires no advierten sino lo extranjerizo" (Borges 1923a, n.p.). (I have rejected the vehement claims of those in Buenos Aires who notice nothing but the foreign.) In the city he will uncover the sacred: "Aquí se oculta la divinidad." (Here the divine hides itself.) He represents himself as one who uses the "primordial" meanings of words, ending with an apparently humble apology that he, not the reader, is the author of these poems. The last two words of the prologue of *Fervor de Buenos Aires* are, however, "my verses." Borges could have used the definite article to depersonalize the work, but he does not. Not surprisingly, he removed this trace of authorial assertiveness from the 1969 reprint of the prologue.

Girondo's prologue to *Veinte poemas* opens with an attack on its audience: "¡Qué quieren ustedes!" (What do you want!) One finds poems, he says, thrown into the middle of the street, "poemas que uno recoge como quien junta puchos en la vereda" (poems one gathers up like scraps of trash from the sidewalk). Do we write to humiliate ourselves? Why publish "cuando hasta los mejores publican 1.071% más de lo que debieran publicar?" (when even the best publish 1,071% more than they ought to?) The argument he makes for publishing his book is surrealist: The everyday is an admirable manifestation of the absurd and cutting through logic is the only way to arrive at true adventure. In an even more surrealist act, he ends by celebrating the contradictions of these arguments. "No renuncio ni a mi derecho de renunciar, y tiro mis *Veinte poemas,* como una piedra, sonriendo ante la inutilidad de mi gesto" (Girondo 1987, 9–11). (I don't renounce even my right to renounce, and I throw my *Veinte poemas,* like a stone, smiling at the futility of my gesture.) If Borges's prologue spiritualizes the nation, Girondo's evokes the nation-bashing of Tzara and Breton. It is not surprising then, given their cultural and historical moment, that Borges becomes the spokesperson of an avant-garde operating in a nationalist age while Girondo is the movement's unruly older brother.

Because the first edition of *Veinte poemas* was published in Paris, it came to Argentina as a European product. Both *Nosotros* and *La Nación,* which were part of the ideological apparatus Girondo attacked in his prologue, published reviews by European critics. Had the production and reception of *Veinte poemas* been a purely national affair—without the cachet of foreign critics and, in the words of Delfina Muschietti, the "mediating and neutralizing"[27] effect of their criticism on scandalous material—it is unlikely Girondo's early work would have been enthusiastically received. His second book, published in Madrid, was also favorably received by the bastions of consecrated culture. European critics, accustomed to the textually outrageous, reacted almost exclusively to the book's aesthetics, calling it "original" and "revealing" and describing it as full of "magnificent explosive images."[28] In contrast, Borges's early work was considered nostalgic (de Torre), dignified (Ramón Gómez de la Serna), and formally classic (Enrique Díez-Canedo) (repr. Alazraki 1976, 21–26, 29–31). Locally, the critical reaction to Girondo's first book was decidedly tepid. Reviews published in *La Nación* in 1923–24 have such titles as "La literatura nacional en el extranjero" and "La literatura sudamericana vista desde París." The emphasis is less on the works themselves than on what the European critics think about them. An angry article appearing in *Martín Fierro* in March 1924 called the newspapers and journals that failed to review *Veinte poemas* "cretinous," an epithet usually reserved for Boedo (20).

Girondo was not so lucky thereafter. *Espantapájaros* (1932) and *En la masmédula* (1954), each more radical than the last and both published in Buenos Aires, were given lukewarm receptions (Muschietti 1985, 160–61). *Espantapájaros* was greeted with silence from *La Nación* and *Sur,* the journal in important ways representative of the avant-garde generation in the 1930s. Arturo Capdevilla repeated in *Nosotros* an Argentine woman's comment that the book was "nasty" (Girondo 1987, prologue). *Espantapájaros* represents a significant rupture in Girondo's work. There are no more foreign travel sketches and few signs that the poetic speaker is upper class. We must ask whether Argentina's elite publications shunned the book in part because its contents reflected little cultural or economic privilege.

Girondo's relationship to the literary market became more unacceptable in high cultural circles as the years went by. He published *Veinte poemas* in two editions aimed at two audiences. The first edition sold for five pesos, the popular second edition—published by Martín Fierro Editorial in 1925—for only twenty centavos. The Parisian printing was a luxury edition, almost certainly paid for by Girondo, who chose to withhold many copies from sale. The majority of the Argentine audience, then, had to wait three years for Girondo's book to become available. In 1932, Girondo made a boldly ostentatious marketing gesture that scandalized the anticommercial cultural elite but was, ironically, aimed at that very elite. To sell *Espantapájaros,* he had a life-size papier-mâché scarecrow driven about for days in a funeral carriage drawn by six horses and accompanied by footmen dressed in the style of the late eighteenth-century French Directory.[29] The scarecrow was dressed in a top hat and monocle reminiscent of the French dandy. Young women hired for the occasion sold all five thousand copies of the unusually large edition from a locale Girondo rented in Buenos Aires's most fashionable neighborhood.[30] Major newspapers refused to cover the event.[31]

Girondo claimed that at age eighteen he had a "sagrado horror" (sacred horror) of publicity (qtd. in J. Schwartz 1987, 43). But he was already familiar with the audience-enlarging strategies of the Dadaists at the time he staged a play that required an actor to insult the audience by calling it "stupid." He also tried to produce a journal called *Comedia,* but the publisher "forgot" to distribute it.[32] By his own account, he then—like Borges—destroyed a lot of work until he published *Veinte poemas.* Because Buenos Aires was not Paris, Girondo was caught in the avant-garde dilemma of wanting to confront a large audience with material it wouldn't tolerate.[33] He struggled to resolve the conflict between the privileges of his class and his desire to democratize the literary market. The title of his first book suggests that it be read in a streetcar, transportation for those who couldn't afford their own automobiles. A *Martín Fierro* article complaining about the lack of recognition by Argentine critics of *Veinte poemas,* however, calls its title ironic. *Espantapájaros*'s subtitle, *Al alcance de todos* (Within everyone's reach) is somewhat ironic, as Girondo did not take the necessary steps to distribute his books to the masses, nor were they likely to find it to their taste.

In the 1920s, Girondo broke rank with his socioeconomic class by satirizing the aristocracy, though he did nothing to undermine the class system itself. He also defied the vanguardia, especially *Martín Fierro* and *Proa,* by declaring himself opposed to state-sanctioned prizes and to writers holding public office. Borges, in contrast, accepted with pleasure the Second Municipal Prize for prose in 1929. He later headed the National Library for the better part of two decades, a post Victoria Ocampo helped obtain for him.[34] Though critical of the upper classes, Girondo did not advance the cause of the Argentine poor. He was a satirist, not a populist or a revolutionary. Formally radical but socially and politically ambivalent, he vacillated between enjoying and denouncing the privileges of his class. He did more than any other Argentine vanguardia writer to force the relationships among literature, institutions, and the market to reveal themselves to the public eye, much as Dadaism forced the European public to confront the crisis of cultural value. In the 1920s, however, he was merely an apprentice in radicalism.

Girondo did not become the avant-garde's second most important poet until well after World War II when his work was "reevaluated." In her prologue to Girondo's *Espantapájaros y otros poemas* (Scarecrow and other poems), Delfina Muschietti dates this reevaluation from the 1960s. Only then did high culture receive him in its center, she says. For decades he was considered a destructive element to be counterposed to the constructive Borges, the lover and preserver of Argentine tradition.[35] Girondo was the cosmopolitan aficionado of speed and modern things who captured images with a mock camera eye and turned cities into postcards. Borges was a slow, nostalgic, willfully *porteño* writer with highly narrative syntax; Girondo was fast, international, and partial to fragmented, cubist images.[36]

Girondo's formal innovations were markedly less well accepted in Argentina than were those of Borges. His use of the prose poem, borrowed from the French symbolists, was new to Argentina and was thus a more radical choice than free verse. Evar Méndez's (1927) article "Doce poetas nuevos" (Twelve new poets) praises Borges even as it puts Girondo on the literary sidelines (17, 26; see also Muschietti 1985, 165–66). The conservative Argentine spirit, says Méndez, sees in Girondo "una amenaza terrible para la estabilidad del lirismo escrito" (a terrible threat to the stability of written lyricisim). Méndez, however, offers only a lukewarm defense of Girondo. Late in life, Borges criticizes Girondo for his market-oriented behavior, calling him the "más flojo" (laziest, weakest) member of the vanguardia (Muschietti 1985, 168). In an important sense, Girondo was too avant-garde for his movement. But if the movement was too conservative to foreground Girondo's poetry, it still found him essential.[37] On trips through Latin America and Spain, Girondo represented five Argentine and two Uruguayan journals, including those of the Argentine vanguardia.[38] Unlike Borges, he did not sign the manifesto he wrote, which—significantly—was also the vanguardia's most important document. The omission of this signature is meaningful in the context of how differently the movement treated the two poets.

Muschietti argues that Girondo's texts corrode the dominant social, literary, moral, and religious premises of Argentine culture. Girondo (1987) once said his aesthetic goal was to "abrir al arte las puertas de la vida" (prologue) (open the doors of life to art) and that "un libro debe construirse como un reloj, y venderse como un salchichón" (Girondo 1968, 146–47; see also 1987, prologue) (a book should be put together like a clock, and sold like a sausage). J. Schwartz (1979) likens Girondo's wealthy casino revelers in "Biarritz" to Eliot's Prufrock: they are mocked and rendered sterile and mechanistic (224). Though he rejects social norms and scandalizes the public, however, Girondo's early revolution is merely *aesthetic*.[39] His satirical attacks—on women, the church, and the lazy rich—neither change nor seriously threaten the norms and institutions that produce Argentine literature. That Girondo remains the *cas limite* of the vanguardia defines the movement's essential conservatism. His sexual rebellion is traditional and machismo-ridden: women are objectified, dismembered, or made crudely animalistic. Like the surrealists, Girondo believed that undermining conventional language will change reality. But, like them, he failed in his mission to revolutionize literary relationships. As Umberto Eco (1983) describes this problem, "Literature says something and, at the same time, it denies what it has said; it doesn't destroy signs, it makes them play and it plays them" (242). The *cas limite* of the Auden group is different. In a decade characterized by extremes, it is occupied by Louis MacNeice, the one who tried to occupy a middle ground. For the surrealists, the *cas limite* is in one sense Breton, whose monomaniacal relationship to the surrealist cause is unparalleled. In another sense, it is the poets who did not fit: Aragon, because he became a devoted communist, and others, who were, in Breton's eyes, followers of literature.

If the differences between Borges and Girondo were noted but not widely discussed during the 1920s, they have since become clear. As Enrique Molina notes, the independent Girondo opted out of the complacent vanguardia well before the end of the decade:

> Volvió la espalda a sus compañeros de generación, que tras proclamar una mistificada actitud iconoclástica, acabaron por ubicarse dentro de las jerarquías tradicionales, pastando idílicamente en los prados de los suplementos dominicales. La efervescencia martinfierrista se diluyó en una mera discusión de aspectos formales. Ajenos a un auténtico inconformismo, la mayoría de los componentes del grupo terminaron en las más reaccionarias actitudes estéticas.[40]

> (He turned his back on generational compatriots who, having proclaimed a falsely iconoclastic attitude, ended up situating themselves inside traditional hierarchies, grazing idyllically in the pastures of the Sunday supplements. The martinfierrist effervescence diluted itself in a mere discussion of formal issues. Unaware of authentic nonconformity, most of the group members ended up with the most reactionary aesthetic attitudes.)

Borges did in certain ways become the aesthetic reactionary described here, and he later saw in these early efforts to be avant-garde a good deal of posturing.

Literary historians tend not to discuss Borges and Girondo together largely because they had little in common philosophically and poetically. However, because they were the two most important leaders of the vanguardia—Borges offering an aesthetics, Girondo the movement's avant-garde gestures and publicity—this is a complex and perhaps strange choice. It is likely that Girondo was marginalized partly because he was too aware of issues of power and privilege to provide the vanguardia with a spokesperson uncritical of the movement's ideology and behavior. The vanguardia chose a leader who would not betray openly the movement's ambivalences and internal divisions; the choice of Borges as spokesperson was as safe as their choice of Boedo as discursive enemy. The two choices worked well together; Boedo enabled the movement to pass itself off as radical, thus allowing it to give Borges a leadership role with less risk of being accused of conservatism. But the vanguardia did not work its magic in a vacuum. Several generations of critics have reinforced the myth. Rhetoric, Eco (1983) argues, is "the ordering and modelizing function of language, which with infinitesimal shifts of accent legitimizes certain relationships of strength and criminalizes others. Ideology takes shape: The power born from it becomes truly a network of consensus" (247). The same literary culture that the vanguardia was unwilling attack in 1924 continues in a new incarnation to reproduce the myth of its own champion. By reevaluating the vanguardia, it is possible to discard outworn myths and substitute a new regime of truth.

Written literature is born already laden with the task of consecration, of supporting the established order of things.

—Italo Calvino

4. Borges and *Sur*

Borges, one of the 1920s' "last happy men," entered the 1930s already established as one of Argentina's most important writers. For intellectuals, this "infamous decade" was devoted largely to a conservative retrenchment of the sort advocated in Benda's *La trahison des clercs* and to looking toward Europe, which increasingly found itself confronting the prospect of war. In the summer of 1930–31, Victoria Ocampo launched the journal *Sur*, which was to survive into the 1970s. Borges's decades-long participation in *Sur*, arguably Argentina's most important cultural journal of the twentieth century, has caused critics to identify the journal and the writer with each other. As cultural institutions in their own right, the parallel fates of the two illustrate the relativism of cultural meaning in a nation becoming progressively more politicized. During the 1930s, the journal and the writer both openly supported the Republican cause in Spain and professed many of the values of liberal humanism. *Sur* in its early years was considered liberal and was accused by the conservative journal *Criterio* of being leftist. Borges, already a known aesthete, was little criticized for his lack of interest in domestic social issues. In the 1950s, however, *Sur* was labeled oligarchic while Borges was the object of harsh criticism for failing to involve himself in the nation's pressing social and political problems. As the country's intellectuals became more radicalized politically, Borges was associated with apathy and irrelevance:

El país entero estaba politizado, la clase obrera en la calle, una revolución parecía próxima. En esas condiciones Borges significaba nada o casi nada. . . . El realismo crítico desplazaba a la literatura de evasión. Atacar a Borges en esas circunstancias era casi como proponerse matar a un cadaver.[1]

(The entire country was politicized, the working class was in the streets, a revolution seemed imminent. Under these conditions Borges meant nothing or almost nothing. . . . Critical realism displaced the literature of evasion. Attacking Borges under these circumstances was almost like resolving to kill a corpse.)

Though high culture tends to react only slowly to changes in political climate, the politicization of the 1950s produced remarkable shifts in long-accepted norms of critical reception.

In contrast to the shifting critical reception of *Sur* and Borges, there has been comparatively little change in the reception of the Argentine vanguardia, which was the last literary generation to be considered almost exclusively within the context of its own project and myth of self. The discrepancy between these two instances of reception suggests that literary groups operating before literary criticism became politicized in Latin America may be subject to critical isolationism, that is, treated separately and not reevaluated by later standards. In the case of ongoing literary phenomena—such as *Sur* and Borges—later standards have been applied to early texts, sometimes distorting the early histories of writers or publications. In the cases cited here, each mode of reception serves critics well. *Sur* and Borges serve as targets for attack by contemporary leftist critics, who see the interwar period through post–World War II eyes. It might appear that there is no point in revising the history of the vanguardia unless the object is to "discredit" it as a movement. But this is to see the problem through the lens of European values. In fact, a revision may emphasize what distinguishes the Argentine vanguardia from European models. The dearth of such revisions suggests that the vanguardia is of little political use to left-leaning critics and that its official history is one many Argentine critics feel deserves to be preserved.

Changes in market "truth" are considered normal, while changes in critical "truth" are problematic. The difference lies in the status held by each in the larger regime of cultural truth. Whereas the market is an independent force controlled by outsiders only with difficulty, the meaning of a literary text often has limited factual content. Reversals—such as that experienced by *Sur* and Borges—often have the effect of undermining all versions of literary truth. The Auden group has likewise been evaluated by very different criteria at different moments, and the criticism of surrealism is largely the product of two very different orientations toward the movement: critics who are deeply sympathetic and critics who are skeptical and sometimes even hostile. By acknowledging the contingency of all interpretation—its dependence on the interpreter's context and needs—we understand better the interests served by literary criticism. The vanguardia, for example, needs to be understood in context. It is constructive, rather than destructive, in intent, and its strong relationship to European influence is not synonymous with wholesale borrowings. The movement is a study in paradox and subtlety; it borrows and then it deforms the borrowed. As we have seen, that process reveals the nature of the borrower.

From the outset, *Sur* was very different in form, content, and intent from *Martín Fierro*. Initially a trimestral luxury journal, it ran nearly two hundred pages and sold for a very expensive two pesos. The luxury format was discarded in 1935 when, after a year of silence, the journal reappeared as a monthly. Waldo Frank, a Yale-educated communist Jew, lectured at Amigos del Arte in Buenos Aires in 1929 and, to hear him tell it, persuaded the wealthy heiress Victoria Ocampo to start a literary journal with a pan–Latin American perspective. Frank's vision of the magazine was not to be. Frank hoped Samuel Glusberg would collaborate with Ocampo, but she found Glusberg socially and ideologically unacceptable and believed that spending her money on the journal entitled her to determine its taste. Like Frank, Glusberg had a more Americanist vision than Ocampo.[2] Ocampo's tastes were not very Americanist, at least in the beginning, though *Sur* (South) had a title reflecting its hemispheric origins and an arrow on the cover pointing down (south). She had little use for European avant-gardism and was in fact uninterested in poetry or fiction for the first several years of *Sur*. Her tastes ran to the personal essay, Europe, and whatever her friends had to say. Journalistic models included André Gide's *Nouvelle Revue Française* and Ortega y Gasset's *Revista de Occidente*. Ortega y Gasset believed that the intellectual's duty was to continue a tradition of preserving cultural value and ensuring that the thinking elite remained a strong influence. His belief in the intelligentsia as a transnational class was often echoed by Ocampo, who felt she and her peers were "desterrados de Europa en América; desterrados de América en Europa" (qtd. in Viñas 1971, 193) (exiled from Europe in America; exiled from America in Europe).

In the beginning, *Sur*'s relationship to things Latin American was disorienting to its Argentine audience. Ocampo wanted to present her continent to European friends; the early issues were populated by full-page photographs of scenic Argentine landmarks and essays about Latin America by European writers who knew little about their subject. It was French orientalism, as analyzed by Edward Said, once removed: instead of seeing North Africa through the fantasy-inspired imagination of nineteenth-century French culture, Ocampo presented Argentina to its own people through the filter of the European gaze. Not surprisingly, this choice provoked a reaction in Buenos Aires. As Borges later recalled,

> Nous étions assez étonnés de voir, dans le premier numéro de cette revue publiée à Buenos Aires, qu'il y avait une photo des Iguazú, une autre de la Terre de Feu, une autre de la Cordillère des andes et une autre encore de la province de Buenos Aires. Je crois encore me rappeler que c'était 'Vista de las pampas' . . . avec ce pluriel! Un vrai manuel de géographie. (*Jorge Luis Borges* 1964, 377)

> (We were rather astonished to see in the first number of this journal published in Buenos Aires a photo of Iguazu Falls, another of Tierra del Fuego, another of the Andes and yet another of the province of Buenos Aires. I believe I still recall that it was captioned "Vista of the Pampas" . . . in the plural! A true geography manual.)

Ocampo defended her choice by saying she wanted to persuade the Europe-oriented *porteños* to think about their own country for a change. But she also indicated that Europe was the vehicle of Argentine cultural truth: "Nada nos pone más seguramente en el rastro de nuestra verdad como la presencia, el interés y la curiosidad, las reacciones de nuestros amigos de Europa" (qtd. in Warley 1985, 28). (Nothing puts us so securely on the track of our truth as the presence, the interest and the curiosity, the reactions of our European friends.) Through much of the 1930s, *Sur*'s content was heavily European, an editorial choice reflecting the intellectual insecurity Ocampo frequently expressed: "En presencia de Valéry, yo, sudamericana, me sentía a mitad de camino entre él y el hombre de Cromagnon" (Ocampo 1946, 125). (In the presence of [Paul] Valéry, I, a South American, felt myself to be midway between him and Cro-Magnon man.) Cultural authority was to be imported to an even greater degree than in *Martín Fierro*. As King (1986) explains, "*Sur* would always see itself as one of the great literary magazines of the period, the *Nouvelle Revue Française* of Latin America, with an editor who knew all the *Nouvelle Revue Française* contributors personally" (45).

In the 1950s, when the acclaimed journal was for the first time frequently identified as "oligarchic," it was in reaction to *Sur*'s perceived devaluing of Latin American writing and to its pervasively Europeanized taste. These criticisms were presented as *Sur*'s failure to be involved in solving Argentine social problems. The gap between the original problem and the latter commonly accepted formulation of the problem illustrates how difficult it is to read except through the filter of our present concerns; in the 1950s, Ocampo's cultural elitism was recast in Marxist terms as socioeconomic elitism. This act of critical revisionism repeats in important ways the gesture of Florida toward Boedo: the true or original concern is obscured by a more current or popular form of protest. Florida projected onto Boedo its anxieties about the boom in immigration and the popularization of the market, but cloaked those concerns in avant-garde rhetoric. One reason why it took more than twenty years for critics to point out that *Sur* and Borges had failed to become involved in domestic social problems is that in the 1930s critics weren't so concerned with such issues. Latin America in the 1950s and thereafter expected of its writers what the Auden poets and the surrealists expected of themselves early on: that they save their societies from ruin. Criticism is thus both contingent diachronically (within a given country over time) and synchronically (across national borders at a given moment).

The first issue of *Sur* is a striking example of how in moments of uncertainty Argentine high culture has defined itself through the perspectives of North American and European writers. In an open letter to Frank thanking him for convincing her to undertake the journal, Ocampo describes America as "hidden treasure." If the rest of the issue is any indication, the "treasure" will for some time be excavated for and by foreigners. Frank's essay "La selva" (The jungle) follows, with grand pronouncements about Brazil's history and racial nature. Because of the hot, humid climate, the black Brazilian has suffered "una disminución biológica de sus funciones psíquicas y nerviosas" (a biological diminution of his psychic and nervous functions). Frank concludes that Brazil is "racialmente, intrínsecamente, la antítesis del progreso" (Frank 1931, 25) (racially, intrinsically, the antithesis of progress) and that its hope lies in its southern part, where Europeans have settled and the climate is more like that of Argentina and the United States. It is hard to imagine what Frank intended by this essay, which clearly is not about literary culture. What it accomplishes, however, is quite interesting: by identifying Brazil as a racially impaired neighbor and Argentina as similar to the United States, he asserts Argentine racial and cultural supremacy. Similarly, Pierre Drieu la Rochelle's (1931) "Carta a unos desconocidos" (Letter to unknown people) admits ignorance about America, but offers the appealing suggestion that the Argentines, like the Europeans, are citizens of the world (53–63).

In "Los problemas del compositor americano" (The problems of the American composer), Swiss composer Ernest Ansermet rejects the use of Incan and other indigenous music in modern Latin American composition as "artificial." Ansermet (1931) doesn't hesitate to play the dictator of taste, emphasizing "quality," a European notion of good music (124). The question of quality continues to haunt the pages of *Sur* for decades. Ocampo (1975) defines the quality she claims has for decades governed her editorial choices:

> Lo fundamental, en una revista literaria, tal como fue concebida la nuestra, es mantener y defender el *standard literario*. En arte no cabe la igualdad ni la caridad. Premiar una obra mediocre porque su autor vive en circunstancias difíciles es inconcebible. La obra está bien o mal escrita, bien o mal pensada. . . . No hay más pasaporte que el talento. . . . Pero a la exigencia de calidad a que yo me refiero se resiste cada vez más el mundo moderno. Es *impopular,* y con eso queda todo dicho. (206–7)

> (The fundamental principle, in a literary journal conceived as ours was, is to maintain and defend the *literary standard.* In art there is no room for equality or charity. To award a prize to a mediocre work because its author lives in difficult circumstances is inconceivable. The work is well or badly written, well or badly thought. . . . There is no other passport than talent. . . . But the urgent need for the quality to which I refer is increasingly resisted in the modern world. It is *unpopular,* and with that everything has been said.)

There is nothing objective to hang on to here; this is a standard created through a group's economic and cultural power to identify its own product as valuable and to evaluate the work of others by its normative taste.

Over the decades, the shifting values of *Sur* map the tension between the need to assert a Latin American identity and voice, and Argentine high culture's continued dependence on Europe for inspiration and self-image. In 1931, Mexican writer Alfonso Reyes writes in *Sur* that America is generally "pathetic," but he argues that it is a mistake to cater to the European expectation of exotic or picturesque cultural products.³ The assertion of a distinctly Latin American voice requires several more years and has much to do with Borges's fiction finding a prominent place in *Sur*. Ironically, the analogue of the vanguardia's infrequently stated goal of gaining a voice in Argentine high culture was for *Sur* in the 1930s the dissemination of Argentine literature abroad.

Though relatively few vanguardia poets published in the pages of *Sur*, there is considerable continuity between the two groups. *Sur*'s national editorial committee was a small, tightly knit group that in the 1930s included Borges, Girondo, Eduardo Mallea, and de Torre. Viñas (1971) emphasizes the vanguardia's and *Sur*'s shared love of Europe, calling the vanguardia "una suerte de club de amigos de París en Buenos Aires" (61–62) (a sort of club of friends of Paris in Buenos Aires). Ocampo refers to *Sur* as a "bridge" between Argentina and Europe. She worked with little early success to promote the translation of Argentine work, especially that of Borges, in Europe. *Sur* made a forte of translating early what were to become famous European works, thus building the credibility of Ocampo's "standard" of quality. Ocampo claims she published Sartre before he was famous in France. *Sur*'s first translation of Faulkner's work, in August 1939, also appeared before Faulkner gained renown in the United States.

There were other firsts as well: Octavio Paz, for example, read Breton's work for the first time in *Sur*.⁴ Borges's work was not available in French, however, until 1944, when Roger Caillois oversaw the translation of short stories for the *Croix du sud* series. Both *Sur* and the vanguardia have been accused of domestic elitism. Whereas the vanguardia excluded the Boedans, *Sur* essentially excluded from its pages Lugones, Horacio Quiroga, and the Boedans, including Roberto Arlt. Ironically, Quiroga was an important influence on Borges's fantastic short stories, which began to appear in 1939 and which helped make *Sur* internationally famous.

If the official history of the vanguardia is largely an insider's story, perpetuating the group's original myth of self, *Sur*'s official history is often told by outsiders whose socioeconomic and political concerns extend beyond the usual scope of cultural magazines. The journal's early emphasis on European literature eventually led to charges that it was *extranjerizante*. Over time, the division by critics of foreign versus national interests became associated with an aesthetics versus politics division. For many contemporary Argentine critics, *Sur* was antinational because apolitical. Jorge Warley (1985) for example, equates politics with national concerns:

A lo largo de su primera década, *Sur* prácticamente no dedicará una linea al comentario político. Habrá sí algunas menciones sobre la guerra en España y denuncias sobre las prácticas de los gobiernos fascistas y el stalinismo; pero ninguna sobre la cuestión nacional. Será a partir de la Segunda Guerra cuando la política *llegue* a *Sur.* (51)

(Through its first decade, *Sur* practically doesn't dedicate a single line to political commentary. There are some mentions of the war in Spain and denunciations of the practices of fascist governments and Stalinism, but nothing on the national question. It is only beginning with World War II that politics *arrives* at *Sur.*)

Sur's editorial choices in the early years are proof enough that the journal was apathetic about or afraid to seek solutions to serious national problems. Warley's view is typical of left-liberal critics who label *Sur* elitist and apolitical. Nicolás Rosa (1971) goes farther to argue that imperialist capitalism has governed Argentina's literary practice, that the historically regressive *Sur* was produced and read by the elite, and that its foreign languages and literatures of choice — French and English — reflect its chronic elitism.

Blas Matamoro's (1971) charge that *Sur* was an organ of the aristocracy takes as its basis Ocampo's money and taste in spite of Matamoro's admission that most of *Sur*'s editors and many of its contributors were middle class (136). In the early 1940s, Ocampo told a journalist that *Sur* lost money every month (Vázquez 1980, 170). Enrique Pezzoni, an editor of *Sur* in its later years, has said that even with Sur Editorial — the profitable publishing house Ocampo established in 1933 — he does not believe Ocampo ever broke even (interview with author, 16 November 1987). Not only was *Sur*'s early goal to provide a cultural channel between two continents; in the 1930s the journal was arguably forced to publish European work in order to gain for itself a large enough audience to accomplish this goal. In contrast, the Auden poets and the surrealists were able to be their own strongest influences. Like its European models, *Sur* did not in its early years value highly — perhaps could not afford to value highly — young, untried Latin American writers. That it translated and published young, not necessarily famous Europeans and North Americans, however, reveals how different the Argentines' circumstances were. It was perhaps out of necessity that Girondo published in Europe. Still, the Argentine journals enjoyed considerable success. *Sur* published five thousand copies at one point, whereas the *Revista de Occidente*'s circulation never surpassed three thousand. Though this is modest compared to the success of the more nationally oriented *Martín Fierro, Sur* appealed to a more elite, more international audience (see Matamoro 1986, 221).

María Teresa Gramuglio (1986) is a rare voice of dissent, reacting against the prevalent pairing of oligarchic with politically apathetic in *Sur* criticism. Construing politics broadly, she argues that *Sur* in the 1930s was a political journal because it took an interest in international political events, especially the Spanish civil war and the rise of Nazism. The fact that the journal had foreign writers (such as Aldous Huxley) publish on issues only marginally relevant to Argentina (such as pacifism) suggests that political debate often had an academic quality. In the spirit of self-preservation that is inherent to all cultures, *Sur*'s position is not surprising given that it saw itself as a minority voice in need of protection.

Gramuglio's view is unusual; more typical among nonleftist critics is an account that closely parallels Ocampo's official history of the journal. Jesús Méndez, for example, argues that "Americanist, cosmopolitan, elitist, and proletarian ideologies all competed for supremacy during the initial founding of the magazine and contributed to its founding." But Waldo Frank and Samuel Glusberg can hardly be called proletarian, and Méndez omits all mention of why Ocampo's vision triumphed over theirs and how money figured in the outcome. More misleading still, Méndez (1981) writes: "The pages of *Sur* remained open to all Argentine intellectuals who wished to contribute to it" (11, 13). Critics of *Sur*—and of Borges—have divided along the line that separated the surrealists in 1929: politics versus aesthetics. By the 1950s, political neutrality was no longer an option for Argentine writers unless they were willing to run the risk of being considered aesthetes associated with elitism, traditionalism, and antinationalism. This fault line between politics and aesthetics, between public and private, arises in other forms in the criticism of the Auden group and the surrealists as well.

Like the vanguardia, *Sur* adopted a defensive stance toward its critics, popular culture, and both ends of the political spectrum. *Sur* represented an outmoded brand of liberalism; its philosophic centerpieces were such timeless values as individual artistic freedom and the notion that intellectuals have an important role as society's moral compasses. Political liberalism in the 1930s was an elitist economic order dependent on foreign capital and markets, especially those of England and North America. As King points out, liberalism in the 1930s "lost any chance of being equated with democracy" (King 1986, 70). In spite of Borges's habit of pointing to the arbitrariness of the linguistic sign and to the arbitrariness of all kinds of argumentation, language and the speaking subject were, for the essentially elitist *Sur,* the unimpeachable conveyers of truth. Some of the journal's editorial defensiveness developed from Ocampo's personal experience as a woman of letters in a patriarchal literary age. Ocampo suffered patronizing treatment from *La Nación* and several male writers. Although Ocampo helped feminize Argentine literature, in 1979 she remained the first and only woman member of the prestigious Academia Argentina de Letras.

Though Ocampo held fast to the idea that the journal's pages were open to those who met a universal standard of quality, regular contributors—including European contributors—were almost always personal friends. Friendship was a strong common denominator in the three groups discussed in these pages: in all three cases, the friendships among the core poets were one of the strongest ties holding the groups together, at least in their early years. While Breton was willing to reject friends he was displeased with, Ocampo made an art form of cultivating foreign acquaintances. Many of her friends introduced her to their friends, until she knew whole groups of European writers. In the 1920s she met Ortega y Gasset, Count Hermann de Keyserling, Rabindranath Tagore, Pierre Drieu la Rochelle, and Paul Valéry. She later met Aldous Huxley, André Malraux, Adrienne Monnier, Sylvia Beach, Virginia Woolf, Jean Cocteau, André Gide, Paul Eluard, Paul Claudel, André Maurois, Valéry Larbaud, and Jacques Lacan (see Meyer 1981, 90, 158, 168–71). Members of the national editorial committee shared Ocampo's ideas about the intellectual elite's mission, but did not manage to create a democratic atmosphere within their own project. On the contrary, they had an internal hierarchy that temporarily placed Eduardo Mallea, whose ponderous essays about Argentine "reality" enjoyed a brief burst of popularity, over Borges, who leaned toward the fantastic, the semiotic, the esoteric, and the universal.

From its first issues, *Sur* attempted to save the West from Spenglerian decline and revealed that its intellectual mission was to lead a historically barbarous society into the humanistic light. Matamoro points out that this notion can be traced back to Sarmiento and the Generation of 1880. In fact, *Sur*'s brand of liberalism bears a remarkable resemblance to nineteenth-century ideals. In this sense, *Sur,* like the "newest generation" of poets that followed on the heels of the vanguardia, represents a reaction to that avant-garde (see Matamoro 1986, 214–15). This reaction reveals just how conservative the Argentine literary landscape actually was, and suggests that if it wanted to survive, its avant-garde movement probably had fewer choices than either the surrealists or the Auden poets. The poets came by their lack of interest in the Continental avant-garde honestly; there was almost nothing in their immediate environment that made it relevant. In fact, as they undoubtedly knew, in its pure form it was a threat to literature as they knew it.

Following the military coup of 1930 that brought Juan de Uriburu to the presidency, rampant corruption was paired with rigged elections. Extremist elements in Argentine society grew more powerful as the decade wore on and an increasingly ugly authoritarian nationalism helped anti-Semitism and fascism become mainstream forces. In such a setting, it was a self-preserving gesture for *Sur* to avoid getting involved in domestic politics, though that was an increasingly difficult task. Gramuglio (1986) points out that *Sur* failed to criticize the repressive violence and illegal imprisonment—including of intellectuals—carried out under Uriburu's and Justo's dictatorships (39). In the late 1930s *Sur* published many articles opposing fascism and Nazism. It also tried to extend tangible help to struggling intellectuals abroad. In the pages following an excerpt of Ernst Toller's play "El Pastor Hall," on concentration camp life in Nazi Germany, the Comisión Argentina de Ayuda a los Intelectuales Españoles requested donations to help Spanish (Republican) intellectuals get out of refugee camps in the Pyrenees.[5]

It wasn't until Juan Perón came to power, however, that domestic politics appeared in its pages. Ortega y Gasset had warned against involvement in issues that would distract intellectuals from their more atemporal duties. Ocampo, who always disliked party politics, distinguished between opinion and political expression: "Claro que los que se ponían al servicio de un partido, y le hacían 'propaganda,' bajan inmédiatamente de nivel. . . . Me refiero a la *propaganda,* no a un expresar honestamente opiniones."[6] (Clearly those who put themselves in the service of a party and produce 'propaganda' for it immediately diminish in level [of quality]. . . . I am referring to *propaganda,* not to an honest expression of opinions.) In contrast to Auden's 1930s, where propaganda was typically defined as rhetorical persuasion in the service of the Communist Party, Ocampo's propaganda is merely any partisan expression of party sentiment. She defines the political subjectively, identifying as "ethical" the public statements she wants to make about political topics. In later years, Borges was still making this somewhat artificial distinction: "Je m'occupe le moins possible de politique. Je m'en suis occupé pendant la dictature, mais cela, ce n'était pas de la politique, mais de l'éthique."[7] (I spend the least possible amount of time on politics. I spent time on politics during [Perón's] dictatorship, but that wasn't politics, it was ethics.)

Unlike the Auden poets, who in the 1930s found political content virtually everywhere, the *Sur* group took the opposite tack: because politics was a dirty word in Argentine society in the 1930s, *Sur* labeled its political interests "moral" or "ethical." Nevertheless, Borges verified in 1941 that even Argentine poetry was rapidly politicized in the course of the 1930s: "Hará veinte años clasificábamos a los poetas por la omisión o por el manejo de la rima. . . . Ahora se prefieren las distinciones religioso-políticas: interminablemente oigo hablar de poetas marxistas, neotomistas, nacionalistas" (Borges, Ocampo, and Casares 1941, 9). (Twenty years ago we classified poets according to whether they did or didn't use rhyme. . . . Today religious-political distinctions are preferred: I hear endless talk about Marxist poets, neothomist poets, nationalist poets.) For the surrealists, the choice between political and aesthetic was more problematic. Breton urged them first in one direction, then in another, expecting them to share in his reactions even though they changed at a rather rapid clip. All three of the groups had unwritten internal rules. The notion that the avant-garde is anarchic and spontaneous is belied by the internal dilemmas of these groups, especially those of the Auden poets and the surrealists. In both cases, there are many signs that they searched individually and collectively for the right way to proceed.

Sur displayed a remarkable ability to collapse binary oppositions that split European literary groups irrevocably in two. While the Auden poets and the surrealists concluded that communism was the only way to fight fascism, was in fact fascism's opposite, *Sur* conflated both ends of the spectrum and clung to the liberal middle ground, rejecting communism and flirting briefly with fascism. Ocampo traveled to Italy in 1934 to meet Mussolini and deliver a lecture titled "Supremacía del alma y de la sangre" (Supremacy of the soul and the blood) in Florence and Venice at the Instituto Interuniversitaria di Coltura. Another tie to fascism in the 1930s was her romantic relationship with Pierre Drieu la Rochelle, a fascist who committed suicide before the end of the decade (Ocampo 1981). In "Literatura individual frente a literatura dirigida" (Individual literature in contrast to directed literature), published in *Sur* in 1937, Guillermo de Torre writes: "En el fondo, comunistoides y fascistizantes de toda laya se dan la mano y se reconocen como hermanos gemelos en el común propósito de aniquilar o rebajar la libre expresión literaria y artística."[8] (At bottom, communist and fascist types of every ilk shake hands and recognize each other as twin brothers in the common goal of eradicating or decreasing free literary and artistic expression.)

It was not until 1937 that *Sur*'s editors came out openly against fascism. By inviting eminent Europeans to participate in discussions of politics, *Sur* raised its own cultural authority and prestige. By choosing the one path that seemed most bankrupt in Europe—liberalism—it expressed an identity and history very different from those of Europe and conflicts very different from those of the surrealists and the Auden group. By the 1940s, the journal was moving toward a more stable American identity. In spite of its dependence on European influence and authors, it did not try to fashion its own social and political circumstances in a foreign image.

Sur occasionally made the ironic gesture of rejecting liberalism itself. In a 1935 article entitled "El escritor de hoy frente a su tiempo" (Today's writer faced with his era), Mallea (1935) writes, "Yo creo que *la muerte del liberalismo* y la crisis del amor humano han cambiado la faz del mundo" (72; my emphasis). (I believe that *the death of liberalism* and the crisis of human love have changed the face of the world.) His perspective is oriented more toward European than Argentine reality, decrying, "Esta crisis, este invierno, esta vacilación entre los dogmas contradictorios, este no poder tomar partido, esta necesidad de quemar en seguida las reservas y lanzarse violéntamente a una creencia" (72–73). (This crisis, this winter, this vacillation between contradictory dogmas, this inability to make a decision, this necessity to burn immediately our doubts and launch ourselves violently at a belief.) Mallea divides writers into spectators and agonists, calling for the ethical writer to intervene in "el conflicto moral de las masas" (73) (the moral conflict of the masses). His rhetoric sounds like that of the Auden group: the era of the aesthete over, it is time for the intellectual to act once again as a prophet and lead his people into a "nueva forma de civilización" (76) (new form of civilization). But no concrete action is advised, no solutions tendered, no alternative philosophies or dogmas proposed. Mallea labels *Sur* an Argentine journal, although he says that only those whose families have long histories in the country ("los viejos criollos" [old criollos]) have the right to judge its merits.

That *Sur* was in important ways more rebellious and independent than the vanguardia journals is ironic in light of their respective histories of critical reception, many of which see the vanguardia as the rebel and *Sur* as the conservative. Criticizing fascism and anti-Semitism in the late 1930s put the journal at odds with many of the most powerful interest groups in Argentine society. During World War II, King (1986) argues, when Argentina became a "hemispheric pariah" for being the only Latin American country not to declare support for the Allies, "*Sur*'s outspoken pro-Allied position was a specifically political intervention" (96). Given this situation, it is hard to argue that *Sur* was "apolitical." Though its politics were sometimes confined to short pieces deep in the journal, they were unmistakably there. In an important sense, *Sur* ran more political risk than the Auden poets did. Like the surrealists, a couple of whom ended up in jail, Argentine writers sometimes found themselves risking retaliation from the government.

Though *Sur* had no use for Marxism, it was in fact left of center in the political climate of the 1930s. But *Sur* rebutted *Criterio*'s charge that it was a leftist journal by claiming to be interested in ethics, not politics. This claim rings somewhat truer than the vanguardia's assertion that it operated totally independently of the literary market. It is similar, however, in its denial of a basic truth: this was an era—a mild version of Auden's 1930s— when refusing to take a stand was in and of itself a political position. As national politics was a divisive and dangerous territory, responsible for the demise of both series of *Martín Fierro, Sur* was wise to approach the political and the literary as parallel but separate discourses. The main risk of mixing them was not state-sanctioned censorship, but rather the interpersonal stress of editors and contributors at odds with one another. Allowing a high cultural journal to be political at this time was to risk having it self-destruct. There were those, of course, who could not abide this separation. Samuel Glusberg withdrew from the second series of *Martín Fierro*—the series discussed earlier—because, in contrast to the political first series (not discussed in these pages), it was going to be largely aesthetic. Ocampo denied Glusberg a role in *Sur* after he chose in 1930 to reprint in his Americanist newspaper, *La vida literaria* (The literary life), an embarrassing list of Floridians—including Borges—and others who had supported Yrigoyen for president of Argentina (see Méndez 1981, 15).

Sur conceived of itself as a voice crying in the moral—not political— wilderness. Ocampo, for example, wrote: "*Sur* se esforzará en revelar valores jovenes, formados en disciplinas nuevas, auténticamente despiertos ante la miseria actual del espíritu."[9] (*Sur* will strive to reveal young values formed in new disciplines, authentically awakened in the presence of the present's spiritual poverty.) But *Sur* avoided literary life at the Universidad de Buenos Aires and insistently created its own public roles and cultural standards. The university-based *Contorno,* a journal oriented toward the political and historical aspects of literature, was founded in 1935 and served for several years as *Sur*'s rival. Ocampo had once wanted to attend the Argentine university, but her upper-class background stood in the way.

Its own strongest influence, *Sur* contains many instances of self-historicization that emphasize its identity as a spiritually elite journal. The tension between Americanism and Europeanism remains unresolved: number 8 contains a list of the twenty Argentine writers published in *Sur* during its three-year history, but when Sur Editorial was established in 1933, the first book published was a translation of D. H. Lawrence's *Kangaroo*. Among the few poems published in the journal are translations of poets such as Langston Hughes, Jules Supervielle, and Edgar Lee Masters. National art is much discussed, but foreign writers continue to tell Argentines who they are and what they should be. Hermann Keyserling's paternalistic "Perspectivas sudamericanas" (South American perspectives), for example, argues that Argentina's lack of initiative, inventive ability, and perseverance make it very different from France. Keyserling's cultural authority grants him the privilege of undermining *Sur*'s own project.[10] That *Sur* chose to publish his essay reveals the degree to which Ocampo was fixated on the authority of European—usually male European—voices.

During the 1930s, Borges explicates and translates poems and reviews texts ranging from *The Adventures of Huckleberry Finn* to the *Arabian Nights* to Chesterton's detective novels. With the appearance of "Pierre Menard, autor del *Quijote*" (Pierre Menard, author of the *Quixote*) at the beginning of the May 1939 issue of *Sur,* a new era has begun: Borges has moved from the margins of the journal to its center by changing his focus from international criticism to presenting his own fiction. As he comes to stand for Argentine literature beyond the nation's borders, he becomes a source of great authority for the journal. In comparison, Auden's shift from England to the United States and from political to more religious poems is less dramatic. Certainly, it had fewer consequences. Breton, in contrast, did not shift significantly in his writing or his philosophy. Surrealism in France changed with the times, finally fading with age.

Ocampo acknowledged years later that Borges represents "un passeport pour la haute société littéraire contemporaine, un laisser-passer pour nous, Argentins"[11] (a passport for high contemporary literary society, an entry permit for us Argentines) to high cultural circles everywhere. Borges came to believe that fiction was his ticket to an international reading public. If he had continued to write poetry and essays, he later argued, "cela ne m'aurait pas sorti de Buenos Aires"[12] (it wouldn't have gotten me out of Buenos Aires). Ultraism's metaphorical play with infinity, replication, time, and space infects Borges's fiction. But the poetry, partly because it is oriented toward argentinidad and is nostalgic and romantic, is of more limited appeal. Formally, it relies too heavily on a limited range of tropes; Borges's frequent insistence on making a new metaphor for each image creates a scattered effect. Many of the early short stories, in contrast, resemble more closely the structure of successful poems in that they take a single conceit—such as the ephemeral boundary between waking and sleep—and extend it throughout the work. Bioy Casares describes Borges, his literary mentor, as a literary conservative in the 1930s. In 1939, Borges participated in making a list of tropes and techniques writers should avoid. Rejected are many of Borges's 1920s' attachments: metaphors in general, especially visual metaphors, local color, and an archaic, latinate, and argentinismo-centered vocabulary.[13]

Going across the grain of Argentine belief, Borges argued at various times during his life against the deification of the author. To reinforce his case against the sanctity of the author-function, Borges even argued that making editorial changes to canonized works, "même faites par un magistrat, peuvent y être bénéfiques"[14] (even [changes] made by a judge, could benefit the work). Late in life, Borges said, "I think poetry should be anonymous. . . . I would like a line of mine, a story of mine, rewritten and bettered by somebody else, to survive, and I would wish my personal name to be forgotten" (Barnstone 1982, 9). Many of his works of fiction allude simultaneously to their status as texts in the imaginary library of all possible books and in the real libraries of the world.

Foucault would have applauded Borges's attempts to examine the problem of the excessive authority accorded the author in literary discourse. But in the late 1930s and 1940s, when Borges and Adolfo Bioy Casares collaborated secretly to produce works published under the name of the imaginary author H. Bustos-Domecq, the Argentine audience was not amused. Having discovered what it considered to be a ruse, the Buenos Aires reading public—which felt it had been ridiculed—refused to read such works as *Seis relatos para don Isidro Parodi* (Six stories by Don Isidro Parodi [1942]).[15] A text that points to its own condition as text or, in the case of "Pierre Menard: Autor del *Quijote*," lays bare its own internal "ruse," was considered acceptable. Tampering with the name of the author was not. This is partly because the Bustos-Domecq device disrupts the circuit of bestowing authority on the author's name, in turn throwing off the critic's authority to offer discursive power to the author. It may also prevent critics from interpreting works through the lens of the author's socioeconomic and cultural background. In the Argentine context, this was a disturbing intervention in the status quo of how literature was evaluated.

Borges's increasing fame did not result in sympathy from Argentine critics. The vagaries of Borges criticism show up in the tendency of critics (especially Argentine critics) to read through the lens of the nation's current concerns. As early as the 1923 *Nosotros* survey, Borges's ultraism was often mentioned as the major influence on his generation of poets. In 1933, *Megáfono*—the organ of the university-based "novísima generación" (newest generation) of poets—published a poll on his role in Argentine literature. Commenting on the poll, Jaime Alazraki (1987) identifies Borges in 1933 as "the most prominent member of the so-called new generation and the most influential force among young writers" (1). Ironically, given the vanguardia's conservatism, the "newest generation" of poets defined itself as more conservative than the Generation of 1922: in the August 1931 issue of *Megáfono* they argued that the vanguardia indulged in the aggressive use of language, excessive use of the metaphor, and "la abolición de toda norma externa" (8:3–8; qtd. in Bastos 1974) (the abolition of all external norms). The *Megáfono* survey indicates that the increasingly conservative writer "Borges" has replaced the Boedo-Florida debate of the 1920s as a polemical topic in its own right. Bastos's 1974 summary of the respondents' comments, however, depicts a different Borges from that evoked by Alazraki's sanguine description. Poll respondents, Bastos (1974) writes, reached the consensus that

> Borges inició un movimiento de renovación de nuestra prosa, pero al cabo de diez años de trabajo . . . su estilo es retórico, complicado y vacuo; Borges no solo carece de preocupación por lo humano sino que da la espalda a los problemas nacionales. (117)

> (Borges initiated a movement to renovate our prose, but at the end of ten years of work . . . his style is rhetorical, complicated and empty; Borges not only lacks a preoccupation with the human, but turns his back on national problems as well.)

Writing in the 1970s, Bastos may be interpreting the *Megáfono* survey comments in light of the view of Borges that has prevailed on the Argentine left since the 1950s. The majority of the 1933 survey respondents do not address the issue of Borges's relationship to national problems. A number of respondents identify him as an important contributor to national culture, and most discuss him only in aesthetic terms, emphasizing his linguistic and stylistic innovations. Social comments are limited to Erwin Rubéns's view that Borges has a static image of the world and vanguardia poet Ulises Petit de Murat's disapproval of the labeling of Borges as "anti-humano" on the grounds that the label is a product of current fashions of word use (Bastos 1974, 104). Enrique Anderson Imbert is the important exception: he remarks that "Argentine reality" is missing from Borges's essays, that Borges is not a "national thinker" (Bastos 1974, 102–20). Imbert seems most annoyed by the essay "Nuestras imposibilidades" (Our impossibilities), in which Borges complains of the "penuria imaginativa" (impoverished imagination) of the Argentine people, their national vanity, and "negligence" of the non-Argentine.[16] Imbert criticizes Borges for an inability to write "works of value" (Bastos 1974, 113) and ends on a nationalist note: those who don't contribute to the culture in a constructive way have no "derecho a ocupar un lugar en nuestra cultura y mucho menos en nuestros corazones" (right to occupy a place in our culture and much less in our hearts). They are, he says, "ausentes del país" (Bastos 1974, 114) (absent from the country).

Imbert's comment is a product of his era, much as Bastos's summary is a product of hers. Bastos's criticisms are more problematic because they impute a post–World War II point of view to prewar writers. In 1933, there is simply no talk of "national [that is, political and social] problems," but only of national reality and national culture. The difference may seem minor, but it is significant because writers in the 1920s and 1930s were not yet trying to solve such problems.

Alazraki represents the "late" international view; Bastos, the national. In the case of *Sur,* he writes, "Su descalificación como 'revista de la oligarquía,' extranjerizante, etc., es una idea que comenzará a procesarse hacia los años cincuenta. En el período anterior, un tono de respeto, e incluso admiración, es utilizado para hablar sobre ella" (Warley 1985, 45). (Its discrediting, as a 'journal of the oligarchy,' foreign-oriented, etc., is an idea that begins to develop around the 1950s. Earlier, a tone of respect and even of admiration is used to speak about [*Sur*].)

Mario Vargas Llosa's recollection of the early days of *Sur* is an important illustration of this early reception. The journal "fue como una brisa de aire fresco para su generación en el Perú, aplastada por un realismo documentario" (Bastos 1980, 126) (was like a breath of fresh air for his generation in Peru, who were flattened by documentary realism). Julio Cortázar concurs: "SUR nos ayudó a los estudiantes que en la década del 30 al 40 tentábamos un camino titubeando entre tantos errores, tantas abyectas facilidades y mentiras" (qtd. in Matamoro 1975, 138–39). (SUR helped us students who in the decade of 1930–40 were trying out a path as we hesitated among so many errors, so many pitifully easy choices and lies.) *Sur*, which differed publicly with the Catholic Church and the government by supporting the Republican cause in the Spanish civil war and warning of the dangers of Nazism, was willing to decry publicly the Argentine right's increasing support of anti-Semitism and fascism.

Though the journal grew more conservative with age, moving from anti-Peronism to being on the right of the Cuban revolution, it did not change nearly so much as its shifting reception suggests. In the 1930s, criticism against Ocampo was limited mainly to charges that she was too oriented toward Europe. French, for example, was her language of choice and in the 1930s she was still not a proficient writer of Spanish. While such criticism was then an expression of cultural nationalism, in the 1970s it became a leftist concern with institutionalized socioeconomic elitism. Matamoro (1975), for example, labeled *Sur* in the 1970s the "máxima expresión institucional de la literatura oligárquica" (136) (highest institutional expression of oligarchic literature). Matamoro's indictment exemplifies the tendency of critics to identify *Sur* with Ocampo, a descendant of the oligarchy of the Generation of 1880. Borges has argued that Argentines tend to value the signature and the person behind the signature more than the literary work itself. The conflation of Ocampo and *Sur*, like the post-1920s confusion of Borges and the vanguardia, illustrates the Argentine emphasis on the individual signature. As King (1986) puts it, "*Sur* is most frequently read as a product of the class background of Victoria" (59). Ocampo contributed to this critical reading by making such statements as: "SUR me ha pertenecido y pertenece, materialmente. En lo espiritual, ha sido compartida por un grupo de escritores." [17] (SUR has belonged and does belong to me materially. In regard to the spiritual, it has been shared by a group of writers.)

The changing reception of Borges similarly illustrates the shifting sands of cultural value. In a 1967 interview, Mario Vargas Llosa told Gabriel García Márquez: "I have always had problems in justifying my admiration for Borges." García Márquez's response identifies Borges as a moral failure: "I have no problem at all. I have a great admiration for him. I read him every night. I just came from Buenos Aires and the only thing I bought there was Borges' *Complete Works*. I carry them in my suitcase; I am going to read them every day, and he is a writer I detest. His is a literature of evasion." This criticism reflects the postwar politicization of Latin American literary culture. García Márquez dismisses the Borges who writes about "mental realities" as "sheer evasion." Julio Cortázar, in contrast, he labels "profoundly Latin American" (quotations are from Alazraki 1987, 5–6), by which I believe he means involved in the social and political problems of the continent. Cortázar, who is thought by some to have supported Franco during the Spanish civil war (see "La guerra civil española" 1986, 6), admired *Sur* during the 1940s, and described himself as having then been a "burguesito ciego a todo lo que pasaba más allá de la esfera de lo estético" (little bourgeois blind to everything beyond the sphere of the aesthetic), became politically active rather late in life. Cortázar described his early literary peers as

> muy snobs, aunque muchos de nosotros sólo nos dimos cuenta de eso más tarde. Leíamos muy poco a los escritores argentinos, y nos interesaba casi exclusivamente la literatura inglesa y la francesa. . . . La gente soñaba con París y Londres. Buenos Aires era una especie de castigo. (qtd. in Avellaneda 1983, 102–4)

> (very snobbish, though many of us realized it only later. We read little by Argentine writers and were almost exclusively interested in English and French literature. . . . The people dreamed of Paris and London. Buenos Aires was a kind of punishment.)

Cortázar's support for the Cuban revolution and his postrevolution politics—not his little-known earlier views—are the focus of García Márquez's comments. Similarly, García Márquez ignores Borges's early anti-Peronism, anti-Nazism, antifascism, and his essays criticizing Argentina's rampant anti-Semitism, focusing instead on the fact that in his later years Borges was on his way to becoming a right-wing political reactionary.

The social-versus-aesthetics division of García Márquez's and Vargas Llosa's comments has survived several decades of Argentine criticism. Alazraki points to a "bifurcation" in Borges criticism in the 1950s. The first critical strand is exemplified by Adolfo Ruiz Díaz's *Borges: Enigma and Clue* (1955) and Ana María Barrenechea's (1957) classic work, *La expresión de la irrealidad en la obra de Borges* (The expression of unreality in the work of Borges). Barrenechea (1957) comments on "la increíble lucidez de Borges en la deconstrucción de pre-conceptos, de ideas recibidas, y de estilos *(solo comparable a su increíble miopía socio-histórica)*" (140; my emphasis) (Borges's incredible lucidity in the deconstruction of pre-concepts, received ideas, and styles [*comparable only to his incredible socio-historical myopia*]). Both Díaz and Barrenechea analyze the aesthetics and ideas of

Borges's work with little consideration of its socioeconomic or political ideology, though Barrenechea advances the post–World War II critical consensus that Borges is theoretically advanced and socially retarded.

The other critical strand, represented by Adolfo Prieto's *Borges and the New Generation* (1954), vilifies Borges for eschewing the social: "Los jóvenes no pueden pensar en Borges como un 'maestro' porque el escritor se ha encerrado en su propio mundo, y llamarlo 'maestro' sería una pública manifestación de nuestra esterilidad" (32). (Young people can't think of Borges as a "master" because the writer has isolated himself in his own world and to call him "master" would be a public demonstration of our sterility.) Prieto's point of view has been assimilated by official Argentine criticism in recent years. But two years before Prieto's book appeared, Enrique Pezzoni argued that Borges had created a self-sufficient verbal universe. Such a view was so unusual in the context of the decade's politicized criticism that Bastos calls it a "defense" of Borges in the face of a wave of resentful criticism. Borges reminded Argentines of the poverty of their literary tradition, Pezzoni suggests, a tradition that left them ill-prepared to understand his work (Bastos 1974, 176–83; Pezzoni 1952, 101–23).

Perhaps because by the 1950s Borges was no longer seen as the guardian of things traditionally Argentine, it was a short step to seeing him as a destroyer. Alazraki (1987) writes that Borges "has come to represent . . . the denial of everything Latin-American, the glorification of the West and the mutilation of that part of the continent alien to or different from what the West has sanctioned as acceptable or civilized" (7). The civilization-versus-barbarism dichotomy had thus survived into the late 1980s, though Borges—the champion of civilization in 1925—had become a cultural wrecking ball. A useful analogy is Schwartz's (1979) analysis of the changing meaning of the word "cosmopolitan." The *Oxford English Dictionary* dates the noun "cosmopolite" to 1598, when it meant a person of universal citizenship. By the mid-eighteenth century, however, it appears in French dictionaries as meaning unpatriotic or antinational. Clearly, being cosmopolitan was acceptable in Argentina in the 1920s, but not in the 1950s (Schwartz 1979, 5). The massive waves of immigration of the late nineteenth and early twentieth centuries had subsided by 1930, but the need to protect Argentine culture from the barbarism of the immigrants gradually metamorphosed into a revalorization of aspects of culture previously considered barbarous. Further, Borges's internationalism is equated with abdication of national responsibility. Alazraki comments that in Europe and in the United States Borges was read as a European or a North American.

Like the Argentine vanguardia, the literary profession is in part a product of its own mythology. It tends to see itself as fair-minded if not downright objective, concerned with real (as opposed to elitist) values, engaged in debate aimed at determining truth of all kinds, including the changeable truths of interpretation. Similarly, the canon it shepherds is (theoretically at least) open to infinite revision. These days it is commonly believed that previously unrecognized—because marginalized—writers will be allowed to enter the canon. But "canon," which comes from the Greek into Latin, where it means rule, model, or standard, is even today defined by the following adjectives: authoritative, authentic, accepted, standard, normative.[18] The reversals in critical reception of *Sur* and Borges illustrate how prevailing views were influenced by the changing political climate in Latin America during the 1950s. They force us to acknowledge that interpretation can be as contingent as cultural values. I would argue that the Argentine vanguardia's myth of itself has remained intact largely because it has helped consolidate the national literature and because it was old news by the 1950s. *Sur* and Borges, figures of greater longevity, in contrast, have been a site of struggle between the conservative literary establishment and the literary left over the proper role of the writer in relation to social issues. Politics in their case is interwoven with the relationship between writer and critic. The Argentine writer's role is, in important respects, the inverse of that of the Auden poets: in the eyes of critics, the older Borges represents the failure to be political; the Auden poets, the failure of an aggressive political agenda—the failure of too much politics.

The Auden Group

Poetry was born from magic: it grew up with religion: it lived through the age of reason: is it to die in the century of propaganda?

—C. Day Lewis

5. The Mutable Myth of Auden's 1930s

In England, the 1920s and 1930s represent two distinct stages of high modernism: the first decade epitomized by T. S. Eliot's *The Waste Land;* the second, by poems about the redemptive power of communism. In Eliot's 1920s, literature and politics still occupied separate spheres. Stephen Spender (1978) points out that this was "demonstrated by the division of the contents of the *New Statesman* and the *Nation* into the front halves, devoted predominantly to politics, and the back halves, devoted entirely to the arts, literature and reviewing" (13). For a number of young Oxonians whose paths crossed during the 1920s, World War I did not leave a stable world. By the mid-1930s, many writers believed the only way to save English poetry from being destroyed along with English society was to enter the arena of public politics and save England. And the only way to save England, Michael Roberts (1971) argued in *New Country,* was to save the world (14). The Auden group's fusion of political and literary discourse was so different from the apolitical aesthetics of nearest ancestor Eliot that the poets were forced to look to themselves for a sense of poetic identity. By 1933, writes Samuel Hynes (1972), "the 'thirties generation was its own influence" (110). To a significant degree, this was true of the surrealists as well.

Michael Roberts (1934), author of the *New Signatures* (1932) preface, often considered a manifesto for the Auden group, describes the feeling that the war destroyed all sense of absolute values:

Those of us who grew up to manhood in the post-war years remember how, in that period, it seemed to us there was no finality. We learned

123

to question every impulse until we became so self-conscious, so hag-ridden by doubts, indecisions, uncertainties that we lost all spontaneity. . . . [B]eyond all this [was] a feeling that the middle-class world . . . was definitely breaking up, and that it would be replaced in the near future by a world of communism or big business. (238; qtd. in Brown 1975, 16)

While this may be an accurate recollection of how these young men felt in the 1920s, it must also be read as hindsight. It was written in 1934, well after Roberts wrote his openly leftist preface to the *New Country* anthology. In 1927, in the first public statement linking their names, Auden and Day Lewis wrote the introduction to and edited the annual number of *Oxford Poetry*. In the introduction, Day Lewis points to three problems troubling the modern poet, all of which emphasize the individual poet's relationship to the world. They are the psychological conflict between self as subject and self as object, the ethical conflict between "Pure Art" and the "exigen-cies" of the "human mind and culture," and the logical conflict between the denotative and connotative senses of words (*Oxford Poetry* 1927/1929, v–vi; 1927 ed. cited). These conflicts prefigure the 1930s preoccupation with individualism as a regressive bourgeois trait and the problem of pure versus social art, as played out in the poetry-versus-propaganda dichotomy that troubled the Auden poets. They set the stage for the Auden poets' ob-session with the political and moral aspects of poetry.

For these young men in the process of constituting themselves as writers, 1927 was still a very private, inward-looking time. MacNeice (1965) writes of his Oxford days, "The only real values were aesthetic. Moral values were a delusion, and politics and religion a waste of time" (100). A 1929 entry in his personal journal finds Auden (1977) philosophizing about life in a private, self-oriented way: "The only good reason for doing any-thing is for fun" (300). By 1933, however, he sounds much as Roberts does in 1934: "We live in an age in which the collapse of all previous standards coincides with the perfection in technique for the centralised distribution of ideas; some kind of revolution is inevitable, and will as inevitably be imposed from above by a minority."[1]

In less than five years, Auden has moved from a private point of view to a public one. The Auden poets were strikingly apolitical while at Oxford. Louis MacNeice (1965) reports that "the most publicised blacklegs" of the 1926 General Strike were the Oxford and Cambridge undergraduates who used it as "an occasion for a spree; a comic phenomenon due to the Lower Classes" (101). Even in 1932, Spender can write, "Taking a neurotic and almost doomed society as his subject-matter, Mr. Auden finds only two ways out for us. The first is satiric. The second is the religious."[2] Spender's goals during the summer of 1929, which he spent in Hamburg, were not very different from Auden's. He confides in his journal, "My own work is to write poetry and novels. I have no character or will power outside my work. In the life of action, I do everything that my friends tell me to do, and have no opinions of my own. . . . My aim is to achieve maturity of soul. . . . After my work, all I live for is my friends" (1953b, 90).

Spender, too, underwent a significant change in the early 1930s. In a now famous passage of his autobiography, he marked this transition as an invasion of the private sphere by the public:

> From 1931 onwards, in common with many other people, I felt hounded by external events. . . . The old world seemed incapable of solving its problems, and out of the disorder Fascist régimes were rising.
>
> There was the feeling through all these years of having to race against time to produce a book or a poem. . . . The life itself out of which the work grew was being borne away from under us. (1951, 117)

As undergraduates, these aspiring writers were concerned primarily with how to become good poets. They were both more preoccupied with their poetic predecessors and less willing to repudiate them than their surrealist cousins. Spender recalls that he and Auden made a list of poets past and present and divided what they considered to be their "competition" into three groups, two of which they had no use for. Those two were the "generally approved Book-Society-Chosen novelists and political poets" and the experimental writers "concerned with being new at all costs, and whom we connected in our minds with . . . new art movements in Paris and Berlin." Auden and Spender thus rejected the conventionally acceptable, the sociopolitical, and the Continental avant-garde writers. The third category included James Joyce, D. H. Lawrence, T. S. Eliot, and Yeats, writers Spender claims were "directly or indirectly concerned with our own problem of living in a history which though real was extremely difficult to apprehend, and with the problems of living real lives" (Spender 1978, 243; also in Spender 1966). The repetition of the word "real" suggests an aversion to what Spender considered to be inauthentic lives and poems. Though the Auden poets were quite concerned with aesthetic questions in their formative days, they placed themselves on the reality side of a reality-versus-aesthetics dichotomy. They were thus on the other side of the fence from the Argentine vanguardia. Day Lewis also reports that when he and Auden measured themselves against the modernists and their predecessors.

> we wrote down the names of all the living English poets we could re-member: we then sorted them out into three columns: in the left-hand column we put those whom we already excelled, in the middle column those we would excel one day, and in the right-hand column (an ex-tremely short one) the poets whom we had little hope of ever equalling. (S. Day-Lewis 1980, 43)

Day Lewis does not list the names in the righthand column, but Eliot was probably their most forbidding competition. Instead of circumvent-ing what Harold Bloom calls the "anxiety of influence" by engaging in a typically avant-garde rejection of precursors, these poets measured the competition and found most of it inadequate.

Though they met informally and became friends at Oxford, Auden, Spender, and Day Lewis were not constituted as a group until after *New Signatures* appeared in 1932. The literary anthology—a traditional form—seems an unlikely catalyst for the group, given that they were only three of nine poets represented. And Michael Roberts's introduction was writ-ten without the help of the poets whose names eventually stood in for his as Borges's name did for the other signatures on the *Prisma* manifesto. The idea for the anthology developed from a conversation between Roberts and John Lehmann, a young Cambridge-educated poet who persuaded Leonard and Virginia Woolf to publish it at the Hogarth Press. Lehmann (1955) wanted to present the poets as a "front" in order to force the public to notice them (Perkins 1987, 113). Looking back, he describes the disillu-sion that followed the general election of 1931, the collapse of the Labour government, and the feeling in Bloomsbury that "more radical measures of Marxism were necessary to . . . stop the drift towards a new war. It was under the first wave of this disillusionment that work on *New Signatures* began" (178). If the anthology was to have been one of these "radical mea-sures," it was not a very innovative one, for it must have appeared—at least to critics—to have been borrowed outright from the elaborately planned Georgian movement, which published five anthologies between 1911 and 1922. Robert H. Ross (1965) reveals that *Georgian Poetry* editor Edward Marsh "planned it to the last detail: which journals would be asked to publish reviews; which among his influential friends would be given pre-publication copies and requested to mention the book publicly . . . and even what tone would be suggested for the review." Marsh named the anthology in the hope of creating a major movement and his first preface is explicitly directed toward that end. Robert H. Ross's account of Marsh's behavior is based in part on a letter Marsh wrote on 11 November 1912 (103). Marsh's appeals for good reviews appear to have capitalized more on personal than professional relationships. This is similar to Victoria Ocampo's management of *Sur* in its early years. Her strategy was to form a personal network of European and Latin American writers and to make connections through her friends.

In his preface to *Georgian Poetry*, Marsh refers to the "new strength and beauty" of English poetry, explicitly suggesting that "lovers of poetry" recognize this as the beginning of another " 'Georgian period' which may take rank in due time with the several great poetic ages of the past" (qtd. in Rogers 1977, 51). Publisher Harold Monro wrote to Marsh to tell him it was a "trade secret" that he had printed several editions at once. Monro said he felt ashamed of the contrived publicity maneuver, but that "exceptional circumstances" (that is, the war-induced paper shortage) forced him into it (see Ross 1965, 106–7). Ambivalence about the literary market was as much an issue for the Georgian anthologies as it was for the Argentine vanguardia; in contrast, as we will see, the Auden poets were unapologetically pro-market. An unsigned review of "Georgian Poetry 1913–1915" that appeared in *The Nation* makes a claim similar to what the Argentine vanguardia says of itself: "These young poets are nearly all young men, and few of them have suffered the mildew of commercial popularity." In another review, Arthur Waugh betrays anxiety that the Georgian poetry may "submerge old standards altogether" and "hand over the sensitive art of verse to a general process of literary democratisation."[3] In the Argentine context, this point of view is similar to Florida's concern about Boedo.

Though the Georgian movement never attained the status Marsh hoped for, the market was responsive and four of the five anthologies had sales of fifteen thousand or more copies.[4] These high figures' correlation with low enduring fame contrasts dramatically with the Auden group's enduring fame and low early sales. *New Signatures* sold only one thousand copies its first year and was never to have the success of the Georgian anthologies. C. Day Lewis's first three Hogarth volumes sold about five hundred copies apiece during their first years (S. Day-Lewis 1980, 63), and by the end of 1933, Auden's *Poems* (1930) had sold only somewhat more than one thousand copies (Symons 1960, 21–22). Many advertising strategies work only in the short term, and the fact that the Georgians have faded into obscurity and the Auden poets remain well known is a sign of who wrote the better poems and of the power of commentary to preserve literature. The market has become a more powerful bestower of authority and prestige than it was in the early part of the century, but the domain of high culture remains remarkably insulated from its effects. In spite of their anticritical rhetoric, the avant-garde poets would have wished it to be this way. All three groups showed anxiety at the prospect of being subjected to the market demands to which popular culture is forced to answer. These groups could not and never would be popular. They were thus forced to depend for survival—in both the short and long term—on the very literary institutions they criticized.

The Auden poets' success was strongly influenced by their commitment to a shared quest. In this, they were quite different from the Georgian poets, anthology denizens in the most traditional sense who never acted jointly in the service of a group project. As Julian Symons (1960) emphasizes, Auden and his group had a mythological quality amplified by "the difference between the sort of language used in [Auden's] poems and the number of people listening to it. . . . One does at times have an uncomfortable feeling that these young writers were laying down rules for talking to an empty room" (22).

The power of their language was such that early in the 1930s they were often more influenced by one another than by other poets, living or dead. Spender later admitted that "the myth of a coherent movement was taken over even by ourselves."[5] Where the Georgians were managed by Monro and Marsh, the Auden poets often acted independently of one another, the Communist Party, and critical opinion. If the Georgians "had as little in common as an average dozen jurymen,"[6] the Auden poets were a somewhat more likely combination. The literary left—including the Auden poets—appeared unified partly because the right was less homogeneous (see Watson 1977, 90). George Orwell (1968) writes: "When one compares these writers with the Joyce-Eliot generation, the immediately striking thing is how much easier it is to form them into a group. Technically they are closer together, politically they are almost indistinguishable, and their criticisms of one another's work have always been (to put it mildly) good-natured" (1:511).

The literary right at the time was older and of more humble socioeconomic origin. Its major figures were Yeats, Eliot, D. H. Lawrence, Waugh, Pound, and Wyndham Lewis. The left, in contrast, was more coterie-oriented, being divided primarily into two groups, the Auden poets and Bloomsbury (including Leonard and Virginia Woolf, Clive Bell, Lytton

Strachey, and Maynard Keynes). In the context of an eclectic and disorganized right, the left-leaning poets looked more like the unified front Lehmann and Roberts hoped to create.

Though *New Signatures* launched these poets as a group, it did not launch their literary careers. By the end of 1932, Auden had published in eleven journals, including *Criterion, New Statesman and Nation, Twentieth Century,* and *Scrutiny.* His first book of poems had been out for two years. Nor did he or his fellow poets have any avant-garde–style qualms about becoming literary professionals. Day Lewis showed no ambivalence about his relationship to the literary market, joining the Society of Authors in 1926. One of his first acts as a member was to ask for an opinion about whether he could switch to a publisher offering more advantageous terms even though he had promised his second book to the press that had published his first (S. Day-Lewis 1980, 44–45). Moreover, by 1932 he had already published in the Hogarth Living Poets series, of which *New Signatures* was number 24. Several of the *New Signatures* poets were already Hogarth "house poets," Auden was favored by Eliot and thus by Faber and Faber, and Spender would soon become a Faber author as well. The Auden poets had nothing against "recycling" their poetry, using anthologies to help increase its literary value. Hynes (1972) aptly comments that "nothing could have been more conventional, or less revolutionary, than the way in which these young reputations were launched" (82).

By alphabetical accident, Auden's poems open *New Signatures.* In the preface, Roberts (1932) argues that "new knowledge and new circumstances" (7) have compelled new thinking, feeling, and language. The purpose of poetry, Roberts explains, is to help us solve our problems. Here is one member of the educated elite speaking to others in an attempt to serve their shared interests. The Argentine *vanguardia* spoke in much the same way; only the surrealists refused to address themselves directly to the edifice of high culture. Roberts (1932) strongly affirms the intellectual as one who "should guide and control those processes which he alone has studied" (9). The poet "is, in some ways, a leader; he is a person of unusual sensibility, he feels acutely emotional problems which other people feel vaguely, and it is his function . . . to find an imaginative solution of their problems" (10).

This sort of message is implicit in the *vanguardia*'s rhetoric and is a subtext of surrealist doctrine as well, though surrealism would not propose that problems be solved by rational means. The poet may not be God, but he—there being no "she"'s—is at least a first cousin. Roberts (1932) rejects esoteric, difficult poetry, recognizes that "progress is illusory" (and thus that liberalism is dying), and addresses the problem of creating a new audience. He offers a bewildering defense of William Empson's dense, enigmatic poems, however, on the grounds that they "do something to remove the difficulties which have stood between the poet and the writing of popular poetry" (12). The word "popular" is a strange bedfellow for the openly elitist projects of Roberts's idealized poet. It corroborates Bauman and Bové's argument that intellectuals tend to assign themselves the task of solving the problems of the entire society. It also identifies the conflict of trying simultaneously to serve elite and popular audiences and to reconcile the demands of the poet's public and private worlds. Finding a proper audience is a major issue in 1932, when Auden comments, "Writing gets shut up in a circle of clever people writing about themselves for themselves" (Perkins 1987, 125).

Roberts (1932) claims that several of the *New Signatures* poets "combine a revolutionary attitude with a respect for eighteenth-century ideals" (18) and reveals his generation's incipient schizophrenia: poets are still very attached to the ideals and upper-class privileges associated with liberalism, but the belief system attached to liberalism is no longer viable. Though he acknowledges the deep literary conservatism of poets such as Lehmann, Roberts (1932) is already putting into place a leftist vocabulary despite the absence of the political orthodoxy one would expect to accompany it. He defines the "communist attitude" as "the recognition that oneself is no more important than a flower in a field," a belief Auden never accepted, and defines poetry as a propaganda of aestheticism: "Poetry is here turned to *propaganda,* but it is propaganda for a theory of life which may release the poet's energies for the writing of pure poetry" (19; my emphasis).

Conservative values and revolutionary rhetoric then are in search of an agenda for action. If the Argentine vanguardia is anti–avant-garde in its conservatism and support of high cultural consecration and elite institutions, the Auden poets break with English poetic tradition. They propose a radically new society and make important formal innovations in their poetry, though they are openly ambivalent about the possibility of losing the privilege their educations and class backgrounds earn them and are unwilling—or unable—to effect the political changes after which they clamor. Throughout the 1930s, pursuing literary careers remained an important priority while the restructuring of society or even of literary institutions came in a distant second. To put the Auden poets' choices in perspective, it is important to recall that some left-leaning English poets of the 1930s did lay down their lives for their beliefs. John Cornford and Julian Bell died fighting for the Republican cause in the Spanish civil war.

While early critics tended to build the Auden group, later critics have been more inclined to dismantle it. Symons (1960) writes that he has "never understood" why *New Signatures* was considered "a landmark" (18) given that the Auden poets had fewer poems in it than did Empson, Julian Bell, and A. S. J. Tessimond, all of whom he claims "had little to do with the Thirties movement." "The Auden Group," writes Symons, "never really existed" (16). Ironically, this dismantling is a constructive gesture, for critics must make the group the object of their discourse—effectively historicizing it—in order to break it apart. Reasons why Auden, Spender, Day Lewis, and MacNeice were associated with one another include the fact that Auden and Day Lewis edited *Oxford Poetry* in 1927 and Spender and MacNeice edited it in 1929. Day Lewis's *Transitional Poem* (1929) was followed by Auden's *Poems* (1930) and Spender's *Poems* (1933). "Immediately," reports Spender (1951) their names were "linked together by the critics" (118). In spite of their very different styles—Spender had Romantic tendencies, Day Lewis's early work was distinctly Georgian, and Auden's vocabulary contained a unique mixture of industrial, psychological, and geographic metaphors—the titles of their books were so bland as to be almost identical, leaving the names of their authors as the identifying marks.

Like the Argentine vanguardia, the Auden poets had many different names. Using the first letters of their surnames, Roy Campbell labels them "MacSpaunday," Lehmann calls them the " 'New Country' group," and MacNeice in *Modern Poetry* calls them the "nineteen-thirty school of English poets" and the "Auden-Spender school of poets." They were also known as the Auden group, the *New Signatures* poets, the Oxford Poets, the radical group, and—in a reference to their poetic diction—the Pylon Poets. Throughout the 1930s, critics built the group, characterizing it as strong and avant-garde. James Burnham, for example, writes in 1934, "[These poets] should be approached as a group. . . . Like young French writers, they publish manifestoes, and proclaim themselves. . . . All of them . . . are or claim to be communists, at least to the extent of accepting . . . a classless society."[7] Auden (1963) however, strongly rebutted this view decades later: "From a literary point of view, the customary journalistic linkage of the names Auden, Day Lewis, MacNeice, Spender, is, and always was, absurd" (48).

When the 1930s had passed, the dismantling began. In the 1950s, a critic was able to write, "Although the names of Auden and Spender are generally coupled as belonging to the generation that incubated around London and the English universities about 1930 . . . their aims and the nature of their achievement have been widely divergent" (Seif 1954, 61).

Even *New Signatures* editor Lehmann contributed to the dismantling process. "I think it was never an entirely coherent movement," he wrote in 1971, though the "various authors who were associated in the mind of the public did have one or two things in common" (qtd. in Haffenden 1983, 160). When the Auden group's most productive moment passed, critics tended to overlook the common motivations of its members and turned to a more pragmatic analysis of the differences among them and their poems, differences that had previously been suppressed. By the 1970s, even Spender, who had done his best to help build the group, professed bewilderment. "In a sense one might describe the thirties as a leader—Auden —with no movement," writes Spender (1978). "Movements have meetings, issue manifestoes, have aims in common. The thirties poets never held a single meeting, they issued no manifestoes" (19). Such amnesia about what has previously been said should make us ask what is at stake in the creation of a given chapter of literary history. What is behind the desire to make avant-garde movements appear to have formed spontaneously? Behind the impulse to erase or rewrite their history? Edward Marsh, the *Georgian Poetry* editor who went to considerable trouble to publicize the anthologies and who publicly stated his grandiose aims for the movement, made this predictable statement in 1939: "I had not the smallest intention of founding a school, or of tracing a course for Poetry to follow."[8] In the context of a group that fails in its aims, such as the Auden poets, the dismantling or dehistoricizing of a group may be a face-saving gesture.

Hynes's (1972) *The Auden Generation* reinforces the canonization of the group while arguing that the *New Signatures* gang was "not so much a generation as a circle of friends." Their poems were "very dissimilar— some public, some private, some traditional, some modern, some difficult, some transparently clear" (79). Later in his book, Hynes writes: "By 1936 the *New Signatures* poets had come to be widely regarded as a group or a school, but in fact they were no such thing. They did not resemble each other in their work (except Day Lewis, who resembled all the rest at one time or another), and they did not have a common theory of literature" (205–6).

In contrast, Katherine Bail Hoskins (1969) erroneously naturalizes the group formation process:

The critics' assumption was based partly on the *accident* that these poets' early works were published about the same time in the same magazines, partly on their references to each other within their poems, more on the recurrence of certain themes and techniques, and chiefly on the political attitudes that the poets appeared to share and that represented a sharp break with both Georgian pastoral and the school of Eliot. (185; my emphasis)

While this is a good summary of the major reasons why the Auden poets were made into a group, there wasn't much "accident" involved. The poets themselves, who stood to gain from the united front, encouraged it when it served their needs and rejected it when it did not. Ironically, Spender is still at work building the group more than a decade after it has disbanded when he argues unconvincingly that the writers of *New Signatures* and *New Country* "wrote with a near-unanimity, surprising when one considers that most of them were strangers to one another, of a society coming to an end and of revolutionary change" (1953b, 118).

"Even before they were quite over," Robin Skelton (1964) observes decades later, "the thirties took on the appearance of myth. . . . It is rare for a decade to be so self-conscious" (13). The avant-garde is by nature self-conscious, but the Auden group was painfully so. Partly as a consequence, the group's self-image, as the poets themselves created it, passed through various stages in the course of a quickly changing decade.[9] The critical myths of the decade focus on value, specifically on approving or disapproving of the choices poets made during the political years. "The Thirties myth," writes Frank Kermode (1988) "goes something like this:

some of the best writers of the time . . . were induced by its unfamiliar political pressures to write against their own bents. Uneasily allured by Communism, they professed a fatal interest in unemployment, the Spanish Civil War, the death throes of capitalism, the imminence of revolution and of world conflict. . . . Quite soon they saw it wouldn't do, left the Party if they had joined it, retreated to Devon or the United States, and expressed shame at their immature follies. (5–6)

Here the Auden poets' idealized myth of themselves in the 1930s has been dwarfed by the embarrassed recantations that followed.

Kermode (1988), who sees the poets' political choices as valuable, seeks to revise this view:

I shall try to offer an alternative myth, in which what that myth calls vices may appear as virtues; in which the literature the common myth condescends to is treated as valuable, and valuable to us, fifty years on. To some of them, it appeared that to stand aside and carry on as if nothing in the world concerned them except their own work, narrowly considered, would cause an injury not only to conscience but to such gifts as they felt they had. And we can't simply dismiss this view as mistaken, even if they themselves came to feel that it was. (6)

Kermode's revised myth is often subscribed to by critics who have valued Auden's 1930s poetry more highly than his later more traditional and religious work. Both myths have been well attended and the group's critical fortunes have risen and fallen over the decades, possibly reflecting the changing rhythm of Cold War politics. "Perhaps the difficulty," writes Kermode (1988),

> is that we are still in some ways close to the writers of the Thirties, some of them still alive, so that it is in that measure harder to think about them without confusing history and value, without allowing our disillusion with their politics to colour our reading of their work—something we manage quite easily to avoid when thinking of more distant times. (62)

Though the Auden group's projects are easily and often held up as an example of the self-delusion of writers abdicating traditional roles, their idealism about the role of poetry in society is widely admired. It speaks, perhaps, to our wish to believe that literature and criticism have as great an impact on the world as the world has on them. In this sense, many of us are part Auden, part Spender.

The rules for evaluating literary discourse were so altered during the 1930s that even now critics struggle with the problem of point of view. Should a work be judged by the reigning values of its moment of composition? Or by the more normative standards of English literature, for which the 1930s represent an anomalous and fascinating moment? Because neither is wholly satisfactory, the debate over the value of the decade's poetry continues. For those (such as George Orwell) who see the Auden group's political commitment as riddled with the hypocrisy of bourgeois writers enjoying the fruits of the system they criticize, the group's rhetoric rings false. Those who take the rhetoric at face value—as many did in the 1930s—or admire the idealism and historical awareness of these poets, tend to consider them avant-garde in their desire to alter relationships between poet, text, and world. Even now, illustrating the appeal of binary logic, few critics straddle the middle line between these opposing views.

What we can call the binary myth of Auden is in fact a somewhat facile skewing of the facts, an avoidance of the ambivalence that plagued these writers and their critics after them. Like the surrealists before them, the Auden poets wanted to create something memorably new. The 1930s in England present a fascinating experiment in literary and political meaning-making and value-making: the political context and demands of the audience changed so fast, writers could barely keep up. The decade is therefore also an experiment in dismantling outworn meaning. But the process was brutal compared to the usual more gradual evolution of ideas and language. The worst blow, of course, was that in an important sense the creations of the mid-1930s did not outlive the decade. And many of those that did became topical artifacts. Because Kermode's two critical myths are opposites and because the writers of the 1930s often spoke in hyperbole, it is difficult to attach consistent, "objective" meaning to the decade's events. Like the critics and historians who accepted too uncritically the Argentine vanguardia's myth of itself, a number of the critics supporting the two myths of Auden's 1930s fail to acknowledge what is at stake when a fragile card-house of meaning falls down.

Literary value, in the 1930s as now, is closely allied with the notion of truth. My aim here is less to decide with Kermode whether the work of the Auden poets during the 1930s deserves to be valued highly—though I would argue that it does—than to examine the relationship between ambiguous, often ambivalent statements by the poets about their public roles and the unambiguous myths that grew up around them at the time. This paradox reveals how the historicization process can elide information that contradicts consistent meaning. Schooled by a decade of polarized concepts, the poets themselves contributed to this massive exercise in elision, an effort matched perhaps by that of Borges. They wanted to believe in their myth of themselves as much as critics sympathetic to them have worked to perpetuate it. At issue is my hypothesis that unstable meaning and value in literature threaten the critic's authority to create and bestow value. Something surely caused critics to opt for black-and-white myths to describe a gray, confusing time.

The Auden group's need to define the poet's role in a crisis-ridden age quickly caused its writing to become infused with the rhetoric of heroic action.[10] A mild dysphoria—the feeling that the private world of the poet was being violently impinged upon—gave way by the mid-1930s to a polarization of choices: political neutrality was no longer an option, just as individual independence was not an option for French surrealists. The vanguardia poets, in contrast, had considerable freedom, though the range of acceptable aesthetics in their country was noticeably narrower. In England, the situation was complicated by the tendency to read along binary lines. Spender (1953b) later remembers, "A pastoral poem in 1936 was not just a pastoral poem: it was also a non-political poem. A poem that rejected the modern consciousness of politics as a universal fate" (215). In 1937, the apogee of the decade's frantic activity, the Madrid Writers' Congress demonstrated that the combination of bourgeois writers and leftist political action had created schizophrenic behavior. Though the majority of writers in attendance had gathered to offer support to Republican Spain, they "rode about in Rolls-Royces, ate well, made speeches, drank champagne, and in several cases became infected with a hysterical sense of self-importance." Julian Symons's rather cynical view is corroborated by Spender, who later called it a "Spoiled Children's Party." But during the schizophrenia of 1937, Symons (1960) points out, Spender spoke of the meeting in heroic and romantic terms (126–27). All three of the avant-garde groups used overblown rhetoric at times, adopting the posture of the grand speaker when in fact the audience was often like-minded and comparatively small.

By 1938, the "public" or political phase was already over and the hurried retreat to the private had begun. The Auden decade can be broken into three discrete pieces, the first of which includes the carefree days of Oxford and Cambridge in the late 1920s, early publishing adventures, and the unexpected success of the poetic anthology *New Signatures* (1932). The second is inaugurated by the strident though often ambiguous social and aesthetic claims of *New Country* (1933) editor Michael Roberts, self-appointed spokesperson for a generation still in formation. In 1938, MacNeice (1968) refers to the *New Signatures* group in the past tense: "Nearly all these poets, though unlike each other, were far more like each other than they were like Eliot" (14). Ambivalence has turned into full-blown confusion as the poets begin to retreat from their rhetorical battlefield.

By the end of 1933, Auden's *Poems* (1930) and *The Orators* (1932) had sold somewhat more and less than one thousand copies, respectively. Symons (1960) notes that there is a significant difference "between the sort of language used in the poems and the number of people listening to it" (22). Given that the Auden poets were trying to reach a large audience in order to influence their entire society, this discrepancy becomes a symptom of the decade's schizophrenia and its writers' relationship to grandiosity. As Symons (1960) puts it, "Nothing is more curious than the disparity between the tone of absolute certainty in which . . . revolutionary sentiments were uttered, and the actual situation" (20). Many leftist writers believed fascist leaders would yield to nonmilitary forces, perhaps even to the sheer force of public opinion and the arguments of intellectuals. As late as 1936, when signs of Hitler's aggressive military intentions were unmistakable, the British and French governments agreed to nonintervention pacts that were soon infringed upon by signatories Italy, Germany, and the Soviet Union. The gap between rhetoric and events, which haunts the Auden group's poetry, can also be found in the "appeasement" fantasies of writers and governments alike. Such fantasies involved illogical thinking: on the one hand, the fascist dictators threatened the very foundation of Western culture. On the other, as historian David Thomson (1965) puts it, an appeasement policy meant "regarding their appetites as satiable, their grievances as legitimate, their objectives as limited" (174; see also 159, 163).

If, as Hynes (1972) argues, the 1930s are characterized by "a sense of being bracketed by wars" (41), the Auden group's myth of itself can also be bracketed by the years 1933, the year Hitler rose to power, and 1938, the year of the Austrian *Anschluss*. This mini-periodization has been incorporated into literary history. The Faber and Faber anthology of Auden's work, *Collected Shorter Poems, 1927–1957*, for example, makes a separate section of the poems written between 1933 and 1938. That a myth based on little more than half a decade of erratic behavior has survived for more than fifty years testifies to the power of rhetoric to create identity and meaning. The criticism that subscribes to this Auden myth is so Auden-centered that George T. Wright (1969) writes somewhat inaccurately: "Two new journals, *New Verse* and *New Writing*, were founded largely to print [Auden's] and his friends' work" (56–57). Symons (1960) concurs, "The primary function of *New Writing* was to provide a bigger audience for writers of the Auden Group" (59). Symons is closer to the truth: while *New Writing* increased the audience for the Auden group, it was not founded with that goal in mind nor was that its primary function. In fact, editor John Lehmann was very interested in providing a forum for left-leaning foreign and working-class writers. As for *New Verse*, it championed Auden, though editor Grigson had little good to say about Day Lewis.

Auden was a leader almost by default. Because he had so much innate authority and was so admired by other poets, he did not have to use strategies to keep others in line with him. In fact, compared to Breton, he cared little what others thought. If Breton was a charismatic authority who worked doggedly at his self-appointed role, Auden and Borges were charismatic figures who did little to maintain a following and were ultimately more concerned with their own work than with any notion of a literary movement. Auden had the advantage of being considered by the literary world and by his peers to be perhaps the best poet of his generation. He did not even function as a leader in the sense in which Borges and Breton led their movements. He was as if elected by writers, editors, and critics, and he had merely to say something—something perhaps entirely personal—either in person or in print to have an impact on those around him.

The 1930s were quick-change years when beliefs and words were frequently retooled to fit the needs of a changing quest. The changing usage of words such as "history," "action," and "war" illustrates the instability and radical contingency of meaning during this era. Many poems by leftist writers reflect the belief that history was on the side of those who trod the moral highroad, that is, on *their* side. Auden, more skeptical than most about this view of history, sounded a note of warning in 1935:

> . . . In the houses
> The little pianos are closed, and a clock strikes.
> And all sway forward on the dangerous flood
> Of *history, that* never sleeps or dies,
> And, *held one moment, burns the hand.*[11]

This anthropomorphized history is dangerous to possess, though the speaker realizes that many people seek to control it. By the time the Spanish civil war is well under way, Auden (1977) notes in "Spain" (1937) that history has returned to a godly realm, but is on no one's side:

> The stars are dead; the animals will not look:
> We are left alone with our day, and the time is short and
> > History to the defeated
> May say Alas but cannot help or pardon.
>
> > > > (212)

In the parallelism of stars, animals, and man, there is a hint of the Christian determinism that characterizes Auden's poetry of the 1940s: people are giving up control over their world. In "The Public v. the Late Mr. William

Butler Yeats" (1939), Auden (1977) moves to a theoretical statement that is in fact faintly Marxist: "Art is a product of history, not a cause" (393). The 1930s "hope for poetry" is revealed: art was to have caused history to be on the side of good causes, whether aesthetic or social. Only in 1939 do the Auden poets—with the exception of MacNeice, who has been saying it all along—admit publicly that the quest has failed. Symons (1960) writes, "By the end of 1939 the great tide of Left wing feeling had receded . . . and the land it covered was as smooth, almost, as though the tide had never been" (170). Consider what conventional, if distinguished, fates befell the Auden poets after 1939: Auden became a United States citizen and visiting professor, Day Lewis a professor of Oxford and the Poet Laureate, Spender an editor and university professor, MacNeice a writer for the BBC.

Action is another of the 1930s' chameleonic concepts. Early in the decade, the Auden poets and their circle begin to urge an audience of peers to resolve the conflict between the private world of the individual and the public demands of a world in crisis. This urging takes the form of a call to public "action." For most of these writers, however, action was not opposed to the life of the mind as it was for Borges, who was nostalgic for the nineteenth century, or for Julian Bell and John Cornford, who interpreted action much more literally than did the core Auden group. As Bell put it, "action is the most potent of drugs, and battlefield and revolutions are usually fairly good at curing romantic despairs—and other diseases incident to life" (qtd. in Stansky and Abrahams 1966, 95; see also 175, 183–84). The Auden poets, it was soon apparent, wanted no such cure. In 1927, Auden offers the belief that the public ultimately determines the private: "All genuine poetry is in a sense the formation of private spheres out of a public chaos."[12] He does not, however, offer a prescription for how this private sphere is to be formed. In 1929–30, he begins to offer directives: "Those who will not act / Perish for that reason."[13] This action as yet has no specific character, though for Auden it soon comes to be the antithesis of "error."

Action thus means correct action, which soon means sympathy for or commitment to communism. By the mid-1930s, in a fulfillment of the 1927 equation, action is associated with the writer's public duties, inaction with the private life. As Auden (1977) writes in "August for the people and their favourite islands," a poem dedicated to Christopher Isherwood,

> So in this hour of crisis and dismay,
> What better than your strict and adult pen

Can warn us . . .
Make action urgent and its nature clear?
Who give us nearer insight to resist
The expanding fear, the savaging disaster?

(157)

In an uncharacteristic display of blunt talk, Auden speaks in the tongue of the writers' myth of themselves: the writer is the professional best qualified in all of England to guide people through a crisis in values and government.

By 1939, however, the word "action" has disappeared from Auden's verse; poetry and by extension poets make nothing happen on the political plane. "Intellectual disgrace / Stares from every human face."[14] No longer does action determine the public realm; instead, "Waves of anger and fear / Circulate over the bright / And darkened lands of the earth, / Obsessing our private lives."[15] The end of "September 1, 1939," far from being a call to action, is merely the poet's wish for hope amid suffering, defeat, and despair. Hynes (1972) points out that even the meaning of war moves through several incarnations in the rhetoric of the 1930s:

> In the early 'thirties, war was a folly to be opposed through pacifist action. . . . Then in the middle years of the decade . . . war became a heroic resistance to fascism. . . . It was still a *choice*. . . . But as the end of the 'thirties approached, war came to seem neither an elected action nor a foreign one, but a catastrophe that could happen right here, in England, and soon. (292)

We find here an echo of the transition between the 1930s emphasis on free will and Auden's 1940 transition to religious determinism. Symons (1960) comments that early in the decade "freedom" appeared to be "an absolute good" (31). By the end of the decade, however, the burden of choice and especially of the failure of choice had become painfully apparent. Auden's transition also marks the abandonment of the decade's greatest project: the attempt to remake meaning through the instruments of value and truth.[16]

During this period characterized by binary thinking, political and politico-literary meaning were being created like paper money in a period of gross inflation. Many of the arguments and choices of the Auden poets were muddled, sometimes embarrassingly so. In *Forward from Liberalism* (1937), for example, Spender contrives to dispose of liberalism by refashioning it into the precursor to communism, though the two have little in common. Spender's argument belongs very much to its time. Watson (1977) argues that even the polarization of Left and Right did not occur before the 1930s. "D. H. Lawrence [who died in 1930], in one of the last essays he ever wrote, speaks of Lenin and Mussolini as if they were distinct but by no means opposite cases" (95). Both Spender and Day Lewis believed they could be simultaneously committed to communism and faithful to the tradition of lyric poetry, a conflict of interest that resulted in their frequently succeeding at neither.

Critical reactions to the poets' work were sometimes as confused as the poets' stands themselves: though Auden flirted openly with fascism and an antiproletarian attitude in *The Orators* (1932), the text was generally thought to have substantial Marxist content. Ironically, MacNeice, the Auden poet most consistent in his points of view, ultimately became a pariah among critics for his failure to adopt a belief system in the 1930s. There are many reasons for this, one of which is that in a decade of binary choices, MacNeice appeared to many to go out of his way to avoid choosing. In fact, he chose what amounted to neutrality at a time when neutrality was unacceptable.

That the decade's literary journals are no less ambivalent or muddled in their conflicting values than the poets are in theirs is another proof of the reductiveness of Kermode's myths. *New Signatures,* an exercise in consecrating poets "new" to the English literary scene, provides an interesting set of contradictions. The opening note announces that sixteen of forty-one poems have already been published elsewhere, that they are in fact recycled discourse. Lehmann and Day Lewis have already published their first books of poems. These "signatures" are thus not nearly so new as editor Michael Roberts would have us believe. Roberts breezes past the problem of industrialization and "difficult" poetry to alight in binary territory, specifically the problem of science versus literature. Science undermines "our absolute beliefs," he argues, by encouraging poets to treat their own truths as "subjective" and thus of lesser value. At the same time, he argues that excessive self-consciousness is debilitating. "We have become too analytical," he writes (1932), "too conscious of our own motives" (9). This subjectivity, however, is also a sign of the poet's superiority over other people: "The poet is, in some ways, a leader; he is a person of unusual sensibility, he feels acutely emotional problems which other people feel vaguely, and it is his function . . . to find an imaginative solution of their problems" (10).

Roberts (1932) thus states for the first time a refrain that echoes throughout the decade: it is the poet's moral duty to solve other people's problems. In his view, the poet must write "comprehensible" poetry that verges on the "popular" by avoiding being "intelligible only to an educated minority" (11). He nevertheless makes a special point of defending the anthology's least accessible poet. Empson's "difficult" poetry, he argues, "repays study" and its obscurity is acceptable because Empson "is definitely trying to say something to an audience" (12). The huge gap between truly popular poetry and the coterie poetry he eschews is neatly elided here. Roberts hints at an audience of peers and directs most of his preface toward likeminded people. As Spender (1978) later writes of the Auden group: "If their poetry strikes one as addressed to anyone in particular, it is to sixth-formers from their old schools and to one another" (23). The unwritten cultural line dividing the like-minded from everyone else, however, is public school which, Auden points out, then educated only 6 percent of England's youth. Kermode comments on the literary-minded products of English public schools in the 1920s: "They invented their own social order. . . . They wrote of and to one another in semi-private languages, played their own quasi-surrealistic games."[17] It is but a short step from this to the Auden poets' fantasized new world. The exclusiveness of their closed groups makes the myth of a communism-based new society all the more interesting and ironic.

Roberts's (1932) preface provides an important preview of the tensions that plague the decade: community is opposed to individualism, determinism to free will, science and politics to literature. The revolution he hints at saves economic standards by bringing everyone up to the level of the bourgeoisie: "It would be possible, if our resources were suitably used, to provide that leisure and wealth of goods without inflicting suffering or want on anyone" (18). In his final paragraphs, Roberts scatters revolutionary vocabulary like birdseed. But his definitions, as we have seen, are more form than content. The "communist attitude" is "the recognition that oneself is no more important than a flower in a field." Poetry is "*propaganda* for a theory of life which may release the poet's energies for the writing of pure poetry" (19; my emphasis). He links "pure poetry" to the need to regain the absolute values and beliefs of the prewar era. At the end of the preface, Roberts (1932) retreats from revolutionary language to claim merely that *New Signatures* contains verse that delights careful readers and sharpens their appreciation of other work (19).

If Roberts waffles on the question of popular poetry, he also contradicts himself on the poet's role. Four pages after arguing that poets should not let science get in the way of literary truth, Roberts urges them to accept the obvious truth of scientific determinism without giving up the free will attached to human action. And though he has argued that there can be no return to the past, he offers Lehmann's neoclassical verse as an illustration of the poetic renewal he claims occurs in *New Signatures*. While one of Lehmann's better poems in *New Signatures*, "This Excellent Machine," uses the metaphor of a dicing machine to treat the horrors of modern war, its rigid form undermines the power of its subject matter. The poem's perfect octaves and nearly perfect pentameter force Lehmann into such emotionally weak and contrived rhymes as button-mutton and convinced-minced. In many ways, Roberts's preface and some of the work in *New Signatures* are an exercise in confusion.

The poetry in *New Signatures* reflects the disparate values of the preface and further illustrates how contradictory the decade's beliefs already were. Julian Bell's neo-Georgian "Still Life," with its "soft yellow light" and "pale blue harebells in their jar" precedes his overtly political "Arms and the Man," a clear, detailed argument against war. That the second poem is nearly ten times as long as the first suggests where Bell's passion lay. Bell, in fact, died several years later, a combat casualty for the Republican cause in the Spanish civil war. Roberts does not require that poems have social content; Empson's poems, for example, contain almost no references to social problems. John Lehmann's split poetic personality, a division between public and private that haunted him increasingly over the years, is already evident: the publicly oriented "Looking Within" precedes "To Penetrate That Room," a personal lament structured by the metaphor of his psyche as a room he is afraid to penetrate. His self-diagnosis is on target: Lehmann's poetry—in contrast to that of the Auden group, which he admired—suffers from an unwillingness to plumb the complexities of his emotional life. Both poems are so saturated with external and impersonal metaphors that Lehmann's self-identified alienation from his feelings comes as no surprise.

The selection of Spender's poems likewise reveals conflicting impulses: "Oh Young Men," addressed to "comrades," is a call to young fellow bourgeois to abdicate the privileges of their class, while "I Think Continually" is an unabashed celebration of the elitism of the "truly great." Day Lewis's poems from *The Magnetic Mountain* can hardly be called leftist and are an odd mixture of archaic and modern images that make no clear argument. In the first poem, the speaker calls to "my kestrel joy" to turn "a corner into new territory"; in the second, he suggests to his "comrade" that "the temporal princes, fear and pain" will inevitably be their lot; in the third, "that miraculous mountain" is an unexplained deus ex machina that will "build right over chaos / A cantilever bridge" (Roberts 1932, 48–51). These poems, numbered 1–3, provide a good introduction to the decade's fascination with disaster and saviors. But there is no clear agent of doom or redemption and the effect is muddled. The vague, ominous danger introduced in Auden's "Ode" is no clearer; it speaks the language of a troubled pylon country without a diagnosis of the problem or a call to action.

The even more wildly eclectic anthology *New Country* marks 1933 as a watershed year between the early aesthetic and later political periods of the Auden poets' 1930s. It emphasizes prose, a medium largely immune to the conventional charges that poetry and propaganda are antithetical and that poetry in the service of a cause is no longer poetry. Roberts stridently calls for an unworkable combination of retrenchment and revolution; that is, the preservation of the writer's status and standards and a new relationship between proletariat and bourgeoisie. He is clearly ambivalent about the relationship of intellectuals to the working class, whose newly gained access to journalistic discourse impinges on the elite: "We see all that we believe in threatened . . . and print, which should be the medium of the man who has something to say, turned into a daily mirror of the public mind" (1971, 10). In the next sentence, Roberts awkwardly conflates the interests of the intellectual and the proletarian: "If our sympathies turn toward revolutionary change it is . . . because we see at last that our interests are theirs." Not joining the Communist Party is a form of "inaction," Marxism is largely "true," and political neutrality speeds the decline of poetry and science. Shifting confusedly back and forth between the first and third persons, Roberts (1971) makes a rallying call to save literature from social chaos:

> The only way of ensuring that a political party shall represent *our* ideals is to work with it now, to help choose its leaders. . . . It is time that those who would conserve something which is still valuable in England began to see that only a revolution can save *their* standards. (11; my emphasis)

The combination of "revolution" and saving "standards" would seem an oxymoron to a serious Marxist, but neither Roberts nor any of the Auden poets approached the consistency of such belief. A number of critics, however, have measured Roberts's anthologies in the coin of their prefaces' arguments. Aney (1954) labels *New Signatures* "largely non-ideological" and *New Country* "Communistic." She is correct up to a point, though both are plainly ambivalent about how to achieve their aims (108).

In the *New Signatures* preface, Roberts speaks authoritatively, referring to the poets in the third person. In *New Country*, in contrast, he deals in the first and second persons plural, badgering his reader. "We" are "poets, schoolmasters, engineers," a group "doomed to sharp extinction" (1971, 9). "We" are a group lacking control over the "system," stable cultural values, and a sense of security, but—paradoxically—"we" are also the group that will solve these problems. The reader is then metamorphosed into the intransigent enemy:

> But if you, reader, stand for the accepted order; if you cannot envisage a state in which resources are used to meet the needs of the community and not for individual profit, please remember that the Union Jack, the British Grenadiers, and cricket are not your private property. They are ours. . . . You're a fool if you think your system will give you cricket much longer. (1971, 13)

Roberts (1971) then switches back to his earlier implied audience, the other "we" of the inner circle of like-minded writers: "But how is all this to affect our writing?" (15). When he is not admonishing England's unconverted writers to pursue leftist politics, he flatters them with a grandiose vision of their role as omniscient seers into the future: "If your writing about a new world is to mean more than buttercup lyricism, you must know how that world is to come into being and precisely what sort of a world it will be" (1971, 17). Shortly thereafter, *New Verse* editor Geoffrey Grigson condemns Roberts for forced group-making: "What joins these writers except paper? How, as an artist, is Auden united with Day Lewis, Day Lewis with Spender, Spender with Upward? . . . Roberts in a long preface 'usses' and 'ours' as though he were G.O.C. a new Salvation Army or a cardinal presiding over a Propaganda."[18]

The poems of *New Country* are as disparate as the strands of argument in its preface. Auden's "Prologue," with its echoes of Nordic sagas and English history, seems to have little to do with Roberts's preface, while "A Communist to Others" is about bourgeois hypocrisy. Medical metaphors dominate the latter, though the language of military action and social unrest is also increasingly present in Auden's work. The speaker addresses an audience of public school and university graduates with diction that, in spite of the slant-rhyme, is barely poetic:

> Among the foes which we enumer
> You are included.
> Because you saw but were not indignant

> The invasion of the great malignant
> Cambridge ulcer
> That army intellectual
> Of every kind of liberal
> Smarmy with friendship but of all
> There are none falser.
> (Roberts 1971, 212)

Auden here indicts the facile liberalism of campus intellectualism, the "we" who are fellow poets, the inner sanctum of sacred peers. His perspective becomes progressively more public, but his point of view remains remarkably private, even when he charges his peers with an excess of individualism:

> Unhappy poet, you whose only
> Real emotion is feeling lonely
> When suns are setting;
> Who fled in horror from all these
> To islands in your private seas.
>
> . . . .
>
> You need us more than you suppose
> And you could help us if you chose.
> (Roberts 1971, 213)

The mention of "real" emotion, which presupposes an unreal or false emotion, is an ironic indictment of the Romantic. Auden is calling back his fellow poets from their flight into the private life in an era of political crisis, but his communism—if there is any in this poem—is about a community formed through the bonds of a transcendent and transpersonal Christian love. His call to action is not a suggestion to join the Communist Party, but rather to trust in a higher power. He ends the poem with:

> Remember that in each direction
> Love outside our own election
> Holds us in unseen connection:
> O trust that ever.
> (Roberts 1971, 213)

A number of period critics chose to focus on "A Communist to Others"' title and the use of "comrades" as proof of Auden's Marxist commitment. But Auden's poems in 1933 lack a communist attitude; rather, they are riddled with the conflict between the small group of like-minded peers and a vaguely defined enemy.

In "Poem," Auden structures a conflict between the Whites and the Reds, two sides in a falling world where all choices have uncertain outcomes. Again, the inner circle is saved by its faith and its willingness to face the future:

> But because of our trust we are free
> Though alone among those
> Who within earshot of the ungovernable sea
> Grow set in their ways.
>
> (Roberts 1971, 215)

This Auden is no communist, though trust among the members of the small group leads to a sort of fraternal communistic microcosm. In this case, however, communism is merely a metaphor, and "the governable sea" can be understood either as generalized social chaos or as the unhappy, clamoring masses. Unlike Day Lewis, who joined the Communist Party in 1935, and Spender, who joined briefly in 1937, Auden did not become a member of the party. Spender announced in 1937 that he had joined in order to prove his loyalty, which was questioned after *Forward from Liberalism* appeared.

Other *New Country* poems reveal the decade's tendency toward hero worship. In the first two of the four poems selected from *The Magnetic Mountain,* Day Lewis twice uses the vocative, once to name the reader "comrade" and once to call to Auden, "lone flyer, birdman, my bully boy!" (Roberts 1971, 223). Because Auden is the only person praised in these selections, the editorial choice hints that he is the savior evoked in the poem. Although the poem praising Auden is number 16 in *The Magnetic Mountain* sequence and the promise of a strange new healer is number 32, in *New Country* they are printed only two pages apart. Skelton (1964) remarks that an "almost Messianic notion of The Leader runs through the poetry of the period, as it does through the politics" (22). In *The Magnetic Mountain* poem that begins "You that love England, who have an ear for her music" and asks "Can you not hear the entrance of a new theme?", a mythical transition is taking place: "Know you seek a new world, a saviour to establish / Long-lost kinship and restore the blood's fulfilment." "You who like peace" are promised relief: "We can tell you a secret, offer a tonic; only / Submit to the visiting angel, the strange new healer" (Roberts 1971,

225–26). Charles Madge's "Letter to the Intelligentsia," also in *New Country,* invokes Auden as hero even more directly. Four people are mentioned by name: Lenin, Trotsky, Kamenev, and Auden. Reading Auden, writes Madge, provoked in him a personal emotional revolution:

> . . . I read, shuddered and knew
> And all the world's stationary things
> In silence moved to take up new positions;
> Dissolved before me the still-wet trees; morning
> Unshaped; the sun thumped; I had had my warning.
>
> (Roberts 1971, 231–32)

Poetry—and Auden as leader—is thus to be the savior of poets.

Though the poets of the Auden generation are by 1933 falling in love with the idea of revolution and their own revolutionary roles, the effect of this infatuation is primarily on language, not on lives. Day Lewis's "Letter to a Young Revolutionary," which opens *New Country,* calls for an "absolute belief in revolution as the way to, and the form of, new life." "You must have a conversion," he says. Communism becomes both religion and morality.[19] But the political activism of Day Lewis, who then earned his living as a schoolteacher and writer, left his traditional career path unaffected. The ability to go about their business as usual, publishing books and getting jobs in teaching and journalism, caused a curious gap between the idealistic language and the conventional lives of these poets. The surrealists would have considered *New Country* and *New Verse* tame stuff indeed compared to their own journals and poems, especially Aragon's "Front rouge" (published in the May 1933 issue of *New Verse* and criticized harshly by Spender), but this is partly because the process of politicizing literature in England was not nearly so advanced as in France. Though *New Signatures* and *New Country* appear to signal a transition from individual-centered to group-centered literary projects, *New Country* in fact merely inaugurates a period of conflict between the poet's traditional lyrical orientation and new political commitment. *New Country* proposes the following for writers: recover belief in standards and values, avoid the "individualist predicament," convince themselves that the interests of the working class are their own, and work toward "social communism" (Roberts 1971, 20–21).

The year 1932 is receding quickly. Though *New Signatures* and *New Country* are published by Hogarth, Roberts (1971) calls Bloomsbury "absurd . . . because of its impotence" (12–13). As we have seen with the

Argentine case, the avant-garde bites the hand that feeds it, but never so badly as to cut off its food supply. These two important anthologies functioned as books but were read as new and provocative journals, complete with manifestos. As onetime anthological events, they had none of the problems of sustaining themselves through a subscription base. Published by a well-known house, they could afford any amount of anti-institutional speech and didn't need to make editorial choices consistent with the agendas of their prefaces. In an important sense, the anthology strategy paid off: as Hynes points out, neither anthology was as important during the 1930s as *New Verse*. But *New Verse* is the less remembered today.

While the openly propagandistic *New Country* is in important ways conservative, the self-identified "apolitical" journal *New Verse* (1933–39) is, in Skelton's (1964) words, closer to a "heresy-hunting inquisitor" (25). The label reflects Grigson's strident criticism of Day Lewis and opposition to writers' accepting state honors or consecrated roles. This oxymoronic quality seems fitting in a decade where things are rarely what they claim to be. In spite of its habit of incisive criticism, *New Verse* isn't free of the period's rampant double-talk. Its opening statement of purpose contains the following piece of confusion:

> Poets in this country and during this period of the victory of the masses, aristocratic and bourgeois as much as proletarian, which have captured the instruments of access to the public and use them to convey their own once timid and silent vulgarity, vulgarising all the arts, are allowed no longer periodical means of communicating their poems.[20]

The masses are diluted here to mean all classes, all equally prone to vulgarizing the arts. Poets are the small group that escapes this classification and must somehow recover access to discourse being denied by the rise of the masses, that is, the nonpoets. Yet the reader senses that the "victory" of the masses—presented as something of a fait accompli—is acceptable as long as the traditional privilege of the bourgeois poet is left intact. How the revolution took place at all and how the poet is to remain unaffected are questions that go unanswered.

In his opening statement, Grigson states that *New Verse* exists to publish "respectable poems" that might otherwise go unpublished and that it belongs "to no literary or politico-literary cabal."[21] But Grigson later allows Spender to criticize Auden for accepting the king's gold medal for poetry and Day Lewis for becoming a Book Society selector. Grigson views the Book Society as "pimping to the mass *bourgeois* mind and employing 'distinguished' members of the literary underworld, *adopters* of literature as a profession, writers each of no more real existence than a tick lost in the last five minutes of a cuckoo clock" (qtd. in Skelton 1964, 25). The political statements of *New Verse,* far from being a call to action, are in fact a warning to writers prone to the excesses of orthodoxy.

By stating that criticism published in *New Verse* must be "of value and not only of propaganda value," [22] Grigson privileges aesthetics over politics while pointing to the omnipresence of propagandistic poetry and criticism. In a review of *The Magnetic Mountain,* he is equally plain about his preferences: "Briefly the best propaganda is art; and Day Lewis is too able to wither himself as a poet by being politically active." [23] Though *New Verse* claims to have no politics, it publishes many poems treating leftist politico-literary issues and functions as an important critic of poets whose politics or poetry are facile. Interestingly, the ambiguous, ambivalent, and sometimes evasive Auden is held up as the model of appropriate behavior. In a positive review of Spender's *The Destructive Element,* for example, Grigson credits Auden for Spender's book: "No one, except Mr. Auden, has written anything so pertinent to the writer's problems now; and no one has written so usefully and convincingly of Mr. Auden himself, whose mind, really, engendered this book as it has engendered something of a poetry revival, half of Mr. Spender and nine-tenths of Mr. Cecil Day Lewis." [24]

In content, *New Verse* promotes the idea of communist revolution more tactfully and, many would argue, more effectively than *New Country.* Auden's "Song," though it ends with the imperative "Go down with your world that has had its day," does not pretend to resolve the intellectual class's alienation from the working class, nor does it look for easy transitions:

> I'll get a job in a factory
> I'll live with working boys
> I'll play them at darts in the public house
> I'll share their sorrows and joys
> Not live in a world that has had its day.
>
> They won't tell you their secrets
> Though you pay for their drinks in the bar
> They'll tell you lies for your money
> For they know you for what you are
> That you live in a world that has had its day.

This portrait of the bourgeoisie's unease with the working class is far less facile than Roberts's unsupported assertion in *New Country* that the interests of the two classes are the same. Auden is willing to let his speaker use the first person and identify the proletariat as more antagonist than friend. He emphasizes the failure of the old system, but does not pretend to have simple solutions to the problems of capitalism:

> It's no use turning nasty
> It's no use turning good
> You're what you are and nothing you do
> Will get you out of the wood
> Out of a world that has had its day.[25]

It is significant that *New Verse,* for all its apolitical values, did not survive the decade. The overtly political *Left Review* (1934–38) had an even smaller window of opportunity, in contrast to the traditional quarterly *Scrutiny* (1932–53), whose values bear a striking resemblance to those of *Sur.* Ironically, *Scrutiny*'s manifesto declares the journal to be both pragmatic and political. In a hyperpolitical decade where neutrality was construed as retrenchment in liberalism or passive fascism, this conservative journal comes closer than many to telling the truth about itself. *New Writing,* edited by John Lehmann, claims in its manifesto to be politically independent, though it is more overtly leftist than *New Verse.* It introduces its contributors by means of their political biographies, and publishes the work of both working-class and Eastern European writers.[26] Why do *New Verse* and *New Writing* hedge about their relationship to political commitment? Most likely because it was still taboo to politicize literature openly. These Oxford- and Cambridge-educated editors were reluctant to acknowledge that politics were sometimes privileged over literary standards or even that politics and aesthetics were in conflict. Grigson liked to point out this conflict in the work of one of his least favorite poets, Day Lewis, but he did not often discuss his own struggles with it.[27]

By 1938 and 1939, the 1930s myth was already impossible: the whole politico-literary climate had changed and experimentation by dynamic literary journals was no longer feasible. Cyril Connolly writes, "When [World War II] started[,] *New Verse* and *The Criterion* were coming to an end—a magazine had to be eclectic to survive. It was the right moment to gather all the writers who could be preserved into the Ark and only then could the Ark get by the Paper Control—by earning dollars or aiding prestige."[28]

By 1939, even the dynamic journals seem scalded by their failures. The new journal *Horizon* (January 1940), edited by Connolly, retreats from political commitment: "The impetus given by Left Wing politics is for the time exhausted. . . . The aim of *Horizon* is to give to writers a place to express themselves, and to readers the best writing we can obtain. Our standards are aesthetic, and our politics are in abeyance" (qtd. in Spender 1978, 87). Connolly sounds strikingly like Victoria Ocampo in *Sur*. Spender, who had a hand in getting the new journal off the ground, later commented that Connolly "published what he liked" but with an eye to what would still be of interest in twenty years (1953b, 254–55). Connolly thus shifts the focus from dealing with present crises to providing for good critical reception in the future.

In the preface to a *New Verse* anthology published in 1939 by Faber and Faber, Grigson (1939) offers only the vaguest patchwork of comments as an apologetic summary of the journal's project.

> *New Verse* is now six years old. . . . I think it is possible to trace in the poems as they came out in *New Verse* this gradual emergence of a criterion, formed by an amalgam of science (in scraps), Freudian theory (in scraps), Marxist thought (in scraps), the political and economic situation in the world, the practice and precept and perspicacity of Mr. Auden (and Mr. MacNeice and Mr. Spender) and the load of reaction and attraction which the time I belong to has inherited. (22)

Compare this to C. H. Madge's insistence in *New Verse* in 1933 that writing poetry is the most revolutionary of human activities, that a successful poem "gives the order to march."[29] Compare also Grigson's pointed rebuke in 1934 to Day Lewis for *A Hope for Poetry*: "Advertising is written to persuade, to sell goods. Mr. Day Lewis . . . has written to persuade others to read himself, Mr. Spender, and Mr. Auden. An inferior purpose has bred an inferior book, evasive on the poet and politics, ridiculous often in judgement."[30]

Grigson fits Argentine critic Beatriz Sarlo's profile of the avant-gardist who is uncomfortable when writers engage in obvious literary marketing or self-promotion. In spite of his reiterated apoliticism, Grigson in the mid-1930s vocally opposes "anthology-making," weak or excessive politics, and what he perceives to be a "nauseating concern" for the fate of poets and poetry. In 1939, in contrast, he conceives his task vaguely and as a sort of fait accompli: "We know [now] with more exactitude, with more health, and less pretentiousness and priggishness how poems come about and how poets should be related to people. We know what a variety of different things some one who can write is free to write" (24). In fact, the problem with the 1930s is that writers *didn't* feel free to write either the exclusively lyric poem or overtly political verse. Theirs was a constant struggle to strike a balance between conflicting imperatives and to locate their true inclinations.

Critics have responded to Grigson's comparative evenhandedness and superior critical skills by calling him and *New Verse* "remarkably objective" (Skelton 1964, 26) and accepting what we might call *New Verse*'s myth of itself. Katharine Bail Hoskins (1969), for example, echoes the early Grigson: "*New Verse* . . . welcomed unOrthodox poets as well as Orthodox, applying no standards beyond the aesthetic" (186). Hynes (1972), more sophisticated and contemporary than Hoskins, makes no such assumption. Grigson, he claims,

> meant to run an elitist, highbrow magazine that would draw up sides in the traditional way—artists against philistines, good art against bad, avant-garde against rearguard—and that would avoid political commitment. But the fact that he chose to put his intentions in the form of such an aggressive manifesto suggests that he knew from the start how strong the political pressures would be, even on a magazine of verse.

Hynes correctly points out that *New Verse* was leftist and propagandistic because its contributors were (114–16). *New Verse,* however, did much to promote the idea that it was fair-minded and apolitical. In late 1936, for example, it defended its repeated attacks on Day Lewis: "*New Verse* was never left wing or right wing. It was not founded as a wing journal. . . . We have not been hounding Day Lewis for an excess of Communist loyalty. We have been attacking him as a bad poet, a muddled writer."[31] Grigson oversimplifies the issue into a Victoria Ocampo–style view that "quality" is the only criterion of value. Earlier, however, he had stated plainly his view that Day Lewis's politics contributed significantly to his problems as a writer. *New Verse* is the *Martín Fierro* of the English 1930s: its view of itself necessarily conflicts with its editorial choices.

The writers of the 1930s were paradoxically attached to the notion of cultural apocalypse.[32] Kermode reminds us—denizens of the nuclear age—that we have "routinized apocalypse" and that in the years preceding World War II it had all the appeal of the new.[33] As Walter Benjamin wrote in 1936, "[Mankind's] self-alienation has reached such a degree that it can experience its own destruction as an aesthetic pleasure of the first order.

This is the situation of politics which Fascism is rendering aesthetic. Communism responds by politicizing art." [34]

In "The Author as Producer," a lecture given in 1934 at the Paris Institute for the Study of Fascism, Benjamin (1978) indicts writers for capitalizing on the pleasures of radical politics: "And I further maintain that a considerable proportion of so-called left-wing literature possessed no other social function than to wring from the political situation a continuous stream of novel effects for the entertainment of the public" (229). Kermode (1988) describes this phenomenon as a tendency to produce "a literature of conscience that is also a literature of fear, and sometimes of a certain pleasure in the fear, even of a wish to be clever about the fear and the pleasure" (42). Symons (1960) concurs: "Slowly, almost imperceptibly, liberals found themselves acknowledging simultaneously pleasure in reading of a thousand dead and sorrow that war meant burned-off lives; swiftly and delicately they touched violence to see if it burned, as a child puts a finger through the flame" (49).

Spender (1953b) illustrates the impetus to produce such a literature: "My inner world became dependent on an outer one, and if that outer one failed to provide me with its daily stimulus of crime and indignation, I felt often a kind of emptiness" (164). Kermode also points out that Auden—who holds himself somewhat aloof from many of the decade's indulgences—recognizes this problem as early as 1933: "For private reasons I must have the truth, remember / These years have seen a boom in sorrow; / The presses of idleness issued more despair / And it was honoured" (Auden 1977, 142). Auden's insight into the conflict between personal truth and the public realm comes remarkably early, as does his awareness of the manufactured quality of certain emotions already being used for political purposes.

These polarized years witnessed a boom in paranoia. In *Inside the Whale,* Orwell complains that during the Spanish civil war, even intellectuals participated in World War I–style war hysteria, including "orthodoxy sniffing (Sniff, sniff. Are you a good anti-Fascist?)" (qtd. in Fussell 1975, 109). The detection of politics in poetry became such a pursuit of critics that Day Lewis (1942) came to find out what he'd written by reading reviews of his work: "When I have expressed some private experience in a poem, I have frequently discovered it to contain a 'political' significance of which I was quite unconscious while writing it" (37–38). He notes that critics "almost to a man" read *From Feathers to Iron,* about the birth of his first child, as political allegory. There is even a shared sense among writers that public drama provides the only interesting raw material for literature. In Auden and Christopher Isherwood's *The Ascent of F6* (1937), private barrenness is eerily combined with the excitement of public disaster:

> Nothing that matters will ever happen.
> No, nothing that matters will ever happen.
> Nothing you'd want to put in a book;
> Nothing to tell to impress your friends —
> The old old story that never ends.
>
> I read the papers; there is nothing there
> But news of failure and despair:
> The savage train-wreck in the dead of night,
> The fire in the school, the children caught alight,
> The starving actor in the oven lying,
> The cashier shot in the grab-raid and left dying.[35]

Auden and Isherwood draw poetic power from ironically opposed lists that point to the (temporary) impoverishment of the lyric poem and to the distinction between the protected private life and wrenching public disaster.

The urge to substitute poetry for religion, which infected most of the Auden poets, easily became the urge to make politics a secular religion. Day Lewis, Grigson, and MacNeice were sons of clergymen. Auden had an Anglo-Catholic mother and both of his grandfathers—and Grigson's father—were Church of England clergymen. Spender's (1935) religion of politics in the 1930s was poet-centered and thus, in an important sense, godless: "If we hope to go on existing, if we want a dog's chance of a right to breathe, to go on being able to write, it seems that we have got to make some choice outside the private entanglements of our personal life. . . . The precise difficulty [today] is to . . . find the real moral subject" (223–24).

In *The Creative Element* (1953), in contrast, the moral has been redefined to exclude the political. "The point really is that a moral view of society can be stated without any concern for social action of any kind, whereas directly politics enters in, social action and taking sides are involved" (1953a, 9).

This revisionism, it should be remembered, is an inversion of the process that took place in Argentina. In the 1930s in Buenos Aires, the moral was still considered by many to transcend politics, while in later decades political involvement was closely identified with moral and social con-

cerns. But in the 1930s in England the poet was his own savior who—
theoretically at least—would be spared disaster by his ability to confront
the moral and political issues of the time. At moments, the Auden poets'
project was surprisingly like that of the Argentine vanguardia. "Communism," writes Spender, "is the struggle to inspire the standards of our
civilization with the political will . . . to survive the attacks of a barbarism
growing up in our midst." Unlike the Argentines, Spender (1937) reveals
that civilization may not be worth saving and that the writer-savior's quest
contains elements of denial and perhaps of hypocrisy: "The European
individualist is in fact a sick soul. . . . To himself, as he often proclaims, he
is civilization" (15, 55). Only the surrealists see themselves as the barbarous
rather than the civilized. And of the three groups, only the surrealists value
the barbarous over the civilized.

Hynes (1972) dates the historical peripeteia, "the point where the action
turned" (193), to 1936, when Hitler occupied the Rhineland, the League of
Nations failed, and the Rome-Berlin Axis was established: "Political commitment had produced no art of any importance, and no aesthetic that
seemed adequate to a generation raised on Eliot's essays and the books of
Richards; everything of importance in those years had been heterodox and
individualist" (206). This is certainly the view held by the Auden poets in
hindsight. But in 1938, the most stubborn of them is still trying to win
the battle. Day Lewis ends "In the Heart of Contemplation" with the line
"Nothing is innocent now but to act for life's sake."[36] And the argument
of "Newsreel" is that proper action will prevent war:

> See the big guns, rising, groping, erected
> To plant death in your world's soft womb.
> Fire-bud, smoke-blossom, iron seed projected—
> Are these exotics? They will grow nearer home:
>
> Grow nearer home— and out of the dream-house stumbling
> One night into a strangling air and the flung
> Rags of children and thunder of stone niagaras tumbling,
> You'll know you slept too long.
>
> (Day Lewis 1977, 106)

Hynes is correct that this sort of message tends to produce bad poetry.
The heavy-handed and overmutable metaphor—virile guns raping the
feminine world turn into exotic species of plants—is not particularly successful either. My point, however, is that while the historical tide began

to turn in 1936, the Auden poets, except for MacNeice, did not turn from their belief in the leftist cause until well into the Spanish civil war.

Auden's language, like that of the decade's journals, makes him a slippery fish politically. Malcolm Cowley (1934) identifies Auden's personal and political ambivalence as the source of his ambiguous language: "He regards himself as a class traitor, a spy, a Copperhead. For this reason he is forced to speak in parables, to use code words. . . . He is on his guard, wary—till suddenly he gets tired of being cautious and blurts out a condemnation of everything he hates" (190).

What makes Auden the decade's best poet is this pained honesty coupled with his talent for expressing himself memorably. As Cowley points out, when Auden tires of ambivalence and guilt, he is brave enough to tell his truth. Like Borges, when he changes his mind, he is plain about it. And like Borges, Auden freely exercises his right to suppress—if temporarily—works he has come to disagree with, such as "Spain." The Auden poets as a group are more soul-searching and painfully self-aware than the surrealists or the vanguardia. In 1938, Auden begins to retreat from enigmatic metaphors of illness to poems about love; his political reversals demand new kinds of poems and the editing of objectionable material from old poems. In "Time of War" (1937), for example, the last stanza:

> Till they construct at last a human justice,
> The contribution of our star, within the shadow
> Of which uplifting, loving, and constraining power
> All other reasons may rejoice and operate.

becomes

> Till, as the construction of our star, we follow
> The clear instructions of that Justice, in the shadow
> Of Whose uplifting, loving, and constraining power
> All human reasons do rejoice and operate.
>
> (qtd. in Beach 1957, 7).

Capitalization and syntax promote the transition between Auden's 1930s commitment to free will and his 1940s attachment to divine determinism. The second version sounds too much like a celebration of human passivity to please those who supported the Auden group's difficult quest. Gone are the human subjects whose place in 1930s poetry and whose free will were already tenuous. In another example, Auden writes, "May this for which we dread to lose / Our privacy need no excuse." By 1950, the original 1936 version becomes its opposite: "May these delights we dread to lose, / This privacy, need no excuse" (Rodway 1984, 45).

The year 1938 is Auden's turning point: in "The Voyage," for example, the sojourner, who, as in many other poems, may stand in for the poet,

> . . . discovers nothing: he does not want to arrive.
> The journey is false; the false journey really an illness
> On the false island where the heart cannot act and will not suffer:
> He condones the fever; he is weaker than he thought; his weakness is
> real.
>
> (Auden 1977, 231)

The poem ends on the wistful and frustrated wish for a true journey characterized by true hearts. The false journey, Auden points out, has produced true weakness.

A number of poems written late in the decade reveal how the prophets of the coming age lose their powers. In "The Ship" (1938), Auden (1977) writes, "Somewhere a strange and shrewd To-morrow goes to bed / Planning the test for men from Europe; no one guesses / Who will be most ashamed, who richer, and who dead" (233). Behind this supremely endowed future that controls the fates of men is a new view of the relationship between literature and history. In "The Public v. the Late Mr. William Butler Yeats" (1939), Auden (1977) explains that art "does not re-enter history as an effective agent, so that the question whether art should or should not be propaganda is unreal" (393). In "September 1, 1939," Auden (1977) emphasizes, "All I have is a voice / To undo the folded lie" (246), and in *New Year Letter* (1940) he confesses to having "adopted what I would disown / The preacher's loose immodest tone" (qtd. in McDiarmid 1984, 77). In the latter he eerily conflates two elements of one of the decade's most important binarisms: "Fascism is Socialism that has lost faith in the future" (qtd. in S. Smith 1985, 143). Art has lost not only its power, but much of its will to power.

The inappropriateness of Spender and Lehmann's introduction to the anthology *Poems for Spain* (1939) illustrates how quickly political reality and cultural meaning change in the 1930s and how a widely circulated belief can be rejected from one year to the next. Spender's introduction reveals how important poets feel poetry to be, even in the context of the threat of cultural apocalypse. The introduction is remarkably poetry- and poet-centered: "Poets and poetry have played a considerable part in the Spanish War, because to many people the struggle of the Republicans has

seemed a struggle for the conditions without which the writing and reading of poetry are almost impossible in modern society" (Spender and Lehmann 1939, 7). However, the vast majority of the at most four thousand or
so British volunteer soldiers in Spain are thought to have been "militant
members of the working class" (Symons 1960, 120).

Spender's introduction goes on to sound horribly ironic in light of the
suffering of the Spanish in a war that killed between 500,000 and 800,000
of their people:

> In a world where poetry seems to have been abandoned, become the
> exalted medium of a few specialists, or the superstition of backward
> peoples, this awakening of a sense of the richness of a to-morrow *with*
> poetry, *is as remarkable as the struggle for liberty itself, and is more remark-
> able than [its] actual achievement.* . . . Occasionally, in a revolution, . . .
> there is a revival of the fundamental ideas and there is actually an iden-
> tity of the ideas of public policy and poetry. (Spender and Lehmann
> 1939, 9–10; second emphasis mine)

Equally shocking is that if this volume had appeared earlier, Spender's
rhetoric would have sounded natural, even commonplace. But the political context for politicized literature is changing so fast that Spender sounds
as if he hasn't yet noticed the death toll or lost cause. The savvier Auden
has by this time moved to acknowledge the political impotence of the
poet, writing in 1939, "For poetry makes nothing happen: it survives / . . .
A way of happening, a mouth."[37]

Spender's personal relationship to the war provides another contrast. As
Symons (1960) writes,

> Spender was unwilling to join the [International] Brigade, but [ac-
> cepted] . . . a post as head of English broadcasting at the radio station
> of the Socialist Party in Valencia. . . . When he got to Valencia he found
> that the Socialist station had been abolished, and he devoted much time
> and energy to attempt to get [his secretary and former live-in compan-
> ion] Jimmy Younger out of the International Brigade. (125)

Only many years later does Spender (1978) offer a revision of the poet's
self-centered obsession with his role in the face of human tragedy:

> One became more and more aware [in the 1930s] of the indescrib-
> able suffering of victims—of an incommunicable reality which was the
> truth of history in this decade. Compared with it, a literary movement

like that called "The Thirties" was a mockery, like a parrot imitating the screaming of a prisoner being tortured. I think we felt this. (22)

In *World Within World,* however, Spender (1953b) admits to a rather different experience of the 1930s: "When my book of poems was published [in 1933] I began to lead a literary-social life of luncheons, teas, and week-ends at country houses. . . . The middle years of the 1930's were symbolized in England not by Hitlerism or even the Spanish war, but by the Royal Jubilee" (122). Given the unsettling mixture of private pleasures and public horrors in this decade, it is hardly surprising that its writers' accounts of it have a schizophrenic quality. In light of the Auden decade's myth-making tendencies, the "truth" of their experience was hard even for them to locate. It appears to have been a plural truth: there was concern for suffering and there was the Royal Jubilee.

Roberts is perhaps the decade's most emblematic turncoat: actively selling communism in 1933, he is already frantically backpedaling by 1936. In the preface to *The Faber Book of Modern Verse* (1936), he writes: "Writing may be poetic without being either moral or didactic. . . . Primarily poetry is an exploration of the possibilities of language" (1982, 3). He ends by quoting the overtly antipolitical view of Dr. Johnson: "The poet must divest himself of the prejudice of this age and country; . . . he must disregard present laws and opinions, and rise to general and transcendental truths, which will always be the same" (34). It is significant that the preface of this book received remarkably little attention from critics fascinated by Roberts's other anthologies, though the book sold more than four thousand copies its first year. Given the low circulation figures of the decade—*New Verse*'s circulation, for example, did not generally exceed fifteen hundred—Roberts's message of retrenchment was, comparatively speaking, widely circulated. I would argue that because Roberts's preface was a premature abdication of his views in *New Country,* critics on the leftist bandwagon as well as those who liked to bash it had every incentive to ignore the change of tone. It was, after all, a voice like many they had heard before, and they preferred the novelty and drama of the political Roberts. Critics, in other words, were perhaps as preoccupied with their own agendas as the poets were with theirs.

It is important to ask in this context why so many critics—Hynes being an admirable exception—have mimicked the schisms and myths of a confused decade. Most acknowledge that the 1930s witnessed the temporary politicization of English literature. But they acknowledge less frequently the active "literization" of politics, the attempt by the literary establishment to acquire a new domain of power and discursive possibility. As Bové would argue, there is little incentive to speak of a failed attempt to annex foreign discursive territory. In late 1933, Julian Bell had remarkable insight into the quest by 1930s writers to appropriate power not usually accorded the literary profession. In a letter to *The New Statesman and Nation,* he remembers the Cambridge of 1929 and 1930 when "we hardly ever talked or thought about politics." Times had changed by 1933: "It might, with some plausibility, be argued that Communism in England is at present very largely a literary phenomenon—an attempt of a second 'post-war generation' to escape from the Waste Land." [38] Instead of plugging the choice of direct political action, to which he was deeply committed and for which he later died, Bell speaks of the "very large element of rather neurotic personal salvationism in our brand of Communism" (Stansky and Abrahams 1966, 109).

In 1934, John Cornford, another poet who later died fighting for Republican Spain, attacks one of the decade's most insistent blind spots: "Literature stands above or outside the class struggle. The struggle for power between the bourgeoisie and proletariat which has included every other field of human activity, has somehow kept clear of the sacred precincts of literary traditions." [39] Cornford is here paraphrasing what he considers to be Bell's faulty logic, though Bell has stated that he sees poets to be of little use in revolutionary politics. Cornford's observation is on the mark. At no time do the Auden poets take important steps toward making major changes in their relationship to society. In France, the separation between literature and politics has always been less clear than in England, and in Argentina it grew markedly less clear as the twentieth century progressed.

"When and why did such men join and leave communism?" asks George Watson (1977), who argues that they understood its limitations long before 1939 (58). We should ask instead whether the Auden poets seriously intended to accomplish anything revolutionary. In 1939, when the recantations flowed surprisingly easily from their pens, little had in fact changed. The writers pursued their professional paths somewhat more peacefully than before. David Thomson hints (1965) that perhaps the 1930s are best remembered as a decade of escapism: "The essence of the spirit of the thirties was not apathy but inertia: an incorrigible *immobilisme* in State and society, a structural resistance to change, and especially to any radical improvement. . . . The sense of helplessness and drift" (181).

But Spender, even as late as the 1950s, insists on a different experience:

"The 1930's saw the last of the idea that the individual, accepting his responsibilities, could alter the history of the time." For Spender, the 1940s were a time when writers were convinced they were no match for political crisis. The Auden movement had "been made bankrupt by events" (1953b, 251, 257). The gap between Spender's and Thomson's vision is precisely the problem of the 1930s. Neither is right; the two realities in fact coexisted. As Kermode's two myths suggest, there has also been a certain schizophrenia in the writing of this history. At stake are the creation and status of truth, value, and belief.

After the war, when I was being entertained by a group of Cambridge undergraduates, one of them, obviously speaking for all of them, said "Tell us about the Thirties." I asked why he and his friends were so interested in this troublous period. "Because," he replied, "it seems to be the last time that anyone believed in anything."

—C. Day Lewis

6. The Struggle Over Value and Belief

"Today," C. Day Lewis (1960) wrote, "the Thirties might well seem to those who were unborn then, if not an age of faith, at least an absurdly credulous one." The Auden generation's need to rebuild a belief in values destroyed by the shock and senselessness of World War I resulted in a frantic effort to create new and rehabilitate traditional values and beliefs. Eliot's *The Waste Land* is the text whose crisis the Auden generation tries to resolve. As Auden later explained: "Dr. Richards once said that *The Waste Land* marked the severance of poetry from all beliefs. This seems to me an inaccurate description. The poem is *about* the absence of belief and its very unpleasant consequences; it implies throughout a passionate belief in damnation: that to be without belief is to be lost."[1]

Spender's (1935) comment on Eliot's text is even more revealing: "*The Waste Land* is an example of a long poem without any subject, or in so far as there is any subject, it is the conscious lack of belief" (189). In their interpretations Spender and Auden choose to disregard Eliot's statements about his work. Eliot wrote: "I cannot see that poetry can ever be separated from something which I should call belief."[2]

By identifying the poetic subject of the 1920s as a lack of belief, Spender hints at the 1930s' choice of belief as the supreme poetic subject. Indeed, the Auden poets' quest for values and belief is the mired center of the decade's problems. If belief is to be convinced of the truth of something, and truth in the modern age is located less in facts than in belief, the two words form a sort of tautology. The Auden poets fell into the trap of relying on history to prove the truth of a valuable but contingent system of belief.

Spender (1934a) voices the fear that history will betray writers: "Is history ungrateful? Do books / Ignore us?" (15). History, as we know, failed to perform. For the Argentine poets, success was measured through respect and recognition. For the surrealists, there was no clear notion of what would constitute success; the goal was as undefined as the revolution itself.

The equation of truth with political and historical success forced the Auden poets to confront the unhappy fact that their truths were unstable and contingent. Michel Foucault would argue for a more radical view of truth as an organized set of procedures for producing, circulating, and regulating statements, and as the product of the interests of political, economic, and cultural institutions. He would also advance the view that there is no such thing as transcendental truth, an argument I believe is problematic (see, for example, Foucault 1979, 46–47). As the experience of the Auden poets illustrates, absolute beliefs and truths play an essential role in structuring and preserving culture. While the Auden poets want to rehabilitate something valuable and the Argentines seek to create value for the first time, the surrealists are unsure about what is worth preserving. Breton favors correct syntax, a few rhetorical tropes, and his own authority. Like the Auden poets, he needs to believe in something, but that something need not exist in the culture at large.

Literary groups—such as the Argentine vanguardia—are often viewed as spontaneous comings together of like-minded people. The Auden group's beliefs have been treated as a sort of spontaneous reaction to their historical moment. It is useful, however, to analyze these beliefs as problem-solving tools the poets chose from among a number of options. In hindsight, a decade characterized by binary logic—communism versus fascism, us versus them—appears to offer few choices. It is easy to forget, however, that these poets played a role in shaping the decade's binary choices. Why did they make these choices and how did their choices serve them? One answer is that binary logic contributed to fantasies of grandeur. Implicit in the 1930s notion of the poet-prophet is the idea that everyone and everything—perhaps meaning and value themselves—need to be liberated. Spender (1934a) idealizes himself as the liberator of imprisoned truth who, through his writing, will free history (or at least himself) from the forces of darkness:

> I suffer like history in Dark Ages, where
> Truth lies in dungeons, from which drifts no whisper.

. . . .
This writing is my only wings away.

(41)

The poet becomes the supreme historical agent: a transcendental subject in an age that no longer has a place for such a subject.

On a more practical level, leftist politics, as Day Lewis openly admitted, promoted these poets far more effectively than did their poems. In fact, becoming a leftist was a sort of marketing strategy for young poets: "It is difficult not to suspect that renewal of interest in poetry proceeds largely from an interest in the social connections to be found in much 'left-wing' work; that it is the communist or fascist tendencies, the up-to-dateness of the imagery, the preoccupation with specifically modern problems which attracts, and not the poetry itself" (Day Lewis 1942, 28).

The literary market was never far from these writers' minds. Day Lewis, as we have seen, was so easily swayed by critics that he began to see in his work what they saw. Spender (1953b) was also susceptible to this influence: "I have wasted time by paying heed to criticisms that I had no skill in employing rhyme. This led me to try rhyme, whereas I should have seen that the moral for me was to avoid it" (147). If the Auden poets were ambivalent about propaganda in the service of politics, they hardly hesitated before using it to promote their careers. Day Lewis, in a moment of candor, confided to Grigson—who was then preparing *New Verse*—that he had no qualms about propaganda in the service of marketing:

> I am for anything that will help to throw open the park to the public: it makes one despair to think that one is preserved for an aesthetic aristocracy. . . . I don't mean that we should go about distributing our work in tube trains: but that contact should be made between us and the sort of people who are at present being spoon-fed out of novels and wireless talks. . . . *As you know, our writing is half propaganda:* we can't help it. . . . And it's so silly to be spilling propaganda only into the mouths of a few incurable neurasthenics. I feel somehow that *it is really quite a practical matter, the purveying of our brand of salvation—a matter of distribution and advertisement and business methods.*[3]

This is the same Day Lewis who says he was unwilling to join the Communist Party until "I was making enough money to be able to assure myself that I was joining from disinterested motives, not as one of the lean and hungry who would personally profit by revolution" (qtd. in S. Day-Lewis 1980, 94). When he is the capitalist bourgeois, he plays the role to the hilt; when the communist, he apologizes for a profit motive that could hardly have attended a real revolution.

The Auden group's choices also helped clarify the poet's role in society and investigate a number of the poet's problems. As David Daiches (1940) points out, the interwar poet had little firm ground on which to stand: "The audience for poetry was neither as distinct nor as homogeneous as it had been in Tennyson's generation; both the function of poetry and the poet's place in society were in doubt; the sources of imagery which had been traditional for English poetry for generations had for a variety of reasons become dried up" (35–36).

By the end of the 1930s, it was clear that while English poetry had expanded its vocabulary and subject matter, it had failed to give poets new roles or substantially larger audiences. Skelton (1964) accuses the Auden poets of rhetorical inflation, of having "discovered a drama and invented an audience." Their political poems "were almost all aimed at people who did not exist, at least in the roles assumed in the poems. Their assurance and poise is a pretence. Their prophecies are made to a handful of the converted" (36–37). Like the surrealists, the poets who wanted a large audience were unwilling or unable to speak in language accessible and of interest to working-class people. Paradoxically, inflated rhetoric typically went hand in hand with the tendency to preach to the converted. Symons explains the political-artistic movement of the 1930s with a pyramid structure. England's intelligentsia, which he estimates numbered around a million people, forms the base. The "Pragmatists" are the fifty thousand people who probably looked at the Auden group's work at one time or another. Perched precariously at the top are the one thousand writers and artists who spoke primarily to and for one another (Symons 1960, 37–39).

A new role was perhaps not what the poets most wanted. Their early poems offer abundant proof that they were not naturally inclined toward politics, but rather that they made great efforts to adjust their original goals to fit an unusual historical moment. MacNeice (1987) admits the problem: "The paradox of *my* generation, who were aged about eighteen in 1926, is that while . . . we were at heart romantics . . . the date of our birth had deprived us of the stock, i.e. the Nineteenth Century, 'romantic' orientation" (149). Grigson (1939) concurs: "If Spender had been born about 1890, nothing, I repeat, could ever have saved him. He would have frittered himself away into vagueness and reaction" (18). Poets on the right—such as Yeats and Eliot—were not associated with the 1930s as a period largely because they had not collaborated noisily on a project. That the leftist poets' ambitious project turned into a memorable failure only exacerbated critics' tendency to think of the right as a collection of individuals whose politics didn't much affect their work. MacNeice (1965) recalls an aesthete-versus-leftist split: "Literary London as I met it fell in two categories; there was the old gang who were just literary and there was the new gang who were all Left" (165). Watson (1977) suggests that the "contest of the Thirties smacks strongly of a generation struggle" (89). But that is not altogether true. Rather, the literary left and right never formed a real opposition because the right cared little for the left's value-making project, preferring to stick quietly to its tradition of individual truths. And when the left spoke of enemies, it rarely mentioned the literary right directly.

At the end of the decade, after the Auden poets recanted their political views, they did not acknowledge how well their strategies had served them. Though some of their books failed to be good poetry or successful propaganda, their chameleonic voices and roles caused critics to go into a debate about value that continues even today. I would argue that our enduring fascination with the 1930s is rooted in the problem of belief and the creation of value, specifically the critic's need to affirm either critic or writer in the role of primary creator of value. Those who affirm the critic in this role tend to adhere to Kermode's first myth: the view that the Auden poets were wrong to attempt to make for themselves a role in politics. The adherants to the first myth are more likely to have sympathies in common with F. R. Leavis, who locates morality more in his own practice than in the work of the writers he treats. To understand the critic's stake in this, it is helpful to substitute value creation for politics in the formula of Kermode's myth. For when the Auden poets involved themselves in politics, they chose it as a means to work for social justice, the prevention of war, and the solution to the bankruptcy of cultural value. It follows that critics who affirm the poet in the role of primary creator of value subscribe to Kermode's second myth: the legitimation of writer as prophet and activist. Many critics, myself included, have chosen to value highly the Auden poets' quest to relocate truth and value. I believe this is partly because the poets produced memorably good poetry and partly because their project, which was not without emotional costs, speaks to a basic human need to locate value in culture.

As critics subscribing to both critical myths have recognized, the "truth" of the Auden poets' belief systems did not hold up well under the many abrupt acts of devaluation to which it was subjected. Kermode (1988) concurs that the tendency to have sudden changes of heart undermined the poets' credibility: "Auden is said never to have read a newspaper before 1930, Christopher Caudwell was apolitical until his sudden conversion to Communism in 1935. . . . Such political *coups de foudre* lent an air of wildness and extremity to the subsequent remarks of the stricken" (37).

That these sudden conversions did little to dissuade a number of critics from valuing highly the political cause suggests that *belief* itself was at stake, especially the belief in taking steps to save civilization by all possible means. There are, however, signs that *believing in something* was at moments more important to these writers than any given belief. The critical reception of Louis MacNeice (see Chapter 7) is one of the more enduring signs. The poets believed passionately in belief itself. In important ways, the ideologies of the 1930s functioned as substitute religions and these poets tripped from faith to faith—from aesthetics to politics to church—as though the beliefs were interchangeable. Skelton (1964) suggests that the reader of Auden-group poetry written in the early 1930s "becomes more and more astonished by the narrow range of its attitudes" (15). Politics reached both to the heart of human belief, religion, and to the whims of fashion. Between 1935 and 1939, writes George Orwell (1968), "it became as normal to hear that so-and-so had 'joined' [the Communist Party] as it had been a few years earlier, when Roman Catholicism was fashionable, to hear that so-and-so had 'been received'" (1:512). Auden, as we know, came full circle back to a serious commitment to Christianity in 1940. Day Lewis (1960), who was a Communist Party member from 1935 to 1938, calls his own withdrawal from communism a "revulsion" that was nothing short of "apocalyptic" (222). He discovered halfway through delivering an anti-fascist lecture that he had ceased to believe in himself as a political activist. In 1940, Spender, an avowed agnostic, made the uncharacteristic statement that political orthodoxy was flawed because "it leaves nothing to the imagination," while religious orthodoxy was "a structure within which great art can exist."[4]

The need to locate and redeem belief took a heavy toll on these poets. At moments, when the pressure of the quest was great, they retreated from belief (or the appearance of belief) altogether. Auden, for example, was willing to write at the height of leftist fervor in 1936: "If you asked any artist why he works, I think he would say, 'To make money and to amuse my friends.'"[5] Most of the time, however, the poets were busily coping with the problems of a system of poetic valuation made chaotic by the competition of two very different types of value: "poetry," associated with aesthetics and escape from reality, and "propaganda," associated with social action. The conflict between them raised the questions, What is the proper subject of poetry today? And what is the proper role of the poet? The 1930s short-lived answers to these questions were: the world and the prophet. The 1930s placed these questions in a moral framework and asked: At what price does one fail to believe in these roles? The critical view of Louis MacNeice as one constitutionally incapable of believing in anything is true only within the polarized value system of the 1930s where neutrality and ambivalence were untenable positions. Day Lewis, who was charged with having an excess of belief—belief that caused the quality of his poetry to decline—has generally fared better with critics than MacNeice. In the world of literary humanism, it is perhaps better to believe wrongly than not to believe at all. In contrast to MacNeice and Day Lewis, Auden waffles on the question of poetry's role as moral leader. "Poetry is not concerned with telling people what to do," he writes mid-decade, though he goes on to undermine his assertion. Poetry extends "our knowledge of good and evil, perhaps making the necessity for action more urgent and its nature more clear, but only leading us to the point where it is possible for us to make a rational and moral choice."[6] Auden's statement about the poet's merely making choice possible is a hedge. Society was diseased, Auden repeatedly suggests, and urgently in need of diagnosis and treatment.

The fear that plagued the 1930s, I suggest, was less the fear of war or revolution than apprehension about what the absence of humane values does to human behavior. As Auden writes in 1939, "We have the misfortune or the good luck to be living in one of the great critical historical periods, when the whole structure of our society and its cultural and metaphysical values are undergoing a radical change. It has happened before, when the Roman Empire collapsed, and at the Reformation, and it may happen again in the future."[7]

Placed in this context, the 1930s poet's self-appointed role as prophet and leader is indeed of staggering importance, at least in the eyes of the decade's poets. These writers—perhaps for the first time in the history of English verse—state openly that they want to preserve and revamp their whole civilization. They attempt to go far beyond Wilfred Owen's advice: "All the poet can do to-day is to warn. / That is why the true Poets must be truthful" (qtd. in Day Lewis 1942, 14). Their prophet-poet is both political and spiritual. The object of Spender's (1934a) poem "I think continually of those who were truly great," for example, can be read as the few divine poet-speakers

> Who, from the womb, remembered the soul's history
> . . . Whose lovely ambition
> Was that their lips, still touched with fire,
> Should tell of the Spirit clothed from head to foot in song.
>
> (45)

Day Lewis (1942) has a vision of the supremely endowed poet: "It is the nature of the poetic vision to *perceive those invisible truths* which are like electrons the basis of reality. . . . *If the poet is not clairvoyant, he is nothing*" (75; my emphasis).

The Auden poets are not consistent in their self-appointed roles, nor are they clairvoyant. Roberts (1980) writes in 1935: "The poet, or prophet, is engaged in defining the political issues of to-morrow" (98). In an earlier review of *The Orators,* however, he argues just the opposite: "The poet is under no obligation to provide his own or any generation with a meta-physical system or a prophetic message" (1980, 57). At moments, these writers act as verbal tricksters, using political language to promote conventional beliefs. Linguistic sleight-of-hand, kicked off by Roberts's identification of poetry as "propaganda for a theory of life," is common. Spender, for example, plays with the word and concept of the revolutionary:

> Although a poet might conceivably write from a truly revolutionary standpoint, it is unlikely that he would do so, as to the true revolutionary the creation of poems would seem a dishonest means of expression. For this reason most poets, as with Mr. Auden, are forced into an attitude which is really religious or mystical. . . . But in another sense a poet like Mr. Auden is inevitably a revolutionary: that is, because nothing is more revolutionary than to tell the truth.[8]

The politically committed poet, Spender suggests, is caught between being the "true" but dishonest revolutionary or the poet who tells the truth. The play on the word "revolutionary"—which slips from noun to adjective—privileges the latter while minimizing the fact that its revolution may be apolitical. Day Lewis (1942) makes the same gesture, labeling "a true revolutionary" the poet who is "always breaking up and melting down the inherited forms of language" (12).

Spender (1964) admits that "in fighting Fascism we felt that in the last analysis we were struggling for our own freedom to write non-political poetry" (90), a revealing irony in light of the 1930s clamoring to have political poetry taken seriously. And though this comment is fed by hindsight, it rings true: the Auden poets wanted to be able to write anything they chose and Spender, to the end, was unmistakably Romantic in his approach. "Spender," Hynes (1972) argues, "in urging the function of poetry as a preserver of pure meanings, was being conservative and counter-revolutionary, in spite of his expressed political sympathies." Hynes also notes that "the most striking thing about [Day Lewis'] *Transitional Poem* [1929] is how conventional it is, how well it attaches itself to the English tradition: the verse forms are regular, the allusions are classical, the natural details are Romantic. Romantic, too, is the constantly present 'I' " (45).

Similarly, Day Lewis wrote traditional, quasi-Georgian poetry until well into the decade, and Lehmann and Roberts never managed to give up their attachment to traditional poetic forms. Lehmann found it impossible to write good political poetry and eventually to write poetry at all. He exemplifies the poet who becomes alienated from his natural inclination. That even the surrealists worked against their inclination is suggested by the kinds of poems they wrote after they felt liberated from surrealism. The traditional poems Aragon wrote during World War II are a case in point.

The English writers tried so hard to believe something publicly useful, they lost touch at times with what they themselves believed. As Auden (1977) confesses in the searing opening of "September 1, 1939":

> I sit in one of the dives
> On Fifty-Second Street
> Uncertain and afraid
> As the clever hopes expire
> Of a low dishonest decade.
>
> (245)

Skelton (1964) points out that "some of the propagandist poems convince us more of the writer's belief in the importance of writing propaganda than of his emotional commitment to his statements" (30). In *The Magnetic Mountain*, Day Lewis's (1977) utopian promises ring hollow:

> I know a fairer land,
> Whose furrows are of fire,
> Whose hills are a pure metal
> Shining for all to share.

And there all rivers run
To magnify the sea,
Whose waves recur for ever
In calm equality.

Hands off! The dykes are down.
This is no time for play.
Hammer is poised and sickle
Sharpened. I cannot stay.

(67)

The urgency of the short lines and strong message is undermined by the lulling quality of the trimeter and rhyme. The promised utopia, its hills full of a "pure metal" for everyone, sounds more like a Shangri-la than a hard-won socialist state requiring sacrifices by the wealthy.

An early reviewer of *Vienna* (1934) charges that Spender fails to produce either good poetry or good propaganda, citing "lines, passages, images, and clusters of images of a falsity and affected ugliness."[9] The description of the unemployed, for example, feels romanticized:

We can read their bodies like advertisements
On hoardings, shouting with common answers.
Not say, life is happy, unhappy is ill,
Death is reward, law just, but only
Life is life, body is body, a day
Is the sun: there is left only beauty
Of merest being, of swimming, of somehow not starving.

(Spender 1934b, 15–16)

The speaker seems often to be beyond himself, reaching for metaphors and allusions irrelevant to the subject:

I reached the ambition to despair.
Ignorant of history, all the day
Traffic shivered my bones like a malaria.
Time seemed foreshortened and confused with change
Not seen monstrous with slowness like the Himalayan range.

(35)

Syntactically weak, these lines combine too many geographic zones with a strange goal—an ambition to despair. The emotion is forced and the passage is a good illustration of the type of poetry to which Grigson objected.

At its worst, such poetry denaturalizes horrific realities until they no longer seem real. In *Vienna,* Spender's images have a mixed effect. "A waste canvas sky, uniformed nuns, / Streets tinkling with the silver ambulance" (12) sounds more like a set for a theatrical production about war than the description of a city after attack. But Spender also explores the differences between ways of living and the problem of finding value in one's life. When the invading guns utter: "How can we kill these dead? O, kill their worth" (12), the effect is as powerful as many of Auden's best lines.

While still at Oxford, the Auden poets were not at all sure about the proper role of the poet and tended to flip-flop among several choices. Spender reports having wavered between a Keatsian shutting out of the real world and casting himself as one of Shelley's unacknowledged legislators of mankind. Finally, he settled down to a third choice. The poet "was now a *translator* of the world which man projects around him through the actions of his will" (1951, 81; my emphasis). Auden held court like a lord instructing his serfs. He loved to play the leader and offer advice such as: "The poet is far more like Mr. Everyman than like Kelley and Sheats. He cuts his hair short, wears spats, a bowler hat, a pin-strip [*sic*] city suit. He goes to the job in the bank by suburban train." Spender reports that Auden also told him at Oxford that "in a revolution," the poet "shoots across the lines at his best friend" and that his sympathies "are always with the enemy." "At this time," adds Spender, "Auden had fantastic fads [and] sometimes carried a cane and even wore a monocle" (1953b, 53–54). MacNeice, finding he didn't fit in among the Oxford crowd, opted out of role-playing and — by his own account — took to drink. As an undergraduate, Day Lewis (1960) recalls having "tried on bits of various disguises: I even experimented with my walk, and gave myself a fright one day when I found I could not remember which gait was my natural one. At times . . . I assumed the role of the Fool, the simpleton, exaggerating my naiveté in order to conceal it" (156).

The harmless experiments with identity became more serious when the poets' ambivalence about commitment to political and aesthetic views found expression in their poems and critical writings. Day Lewis (1960) acknowledges that he and Auden avoided taking responsibility for their literary beliefs in *Oxford Poetry* (1927): "A note of buffoonery runs *throughout* the introduction: the editors were in deadly earnest, but they took out an insurance policy, in the form of deliberately portentous prose styles carrying pastiche to the edge of burlesque, against any risk of solemnity or self-importance" (179).

For a decade committed to the reaffirmation of belief, this provides an unsettling beginning. The love of metamorphosis, of quickly changing forms and beliefs, became something of an addiction. The poets took on the roles of public witness and interpreter, believing for years that the highest form of authenticity was lived experience. Spender (1953b) remembers that at Oxford he and a friend located reality in the lower classes: "We thought that perhaps being a working man, or perhaps even making love with a prostitute, was to be *real.*" Oxford, in contrast, was like "living in a vacuum" (34–35). Grigson (1939) is able to refer to poems published in *New Verse* with this idea in mind: "In substance these poems do strike me as being for the most part genuine: something actual has happened to the writers" (23). In a late 1936 or early 1937 letter to E. R. Dodds, Auden (1977) expresses a desire for firsthand experience of the Spanish civil war: "I do believe that the poet must have direct knowledge of the major political events. . . . I shall probably be a bloody bad soldier but how can I speak to/for them without becoming one?" (xviii). Auden never did obtain this experience and was scalded late in the decade by Orwell's stinging rebuke for "Spain" 's glib reference to the "necessary murder."

The "chief use of the 'meaning' of a poem," T. S. Eliot has argued, "may be . . . to satisfy one habit of a reader, to keep his mind diverted and quiet, while the poem does its work upon him: much as the imaginary burglar is always provided with a bit of nice meat for the house-dog." [10]

In contrast to Eliot, after 1932 the Auden poets did not aspire to deceive through skill or cleverness, but rather to convince through the sheer rightness of their message. To this end, they argued incessantly over the qualities of propaganda. As late as 1938, MacNeice (1968) is still defending poetry from the charge that it is propagandistic: "The propagandist is consciously and solely concerned with converting people to a cause or creed. . . . The fact that a poem in which a belief is implicit may convert some whom direct propaganda does not touch, far from proving that that poem is propaganda, only proves that propaganda *can* be beaten on its own ground" (201).

This distinction appears to be based on the intention of the poet: propaganda is overt, dishonest, and manipulative; belief is sincere and valuable. Even MacNeice, the most consistent of the Auden poets, revised his view of the MacSpaunday poets' relationship to belief. In 1938, he writes:

Poets like Auden, Spender, and Day Lewis have adopted a system of belief which they have not yet quite grown into. But on the whole they do not state such beliefs more explicitly than is warranted by their natural emotional reaction to them. Only Day Lewis's sermonizing appears sometimes too *voulu* (commensurately with his technique). (1968, 204)

A decade later, he sees things differently:

The thirties poets . . . quite often overplayed their hand and lapsed into mere propaganda, and by this I mean that they stated an opinion or introduced an image not because it came from their experiences, but because it was the thing to do. But a poet should never, never, never, fake his reactions. (1948, 347)

As Day Lewis (1942) writes in 1934, "There is poetical truth, and there is common honesty; they are very distant relations" (15). At the end of the 1930s the Auden poets began to admit that their will to believe had in many cases been stronger than their actual belief and that they had in fact experimented with faking their reactions. Giving up the habit of forced belief did not mean relinquishing the need for a cause and attendant values. It merely meant living by beliefs more consonant with their personalities, vocation, and socioeconomic backgrounds. It meant being honest. Though their orientation and strategies could hardly have been more different, the surrealists shared the Auden poets' quest for truth and honesty. The question that lingers long after they wrote is whether poetry is a capacious enough vehicle of truth. In a historical sense, could it serve as the central tool of the avant-garde's mission? Insofar as the avant-garde's goals are social as well as aesthetic, the answer was found to be no.

If, as Robert Scholes (1989) argues, "*hermeneutics* refers to the search for truth or grounded meaning in texts . . . and *nihilistic* refers to the view that truth . . . can never be attained" (57), Auden's 1930s represent a cycling between the two positions. Scholes' (1989) statement that "in a world without truth all interpretations would be equal" (58) uncovers the 1930s' greatest unspoken fears: that fascism would prove to be the cousin of communism, that meaning was contingent and relative after all, and that there were no absolute values or truths. These fears were well warranted given the way writers obscured their own distinctions through carelessness and rhetoric. At the First International Congress of Writers for the Defense of Culture, held in Paris in June 1935, Italian historian Gaetano Salvemini warned that if the label "fascism" were used too freely, there would be no way to distinguish between genuine fascism and anything else. His definition of a fascist country—"a bourgeois society which has suppressed the very possibility of cultural freedom"—bears little resemblance to how the word was used in England during the mid-1930s (qtd. in Shattuck 1960, 21). Walter Benjamin pointed out that too much crying wolf is dangerous. "One reason why Fascism has a chance," he warned, "is that in the name of progress its opponents treat it as a historical norm."[11]

The fear that at bottom these related belief systems were similar greatly exacerbated the decade's binary habits. Edward Callan points out that Auden eventually came to an understanding of the similarities of what were held to be opposites: "In time he became acutely conscious of a kinship between the cult of the poet as national Bard and the cult of the 'inspired' national leader—Hitler, Mussolini, Stalin—that threatened the survival of European democracy in the thirties."[12] Barbara Herrnstein Smith (1988) argues that value is often created by "discounting or pathologizing" (41) other, related values. This is especially true of the avant-garde's value-creating strategies. If the Argentine avant-garde was willing to consider Boedo's social realism—which it disdained—"art," it is partly because it was then easier to valorize what it considered to be the better, truer art of Florida. But value created hastily through such oppositions has a tendency to reveal its own constructed and thus sometimes transitory character. Symons (1960) offers an illustration of the kind of leftist logic proved false by 1939: "A Popular Front is the only way of combating Fascism: the support of the Soviet Union is necessary to such a Popular Front: therefore any criticism of the Soviet Union is in essence pro-Fascist" (105).

In the poetry-versus-propaganda debate of the 1930s, every answer felt inadequate. The poets "found themselves uncomfortably confined both by Left wing orthodoxy and by the sharp discouragement of vague poetic feeling in *New Verse*. That *nauseating concern for poetry* was being felt again" (Symons 1960, 144). In the value scheme of traditional English poetry, propaganda cannot also be poetry because poetry is not performative language and is both nonmanipulative and self-contained. Kermode (1988) phrases it this way: "Can literature participate directly in social or political action if it is truly literature? Isn't literature that is truly literature silently defined as writing which can't do so?" (86). The question is: How do we define action? Scholes (1989) reminds us that Aristotle believed rhetoric and poetry to be closely allied, using similar means to arouse the passions (107). "Every poem wants to be loved for its own verbal body and not for whatever message it conveys," writes Scholes (1989, 133). But the political poetry of the 1930s wanted to be loved for both of these qualities, especially its moral content. Before the decade even began, Auden (1977) expressed his fear of moral error:

> Their fate must always be the same as yours,
> To suffer the loss they were afraid of, yes,
> Holders of one position, wrong for years.
>
> (45)

Silence became an alternative to overt error: when Auden returned from a brief and disillusioning visit in 1937 to Spain, where he had planned to work as an ambulance driver, he chose to remain silent about what he had seen in order not to undermine Republican Spain. In contrast, Orwell, who fought in Spain, refused to delay publishing *Homage to Catalonia* (1938) because it might hurt the Republican cause. He wrote by way of explanation, "I hold the outmoded opinion that in the long run it does not pay to tell lies." [13]

By then, Auden had also realized that the decade's commitment to willed belief was a bankrupt choice. His candid statement of nonresponsibility in "The Public v. the Late Mr. William Butler Yeats" expresses a certain relief that the artist has relinquished his political hat: "The *honest truth*, gentlemen, is that, if not a poem had been written, not a picture painted, not a bar of music composed, the history of man would be materially unchanged" (1977, 393; my emphasis). Auden's redundant adjective "honest" tips the hand of a sometimes hypocritical decade's dishonest relationship to "truth." Spender identifies the problem of the hypocrisy of falsified "truth," but admits he has no solutions:

> . . . I look at you and through as if through glass
> And do not say "you lie."
> . . . you trust belief
> Of the lean spectator living on illusion.
> This delicate smile that strokes my arm I cannot
> Break. It is your truth's invisible creation.
>
> (Roberts 1971, 242).

Years later, Spender (1964) writes, "I cannot see that we are to be envied in having been diverted from exploring fundamental truths which have nothing to do with the politics of that time" (92).

Not all leftist writers of the 1930s were quick to give up their belief, even in the face of André Gide's unhappy report of the Soviet Union. It is not difficult to argue that the poets themselves bear considerable responsibility for what Spender calls the "diversion" from "fundamental truths." "The impulse that led them to express faith in the Soviet Union after the Moscow Trials had no better motive than self-preservation," Symons (1960) writes. "Twitch away this blanket of belief, and they would be left naked and shuddering to face the winter wind of reality" (142–43).

As Auden confesses in 1939, "There has never been an age when it was more necessary to look after one's health and keep an honest diary."[14] Looking back at the beginning of the decade, one is eerily reminded that the choice has not yet been made and that those who make it are aware of the risks. In the prologue to *The Orators* (1932), Auden (1967) writes:

> And yet this prophet, homing the day is ended,
> Receives odd welcome from the country he so defended:
> The band roars "Coward, Coward", in his human fever,
> The giantess shuffles nearer, cries "Deceiver."
>
> (3)

If we read "prophet" to mean the poet—as it so often did during the 1930s—it is also possible to see the "band" and "giantess" as public and critic, respectively. The roles are less important, however, than the possibility that Auden imagined a future when he and his fellow poets would be accused of dishonesty, bad judgment, and the abandonment of the English cause. In 1940, the press asks: where are the poets who gave so much to the cause of the Spanish civil war? Why is Auden, who looked to save England, in New York? In "Address for a Prize-Day," another section of *The Orators,* Auden (1967) predicts and asks for delivery from the sequence of events that occurs in the 1930s: "In the moment of vision; in the hour of applause; in the place of defeat; and in the hour of desertion: / O Holmes, deliver us" (9). Much later, in *The Dyer's Hand* (1963), Auden repudiates the poet as prophet and public speaker: "The characteristic style of 'Modern' poetry is an intimate tone of voice, the speech of one person addressing one person, not a large audience; whenever a modern poet raises his voice he sounds phony" (qtd. in Partridge 1976, 261).

Replogle argues that the young Auden rarely settled down to the business of plain statement, preferring to waffle between the serious voice of the "Poet" and the ironic and undercutting safety valve of the "Antipoet." While (or perhaps because) Auden plays with the speaker's authority and reliability, he is willing to make statements of personal feeling that other poets avoid. Auden experiments with syntax and registers of diction in the quest for ambiguous meaning; his speakers regularly elide subject pronouns, articles, and prepositions. The disconcerted reader wonders precisely whom Auden is addressing and who is speaking. In an early poem, Auden writes:

> I shifted ranges, lived epochs handicapped
> By climate, wars, or what the young men kept,
> Modified theories on the types of dross,
> Altered desire and history of dress.[15]

This speaker is perhaps part God, part earth, an energy that affects plate tectonics, human fashion, and ideas, but that nevertheless lives "epochs handicapped." In many of Auden's poems, adjectives and adverbs appear as modifiers in unlikely places, reflecting the influence of Anglo-Saxon inflection on Auden's modern idiom. His choices sometimes resemble Borges's oxymorons: prizes are given to "ruined" boys and one escapes "humming" down arterial roads.[16] The mixture of pleasure with pain and fear creates a menacing tone appropriate to the bourgeois audience's plight during the 1930s: life is pleasant enough, but it may not be that way for long. Similarly, private language and allusions are mixed with public forms and ballads tell un-balladlike stories. Auden likes to subvert the normal status of the subject, and for him language is the coin that—well invested—multiplies and creates value. He ends "Letter to Lord Byron" with a rare—and ironic—allusion to the poem as permanent text:

> But here I end my conversational song.
> I hope you don't think mail from strangers wrong.
> As to its length, I tell myself you'll need it,
> You've all eternity in which to read it.

> (1977, 199)

In matters of style and politics, Auden is a brilliant middleman, wavering between commitment and abstention as well as innovation and traditionalism.

Auden's imperfect solution to the conflict between the demands of the private and public realms, as between life and art, is to hedge his bets. As Replogle writes of Auden's moral dilemma, "If the Poet preferred Art, the Antipoet felt 'deep abhorrence' when he 'caught anyone preferring Art / To Life and Love.'"[17] Auden wavers between seriousness and farce and between choosing as his subject social issues and the enduring apoliticism of love. Compare, for example, Day Lewis's "The Conflict" and Auden's "Five Poems," which appeared in consecutive issues of *New Verse*. Day Lewis's poem is heavy-handed in its use of binarisms and political symbols:

> Yet living here,
> As one between two massing powers I live
> Whom neutrality cannot save
> Nor occupation cheer.
>
> None such shall be left alive:
> The innocent wing is soon shot down
> And private stars fade in the blood-red dawn
> Where two worlds strive.[18]

We now know to what degree Day Lewis overstates his case in this poem, for MacNeice did in fact choose a form of neutrality that had few ill effects aside from personal pain and a barrage of unfriendly criticism. It is 1933 and the conflict is as yet a psychological, not a political reality; Day Lewis's choice of an external, public conceit is melodramatic. In an important sense, poems such as this created the binary divisions that left the 1930s poets feeling helpless. The gap between Day Lewis's poetic theory and practice shows in the contrast between "The Conflict" and his conservative statement: "Propaganda verse is to be condemned when the didactic is achieved at the expense of the poetic: poetry, in fact, whatever else it may or may not be, must be poetry" (1942, 49). Though Auden's "Five Poems," on the theme of love, address many of the same issues, Auden chooses instead a personal voice and an enigmatic message:

> Sleep on beside me though I wake for you:
> Stretch not your hands towards your harm and me,
> Lest, waking, you should feel the need I do
> To offer love's preposterous guarantee
> That the stars watch us, that there are no poor . . .
> Turn not towards me lest I turn to you.

In the second of the five poems, Auden hints at a public wounding of private love:

> There is a wound and who shall staunch it up?
> Deepening daily, discharging all the time
> Power from love.[19]

Where Day Lewis dramatically describes the helplessness of the bystander, Auden asks the more practical and pressing question: Whose responsibility is civilization's mess?

The 1930s were characterized by a strong inclination to romanticize the working classes. John Lehmann searched for working-class writers to publish in *New Writing,* perhaps to prove that they did in fact exist. The romance of the proletarian writer certainly affected the historicization of D. H. Lawrence. Watson (1977) argues that the critics' image of Lawrence—whose humble early years quickly gave way to a middle-class existence—was somewhat contrived: "By the late Thirties, though no earlier, Lawrence's status as a working-class novelist is beginning to be taken for granted, and by the Forties it is a commonplace" (115). Similarly, Mac-Neice (1965) reports that in 1936 "literary London, hungry for proletarian literature, assumed that the Birmingham novelists were proletarian. Birmingham denied this" (154). Auden and Day Lewis's relationship to the working classes is tinged with patronage and fear. Auden (1977) wonders about "Engine-drivers with their oil-cans, factory girls in overalls / Blowing sky-high monster stores, destroying intellectuals?" (49). Day Lewis (1977) asks:

What were we at, the moment when we kissed—
Extending the franchise
To an indifferent class, would we enlist
Fresh power who know not how to be so great?

(47)

In 1936, at the height of leftist literary fervor, Auden (1977) writes: "Personally the kind of poetry I should like to write but can't is 'the thoughts of a wise man in the speech of the common people'" (360). Among other things, Auden is suggesting that common people aren't wise.

Looking back from the 1950s, Spender (1953a) writes, "My Spanish war poems were written on the hypothesis that if the cause were just then the particular truths of experience could not hurt it" (153). Perhaps we should ask whether the particular truths of Spender's lack of direct relationship to the war hurt his own cause. "Port Bou" ends with the lines:

. . . The machine gun stitches
My intestines with a needle, back and forth:
The solitary spasmodic white puffs from the carbine
Draw fear in white threads back and forth through my body.

(1986, 67)

This machine-gun fire as sewing needle is an effective metaphorical evocation of gut-wrenching fear, but it sounds like an image conjured by a person far from the bloody front, a person who has not witnessed how unlike a needle a bullet really is. Compare John Cornford:

> We buried Ruiz in a new pine coffin,
> But the shroud was too small and his washed feet stuck out.
> The stink of his corpse came through the clean pine boards
> And some of the bearers wrapped handkerchiefs around their faces.
> Death was not dignified.
> We hacked a ragged grave in the unfriendly earth
> And fired a ragged volley over the grave.
>   (qtd. in Stansky and Abrahams 1966, 353)

Cornford does not need metaphor here: plain description is enough. His poem is unusually clear for an era of difficult poetry full of private allusions.

Before the Auden poets graduated from Oxford, I. A. Richards wrote in the *Cambridge Review:* "Modern verse is perhaps more often too lucid than too obscure. It passes through the mind . . . with too little friction and too swiftly for the development of the response. Poets who can compel slow reading have thus an initial advantage" (qtd. in Gardner and Gardner 1978, 22). Richards advocates a poetry for a small, highly educated audience attended by helpful critics. The Auden poets claimed they wanted a large audience, but they never produced the right kind of poetry. Though the Cambridge New Critical movement had comparatively little direct effect on these Oxford-based poets, its central impulse—to find an objective, quasi-scientific measure of truth—was shared by them and the rest of England by the late 1930s. For those looking for an anchor for newly created meaning that extends beyond language itself, science offered the best tools. Referring to the theory of Roland Barthes, Italo Calvino (1986) argues:

> For literature, language is never *transparent,* and is never merely an instrument to convey a "meaning" or a "fact" or a "thought" or a "truth"; that is, it cannot mean anything but itself. Whereas, on the other hand, the idea of language given by science is that of a neutral utensil that is used to say something else, to mean something foreign to it. (29; my emphasis)

The Auden poets wanted very much for literary language to mean more than itself. But they did not want it to be a hollow tool, either; their quest was to combine the art of literature and the truth value of science.

Spender (1937) associates "reality" with disinteredness, objectivity, and truth, and tries to convince his reader that truth is now solidly located outside subjectivity: "I am a communist because I am a liberal. Liberalism seems to be the creed of those who . . . are disinterested, if by disinterestedness one understands not mere passivity but a regard for objective truth, an active will towards political justice" (189).

The fetish of objectivity is at its apogee in 1937: the "Oxford Collective Poem," conceived by Charles Madge and composed systematically by a group of Oxford undergraduates, promotes the idea that a group's truth, especially a group operating on the principle of consensus, is more universally valid than that of a single individual. The poem was thought by many to be a sort of "collective account" of Oxford.[20] Mass Observation, an "objective" method of investigation, also appears that year, sharing New Criticism's valuing of the "scientific" truth of nonscientists.

> The hope [of Mass Observation] was that by means of the detailed account of the observations of hundreds of fact-gatherers, using interviews, questionnaires, applause meters, and similar devices, social engineers could "discover the nature of the mass-life of the mass-man from the cradle to the grave."[21]

New Verse complained that the "immediate effect of MASS-OBSERVATION is to de-value considerably the status of the 'poet.' It makes the term 'poet' apply, not to his performance, but to his profession, like 'footballer.'"[22] Mass Observation was uncomfortably democratic in its approach and value scheme; "ordinary" people were asked to write extensive accounts of their lives one day a month, and all experiences and roles were held to be essentially equivalent. It is no small irony that the poets working toward a new socialist state would be made unhappy by such a suggestion of democratic leveling. The 1937 love of consensus as a measure of objectivity, however, is a sign that the Auden poets had managed to diagnose their decade's ills. As Thomson (1965) suggests, "the cult of 'facts'"—illustrated by a rise in documentary films and publications and by the appearance of the leftist journal *Fact*—"perhaps betrayed less a scientific faith than a loss of all faith" (183).

I have argued that critical approaches need to be evaluated as tools in the promotion of larger issues. Kermode (1985) makes the point that

> the success of interpretative argument as a means of conferring or en-
> dorsing value is . . . not to be measured by the survival of the comment
> but by the survival of its object. Of course, an interpretation or evalua-
> tion may live on in the tradition on which later comment is formed,
> either by acceptance or reaction; but its primary purpose is to provide
> the medium in which its object survives. (67)

The Auden group's strategies—the choice of politics and propaganda as well as the decision to recant—were successful, if painful, means of cata-pulting their poetry into several decades of critical debate about its value and meaning. Though such choices were clearly made possible by an un-usual historical moment, it is important to keep the issue of free will in mind: Auden and his peers made these choices for self-interested as well as community-oriented reasons. It is a fact that their temporary failure of belief speeded their acceptance in the permanent literary canon. Barbara Herrnstein Smith (1988) argues that canonized works "would not be found to please long and well if they were seen *radically* to undercut establish-ment interests or *effectively* to subvert the ideologies that support them" (51). The emphases here are Smith's and her point is essential: the Auden poets' work of the 1930s pleases partly because it did not accomplish these goals. Many comments made by these poets during the 1930s suggest that it was never intended to do so.

The group's experiments with propaganda successfully expanded the range of poetic subjects in the English tradition.[23] At the same time, the poets recognized the inadequacies of their strategies. Auden (1977) refers in 1933 to "the common language of collective lying" (143), but like other writers whose profession involved the creation of meaning and value, he was forced to deal with the conflict between (perceived) public needs and private belief. Spender's anecdote about the Auxiliary Fire Service for which he worked during World War II illustrates his ambivalence about the role of propagandistic language in creating personal reality:

> One man, Ned, had a secret cause of shame. He could not read or
> write. . . . Because of his illiteracy he was the only man in the sta-
> tion who told the truth about his fire-fighting experiences. The others
> had almost completely substituted descriptions which they read in the
> newspapers or heard on the wireless for their own impressions.[24]

It is important to keep in mind that the Auden poets began systematically to pursue fame before they left Oxford and even to compete among themselves. In a September 1932 letter to Grigson, Day Lewis writes:

> I see from the *Bookman* that you have now arranged us in the correct order—1, Auden; 2, Day-Lewis—but I shall chase him home, you can rely on that, and I think we'll make the pace pretty hot between us. . . . My final order—another professional weakness!—is 1, Auden, 2, Day-Lewis, 3, Spender. (qtd. in S. Day-Lewis 1980, 71–72)

On the strength of their belief, these poets managed to change the face of English poetry. The measure of this belief, which brought these poets both tangible and intangible rewards, can be seen in the bitterness of its short-term failure. Spender (1986) ends "The Double Shame" with one such message of regret and reproach:

> You of the double way of shame:
> At first you did not love enough
> And afterwards you loved too much
> And you lacked the confidence to choose
> And you have only yourself to blame.
>
> (85)

Reading has two faces, looks in two directions. One direction is back, toward the source and original context of the signs we are deciphering. The other direction is forward, based on the textual situation of the person doing the reading.

—Robert Scholes

7. MacNeice, Empson, and Auden:
A Politics of Reception

"Notions of value in literature more often than not involve, as a rule rather obscurely, our views of the relation of a work to its historical context" (Kermode 1988, 108). Frank Kermode alludes here to an unspoken rule of literary criticism and history: there are proper and improper choices for writers born into different moments and places. Where Borges and *Sur* were for a time thought by critics to have made the right choices, later scrutiny revealed them to have been sorely lacking. Sometimes a poet is taken out of context and studied primarily as an individual, and sometimes a peer of such a poet is examined for his or her role as a cog in a large poetic machine. Surrealists tend to be evaluated according to whether they fulfilled their self-identified mission. Where their individual poetic oeuvres are the subject of study, the issue of surrealism suddenly becomes mere background noise.

Oxford-educated Louis MacNeice is nearly always discussed in the context of issues raised by the Auden group during the 1930s, while Cambridge-educated William Empson, also an important poet of the 1930s, usually escapes being judged by the critical values applied to the "social" poets. The former is seen largely as a group member, the latter as an individualist. Empson, of course, was not part of the "MacSpaunday" group that was named after the four central Auden poets. Nor did he fit their pattern: Empson's *annum mirabilis* came early, in 1928, and the early 1930s found him teaching English in Tokyo. Late in the decade, he was in China, moving with the students from campus to campus in an effort to stay ahead of the Sino-Japanese War. Empson not only missed a lot of the 1930s but composed most of his poetry before the decade began. Referring to the Auden group's projects of the 1930s, he once wrote, "I agreed with the pylon poets entirely. I've always felt I ought to make that point plain whenever I had the opportunity. . . . I'm very sorry I wasn't in on it" (1963, 32–33). But because his two books of poems were published in 1935 and 1940 and he wrote very little poetry after 1940, he is nothing if not a 1930s poet.[1] He has, for example, six poems in *New Signatures,* while MacNeice has none. Neither is represented in *New Country.* In 1931, in an important review of Auden's *Paid on Both Sides,* he praises Auden for putting psycho-analysis and surrealism in "their proper place," and sees the play, already read by others as a political parable, as a warning about cultural tragedy. Most important, he helps promote the idea of a poetic generation, of Auden as the seed of the Auden group. *Paid on Both Sides,* he writes, "has the sort of completeness that makes a work seem to define the attitude of a generation."[2] Empson's first volume of poetry, *Poems* (1935), appeared well after he completed the poems, leading period critics to read them with at least a hint of the political orientation that characterized the middle of the decade. Strangely, there is no myth of Empson in the 1930s. He was a brilliant scholar whose undergraduate thesis became his first book, *Seven Types of Ambiguity* (1930), and whose difficult metaphysical and quasi-scientific conceits belong more to the 1920s than to the 1930s. Critics have tended to accept him as the proper product of I. A. Richards's Cambridge in the late 1920s: a good, if difficult, poet whose theoretical writings continue to serve formalist critics well.

Both Empson and MacNeice failed to fit the mold of the political poet of the 1930s. For this, MacNeice has been roundly criticized. Empson, in contrast, has not been charged with a failure to commit himself to politics or any other belief system. This is largely because these poets were products of different environments and critical contexts. As Gardner and Gardner (1978) write, "Empson's early poetry and reputation owed much to their time and place: the Cambridge of the mid-twenties, excited by the expanding horizons of science, by literary innovation, and by the rediscovery of the Metaphysical poets, whose work seemed to fuse intellect and emotion" (21).

Empson was largely evaluated on his own terms. MacNeice, in contrast, was viewed as the dissenting member of a group he had done relatively little to promote and which, at least during the 1930s, he tended to refer to in the third person. MacNeice was also very willing to criticize the group's members. In 1935, he labeled Day Lewis inferior to Auden and Spender. Spender, he wrote, "is a naif who uses communism as a frame for his personal thrills" (MacNeice 1987, 26). Grigson, a voice of reason, once referred to the Auden poets as "the Three and Mr. MacNeice." [3]

Just as there are two competing myths of the Auden group, so there are two myths of MacNeice himself. The dominant myth identifies him as having been unable to commit himself to idealistic belief and political action. The less-popular myth holds that MacNeice was a sophisticated skeptic who deserves to be respected for avoiding the traps into which the other Auden poets fell. Underneath the suggestion that MacNeice was actually deficient—*unable* to commit himself—is the idea that his flaw was a failure of the *will* to believe. In this context, which illustrates the degree to which critics have invested themselves in the Auden group's need for belief, MacNeice has failed a moral test.

Contemporary critics have softened up on MacNeice. Kermode (1988) for example, describes him as a sometimes lazy, sometimes honest hedonist: "He was willing to call himself a snob; he liked pleasant places to live, wine, poetry, upper-class women, Greek and Latin classics, in-jokes . . . and he was reluctant to give them up though sure that they must be given up" (66).

Earlier critics, such as D. B. Moore (1972) are less tolerant: "By nature [MacNeice] resented and indeed rejected the idea that in politics one must 'take one's stand.' Both the rejection and the resentment are stated clearly in . . . 'For we are obsolete who like the lesser things / Who play in corners with looking-glasses and beads'" (52). Moore's interpretation of these lines from "Turf-Stacks" is problematic, for in this poem MacNeice takes a stand against belief systems he finds facile and dogmatic. He locates his poem where there "is no mass-production of neat thoughts / No canvas shrouds for the mind nor any black hearses." In the rest of the poem, MacNeice sets forth two courses of action for those who feel as he does about the pressure to support political beliefs they find unconvincing or problematic: avoid them and defend yourself against them or work actively to dismantle them. Though MacNeice is openly antifascist, "Turf-Stacks," in its reference to "peasant's conspirators," perhaps speaks more to the problem of protecting oneself from the pressure to believe in communism:

> But those who lack the peasant's conspirators,
> The tawny mountain, the unregarded buttress,
> Will feel the need of a fortress against ideas and against the

Shuddering insidious shock of the theory-vendors,
The little sardine men crammed in a monster toy
Who tilt their aggregate beast against our crumbling Troy.
For we are obsolete who like the lesser things
Who play in corners with looking-glasses and beads;
It is better we should go quickly, go into Asia
Or any other tunnel where the world recedes,
Or turn blind wantons like the gulls who scream
And rip the edge off any ideal or dream.

(1949, 75)

Read in context, the two lines cited by Moore sound different. Instead of rejecting and resenting the notion that one must "take one's stand," Mac-Neice argues that those who like "the lesser things" and dislike idealized theory-vending must decide how to cope with the fact that they hold a minority point of view. Robyn Marsack (1982) however, concurs with Moore, seeing avoidance of responsibility and a first person confession in "Turf-Stacks": "He deliberately trivializes his own preoccupations . . . forestalling criticism by admitting a penchant for things shining, multi-coloured, narcissistic, confessing the insidious attraction of intellectual theorizing" (8).

Moore appears to subscribe to the second Auden group myth, the one where idealized political belief is a virtue. A discussion of MacNeice's *Autumn Journal* (1939) suggests as much:

> MacNeice in his attitude . . . mirrors the attitude of a large section of the contemporary intelligentsia. Despairing of achieving action, or influencing political thought, the critical analysis is drained of hope. . . . There is an overriding sense of failure. Though this has made poetry in *Autumn Journal,* there will always be those who find its lack of positive idealism a factor which limits their appreciation. (Moore 1972, 91)

Moore is correct that MacNeice "never believed that salvation lay in any system either religious, philosophical, or political" (100). The key word is salvation: MacNeice had beliefs, but not in miraculous or transcendental solutions. In his final indictment, Moore speaks for many other critics who attack MacNeice for "his *inability* to make the *intellectual effort* either to achieve faith, to deny all belief, or to systematize his agnosticism. . . . So MacNeice . . . relied instead on the conflicts of indecision." Moore's interest in MacNeice is largely moral, and MacNeice has failed the morality test. Significantly, Moore does not hold MacNeice altogether responsible, as the failure is due to an "inability to make the [requisite] intellectual effort" (243; my emphasis). Marsack (1982), too, identifies his failure as "an *inability* to subscribe to even Auden's seductive moral imperatives" (22). Marsack and Moore could as well have said "unwillingness" in place of "inability," but they assume that MacNeice wanted to believe.

Though there are signs that MacNeice did want to fit better into the Auden group and the prevailing ideologies of the 1930s, most of his writings point to a carefully considered belief system that did not allow such choices. He experimented with adopting leftist beliefs but learned quickly that it did not work for him. Looking back, he voiced a conclusion ultimately shared by Spender and Day Lewis: "I myself . . . suffered . . . when I forced myself to feel things that in fact I merely thought; feelings are one's own, but thoughts come from the group."[4] MacNeice here identifies the form of dishonesty common to the 1930s, the malaise of choosing between public exigence and private feeling. In a note accompanying *Autumn Journal,* he spells out his choice: "In a journal or a personal letter a man writes what he feels at the moment; to attempt scientific truthfulness would be—paradoxically—dishonest. . . . Poetry in my opinion must be honest before anything else and I refuse to be 'objective' or clear-cut at the cost of honesty" (1967, 101).

Auden was making similar statements—albeit less directly—by this time, March 1939. It is important to remember that MacNeice participated directly in the issues that engaged the Auden poets earlier in the decade. In "Ode," written in 1934, MacNeice (1967) spoke much as the other Auden poets did about the necessity of taking action:

> Trains leave in all directions on wild rails
> And for every act determined on and won
> There is a possible world denied and lost.
> Do not then turn maudlin or weathercock,
> We must cut the throat of the hour
> That it may not haunt us.
>
> (56)

But already he hints at the hypocrisy of newly minted belief systems:

> I cannot draw up any code
> There are too many qualifications . . .
> But as others, forgetting the others,
> Run after the nostrums
> Of science art and religion

So would I mystic and maudlin
Dream of both real and ideal
    Breakers of ocean.
I must put away this drug.

(58)

Assuming his role as diagnostician of the decade's ills,[5] MacNeice makes
the unusual choice of hinting at the role of the poet-speaker as the creator
of the "codes" of belief systems. He already suspects that for him pursuing idealized belief systems could amount to a sort of drug, as it did
for Spender and Day Lewis. And he is suspicious of the new language in
which such belief is framed:

With all this clamour for progress
This hammering out of new phases and gadgets, new trinkets and
    phrases
I prefer the automatic, the reflex, the cliché of velvet.

Such new language — that of "flattery logic seduction or wit" — is perhaps
too prone to change: "the pattern and the patina of these / Are superseded
in the end."[6]

In *I Crossed the Minch* (1938), MacNeice states that he believes in the
leftist cause "on paper and in the soul," but not in his "heart or guts." In an
oft-quoted admission, MacNeice claims his "soul is all for moving towards
the classless society," but admits that he is "both a money snob and a class
snob."[7] While Spender was quite ambivalent about the anti-individualist
demands of the Communist Party, MacNeice writes in his autobiography
that he was attracted by the challenge: "The strongest appeal of the Communist party was that it demanded sacrifice; you had to sink your ego."
He admits to having wanted to participate in communism but to finding
he could not abide the "wishful thinking and over-simplification" that accompanied the choice (1965, 146). MacNeice is better at sinking his ego
than are his peers, but he is not so different from them. Spender, for example, admits that he hopes to "purge myself of an abnormal individuality
by cooperating with the Workers' Movement" (qtd. in Aney 1954, 37).
Unlike the other three MacSpaunday poets, MacNeice refrains from com-
petitive statements about becoming the best poet of the decade. And he
attributes his "First Class in Honour Mods." at Oxford to his skill as "an
intellectual window-dresser" (1965, 113).

In "Les neiges d'antan," MacNeice addresses the loss of the private life and the growing risk of social violence or, as some readers have argued, revolution. But even with the thrice-repeated line "FIRE FIRE FIRE FIRE," this is not leftist in the manner of Day Lewis's *The Magnetic Mountain*. In *Autumn Journal,* MacNeice openly confronts the conflict between his social awareness ("ninety-nine in the hundred who never attend the banquet / Must wash the grease of ages off the knives") and his feeling that in order to "preserve the values dear to the élite / The élite must remain a few." Having confessed his fear—shared, we must remember, by all of the Auden poets—of a "fall in the standard of intellectual living," MacNeice (1949) argues that these fears "must be suppressed" (125). The lines about the unfair distribution of wealth are rarely mentioned by critics, while those about the elite remaining a few are among the most frequently quoted. Similarly, MacNeice's comment that such fears must be suppressed is infrequently quoted, let alone analyzed. Because the oft-cited passage is sandwiched between two modifying statements, I believe critics have quoted MacNeice both out of context and unfairly.

There is ample evidence that critics condemning MacNeice have taken their evidence from the confessions that abound in his poems. *Autumn Journal* contains the lines: "None of our hearts are pure, we always have mixed motives, / Are self deceivers" (1949, 126). MacNeice also comes to write that *Autumn Journal* "fails in depth," agreeing with early reviews by leftist critics. John Lehmann (1940), for example, writes that *Autumn Journal* is "facile . . . never very deep or certain in thought, rather too conspicuously elaborating the picture of an easy-going but attractive personality" (116). He says this of a work that MacNeice once called his "best work to date . . . a confession of faith."[8] Marsack attributes responsibility for MacNeice's critical fortunes to *Modern Poetry,* where MacNeice denies that the poet is either a legislator or a prophet and identifies him instead as one whose product is thoroughly imbued with personal emotional reactions to experience. This is not a view destined to find favor in the 1930s. "This characterization," writes Marsack (1982), "inescapably set the pattern for criticism of MacNeice" (42).

Edward E. Smith (1970) subscribes to Kermode's hedonism theory and the view of MacNeice as a moral failure. He depicts MacNeice as a helpless and hopeless upper-class writer who, after the Spanish civil war and Munich, "is amazed and shocked that an alien scale of values *should have the temerity to threaten his pleasant, indecisive life." Autumn Journal* he finds to be full of "technical brilliance and badinage," but sorely lacking in social content and commitment. What can the intellectual do to help the world,

Smith asks, answering: "The manifest evasion of the poem makes the answer clear: Nothing" (83; my emphasis). Looking back, Cyril Connolly accuses MacNeice of passionlessness. He "had no enemies, his love poems are without lust, his political poems without rancour" (Connolly 1973, 364). *Autumn Journal,* however, contains statements of rebellion against the pressure to conform to prevailing beliefs:

> The order of the day is complete conformity and
>> An automatic complacence.
> . . . at times
>> The Fool among the yes-men flashed his motley
> To prick their pseudo-reason with his rhymes.
>> (MacNeice 1949, 141)

When MacNeice (1949) goes on to ask "which disease / Is worse—the Status Quo or the Mere Utopia" (149–50), it is clear that he doesn't believe communism can deliver on its promises. It is hard to dismiss all this rumination and self-questioning as merely "indecisive," for MacNeice, after much struggle, makes up his mind about how to believe, asserting optimism about the power of free will and personal action later even than Auden. In *Autumn Journal,* he complains of England's "spiritual sloth": "Most of us lack the right discontent, contented / Merely to cavil." He goes on to warn about the pressing weight of impending historical disaster:

> We have not even an hour to spend repenting
>> Our sins; the quarters chime
> And every minute is its own alarum clock
>> And what we are about to do
> Is of vastly more importance
>> Than what we have done or not done hitherto.

MacNeice alludes to concentration camps and implies that it is partly England's fault that vultures are picking "corpses clean in Macedon." He chides the English for "renounc[ing] their birthright, / The responsibility of moral choice" and hints ominously that within a few years few people will see the sun shine. It is very hard to argue that MacNeice does not contribute to diagnosing the decade's problems and suggesting that action—political and possibly military—be taken.[9]

In the small critical camp that does not find MacNeice constitutionally deficient, one finds Terence Brown (1975), who argues that MacNeice is a sophisticated philosophical skeptic: "It is this basic scepticism which,

I feel, has confused critics. They have too easily assumed that its result—a lack of simple dogmatic creed—is of the same kind as their own liberal confusion. It was deeper, more rigorously held and applied, than they perhaps realise" (2). Brown also describes the majority of critics as believing that MacNeice "is a gay conjuror with images, a poet of cunning *legerdemain* and deception. His poetry is a shallow trick, too clever by half" (125).

I subscribe, however, to the view that MacNeice was a careful thinker who knew his own nature better than some of his fellow poets knew theirs. I base my view on MacNeice's critical and poetic writings. In response to a 1934 *New Verse* survey, MacNeice clearly identifies political dogmatism as a flaw. Asked whether he believes in any party or creed, he answers "No. In weaker moments I wish I could." On what makes a poet different from other men, he writes, "Dissatisfaction with accepted formulas. But most of the time one is not a poet and is perfectly satisfied." [10] None of the other core Auden poets responded to the survey, thus sparing themselves the risks involved in answering these questions directly. In his critical writings, MacNeice (1968) repeatedly demystifies the role of the poet, accusing him of often being "both a 'rebel' against and a parasite upon his community" (2). MacNeice here puts his finger on one of the central contradictions of the avant-garde: the habit of rejecting society but simultaneously demanding its support. Though he commends other poets for locating the poetic subject outside themselves, he believes most write in order to arrive at a deep understanding of themselves (1968, 64). He also argues that the capacity for writing poetry exists in all men, a paradoxically anti-elitist view. "Nothing," he writes, "could be more vicious than the popular legend that the poet is a species distinct from the ordinary man" (1937, 145). MacNeice contradicts the prevailing 1930s view of the poet as prophet and leader and in *New Verse* makes a stronger argument: the artist's "morality must be honest; he must not merely retail other people's dogma. . . . Propaganda (unless you use the term, as many do, very, very loosely indeed) is not the poet's job." [11] MacNeice takes on the role of group diagnostician, being one of the first to note that the Auden "poets make myths of themselves and of each other" in an absurd way.[12] MacNeice here writes as though from a great distance, not as a member of "MacSpaunday." At moments like these, it is hard to imagine that he ever meant to be part of the group.

In 1935, MacNeice takes the bold position that binary thinking is deeply flawed. "The individualist is an atom thinking about himself (Thank God I am not as other men); the communist, too often, is an atom having ecstasies of self-denial (Thank God I am one in a crowd); and this too is attitudinizing." MacNeice also writes: "At the moment, even the most intelligent communist tends to relapse into crude generalizations."[13] In *The Arts To-Day*, MacNeice dismantles the communist-bourgeois opposition and, as Walter Benjamin has done, accuses the "would-be communist poets of playing to the bourgeoisie." He goes on to name Auden, Spender, and Day Lewis, remarking that "like all propagandists (cp. Shelley) they sometimes make themselves ridiculous."[14] By 1940, his assessment of leftist literary fantasy is even less tolerant, as when he describes a novel by Edward Upward in which a "neurotic young man . . . sees the light and goes off 'to find a worker'—as if that would solve everything. The Proletariat had become the *Deus ex Machina*."[15] Ironically, Spender describes doing something similar in his guilt-ridden romantic relationships with working-class men in Berlin earlier in the decade. In 1940, MacNeice again stands apart from the recanting majority by defending the Auden group from Virginia Woolf's accusation in "The Leaning Tower" that the privileged bourgeois poets are trying carelessly to tear down a society for which they have no replacement.[16]

That period critics were easier on MacNeice than were their successors is an important sign of critical revisionism. Grigson, for example, held the view that MacNeice was a talented and effective poet. "As far as it is possible to judge now, I should say that there were no better poets in England, after Yeats and Eliot, than Auden and Louis MacNeice. Both have this exact, material view. Both are champions of common sense." Grigson (1939) labels MacNeice a social and moral realist (19–20). Francis Scarfe (1942) forgives him for failing to participate in the 1930s mix of literature and politics on the grounds that he is "damnably Irish" and not up to it. Scarfe refers to MacNeice as "struggling vainly to repress his feelings" and, like Auden, "trying to give a casual air to his most sincere opinions" (62). And in the heyday of political activism, Spender self-consciously avoids criticizing MacNeice for anything more serious than a dearth of "hard statement[s]." MacNeice's poetry, writes Spender, "is difficult to 'place,' which means that it is impossible for a contemporary to criticise it."[17]

Little noted except by Grigson is the fact that MacNeice and Auden had much in common. Among these things were a sharp, questioning intelligence and a consistent sexual identity. The latter was a rather rare thing amid the fluctuating orientations and ambivalences of many left-leaning poets of the 1930s. MacNeice was as consistently heterosexual as Auden was consistently gay. More to the point, the two shared a deep, often ironic skepticism. In 1936 both wrote poems warning of the dangers of complacency. Auden (1977) undermines the average man's somewhat blind sense of personal success:

> As it is, plenty;
> As it's admitted
> The children happy
> And the car, the car
> That goes so far
> And the wife devoted:
>
> . . . .
>
> Give thanks, give thanks.

But then he warns:

> Let him not cease to praise
> Then his spacious days.
>
> . . . .
>
> Lest he see as it is
> The loss as major
> And final, final.
>
> (163–64)

In "Hidden Ice," MacNeice (1967) addresses the same issue of domestic tranquility and mediocrity in the midst of threats to civilization.

> Those who ignore disarm. The domestic ambush
> The pleated lampshade the defeatist clock
> May never be consummated and we may never
> Strike on the rock beneath the calm upholstering.
>
> But some though buoyed by habit
> . . . have lost their bearings
> Struck hidden ice or currents no one noted.
>
> (77)

Auden's poem is much the more threatening of the two, indicating that some disaster is inevitable. MacNeice, on the other hand, suggests that many people will escape this vague threat, especially those who are vigilant. Auden's short lines and straight talk are more effective than MacNeice's long, metrically irregular lines.

Whether MacNeice's poetry is substantially less "social" or "political" than that of his peers is an open question. By MacNeice's own count, at least fifteen of the thirty-three poems in Spender's *Poems* (1933) are not social or political. For Auden's *Look, Stranger* (1936), fifteen of thirty-one are neither. For his own *The Earth Compels* (1938), the figure is at least thirteen of twenty-four. MacNeice (1987) acknowledges that even the poems he labels sociopolitical "remain, to my mind, highly personal . . . and often even 'romantic'" (208–9). This exercise in counting raises two important issues. If the poetic norm in England at this time had been political poetry, the Auden poets might have been considered aesthetes. And the careful reader of MacNeice's poetry will concur that it was not that much less sociopolitical than the work of Auden and Spender. What divides his poetry from theirs, of course, is a difference of attitude toward his subject. Spender actively promotes communism in a number of poems, Auden uses ambiguous language that sounds pro-leftist, and MacNeice, while agreeing with their view of the problem, openly questions the wisdom of proposed solutions.

Like MacNeice, Empson was sympathetic to the leftist cause. But neither quite belonged to his time: MacNeice reminded critics of eighteenth-century poets while Empson reminded them of John Donne. Empson complicated the matter further by being overseas much of the decade. Lehmann, for example, had asked him for a contribution to *New Country,* but Empson didn't get it to him on time. Empson's major critical writings were largely apolitical and he was fascinated by "irreconcilable opposites," including those of the scientific variety (see Kermode 1988, 32). In a 1928 review of *Opposite Things* by M. Carta Sturge, for example, Empson shows a fondness for the coexistence of discordant opposites: "Extremely often, in dealing with the world, one arrives at two ideas or ways of dealing with things which both work and are needed, but which entirely contradict one another."[18] His interest in the major political binarism of the decade appears to have remained somewhat theoretical. In a villanelle long unpublished, Empson's (1988) tone betrays emotional distance from his subject:

> The ages change, and they impose their rules.
> It would not do much good to miss the bus.
> We must endure, and stand between two fools.
>
> Two colonies of Europe now form schools
> Holding absolute power, both of them fatuous.
> The ages change, and they impose their rules.

One claims the State is naked between ghouls
The other makes it total Octopus.
We must endure, and stand between two fools.

.   .   .   .

There is world and time; the Fates have got large spools;
There need not only Europe make a fuss.
The ages change, and they impose their rules.
We must endure, and stand between two fools.

(121)

Written while Empson was at Cambridge, this poem trivializes a contemporary subject by historicizing it and placing it in a temporally vast
context. The colonies of Europe are diminished into "schools" imposing
their "rules." In a metaphorical trick like that used by the young Auden,
Empson here uses a public school vocabulary to describe world events. The
speaker also distances himself from his subject through caricature ("naked
between ghouls . . . total Octopus") and by looking at European politics
as though through a telescope. While MacNeice also sometimes distances
himself from his subject, he is less likely to camouflage his message with
a child's metaphor. He shares with Empson a broad historical perspective
and manages always to be more personal, though he too sometimes enjoys
adopting a patronizing tone. In the brief "To a Communist," MacNeice
(1949) warns

But before you proclaim the millennium, my dear,
Consult the barometer—
This poise is perfect but maintained
For one day only.

(78)

MacNeice's "Wolves" offers an assessment of the cost of self-delusion at a
time of many threats:

Come then all of you, come closer, form a circle,
Join hands and make believe that joined
Hands will keep away the wolves.

(1949, 86)

Many early Empson poems, though rich in allusions that could be developed into political or social themes, are instead scientific or metaphysi-

cal. "The World's End," first published in 1928 as "Relativity," is about the geometric paradox of a world that seems to "end" but can't because it is curved. The note accompanying "To an Old Lady" contains a topical reference that partially rejects its own topicality: Empson (1955) refers to "our earth" as a planet lacking a god's name that he compares with "some body of people (absurd to say 'the present generation') without fundamental beliefs as a basis for action" (98).

Unlike much of the decade's poetry, these poems do not address the question of the subject of poetry and the poet's proper role. As early as 1934, in contrast, MacNeice identifies poetry as a moral healing force and a bridge between unconnected things.[19] He attacks the moral weakness of the bourgeoisie, who must have their false idols and the "flotsam of private property."[20] Where MacNeice repeatedly refers to the effete aspects of a class-riven world, Empson's conceits bring magic to such asocial events as a young woman brushing her teeth and spitting into a lake. Empson's repeated use of traditional forms such as villanelles and aubades, his regular stanzas and frequent use of pentameter and quatrimeter, and his attraction to rhyme distinguish him from MacNeice, who, though skilled in traditional forms, much more frequently chooses to write long poems of comparatively undisciplined free verse. Even where Empson seems to be talking about emotional issues, his primary emphasis is nearly always on language. "Letter III," about nightmare and death, contains the admission, "My pleasure in the simile thins" (1955, 31). "This Last Pain," first published in 1932, retreats in the end from its serious subject—the human desire (and failure) to attain divine states—to powerful, but obviously writerly advice: "And learn a style from a despair" (1955, 33). "Note on Local Flora" offers a rare Empsonian reference to the apocalyptic fervor gripping the 1930s; Empson feels compelled to explain in a note that "forest fire" is a reference to the end of the world. But the poem, with its references to Bacchus and Semele, sounds inconsistent when Empson ends with a final, and unilluminated, reference to "the Red Dawn" (1955, 36, 103).

Empson's *Poems,* its contents already dated, did not fare especially well when it appeared in 1935. MacNeice, reviewing for *New Verse,* accuses Empson of writing "inhuman poetry" at a time when such poetry is inappropriate.[21] MacNeice makes a point of saying that clever poetry is fine, if presented at the right moment and in the right context. In another critical response to Empson, MacNeice hits a distinctly clinical note, describing the meaning of Empson's poems as "disguised in an unfamiliar algebra" borrowed from science and accusing him of not participating in the problems of the real world. As MacNeice (1968) puts it, "Empson is interested in formulas for objects but not in anything he can handle. He studies science from an arm-chair. He is no participant" (105). Reviewing *Poems* (1935), Michael Roberts forgives Empson for a trait little admired in this polarized decade. Where Empson sees "that three quite different things are true and relevant, he tries to force his poem to say all three things at once" (Roberts 1980, 111). Indeed, the fact that Empson specializes in apolitical ambiguities seems to have led critics not to address the question of his political beliefs. As with Roberts, who forgives even Empson's renowned obscurity, the question of Empson's ideological belief rarely arises.

Empson showed signs early on of having incipient leftist sympathies. At school he debated in favor of Britain's recognizing the government of the Soviet Union and of opening the English public schools to the lower classes (see Gardner and Gardner 1978, 15). Once at Cambridge, Empson was quickly taken over by the sort of critic who disliked the Auden poets. In 1929, Leavis wrote in a review that "Mr. Empson commands respect (Gardner and Gardner 1978, 21). His tutor, I. A. Richards, actively encouraged him to write difficult poetry. Thus, at a young age, Empson was strongly affected by two influential critics. As he moved out of the protected atmosphere of Cambridge and realized he was something of a misfit, he started to become apologetic about his poetry's obscurity and to show a vague interest in social issues.[22] Terence Brown (1975) writes that MacNeice is "only slightly related to the left-wing movement of the thirties," but goes on to allude repeatedly to this relationship (53).

In the critical anthology *William Empson: The Man and His Work,* in contrast, leftist politics are barely mentioned. Where they come up, Empson's choices are commended. Kathleen Raine, for example, argues that Empson was interested in the world and therefore in Marxism, but that "his intellectual poise and detachment *would of course no more have committed him to the brash utopianism* which captures so many of our contemporaries than he could have committed himself to Buddhism."[23] Raine sounds congratulatory about Empson's unwillingness (not, as in MacNeice's case, perceived inability) to adopt either a political or religious belief system. M. C. Bradbrook has no condemning statement to make about Empson's "cool and carefully distanced" relationship to his reader or the casual tone he uses to give the "brush off" to hostile critics.[24] George Fraser compliments Empson on his failure to promote political action at mid-decade. Referring to *Poems* and *Some Versions of Pastoral* (1935), he writes, "There is an astonishing new social maturity of tone . . . a refusal to be either panicky or utopian: he knew that we were in for a bad time, in these islands, but felt that we would get through it."[25] This sort of passive optimism (or is it apathy?) that "we would get through it" is part of what got MacNeice into trouble.

American critic Stanley Hyman, a rare voice of dissent in Empson criticism, calls *Some Versions of Pastoral* (1935) "implicitly Marxist throughout" (qtd. in Day 1984, xxv). It is noteworthy that Hyman wrote during the anticommunist mid-1950s. For the reader of the 1930s, the first essay in *Some Versions of Pastoral,* "Proletarian Literature," is tame stuff indeed. Empson (1974) says that proletarian art is generally bad and that propaganda—broadly construed as the effort to convince—is often good. The thrust of his argument could hardly be more conservative: "Good proletarian art," writes Empson, "is usually Covert Pastoral" (6). Pastoral, by his definition, means making the complex simple so that its ideas are both valuable and enduring. This argument undermines the definitions and ideas that Spender and Day Lewis are working to legitimate by narrowing them excessively: "One might define proletarian art as the propaganda of a factory-working class which feels its interests opposed to the factory owners'; this narrow sense is perhaps what is usually meant but not very interesting. You couldn't have proletarian literature in this sense in a successful socialist state" (Empson 1974, 6).

Empson's attitude here is not so different from something Auden might feel, if not say. But in the remaining essays of *Some Versions of Pastoral,* his view of poetry is quite traditional: pastoral has been with us a long time and good pastoral is both timeless and classical. A statement about the appeal of communism reveals his detachment from the political frenzy of mid-decade: "When communists say that an author under modern capitalism feels cut off from most of the life of the country, and would not under communism, the remark has a great deal of truth, though he might only exchange a sense of isolation for a sense of the waste of his powers" (1974, 18).

This weighing of the pros and cons of an issue is a trait shared by MacNeice, to different effect. MacNeice is both more personal and analytical about the 1930s' construction of such politico-literary problems. Critics are generally tolerant of Empson's making such statements in the middle of the Spanish civil war as: "The first or only certain reason for writing verse is to clear your own mind and fix your own feelings." [26] *Seven Types of Ambiguity,* as Fraser points out, is a sort of companion volume to I. A. Richards's *Practical Criticism* (Gill 1974, 55).

Empson and MacNeice, by virtue of their university backgrounds and temperaments, fall on opposite sides of a decade's choices. One of the major reasons why Empson escapes 1930s-style criticism is that he does not take the same emotional and political risks as MacNeice. In "Aubade" (1937), he uses nature metaphors to speak of Europe's ailments and—if the poem is read as a personal statement—concludes that it is best to be gone to China:

> Tell me again about Europe and her pains,
> Who's tortured by the drought, who by the rains.
> Glut me with floods where only the swine can row
> Who cuts his throat and let him count his gains.
> It seemed the best thing to be up and go.
>
> A bedshift flight to a Far Eastern sky.
> Only the same war on a stronger toe.
> The heart of standing is you cannot fly.
>
> (1955, 49)

In contrast, in 1937 MacNeice is willing to try to stand in the moral center of the decade's disasters. MacNeice's "The sunlight on the garden" does not consider escape an option:

> When all is told
> We cannot beg for pardon.
>
> Our freedom as free lances
> Advances towards its end . . .
> And soon, my friend,
> We shall have no time for dances.
>
> (1967, 84)

Poems Empson wrote during the Spanish civil war years display unusual forms of alienation from the historical drama at hand. "Ignorance of Death," which addresses the very important issue of the decade's infatuation with dying, includes the lines:

> The Communists however disapprove of death
> Except when practical. The people who dig up
> Corpses and rape them are I understand not reported.

Empson brings up difficult subject matter, shows himself to be less than a communist convert, and lets his reader draw her or his own conclusions. The poem ends, however, with the incongruous comment that death is a subject "that most people should be prepared to be blank upon" (1955, 58–59).

Empson's abstention from the Auden group's beliefs was a willed act, and his historical awareness, it turns out, was quite acute. Much as MacNeice's "Bagpipe Music" is an indictment of the bourgeoisie's worn-out pleasures and coping mechanisms, Empson's "Just a Smack at Auden" (1938) is an account of the Auden group's failures. "Bagpipe Music"'s ironic barbs are directed at a whole class of Englishmen:

> It's no go the merrygoround, it's no go the rickshaw,
> All we want is a limousine and a ticket for the peepshow.
>
> It's no go the Yogi-Man, it's no go Blavatsky,
> All we want is a bank balance and a bit of skirt in a taxi.
>
> It's no go my honey love, it's no go my poppet;
> Work your hands from day to day, the winds will blow the profit.
> (1959, 61–62)

"Just a Smack at Auden," in contrast, has a more poet-directed and ominous vision:

> It has all been filed, boys, history has a trend.
> Each of us enisled, boys, waiting for the end.
>
> What was said by Marx, boys, what did he perpend?
> No good being sparks, boys, waiting for the end.
> Treason of the clerks, boys, curtains that descend.
> Lights becoming darks, boys, waiting for the end.
> (1955, 63)

While he may have "missed out" on their quest, Empson's jibes show he understood it quite well: the association of history with success, for example, was a mistake; Auden's later admission of his guilt as a treasonous clerk is foreshadowed; and "lights becoming darks" suggests that Empson is as aware as MacNeice of the arbitrariness and tenuousness of the decade's ideologically structuring binarisms. The difference between the poets in these two poems is that MacNeice includes himself in the group being indicted for its excesses and failures, while Empson stands above the object of his attack. "Autumn on Nan-Yueh" (1940) is a belated and generally uncharacteristic attempt at plain talk about the previous decade. Empson reduces the issues to a metaphor about useless language:

> Besides, I do not really like
> The verse about "Up the Boys,"
> The revolutionary romp,
> The hearty uproar that deploys
> A sit-down literary strike. . . .
> But all conventions have their pomp
> And all styles can come down to noise.

He goes on to suggest that while politics is a proper subject of poetry, he questions whether it does "much good" to address the issue by such a means. He hints strongly that the appeal of the "Red argument" lies in the shared desire that "the whole system should not stall" (1955, 76–78). This is the kind of comment that MacNeice might have made—that the 1930s' infatuation with communism was ironically a desire by many to maintain bourgeois society in its current form.

Why were Empson and MacNeice treated so differently? One answer is that they came from different universities, wrote different types of poetry, and attracted different critics. By publishing little poetry during the 1930s and by displaying relatively little angst about social problems in his poems, Empson clearly set himself up for less criticism of a social nature. A more problematic answer to this marked difference in critical reception is that critics sometimes participate in coteries much the way writers do and that these two poets attracted different groups of critics. It is certainly relevant to this question that MacNeice revealed the flaws of the 1930s' belief systems of choice, while Empson did not. MacNeice is thus more traitor than supporter of the decade's central myths. By pointing out the excessive, forced effort to believe in sometimes flawed binarisms and dogma, he threatens those who subscribe to these myths. Maxwell's (1969) comments, for example, suggest this sort of frustration: "MacNeice's poem 'To a Communist' testifies to his unregeneracy. After some ironical praise of the beautifully methodising power of marxism it repudiates the philosophy because its symmetry depends on abstractions" (178). By being a member of MacSpaunday, MacNeice's betrayals of the prevailing faith are impossible to ignore. He attracts the scorn of critics supportive of the Auden group's political choices.

On the other hand, it is possible and even easy to consider Empson's

poetry outside the context of the 1930s. Those looking for historical set-
tings for it are likely to choose either the university-based Empsonian
revival of the 1950s or the debate over how Empson fits into the establishment of New Criticism (see, for example, Norris 1978). Hugh Kenner's
identification of Empson's poetry as belonging to its period is something
of a rarity: "The poetry and the criticism alike are the products of a single,
disciplined, but *'period,' sensibility for which anything may mean anything
because nothing has ontological meaning;* and endless logical constructions
are the sum of all human activity."[27] The reference to the thirties, here
quoted in Frank Day's (1984) *Sir William Empson: An Annotated Bibliography,* is immediately corrected by Day: "One might quarrel with 'period'
perhaps" (xxii). The general failure to use the same sorts of criteria to
evaluate both 1930s poets illustrates the sort of inconsistency that arises
from criticism heavily based on context—in this case, Cambridge versus Oxford, independent versus MacSpaunday. The political judgments of
critics are very much a function of their expectations of a writer.

Auden's fate with critics presents a somewhat different case. Structured by
the division between those who believed in the utopian myth of the 1930s
and those who rejected Auden's early political discourse, its changeable
course reflects the degree to which critical orientations, personal values,
and political context affect evaluations of literary work. Malcolm Cowley
(1934) writes that neither Auden nor Spender "has yet written a long poem
that belongs with the English classics, even with those of the second rank"
(189). Auden is criticized for "damnable and perverse obscurity" and for
writing poetry with "the irresponsible savagery of the Dada Manifesto"
(Cowley 1934, 190). He is a beast that needs taming.

Across the Atlantic, however, American critics are eagerly awaiting
someone who will redeem the "embarrassing and pathetic" state of English
poetry. John Finch goes on to reveal how value, once created, can be passed
almost unquestioned from one critic to the next and even from country to
country. Referring to the 1930s poets, he calls Spender and Auden "probably the most important members of this group. *At any rate, they are the
first whose work has reached the American audience.*"[28] Finch (1935) is typical of 1930s critics who value most highly the quest for belief. He calls
Spender's work "remarkably finished and mature" and identifies its subject
matter as the selection of personal values in a skeptical era. "The poems,"
he writes, "are records of the process by which [this faith] was reached. . . .
In other words, the lyrical process" (121–22). American critics aware of

Auden's political caginess seem to want him to be communist: "Auden, too, should probably be enrolled under the Communist banner . . . [though] he has seldom written what could by any stretch of the imagination be regarded as direct proclamations of Communism" (Flint 1938, 514).

Though Auden had harsh critics during the 1930s, he was highly respected. A new note is sounded in the 1940s: the hope for English poetry has suddenly become sloppy and immature. His innovations are now seen as clichés and, according to Scarfe (1942), he exhibits "the cheapness, the jazz, the slang, the easy thrills, the disrespect and slovenliness of a muddled age" (11). F. R. Leavis (1943) writes that Auden is still "at an embarrassing stage of immaturity" (212–15). Randall Jarrell's (1941) apology for Auden's political interests of the 1930s consists mainly of denying that Auden had these interests. "There is hardly more politics in early Auden than in G. A. Henty; what one gets is mostly religion, hero-worship, and Adventure, combined with the odd Lawrence-Nazi folk-mysticism" (331).

During the 1950s and 1960s, critics line up on both sides of the Auden myth. Morton Seif (1954) writes that "Auden has always been profoundly social," involved in issues of the artist's responsibility (64). Cleanth Brooks (1964) agrees: the early Auden is "pre-eminently the poet of civilization" working "to help reestablish the just society" (173). Justin Replogle (1965), in contrast, rationalizes Auden's Marxist tendencies by correctly observing that "in the 1930's merely to be young, socially conscious, and outspoken was enough to mark one as a Marxist, or at least a 'leftist,' and Auden was all these things" (584). Replogle's project is to determine whether the labeling of Auden as a Marxist is reasonable or not, and to this end he counts the "Marxist" poems in Auden's work. In 1933, he finds one Marxist poem; in 1934–36, none; in 1937, only "Spain," with its "freedom-necessity-choice" argument, is clearly Marxist; in 1938 and 1939, there is no Marxist content, "not even dribbles."

Replogle's Marxism-counting exercise illustrates the problem of finding the political content of Auden's poems. Is parable enough? Certainly our vastly changed social context permits us to see less Marxist content in Auden's work than period critics did. Replogle's (1965) quantitative study is important primarily as a proof of how hard it is to escape the influence of the moment in which we read a text (590–94). For Replogle (1964), Auden actually was a Marxist. Of the post-1930s changes in Auden, he writes, "The change of meaning is tremendous; Auden had changed from a Marxist empiricist to a Christian existentialist" (148). Marxism thus takes on a circumscribed, contextual meaning.

By 1968, critics are ready to address directly the question of the critical revision of "Auden." Robert Bloom (1968) sets out the opposing camps:

> Unlike Yeats's critics . . . Auden's have until very recently almost universally disapproved of his development, seeing in it, most often, evidence of a poetic decline induced by the unfortunate encroachment of religious ideas or by the passage of time. The exceptions occur primarily in recent work by Frederick P. W. McDowell, Justin Replogle, Monroe K. Spears, G. S. Fraser, John G. Blair, and George T. Wright. (443)

This said, Bloom gets down to his own plug for the post-1930s valuing of Auden: the poems of the 1940s show a "humanization" of his style that make them superior to the earlier work. Bloom rebuts the majority opinion that Auden's poetry "declines steadily" after "the brilliant, compelling achievements of the early thirties" by arguing that the idea of decline "is based on a tendency to overvalue the poetry of the early thirties." And this overvaluing is in turn based upon "extraliterary" issues, namely that Auden was taken to be the "real or assumed spokesman of the left" at a time when the Left was sorely needed (1968, 449). Bloom would have us believe that most value created by critics is not and should not be a product of extraliterary or contextual concerns. The premise that the nondiscursive does not affect the discursive is one of the most problematic aspects of criticism's myth of its own objectivity. I would argue that there is no criticism that resists the ideological pressures of its moment.

The crisis of belief and values was so threatening to the literary profession that the period between the world wars witnessed a series of attempts to institutionalize literary meaning. In the years immediately following World War I, university scholarships were offered in English literature for the first time and important bibliographies and professional organizations were established. I. A. Richards's New Criticism helped reinforce the critic as the ultimate arbiter of meaning:[29]

> The expert in matters of taste is in an awkward position when he differs from the majority. He is forced to say in effect, "I am better than you. My taste is more refined, my nature more cultured, you will do well to become more like me than you are." It is not his fault that he has to be so arrogant. He may, and usually does, disguise the fact as far as possible. (Richards n.d., 36–37)

Bové (1986) writes that Richards "appears at precisely the historical moment when academic criticism is struggling to be born; in a sense, if

Richards had not existed, the university system and the culture that supports it would have been forced to invent him" (40). Certainly Richards's method helps the literary professional recover authority lost in the aftermath of World War I by placing criticism in contexts that still have authority: science and the university.

If Richards's ideal critic helps determine the objective meaning of literary discourse, Leavis's seeks to influence in a positive direction the moral development of writers' work. Leavis accuses Auden of stunted growth, a failure to mature as he should have, justifying his view by pointing out that several critics have argued the same thing in *Scrutiny*. He thereby illustrates the tendency of critics to locate value in the consensus view of a given time and place (1960, 227). What bothers him most is that Auden rocketed to international fame so quickly. The blame, he says, belongs to critics for not having managed Auden well enough:

> Greater gifts than Auden's might have lost, in such a success, their chance of coming to anything. His misfortune, in fact, brings vividly before us the conditions that, in our time, work against the maturation and development of any young talent. They may be seen, simply, as the failure of the function of criticism. (1960, 229)

The complaint, then, is that Auden was accorded too much fame before he had complied with the consecrated literary culture's standards of poetic maturity. MacNeice's reception, in turn, illustrates how membership in a discursive group affects critical treatments of individual poets. Leavis (1960) complains that "a coterie naturally protects itself and its members, as far as it can, from the severities of criticism: where the whole literary world . . . falls virtually under the control of something in the nature of a coterie, then the conditions for the development of creative talents are very bad indeed" (230). Referring to the Auden group, this comment suggests a power struggle between critic and writer. Leavis does not want critics to be prevented by writers from performing their duties as molders of talent.

Even a cursory review of the body of early Auden criticism reveals an unmistakable map of the changing values of the 1930s. In fact, these contextual criticisms closely parallel the changing concerns and language of the Auden group itself. Early reviews of *Poems* (1930) address aesthetic issues only. In reviews of *The Orators* (1932), terms such as "revolutionary" begin to appear, but they lack real political content. A. C. Brock finds Auden plainly contemptuous of society, Michael Roberts talks about public school, and Hugh G. Porteus is still wrapped up in aesthetic concerns, especially Auden's fetish of originality (see Haffenden 1983, 99, 109, 119). When *The Dance of Death* appears at the end of 1933, Day Lewis is ready to use his position as reviewer of Auden's work to preach from his own political soapbox: the brief age of propaganda has begun. When *Poems* becomes available in the United States in 1934, critics there are able to detect political content that English critics absolutely did not find four years earlier. Later in the decade, as binary polarization increases, critics are more likely to appropriate the aspects of Auden that speak best to their concerns. Leavis, in *Scrutiny,* sticks to purely aesthetic issues, while Edmund Wilson and Day Lewis discuss Auden's moral views and politics. The left shows itself willing to use Auden as a piece of propaganda in his own right. At the height of the Spanish civil war, the *Daily Worker* prints the following untruth: "The progress made by Auden . . . is due almost entirely to the fact that [he has] been in contact with a mass struggle."[30] In the 1940s, as we have seen, the vocabulary is different again. Malcolm Cowley's comments on *The Double Man* (1941) reflect both the changes in Auden's works and the changing values of critics: "In the first place, [*The Double Man*'s] subject is moral rather than political. All during the 1930's, poets were preoccupied with the possibility of social changes, but Auden wants to begin by changing the inner world."[31]

Auden clearly did want to revise his choices during the 1930s. But if Spender had for a time been an openly committed leftist who remained a closet individualist, Auden was a closet leftist who believed in the cause more than he cared to admit. When his cause failed, Auden sought to erase the traces of his evolution in belief. In this, he resembles the later Borges trying to rehistoricize his early years. "He produced at the end of [World War II] a volume of *Collected Poems* in which the poems were arranged according to the alphabetical order of the first letter of the first line of each poem. In this way all trace of development from poem to poem was suppressed" (see Spender 1953b, 259).

Years later, Auden suggested that his interest in Marxism was more psychological than political. Further, he writes in the middle of the McCarthy era in the United States: "We were interested in Marx in the same way that we were interested in Freud, as a technique of unmasking middle-class ideologies, not with the intention of repudiating our class, but with the hope of becoming better bourgeois."[32] While this statement may be true, it ignores Auden's strong concern in the 1930s that fascism be defeated in Europe and his many early comments that the bourgeoisie was a dying class.

As Edward Mendelson points out, most critics have strongly disapproved of Auden's abundant revisions of early poems.

> Critics who find the changes deplorable generally argue, in effect, that a poet loses his right to revise or reject his work after he publishes it — as if the skill with which he brought his poems from their early drafts to the point of publication somehow left him at the moment they appeared, making him a trespasser on his own work thereafter.[33]

Mendelson argues that this is because Auden has violated the commonly held "romantic" notion that there is an organicism to poetic form that should not be tampered with after a poem has been written (or, where critics are concerned, published). We should recall the many liberties Mendelson took in editing poems for *The English Auden*. Mendelson concludes that in Auden's revisions, "Auden was systematically rejecting a whole range of modernist assumptions about poetic form, the nature of poetic language, and the effects of poetry on its audience."[34]

While there may be significant truth to Mendelson's conclusion, it places the blame for the controversy over Auden's right to revise his own work on the poet. Another way to read Mendelson's comments is to see in them the critic's proprietary relationship to literary works. What we have here is essentially a battle over custody: Whose property is a poetic text once it is published? Mendelson suggests that for many critics it becomes part of the public domain. Clearly, though, that is often taken to mean the property of critics who have invested their energies in the creation of a text's value. Changing the text disrupts the evaluation process and wrests power over a text away from the critic. If anything, Auden — like Borges — is a traitor to the unwritten contract that exists between writers and critics. Both of these poet-critics did much to disrupt the status quo power relationships of the profession. Ironically, this disruption may have been their most truly avant-garde choice in the context of two traditional careers.

The French Surrealists

"The lyric work is always a subjective expression of a social antagonism."
—Theodor W. Adorno

Celui qui croit écrire pour détruire tous les livres écrit encore pour être lu.
—Gaëtan Picon

8. The Surrealists' Search for Authenticity and Independence

The breaking down of basic mental structures, central to surrealism's project of freeing people from the shackles of reason, hinges on the dismantling of "binary logic" or dichotomous thinking. Mary Ann Caws (1970) argues that "surrealism is based on a permanent movement of unification, in which the distance between the perceiver and the perceived, reality and the imagined, the abstract and the concrete, thought and the illogical image is drastically reduced and even, under ideal conditions, suppressed altogether" (204; translations of all excerpts from this work are Caws's). But surrealism's quest—especially insofar as it retains its Dadaist roots—also includes a much more radical attempt to detach art from its role as a commodity in bourgeois culture. In contrast, the Argentine vanguardia is more nearly pre-bourgeois; it sees the market expanding and catering more to the working classes, and it seeks to impede the progress of this trend.

Modernist art, Terry Eagleton suggests, looks for a way out of art's habit of compromising itself in ways that force it to give up both aesthetic and political independence. Eagleton (1990) pursues a line of thought similar to that of Peter Bürger, arguing that the only free art is art that implicitly or explicitly criticizes its own mechanisms of production.

Art can only hope to be valid if it provides an implicit critique of the conditions which produce it—a validation which, in evoking art's privileged remoteness from such conditions, instantly invalidates itself.

Conversely, art can only be authentic if it silently acknowledges how deeply it is compromised by what it opposes; but to press this logic too far is precisely to undermine its authenticity. (349)

This is the paradox of which all true avant-garde movements are aware. Eagleton sees the avant-garde as having two choices about what to do about the paradox, a positive and a negative moment. The avant-garde sometimes chooses both paths by pursuing one and then the other. In its negative moment, the avant-garde attempts to destroy conventional meaning, either by deforming known artistic conventions, making art out of garbage or other cultural refuse, or making a point of not leaving any lasting artifacts. Eagleton (1990) explains this anti-aesthetic aesthetic: "The problem of art is art itself, so let's have an art which isn't art. Down with libraries and museums, paint your pictures on people's pajamas, read your poetry through megaphones in factory yards" (370).

The problem with this—as the future surrealists discovered during the heyday of Dadaism—is that it doesn't produce either good art or an effective critique of art's compromised conditions of production. Left with "anti-art" or art that "isn't art at all," this avant-garde still finds itself grappling with issues of form and with the need to continue to resist institutionalization and the routinization of its artistic gestures.

The plasticity of modern society allows Western cultures to absorb significant amounts of intentional deviance and normalize them—which is why Dada was constantly on the move, searching for new ways to *épater les bourgeois,* and why, ultimately, it ran out of ideas. In its positive moment, in contrast, the avant-garde pursues less radical forms of resistance and is sometimes willing to admit that it is nearly impossible to prevent bourgeois culture from appropriating its artistic products. The Auden poets were quite open about their enthusiastic relationship to the literary market and their role in creating what they hoped soon to make available as a product. While Eagleton's theory is more elastic than some, it is still largely Eurocentric in its focus. In *The Ideology of the Aesthetic,* he discusses avant-garde art as a general category although his focus, as even a quick look at the index shows, is nearly exclusively on European (and occasionally North American) writers and thinkers. Though Girondo's work can be described as belonging alternately to Eagleton's negative and positive moments, Borges and most of the other members of the *vanguardia* (Jacobo Fijman excepted) fit neither model.

André Breton had the insight to understand that art tends to reproduce

what it resists. His and his fellow surrealists' famous solution to the problem was to attempt to avoid institutionally embedded modes of thought
by freeing the mind's deeper resources and structures through automatic
writing. The conceptual framework for this practice, however, was not
anarchic; by the late 1920s, Breton realized that artists must consciously
work against their indoctrination. In an attempt to dismantle habits of binary logic, he emphasized in the *Manifeste du surréalisme,* surrealism must
explore the conceptual and imagistic space between two very different objects, images, or ideas. Surrealism's binary paradox was made all the more
complicated, however, by the movement's commitment to the impossible
goal of separating itself from the context from which it sprang. Surrealism sought simultaneously to arise ex nihilo and to alter known modes of
thought and artistic form.

What the movement largely accomplished was to separate its politics
from its poetry. The Communist Party's stance shows why this was necessary; one French party official told Breton, "Si vous êtes Marxiste, vous
n'avez pas besoin d'être surréaliste" (qtd. in Browder 1967, 26). (If you are
a Marxist, you don't need to be a surrealist.) It is important to remember
that Breton purged fellow poets from the movement for all sorts of behavior—including for publishing in mainstream journals—but never for the
contents of a poem. Even Aragon's overtly communist "Front rouge" (Red
Front) proved worthy of Breton's defense. What he could not tolerate,
however, was disloyalty in the realm of politics: poets should not sign their
freedom away to the Communist Party, nor should they publish in journals Breton deemed ideologically offensive. He separated issues of poetic
integrity and independence from his standards for political discourse and
behavior, tolerating a range of expression in the former that he would not
tolerate in the latter. Poetry must not become corrupted, though Breton
revealed a willingness to let surrealism be politically inconsistent in its
search for a viable ideology. This inconsistency of political ideology is re-
played countless times in surrealist documents. In "La révolution d'abord
et toujours" (The revolution in the beginning and forever after), for example, the poets proclaim their "absolute detachment" from the ideas and
history of Western civilization, yet support Lenin and oppose both the
Moroccan War and France's existence as a nation.[1]

Surrealism's goal of collapsing the binarisms that structure Western
thought comes to fruition in its associative and metaphorical poetry, in
which there is no *overt* gesture of protest against such thought or against
the bourgeois constraints on art. Unlike the work of the Auden poets, this

poetry makes its point by showing (or, rather, by *being* the thing it admires) rather than by telling or giving way to a didactic impulse. Because of this, the poetry is largely successful. Eagleton (1990), however, argues that such success has problematic side effects:

> The more the work of art seeks to liberate itself from external determinations, the more it becomes subject to self-positing principles of organization, which mime and internalize the law of an administered society. Ironically, the "purity" of the modernist work's form is borrowed from the technical, functional forms of a rationalized social order. (351)

Maurice Nadeau (1989) argues that the crisis of 1929, in which the surrealists publicly divided into factions over whether to privilege politics or aesthetics, resulted from an excess of group interaction and an uncomfortable amount of pressure to conform to a group norm: "After having exhausted the joys of automatic writing and dream narratives, they felt they possessed creative forces which the atmosphere of the group prevented them from releasing. Let us venture the word: they no longer felt *free*" (165). The late 1920s surrealist goal of combining materialist politics with an aesthetics of freedom appears now to have been an impossible goal. Ironically, by appropriating some of the behavior of fascist leaders and borrowing repressive tactics from the Communist Party, Breton came dangerously close to imitating some of the more extreme political behavior of his age.

It is not in the *poetry* that this repression occurs; rather, it occurs in every other discursive realm in which the surrealists participate: critical essays, manifestos, internal communications, and so forth. The poetry exists without obvious agenda, yet in its stream of linguistic and conceptual surprises, it alters our conception of the lyric poem and detaches poetic speech from mimetic referentiality. Insofar as art indulges in what Eagleton calls an "irate polemic," it tends to become time-bound and of interest primarily as historical artifact. Breton wisely uses his *Manifestes* and critical essays as the place to rail against the tides of history. Creating a bifurcation between politicized prose and largely apolitical poetry was to row against the tide of these highly politicized interwar years and to make a strong statement about what poetry should be.

In Dadaism's pre-surrealist heyday, nothing could have been further from the agenda than solving political problems. Critics have argued that the term "Dada" is a sort of baby talk, pure sound that delights because it signifies almost nothing. Tristan Tzara's "Dadaist Disgust" manifesto defines the movement in part as "protest by fists with all one's might in taking destructive action" (Lewis 1988, 4–5). And in the May 1920 issue of the ironically titled journal *Littérature,* Breton writes, "Naturally, we cannot believe in any possibility of ameliorating social conditions."[2] Unlike the Argentines, who were largely unaffected by World War I, and unlike the Auden poets, who regretted having been born too late to be men of action, many of the generation of young men from which Aragon and Breton came were injured or killed during World War I.

> [Aragon's] friend, Paul Eluard, had been gassed; Philippe Soupault had also been invalided out of the Army; while André Breton, as a medical student, had worked in the bedlam of hospitals for the shell-shocked and crazed soldiers. Meeting together at the end of the war, these young men of letters found that they had in common an overwhelming sense of revulsion against the "culture" of their country and their time. (Josephson 1962, 111–12)

The physical and emotional horrors of war and the feeling that there were no worthwhile values to cling to inspired these poets to make war against culture. An early Dada manifesto expresses this revulsion: "Let each man proclaim: there is a great negative work of destruction to be accomplished. We must sweep everything away and sweep clean" (Josephson 1962, 112). Had they been born at another time, the surrealists might have been middle-class doctors with middle-class tastes. As it was, they were university-educated, science-oriented young men who rejected not just medical careers but careerism in general.

The notion of exclusive group affiliation—one was not a Dadaist and a surrealist at the same time—is a trait of the avant-garde. It is difficult, however, to point to an event that marks the beginning of a group. Is it when its name goes into circulation? When the first statement of purpose is published? In the case of surrealism, there is a significant gap between the two events. The fact that critics and the poets themselves don't agree on dates or significant events supports the idea that the histories of groups may be, in part at least, strategically constructed to serve certain ends. Aragon claims he and Breton were Dadaists from January 1920 until sometime in 1921, though he says surrealism developed in the spring of 1919. Many critics link the beginning of surrealism to the *Manifeste du surréalisme,* which appeared in 1924.[3] English surrealist critic David Gascoyne, however, dates

French surrealism to November 1922, when Breton defined the word "surrealism" in the journal *Littérature.* Poets, too, construct their discursive selves with care. Breton (1988) for example, appears to have arranged for his book of poems, *Claire de terre,* to appear at the same time as *Les pas perdus* (1924) so that he would not appear to be primarily an essayist (1181).

Literary historians quick to adopt the avant-garde's binary habits have tended to see Dadaism and surrealism either as a continuous development or as opposites: those in the second camp often view Dadaism as nihilistic and surrealism as a constructive movement. Alexandrian, however, argues for the continuity theory on the grounds that Breton uses the word surrealist in his early manifesto "Pour Dada" and that he outlines its method before becoming involved in the movement. Poggioli (1968) concurs: "Avant-garde nihilism was not exhausted in dadaism. . . . The tendency . . . passed . . . , almost intact, to surrealism" (63). Breton claims that surrealism's "intuitive period" spanned 1919–25, a period that includes Dadaism. Alexandrian (1971) is willing to accept these dates: "Dada à Paris, ce n'est plus Dada, c'est le début du surréalisme" (24). (Dada in Paris is no longer Dada, it's the beginning of surrealism.) Though he claims that Dadaism is a state of mind, not a movement, Breton (1988) variously dates the end of Dadaism to May 1921 and early 1922 (260, 816). At stake in this debate is intellectual property, an issue Dadaists claimed to have no relationship to, given that they were all "presidents" of Dada. In an article appropriately titled "Après dada" (After Dada), however, Breton (1988) takes credit for the movement away from Tristan Tzara: "M. Tzara n'est pour rien dans l'invention du mot 'Dada' . . . [et] il est sans doute pour très peu dans la rédaction du *Manifeste dada 1918*" (259). (Mr. Tzara had no part in the invention of the word "Dada" . . . and there's no question that he had very little part in the composition of the *Dada Manifesto of 1918.*)

Interested in acquiring the power that comes from creating a literary movement, the Dadaists implemented carefully planned strategies to find a large audience and to force the consecrated literary establishment to notice them. The publishing of the manifesto "Pour Dada" (For Dada) in the *Nouvelle Revue Française,* for example, is remarkably similar to Borges's choosing to publish his manifesto on ultraism in the elite journal *Nosotros.* The appeal of Dadaism, as Breton later explained, was to stir up polemics and to get the public's attention.

Je me borne à rappeler en quelques mots quelle était en 1919 la situation des poètes français par rapport au public: journellement des vers de

Guillaume Apollinaire, de Blaise Cendrars, de Pierre Reverdy, de Louis Aragon, de Philippe Soupault et de moi-même étaient lus dans une salle quelconque. . . . L'ennui profond que se dégageait de ces séances . . . enfin l'impossibilité d'atteindre autre chose que le public désoeuvré des cinq à sept littéraires nous disposèrent à accueillir favorablement Dada qui, lui, promettait de vives polémiques et de grandes assemblées.[4]

(I'll limit myself to recalling in a few words the relationship in 1919 of French poets to their audience: every day verses of Guillaume Apollinaire, Blaise Cendrars, Pierre Reverdy, Louis Aragon, Philippe Soupault, and of mine were read in some room somewhere. . . . The deep boredom that came out of these sessions . . . the impossibility of achieving anything other than a listless audience for five to seven literary types disposed us to welcome Dada, which promised lively polemics and large gatherings.)

In December 1920, Breton, Aragon, and others decided to ban poetry from *Littérature* because it too closely resembled "literature" (see Somville 1971, 180). "Literature" became a synonym for the work of the professional *littérateur* who gave in to market pressures and the requirements for consecration. Another explanation of how "literature" came to be a dirty word can be found in the pre–World War I "quarrel" of the banks of the Seine. The Right Bank stood for tradition and was exemplified by the Académie Française. The Left Bank, predictably, stood for youth and rebelled against "literature."

The Dadaists' ambivalence about famous authors may be a reaction to their own early choices. The first issue of *Littérature*, for example, had work by André Gide, Paul Valéry, and Jean Paulhan. Only toward the end of the issue did the work of Breton and Aragon appear. Early issues, which included the work of authors already dead, were anthological. This suggests that *Littérature* was a journal in search of an avant-garde project and that, lacking that project, it had turned to consecrated methods in an effort to build credibility and readership.[5] Ambivalent about how to relate to famous writers, the Dadaist-surrealists evaluated themselves and consecrated authors with a scale from –25 (greatest aversion) to +20, with 0 representing "absolute indifference." Authors evaluated included Claudel, Baudelaire, Aragon, Breton, Apollinaire, Paul Fort, Max Jacob, Reverdy, and Francis Picabia. Baudelaire and Apollinaire received approving marks from Aragon and Breton and predictably low marks from Dadaist Tzara. The contrast between the future surrealist and current Dadaist leaders shows that Aragon and Breton were already breaking away from Dada's negativism. Breton also engaged in an exercise quite similar to Auden's and Day Lewis's ranking of authors they had surpassed, would surpass, and could never hope to surpass. Answering the survey question in *Le Figaro*, "Quels mouvements principaux distinguez-vous dans la jeune poésie française?" (What are the main movements you see in young French poetry?), Breton (1988) shows himself to be at least as immodest as his young English counterparts:

> 1. Tous les artisans de plume sans distinction. 2. Ceux de nos jeunes poètes qui . . . sont en train de rentrer dans la catégorie précédente. . . . 3. Ceux du sort de qui je ne désespère pas encore complètement: trois ou quatre, en m'y comprenant. (268)

> 1. All of the artisans of the pen without distinction. 2. All of our young poets who . . . are in the process of joining the preceding category. . . . 3. Those of whom I don't completely despair: three or four, including myself.

Though the surrealists are less charitable toward literary predecessors and more inclined to locate their competition in living poets than are the Auden poets, they betray a preoccupation with status and hierarchy they claim not to feel. All three groups admire certain near ancestors. The three present a spectrum of accommodation of the past: with few reservations, the Argentines embrace it and want to build on it; the Auden poets want to participate in it and outclass contemporary poets they perceive as their competitors; and the surrealists, though capable of admiring others, including Baudelaire and Apollinaire, prefer to repudiate the past. In general, however, their energies are not focused on the past; their interest is the present and the future.

In typical avant-garde fashion, the Parisian Dadaists begin by defining themselves through how they differ from others. "Le cubisme fut une école de peinture, le futurisme un mouvement politique: DADA est un état d'esprit. Opposer l'un à l'autre révèle l'ignorance ou la mauvaise foi." (Cubism was a school of painting, futurism a political movement: DADA is a state of mind. To compare one to the other reveals ignorance or bad faith.) That Poggioli's book engages in such an act of bad faith is something for which we should be grateful. Adding surrealism to the three,

Poggioli (1968) comments that these movements were "not only the showi-est but also the most successful of all" (146). Breton (1988) reinforces Dada's identity based on self-differentiation in the "Appel du 3 janvier 1922" (Appeal of 3 January 1922):

> Les signataires de cet article n'ont nullement l'intention, par-delà . . . d'écoles dont nous avons l'exemple en art avec l'impressionisme, le symbolisme, l'unanimisme, le fauvisme, le simultanéisme, le cubisme, l'orphisme, le futurisme, l'expressionisme, le purisme, Dada, etc., de travailler à la creation d'une nouvelle famille intellectuelle et de resserrer les liens que beaucoup jugeront illusoires. Nous n'entendons, en effet, former ni ligue ni parti. (434)

> (The signatories of this article have no intention, beyond . . . schools of which we have in art, for instance, impressionism, symbolism, unan-ism, fauvism, simultaneism, cubism, orphism, futurism, expressionism, purism, Dada, etc., of working toward creating a new intellectual family and of tightening bonds that many will judge illusory. We intend, in effect, to form neither an alliance nor a party.)

Most contradictory of all is the Dada manifesto's dictum that "Il est in-admissible qu'un homme laisse une trace de son passage sur la terre." (It is unacceptable that a man leave a mark of his passage on the earth.)[6] A manifesto is a discursive trace of the most indelible kind and this one is full of memorably strong language and rules of order. Dada rejects inter-pretation, self-control, morality, and taste. It thus rejects, theoretically at least, the critical apparatus that preserves texts by creating value through the exercise of taste and interpretation. Dada's platform is built on reject-ing social norms. In times of peace, writes Breton, Dada's agenda is "La guerre à tout prix" (War at any price) and vice versa. Dada also rejects the idea of attachment to things. Breton's poem "Lâchez tout" (Abandon everything) advises the reader to give up everything, including Dada.

> Lâchez tout.
> Lâchez Dada.
> Lâchez votre femme, lâchez votre maitresse.
> Lâchez vos espérances et vos craintes.
> Semez vos enfants au coin d'un bois.
> Lâchez au besoin une vie aisée. . . .
> Partez sur les routes.[7]

(Abandon everything.
Abandon Dada.
Abandon your wife, abandon your mistress.
Abandon your hopes and fears.
Sow your children in the corner of the woods.
Abandon if necessary the easy life. . . .
Take to the road.)

This call for the abandonment of conventional roles and mores contributed to Dada's appeal. But to whom is Breton appealing here? For how many people could "Lâchez Dada" have meant something? Breton, like the Auden poets, seems to be writing simultaneously for an inner circle and a larger audience. *Littérature,* for example, had about two hundred subscribers and during its second year printed approximately fifteen hundred copies of each issue (Breton 1988, xl).

Breton's early poetic raison d'être—like that of Auden and Spender—is very personal. Though he shares the Auden group's belief in poetry as a means of solving problems, he is not out to solve those of French society. In response to a survey question in *Littérature,* he writes, "La poésie n'aurait pour moi aucun intérêt si je ne m'attendais pas à ce qu'elle suggère à quelques-uns de mes amis et à moi-même une solution particulière du problème de notre vie" (1988, 267). (Poetry would hold no interest for me if I didn't expect it to suggest to some of my friends and to me a specific solution to the problem of our lives.) This statement is reminiscent of Michael Roberts's preface to *New Signatures.* Breton's attitude seems to have been common at this time. In response to a *Littérature* survey asking why poets write, Blaise Cendrars writes merely, "Parce que" (Because). Paul Valéry writes, "Par faiblesse" (Out of weakness), and Francis Picabia responds, "Je ne le sais vraiment pas et j'espère ne jamais le savoir" (I really don't know why and I hope never to know.)[8] In *Sept manifestes Dada* (Seven Dada manifestos), Tzara writes: "L'art est une chose privée, l'artiste le fait pour lui; une oeuvre compréhensible est produit de journaliste" (qtd. in Leonard 1974, 38–39). (Art is a private thing, the artist does it for himself; a work that is understandable is the product of a journalist.)

The Dadaist poets were, however, insistently public in their strategies. Presenting "spectacles" was one of the most important modes of disseminating the group's message and the "entertainment" often consisted of contradicting audience expectations at literary events by doing such things as reading "poems" consisting of a pastiche of randomly chosen newspaper fragments. The movement mocked the market-oriented audience by failing to deliver the goods as promised, sometimes taunting and insulting its audience. Dada's rebellion against the market took the form of adopting contemporary advertising techniques and then deforming them by placing misleading advertisements in the newspapers. An audience expecting to see Charlie Chaplin was instead subjected to a reading of Dada manifestos (see Browder 1967, 12). The surrealists, many of whom had been Dadaists, were quite similar to the Argentine avant-garde in the frequency of their self-historicizing gestures. Their market-oriented strategies and advertising tactics, however subversive, played a central role in helping consecrate the movement.

Sometimes they weren't subversive at all. *Littérature,* for example, devotes a full page to naming the twenty writers whose previously unpublished poetry and prose the journal printed in its first three issues. On occasion, Breton bypasses the rhetoric of advertising altogether and makes a direct plea for support. In "Les mots sans rides" (Words without wrinkles), for example, he writes, "Je prie le lecteur de s'en tenir provisoirement à ces premiers témoignages d'une activité qu'on ne soupçonnait pas encore. Nous sommes plusieurs à y attacher une importance extrême" (1988, 286). (I beg the reader provisionally to commit himself to these first proofs of an activity of which we earlier had no idea. Quite a few of us believe it to be extremely important.) Such a call for support is characteristic of the avant-garde, though it is most often phrased defensively, as a request to save a movement from its enemies.

Like the Auden poets, the surrealists were ambivalent about the author's role in society. They went farther, however, calling for the radical restructuring of the relationship between art and society. In 1925, Breton writes in *La révolution surréaliste* (The surrealist revolution),

N'est-ce pas nous . . . qui demandons les premiers, non la destruction des musées et des bibliothèques, mais—ce qui est plus grave—l'abolition des privilèges artistiques, scientifiques et autres et, pour commencer, la libération désintéressée, l'isolement de cette subtance mentale commune à tous les hommes, de cette substance souillée jusqu'ici par la raison?[9]

(Aren't we the ones . . . who are the first to demand, not the destruction of museums and libraries, but—and this is more serious—the abolition of artistic, scientific and other kinds of privilege, and, to start with, the disinterested liberation, the isolation of this mental substance all men share, this substance heretofore contaminated by reason?)

"Disinterested" is a word the Argentine poets use to describe their relationship to the literary market, but the freedom to be obtained here is of a more global nature: the freedom from the rational mind. In the journal's next issue, Breton's editorial "La dernière grève" (The last strike) undermines this call to abolish privilege by complaining about how poets and intellectuals are treated in French society. His defense of the right of poets to receive public subsidy is none other than the one advanced in the Argentine avant-garde journal *Martín Fierro,* which ascribes truth and value to the poets' work *because* the poets—in theory—cannot be influenced by the market or by questions of politics and professional status. Breton argues that

> l'insuffisance de repos et de salaire ne sont pas au monde les seules causes de mécontentement. . . . [E]n ce qui concerne *tous ceux qui poursuivent avec un complet désintéressement leur recherche* dans le domaine de la pensée, nous aurions . . . à régler avec la société un conflit autrement grave que celui qui met aux prises employeurs et employés.[10]

> (the inadequacy of leisure time and salary are not the only causes of discontent. . . . [A]s for what matters to *all those who pursue with utter disinterest their research* in the realm of thought, we have . . . to resolve with society a conflict as serious as that which pits employers and employees against one another.)

The suggestion that poets should be paid by society so they can continue to perform disinterested research echoes Michael Roberts's argument that the scholar or writer is a public servant acting in the service of knowledge. The surrealists did experiment with scholarship, opening in Paris in 1924 a "Bureau de Recherches Surréalistes" (Office of Surrealist Research), whose project was to create an archive of surrealist data that would collapse the division between waking life and dreams, subject and object, and reason and the unconscious. The public was invited to participate: "Toutes les personnes qui sont en mesure de contribuer . . . à la création de véritables archives surréalistes, *sont instamment priées* de se faire connaître." (All persons who are in a position to contribute . . . to the creation of true surrealist archives, *are requested instantly* to make themselves known.) [11]

Breton's *Manifeste du surréalisme* is both philosophical and personal. While avant-garde manifestos conventionally use the first-person plural to peddle their wares, Breton (1988) uses the first-person singular, lapsing into personal confession: "Le seul mot de liberté est tout ce qui m'exalte encore" (312). (Only the word liberty still thrills me.) His first gesture is to limit the audience to men: "L'homme, ce rêveur définitif . . . sait quelles femmes il a eues, dans quelles aventures risibles il a trempé." (Man, this definitive dreamer . . . knows which women he has had, in what laughable adventures he has plunged.) [12] He then sets up the central binarisms structuring surrealism: materialism is more poetic than realism, which is the hateful, mediocre mode of journalists; logic is opposed to the imagination; and "les fous" (the crazy) are freer than the sane. Unlike the Dada manifestos' destructive projects, surrealism's *Manifeste* advances a constructive agenda. Breton (1988) argues that dreams can help solve life's most basic problems. "Je crois à la résolution future de ces deux états, en apparence si contradictoires, que sont le rêve et la réalité, en une sorte de réalité absolue, de *surréalité*" (319). (I believe in the future resolution of these two states—in appearance so contradictory—dream and reality, in a sort of absolute reality, of *surreality*.)

Theoretically, surrealism is accessible to all people and will free both the individual and the community from the fetters of institutions and concepts created by the rational mind. Breton's democratic habits in practice, however, can be measured by his two lists of surrealism followers. One is eighteen names long, democratically presented in alphabetical order, while a shorter unalphabetized list names an insiders group Breton identifies as his friends. If Breton's vision of a radical revision of perception and experience were realized, it would amount to massive cultural revolution. But in the same document where he maps out the radically possible, he also pares the audience to that of his male peers, offering them, much as Borges did in his ultraism manifesto, instructions on how to practice a form of writing that by itself does not lead to revolution. He explains the technique of automatic writing and that it evolved from the "pensée parlée" (spoken thought) of the wounded and shell-shocked soldiers he worked with during World War I (1988, 332). Though Breton's attachment to the word "comme" ("like" or "as") in some instances makes surrealist similes less effective than ultraist metaphors, he seeks to collapse the distinction between two very unrelated objects. By extension, he hopes to dismantle the most fundamental binarisms structuring human consciousness and culture. It will take him only a few years to realize that his tools are grossly unequal to the task.

Near the end of the *Manifeste,* Breton (1988) claims that surrealism is characterized by "absolute nonconformity." The definition of a poem has been radically revised: "Il est même permis d'intituler POEME ce qu'on obtient par l'assemblage aussi gratuit que possible (*observons, si vous voulez, la syntaxe*) de titres et de fragments de titres découpés dans les journaux" (341; my emphasis). (It is even permissible to call POEM what one obtains by the most arbitrary combination (*observe, please, rules of syntax*) of titles and fragments of titles clipped from newspapers.) The new definition, however, reflects in miniature a problem that plagues the movement: dedicated to nonconformity, it nevertheless conforms to rules of discourse in essential ways. Not even modernist poetry consistently obeys the rules of syntax, yet Breton directs his followers to obey rules at odds with the unconscious he hopes to liberate.

That such guidelines are clearly directed at an audience of poets is made even clearer by the emphasis on the poetic image, whose value in Breton's eyes increases with the degree of arbitrariness or contrast involved in linking the tenor and vehicle of a metaphor or simile, surrealism's rhetorical figure of choice. In "Signe ascendant" (Ascending sign), Breton writes, "Il est bien entendu qu'auprès de [la métaphore et la comparaison] les autres 'figures' que persiste à énumérer la rhétorique sont totalement dépourvues d'intérêt. Seul le déclic analogique nous passionne. . . . Le mot le plus exaltant dont nous disposions est le mot 'comme', que ce mot soit prononcé ou tu" (qtd. in Briosi and Hillenaar 1988, 78). (It is well understood that next to [metaphor and simile] the other "figures" rhetoric insists on are totally uninteresting. Only the analogic click excites us. . . . The most exalted word we have is the word "like," whether articulated or not.)

Breton's 1924 *Manifeste* identifies him as the uncontested leader of surrealism though, as Anna Balakian puts it, he "made his declarations of theory at an age when he had written little and proved nothing."[13] Where the Auden poets begin by questioning the role of the poet in society, the surrealists question everything, including the nature of a poem. Restructuring the way people experience the difference between the real and the ideal, and between sleeping and dreams, is a revolutionary project. But while it stirred intellectual debate and inspired aesthetic innovation, it failed to change the world. As the work of Freud and Marx proves, discourse alone *can* change the reigning regime of cultural truth. Surrealism, however, did not put forward a compelling methodology that would in any immediate way alleviate social problems or change the role of reason in Western thought. Thus it has remained an aesthetic platform practiced by small groups in many countries over the last seventy years, but that has failed to revolutionize a single one of them.

The surrealists' chosen path to consecration was ultimately not very different from that walked by the Auden poets. Prolific writers, the poets published a plethora of theoretical, polemical, and poetic texts by the mid-1920s. They met regularly and reviewed one another's books, thus helping publicize them. Critics such as Browder (1967) have argued that theirs was a "spontaneous attraction" (18), but their group behavior was cult-like and their leader sometimes fascistic. Browder's characterization points to the tension between the purported naturalness of this attraction and the unnaturalness of the most basic requirements for group membership: "*Naturally* this intense communal experience *required* the presence of *all* at the *daily* gatherings" (18; my emphasis). The naturalness ends where the group begins; though the members shared a quest, the ideological agenda metamorphosed with Breton's changing ideas. In addition, Breton controlled members' behavior, demanded absolute loyalty, and purged those who failed to follow instructions. If Dada claims to have no hierarchy, surrealism is riddled with it.

Though Breton regretted his sometimes hasty judgments, he reiterates in the preface to the 1929 reprinting of the *Manifeste* that he will not sacrifice political goals for personal or sentimental "obstacles." His self-appointed role is that of judge and arbiter: "Je ne m'attarderai pas à juger ceux de mes premiers compagnons qui out pris peur et tourné bride" (1988, 402). (I will not hesitate to judge those of my early companions who have become fearful and turned back.) The language of this preface is clearly religious:

Je ne ferai qu'affirmer ma confiance inébranlable dans le principe d'une activité qui ne m'a jamais déçu, qui me paraît valoir plus généreusement, plus *absolument,* plus follement que jamais qu'on s'y *consacre* et cela parce qu'*elle seule est dispensatrice* . . . des *rayons transfigurants d'une grâce* que je persiste en tout point à opposer à *la grâce divine.* (1988, 402–3; my emphasis)

(I will only affirm my unshakeable confidence in the principles of an activity which has never disappointed me, which appears to me to merit more generously, more *absolutely,* more crazily than ever that one *devote* oneself to it because *it alone bestows* . . . the *transfiguring rays of a grace* which I insist on comparing in all ways to *divine grace.*)

The movement that repudiates church, state, and literature is character-ized not only by signs of secular scripture, but also by those of religious faith. The avant-garde group that appears to have undergone the most spontaneous and natural process of constituting itself turns out in many ways to be rigidly controlled, hierarchy-ridden, and cultlike.

The *Manifeste du surréalisme* conceives of a purely aesthetic movement. As the body of doctrine produced in these early years shows, with the beginning of the Moroccan War in 1925, politics played a progressively more important role in surrealist theory. The movement's early impulse toward internal democracy was abandoned. When there were 391 "presi-dents" of Dadaism, there were strong signs of consensus decision-making. In a "Procès-verbal" (Hearing) in 1920, a group of *Littérature*'s editors and contributors voted on such questions as whether a famous author's work should be included in each issue in order to help market the journal (yes), whether poetry should be published (no), and whether writers should compose as they wish to (no) or as they speak (yes).[14] A massive ranking by individual vote (on a scale of –25 to +20) of authors living and dead pub-licly exposed many Dadaists to evaluation by their peers.[15]

Indeed, political philosophies were identified during the heyday of Dadaism as being coequal. Pierre Drieu la Rochelle defined democracy, aristocracy, and monarchy with the same words: "Gouvernement des uns par les autres" (Government of some by the others).[16] By the end of the de-cade, the situation had changed. What plagued Breton (1969a) as surrealist group leader, he wrote in 1930, "was then, and still is today, a question of trying to maintain a platform flexible enough to cope with the changing aspects of the problems of life and at the same time remain stable enough to attest to the *nonrupture* of a certain number of mutual—and public—commitments made at the time of our youth" (115).

The problem of allowing for ideological change without destroying group cohesiveness led Breton to make a paradoxical set of choices: as surrealist doctrine became more flexible in its ability to encompass leftist revolutionary goals, Breton became increasingly authoritarian in his role as leader. The record of internal doctrinal changes shows an increasingly political search for a means of freeing the imagination from the bonds of logic and reason. Even early on, the natural process of letting one's un-conscious speak unrestrainedly contrasts with the restrictions placed on surrealism's adherents. The *Manifesto of Surrealism* states: "Surrealism does not allow those who devote themselves to it to forsake it whenever they like" (1969a, 35–36). Aragon (1926) hints ominously that successful practitioners of the surrealist "vice" will be persecuted by society much as drug traffickers are (81–82). Individual rights will be revoked and an "anarchic epidemic" will spread. There will be no more universities, families, armies, or careers. Like Auden and Spender, Breton and Aragon have overblown hopes for poetry's role in changing the world. Breton's methods reveal that artistic groups cannot successfully mimic political action groups. The Auden poets discover during the same period that the opposite tactic—remaking politics in the image of literary discourse—brings equally disappointing results.

The *Manifesto of Surrealism* contains a strongly worded doctrine of freedom, both in the unleashing of the unconscious in automatic composition and in the call for antisocial behavior. Breton attempts to define what is surrealist by making the concept wholly new, claiming that the term surrealism "had no currency before we came along" (Breton 1969a, 26). He makes himself an authority on recognizing the true surrealist:

> I would like to stress this point: they are not always Surrealists, in that I discern in each of them a certain number of preconceived ideas to which—very naively!—they hold. They hold to them because they had not *heard the Surrealist voice,* the one that continues to preach on the eve of death and above the storms. (1969a, 27)

In aesthetic terms, that voice is the demanding individual voice of an inner truth free of the constraints of reason. However, in a political and social sense, the voice to which Breton wants the poets to listen is his own. Breton's use of the pronoun "I" as *the* voice of the movement is typical even of the *Manifeste du surréalisme;* as the reactions of other surrealists show, this "I" usually *means* Breton. Unlike other avant-garde movements, surrealism was propelled less by the consensus of a group of friends with shared projects or by the efforts of editors, critics, and journals than by the passion of Breton. The "we" of the Argentine vanguardia and the Auden poets does not appear nearly so often as one would expect in a movement more committed to the life of the group than its English and Latin American counterparts.

Surrealism's liberation is selected for sex. In the first number of *La révolution surréaliste,* twenty-eight photos of surrealists surround the photo of a woman.[17] The caption reads: "La femme est l'être qui projette la plus grande ombre ou la plus grande lumière dans nos rêves."[18] (Woman is the being who projects the largest shadow or the greatest light into our dreams.) The journal's last number frames the intervening five years with a drawing of a naked woman ringed by photographs of well-dressed surrealists with their eyes closed. In "Le dialogue en 1928" (The dialogue in 1928), Breton (1988) replies to Benjamin Péret's question, "Qu'est-ce que le viol?" (What is rape?) with a misogynistic quip: "L'amour de la vitesse" (946) (Love on the run). And though women begin to enter the surrealist ranks during the 1930s, poetic images focusing on the appropriation of their bodies and body parts by men appear often in surrealist journals over the years. In "Recherches sur la sexualité" (Research on sexuality), based on an extensive question-answer group discussion, the surrealists are significantly more conservative and less tolerant in their sexual mores than the Auden poets.[19] Nadja, a woman Breton believed was a visionary and whom he claimed to love, was diagnosed as mentally ill and institutionalized while Breton knew her. The opening line of *Nadja,* the work that grew out of their relationship, is "qui suis-je?" (who am I?). This is the Breton "I," not the "I" of a woman whom Breton imaginatively inhabits. Such habitations were, surprisingly, more foreign to the surrealist mind than to the minds of many conventional novelists. *Nadja* epitomizes the surrealist use of the female as a vehicle for discovering male identity. The surrealists' treatment of women in their lives, in spite of the obvious idolatry, includes disrespect and overt misogyny. Both Elsa Triolet and Frida Kahlo felt badly treated, Nadja was abandoned to a fate of institutional misery, and Breton claimed he divorced Jacqueline Lamda because she wanted to become an artist (see Balakian 1971, 175–76).

In 1924, Breton states clearly that "nous ne devons garder aucun contrôle sur nous-mêmes. Il ne peut plus être question de ces dogmes: la morale et le goût."[20] (we should not exercise any control over ourselves. It cannot be a question of these dogmas: morality and taste.) Maurice Nadeau observes that the 1924 emphasis on "freedom" is replaced in the *Second manifeste* by a different goal, the provocation of a moral and intellectual "attack of conscience." A historicized measure of doctrinal change during the 1920s and 1930s can be seen in Nadeau's division of surrealist history into three periods. The highlights of the "heroic period," from 1923 to 1925, are automatism and trance states, while the Moroccan War ushers in the "analytical period," 1925–30. The crisis of 1929 provokes Breton to write the *Second manifeste* and Nadeau to inaugurate a third period, the "period of autonomy," from 1930 to 1939. Both manifestos emphasize surrealism's quest to achieve truth, beauty, and spontaneity.

As early as 1925, however, the tide is starting to turn from an aesthetics based on freedom to a specific set of political stances. Articles in *La révolution surréaliste* argue in support of working-class strikes, the opening of national prisons, and the legalization of drugs.[21] Breton takes the role of editor from Artaud, Naville, and Péret in 1925 because he wants the journal to have a more political orientation. Aragon reports that he himself was "politically very ignorant" in the early 1920s and that Breton was a strong influence on his becoming communist, not the other way around as is often believed (see Arban 1968, 42, 88). Soupault (1967) later wrote that Breton "convainquit Aragon et Eluard (mais pas moi) de prendre contact avec le group communiste et pseudo-marxiste de *Clarté*" (669–70) (convinced Aragon and Eluard [but not me] to get in touch with the communist and pseudo-marxist group associated with *Clarté*) and that once Breton had himself given up communism, Eluard's rejoining the Party during World War II "lui causa une peine profonde" (caused him deep pain). Breton's need for others to feel as he does when he does is certainly a blessing and a curse, creating strong group cohesiveness that at moments becomes so stifling as to cause members to rebel.

In May 1927, the surrealists called for an eight-hour workday, measures against unemployment, and protection against the militarization of the unions (Breton 1988, 940–41). In the *Second manifeste,* Breton sounds a strident note, claiming that surrealism "expects nothing save from violence" and from a platform of "total revolt" that calls for the destruction of "family, country, religion."[22] Another important index of doctrinal change is the 1929–30 shift in surrealist journals from *La revolution surréaliste* to *Le surréalisme au service de la révolution* (The surrealist revolution to Surrealism in the service of the revolution). An adjective has become a noun, and the goals of the revolution are now very different from the movement's aesthetics-based 1924 goals. The new journal opens with a response to a mock telegram from Moscow in which the surrealists pledge their support for the Soviet regime in the event of "imperialist" aggression. By 1935, however, surrealism is accused of having achieved official consecration. Léon Pierre-Quint argues in *La bête noire* (The aversion) that surrealism has "come into its own in the university" and that young people are no longer interested in it. By 1938, only one right-wing newspaper, *La croix* (The cross), continues to reject surrealism outright (Shattuck 1960, 9–10; Guiol-Benassaya 1982, 134).

In "The Political Position of Surrealism" (1935), socialism is for the first time presented as a fait accompli, not as a goal for the future. In this statement, Breton (1969a) argues immoderately: some intellectuals, he claims, have managed to "make a complete break" with their bourgeois origin; further, it is their duty to teach the proletariat how to achieve its own liberation (208). This is reminiscent of both the Argentine vanguardia's and the Auden group's tendency to patronize what they designate as the "proletariat." A common denominator of avant-garde groups of this period is elitism; whatever its philosophy, the avant-garde believes itself to be more enlightened than others. It is interesting that what it falls back on is not the wisdom of the poet, but the intelligence and right-thinking of the intellectual. In this sense, the interwar avant-garde groups are old-style liberals.

The evolution from idealism to materialism in "The Political Position of Surrealism" is accompanied by signs that surrealism is succumbing to the impulse to consecrate itself as a literary movement. In the "Appel du 3 janvier 1922" (Appeal of 3 January 1922), the surrealists insist they have nothing to do with any movement on the burgeoning list of "isms" and refuse to identify themselves as avant-garde or modernist. They state their goal simply: "Nous n'entendons, en effet, former ni ligue ni parti" (Breton 1988, 434). (We intend to form neither league nor party.) In "The Political Position of Surrealism," in contrast, there is a detailed complaint that Paul Claudel's *L'annonce faite à Marie* (Declaration made to Marie) has been labeled avant-garde and is being staged in the Soviet Union (Breton 1969a, 214). A reasonable inference is that the conservative Claudel's association with the revolutionary avant-garde is an invasion of surrealist turf. Breton's willingness to place surrealism in a context of historical materialism reaches its apogee in the 1946 preface to the *Second manifeste,* where he attributes the "violence of expression" in early surrealist attacks to the interwar period itself: "The blame for it must be placed squarely upon the period itself and also upon the formal influence of a good portion of revolutionary literature which allowed . . . a profusion of aggressive offshoots of mediocre importance" (1969a, 115).

During the years of doctrinal flux, Breton's strong role is institutionalized by the group itself and becomes one of the few constants of the movement. Absolute commitment to an agenda as yet undetermined is demanded in the "Intervention à la réunion du 23 janvier 1925" (Intervention in the meeting of 23 January 1925):

Rappelons que le surréalisme suppose, pour exister, une évolution particulière dont nous n'entrevoyons encore rien et dont il faut avant tout que nous soyons prêts à subir toutes les conséquences—conséquences morales, *participation éventuelle à une action très différente de la nôtre jusqu'ici, politique, sociale, religieuse, antireligieuse, n'importe.* (1988, 482; my emphasis)

(Remember that surrealism, in order to exist, is premised on a particular evolution, of which we as yet foresee nothing and for which we must absolutely be ready to experience all consequences—moral consequences, *possible participation in activities very different from what we've done up to now—political, social, religious, anti-religious, whatever.*)

Because Breton monitored closely all deviance from the movement's platform, this cultlike adherence proved a risky proposition for members who wanted to maintain personal independence. He is reputed to have instructed group members—who were often hard up financially—to avoid traditional careers and to marry rich women. Those who chose the most obvious employment for writers with their skills—journalism—were subject to criticism and sanction (Josephson 1962, 120). Matthew Josephson (1962) describes a "very close-knit communal life resembling that of some religious order, such as the Franciscans or, more nearly, the Jesuit societies. They would meet at regular intervals almost every day, at the same hour of the afternoon, at the same café." (119).

In spite of—and soon because of—this structural rigidity, however, nearly every year has its share of new members, reconciliations, quasi-separations, and permanent ruptures. There are so many comings and goings between 1922 and the beginning of World War II that Breton is one of the few important poets to remain a surrealist for the entire period: among many other breaks, there are ruptures with Philippe Soupault in 1927 and again in 1929, Robert Desnos in 1929, Louis Aragon in 1932, and Paul Eluard in 1938. Of Desnos, Breton (1988) writes early in the 1920s:

A notre époque, dans le domaine intellectuel, il existe à ma connaissance trois fanatiques de première grandeur: Picasso, Freud et Desnos. . . . Symbolisme, cubisme, dadaïsme sont depuis longtemps révolus, le *Surréalisme* est à l'ordre du jour et Desnos est son prophète. (473)

(In our era, in the intellectual arena, I am aware of three fanatics of the first order of grandeur: Picasso, Freud and Desnos. . . . Symbolism, cubism, Dadaism, have been over for a long time; surrealism is the order of the day and Desnos is its prophet.)

In *Entretiens* (Discussion), however, Breton charges Desnos with having a penchant for fixed—and therefore stagnant—poetic forms and with being too attached to his own talent.[23]

In the *Second manifeste,* Breton demands of surrealism's members an "unflagging fidelity" of which few prove capable. Nadeau (1989) articulates Breton's obsession with personal loyalty:

> It was not respect he demanded, but a sense of seriousness in love. And all these men loved him madly: "like a woman," as Jacques Prévert was to say. . . . [They] were ready to sacrifice everything to him: wife, mistresses, friends; and some, in fact, did sacrifice these things. They gave themselves entirely to him and to the movement. (86)

In 1929, Breton (1969a) is willing to "abandon silently to their sad fate" (129) those who fail in their commitment. Breton lists the names of acolytes in disfavor and details their more egregious errors,[24] which include displaying a desire for literary fame, earning a living as a journalist, publishing in the wrong reviews, and having nonsurrealist loyalties. Explaining Artaud's and Soupault's expulsion from the ranks, Breton (1988) emphasizes their "manque remarquable de rigueur" and "la poursuite *isolée* de la stupide aventure littéraire" ("remarkable lack of rigor" and "*isolated* pursuit of the stupid literary adventure" (928; my emphasis). Members and former members reciprocate by making violent statements rejecting Breton. The inner circle's gossip, divisiveness, and name-calling habits are reminiscent of the carefully chosen epithets and insults of the Argentine vanguardia's Boedo-versus-Florida conflict. Eluard, for example, refers in *Au grand jour* (In the open air) to Artaud: "Today, we have vomited up this vile dog . . . we don't see why this stinking corpse waits any longer . . . to declare himself a Christian" (qtd. in Lewis 1988, 64). In the *Second manifeste,* Breton (1969a) frames the failure to meet surrealism's standards as a moral failure: "I judge that I am not authorized to let cads, shammers, opportunists, false witnesses, and informers run around loose" (135). He makes no attempt to hide the nature of his role, writing in a footnote: "Since these lines first appeared in *La révolution surréaliste,* I have been the target of such a chorus of imprecations that, if there is in all this one thing to my credit, it is that I put off this mass slaughter for some time" (135). In contrast, it is hard to believe that either the vanguardia poets or the Auden poets would allow their leaders—insofar as they had leaders—to have this much power over them.

When Breton (1969a) hopes to find common ground with communism, he portrays a communism that is surrealist in its values: "I really fail to see . . . why we should refrain from supporting the Revolution, provided we view the problems of love, dreams, madness, art, and religion from the same angle [as the Party]" (140). Unlike Spender and Day Lewis, who suggest that a Marxist revolution is under way in England (though England has come much less close to actual revolution than France), Breton is more realistic about the actual state of affairs. In the *Second manifeste,* he writes that a proletarian literature is not yet possible because France is still "en période prérévolutionnaire" where "l'écrivain ou l'artiste [est] de formation nécessairement bourgeoise" (1988, 804). (in a prerevolutionary period [where] the writer or the artist has an unavoidably bourgeois background).

Surrealism's internal conflict about which doctrines to support is manifested at the First International Congress of Writers for the Defence of Culture (1935) as a public polarization of the movement's leaders. In the contrast between Aragon's call for the universal adoption of Soviet realism and Breton's statement (read by Eluard) that propaganda leads poets down the wrong path (see Shattuck 1960, 20–21), one sees proof of Breton's unwillingness to do anything that seriously compromises the movement's freedom. In a public act of dissent, Aragon quotes from Lautréamont's *Poésies,* describing the surrealists in his speech as "debased writers, dangerous jokers, two-bit fools, solemn mystifiers, veritable lunatics, who deserve to be in an asylum" (qtd. in Shattuck 1960, 20).

Ironically, the Communist Party's impact on Breton may have been to make him pursue more aggressively his quest for charismatic authority. He was subjected to three long interrogations at the hands of the French Communist Party. Desnos later said of Breton: "Rare are those who have been able to survive the pitiless interrogations that he holds, and one might say that to be the friend of Breton is one of the moral horrors of the times" (qtd. in Caws 1970, 11). What the Communist Party demanded of Breton—that surrealism have no values or goals other than those of the Party—is analogous to what Breton demanded of surrealism's membership. A letter dated 12 February 1929 was sent to surrealists and their supporters asking for clarification of their ideological views. Browder's (1967) account emphasizes the punitive aspects of what ensued: "Designed as it was to unmask the dissidents, this letter had the immediate effect of eliminating all who failed to reply or whose answers were judged unsatisfactory: Artaud, Vitrac, Leiris, Masson, Picabia, the editors of *Clarté* and *L'Esprit,* and others" (27–28).

In a similar vein, *Le surréalisme au service de la révolution* opens with what amounts to a description of Breton's self-assigned role for the 1930s. The twenty signatories are "Solidaires en tous points d'André Breton et résolus à faire passer en *application* les conclusions qui s'imposent à la lecture du SECOND MANIFESTE DU SURRÉALISME" (In solidarity on all points with André Breton and resolved to achieve the *application* of all convictions reached by reading the SECOND MANIFESTO OF SURREALISM). In the manifesto of "Contre-attaque" (Counterattack) (1935), signed by Breton and fourteen other surrealists, one finds overtly fascist language: "What will decide social destiny today is the organic creation of a vast composition of forces, disciplined, fanatical, capable of exercising, when the time comes, a pitiless authority."[25] On the heels of the Affaire Aragon, Breton wrote an oath of absolute loyalty to surrealism, demanded that all surrealists sign it, and purged two members who refused.

Breton's leadership role was perhaps more an internal than an external affair. In any case, it did not arouse much public interest in him. During the 1920s and 1930s, the *Nouvelle Revue Française* published articles about and texts by Artaud, Eluard, and Delteil more often than it focused on Breton; provincial reviews were more interested in Soupault and Eluard than in Breton (see Bridel 1988, 175, 177). Acceptable standards for surrealist publishing were made stricter when it was decided at a December 1932 meeting that permission must be obtained by majority vote before a surrealist would be allowed to publish in a special surrealist number of a nonsurrealist journal. Breton had also demanded that Tristan Tzara apologize publicly for having published in the "counterrevolutionary" Belgian *Journal des poètes*.[26] By 1935, even the difficult alliance with the Communist Party and affiliated groups prove definitively expendable. As Shattuck (1960) puts it, "The only organized group of self-professed Marxists to withdraw firmly and stridently from the Party, after having signed up, was the Surrealists. They contrived to be *plus royaliste que le roi*" (9).

In discussing the avant-garde, Eagleton points out the difficulty of finding a language of self-expression independent of that of bourgeois society. Breton's awareness that most European poets were of "bourgeois formation" led him to pursue a variety of strategies to promote the discarding of conventional concepts and language. Eagleton (1990) describes this sort of "war on culture" as

the guerilla tactics of secret subversion, of silent resistance, of stubborn refusal. Art will pulverize traditional form and meaning, because the laws of syntax and grammar are the laws of the police. It will dance on the grave of narrative, semantics and representation, celebrate madness and delirium, speak like a woman, dissolve all social dialectics into the free flow of desire. (369)

However, the language of the 1929 preface to the *Manifeste du surréalisme* shows how difficult it is even to avoid using traditional metaphors. Breton uses politico-military language such as "the struggle," "conquered territory," and the "ancien régime" to describe surrealism's quest. Breton's (1969a) other metaphors include his claim that freeing the imagination from a "state of slavery" can bring a sense of personal "justice" (4–5). Nor is he consistent in his use of conventional metaphors. Though patriotism is pejoratively labeled "a hysteria" in an early issue of *La révolution surréaliste,* hysteria is celebrated as "a supreme means of expression" a few issues later.[27] Critics have assimilated much of the political and military language. Philippe Audoin (1973) introduces surrealism's early leadership as a "triumvirate" consisting of Breton, Aragon, and Soupault (10). Browder refers to Breton in the title of his book as the "Arbiter of Surrealism." Dissent within the ranks is identified as "acts of sabotage." And Shattuck (1960) refers to Breton heading "his own Surrealist party" (29).

The dilemma of how to dismantle the influence of bourgeois society extends well beyond metaphor. Though the poets claimed to be violently opposed to the Roman Catholic Church, their nomination of the Dalai Lama as the "Pâpe en Esprit véritable" (pope in true spirit) does nothing to dismantle the notion that popes are acceptable.[28] Nor is the movement's anti-Christian stance served by the representation of Breton wearing a crown of thorns in an article responding to *Un cadavre* (A corpse) (1929), a collaborative insult by a number of former acolytes who claim to be disgusted by Breton and who are angry about his insults to them in the *Second manifeste* (Aragon 1931, 3).

Although early surrealism proclaims a commitment to a universal revolution of the mind, the surrealists occasionally indulge in nationalist protectivism. In 1931, an anticolonial photo essay is preceded by a Swiftian, though not entirely tongue-in-cheek proposal by Georges Sadoul that vast numbers of foreign workers—largely from French colonies—not engaged in the kind of work French citizens refuse to do be kicked out of the country.[29] Like the Auden poets, the surrealists suffer from ambivalence about their bourgeois roots, participating in institutions they claim to want to destroy: universities, armies, families, and professions. Their vocal rejection of such institutions and their antisocial behavior, however, cause them trouble with the government. Eluard was prohibited by the police from leaving France, Sadoul was sentenced to prison, and Aragon was threatened with prosecution for "Front rouge." In a familiar sort of irony, surrealism's more outlandish and public episodes piqued the interest of consecrated literary journals. Even during the 1930s, the *Nouvelle Revue Française* published an average of seventeen pieces a year that dealt in some way with surrealism (see Bridel 1988, 174).

Surrealism's earliest poetic texts illustrate the difficulties inherent in making conscious efforts to free the powers of the unconscious: a lack of punctuation is paired with fairly consistent capitalization of the beginnings of sentences, and unusual images often coexist with regular syntax. Describing his early experiences with automatic writing, Breton claims that "ces phrases, remarquablement imagées et d'une syntaxe parfaitement correcte, m'étaient apparues comme des éléments poétiques de premier order" (these sentences, remarkably imagistic and of perfectly correct syntax, appeared to me as poetic elements of the first order). At the least, this automatism involves linguistically competent people with a highly verbal unconscious (Breton 1988, 274). In their automatic writing texts, we can see the surrealists' metaphorized hope for the movement's future. Aragon writes:

> Au grand saisissement des nuages la main blanche s'était arrêtée au dessus des boulevards extérieurs faisant de grands gestes de ses articulations claquantes qui emportaient l'esprit vers une région d'épidémies et de drapeaux Par intervalle des phalanges un rayonnement violet s'abattait comme une trombe en mer.[30]

> (In the great seizure of clouds the white hand stopped above the outer boulevards making great clapping movements which carried the spirit toward a region of epidemics and flags From time to time from the armies a violet burst of light collapsed like an ocean hurricane.)

A divinely imagined white hand—the hand of God perhaps—enters the urban realm to redirect the human spirit. In the *Manifeste du surréalisme*, however, Breton (1969a) suggests that dreams can be used "in solving the fundamental questions of life" (12) and that "absolute reality" or "surreality" is so beautiful, marvelous, and natural that all people are capable of recovering their capacity for it.

In theory, perhaps because it initially claims to have a democratic orientation, surrealism is not concerned with the quality of literature. The

Declaration of 27 January 1925 by the Bureau of Surrealist Research affirms that surrealism is "not a new means of expression. . . . It is a means of total liberation of the mind."[31] But Breton's discussion of automatism, a rapid and unrestrained flow of writing "akin to *spoken thought*," suggests a conflict between the desire to transcend literary value and the desire to produce memorable, beautiful images. In the *Manifeste du surréalisme*, Breton (1969a) praises Soupault for creating texts whose value lies entirely in the naturalness of spontaneous composition: "I must give credit where credit is due and say that he constantly and vigorously opposed any effort to retouch or correct, however slightly, any passage . . . which seemed to me unfortunate. In this he was, to be sure, absolutely right" (24).

Breton (1969a) has already referred to his and Soupault's "praiseworthy disdain for what might result [from automatic writings] from a literary point of view" (23). But in another forum, he reveals a traditional view of talent as a natural quality unequally distributed. Referring to Soupault, he writes: "La poésie est un produit si naturel de son cerveau que ceux qui le connaissent tiennent de sa part la publication de livres pour une simple formalité" (Breton 1988, 612). (Poetry is such a natural product of his brain that those who know him consider his publishing of books to be a simple formality.) In instructions on how to write an automatic text, Breton (1969a) reveals his ambivalence about the question of talent: "Forget about your genius, your talents, and the talents of everyone else. Keep reminding yourself that literature is one of the saddest roads that leads to everything" (29). Referring to automatism as serving a noble cause, he writes, "thus do we render with integrity the 'talent' which has been lent to us," only to correct himself: "We do not have any talent; ask Philippe Soupault" (1969a, 28).

Shattuck (1960) points out, however, that the surrealists "rarely abandoned a strong sense of decorum" partly because they wanted "to be able to violate it" (50). Certainly their acts of rebellion and strategies of poetic innovation were carefully considered against a backdrop of historical conventions. Eagleton's statements about the aesthetic anarchy of the avant-garde are somewhat overblown, even in the case of the surrealists. The question arises, as it does with the Auden poets, whether the surrealists truly wanted to destroy the system that was bringing them fame, if not fortune. Though they had a strong political agenda for a time, they did not attempt to fashion themselves into a proletariat or even to give up poetic freedom for their cause. Caws (1970) aptly comments that surrealism, with "its horror of *le travail* and *le métier* and its latent appeal to a certain intellectual snobbism and a certain leisured class . . . can scarcely be thought of as a valuable discipline for the 'anticapitalist' mind" (38).

Surrealist poetry also preserves certain traditional structures of thought even as it forges a wildly new well of imagery and range of rhetorical strategies. Most surrealist images are visual; the poem's speaker is nearly always gendered male and the poem's image-object, if human, is often female. The characteristic domination of female objects by male subjects creates a sort of human colonialism, redeemed for some readers perhaps by the mitigating power of love.[32] Such poems are often in the first person. Blaise Cendrars's "Sur la robe elle a un corps" (On the dress she has a body), for example, combines the surrealist-Dadaist love of turning the world upside down with a traditional relationship to woman as the source of the male poet's inspiration. Though the poem was published in 1919, three years before surrealism officially separated from Dadaism, its metaphors predict Breton's commandment to fashion images from vastly different elements. While Cendrars writes such metaphorically innovative lines as "Mes yeux sont des kilos qui pèsent la sensualité des femmes" (My eyes are kilos that weigh the sensuality of women), he ends the poem by appropriating his female subject with a personalized cattle brand: "Et sur la hanche / La signature du poète" ("And on the hip / The signature of the poet).[33] This combination of linguistic innovation and traditional material is typical of the surrealists' poetic treatment of women. Where women are not involved, the work tends to be more innovative still, approaching the verbal counterpart of surrealist painting. Consider, for example, the following visual images from Breton's (1988) *Les champs magnétiques* (The magnetic fields): "Les égoutiers du paradis connaissent bien ces rats blancs qui courent sous le trône de Dieu" (The sewers of paradise know well these white rats which run under God's throne) and "Le jour des Morts, je naissais dans une prairie affreuse parmi les coquillages et les cerfs-volants" (87) (The day of the Dead, I was born on a terrifying prairie among seashells and paper kites). Breton's poetic oeuvre shows that he did not grow tired of playing with language and inventing puns. At the end of the Dadaist "Clé de sol" (Sun key), his untranslatable homophonic pun provides the poetic pleasure: "La porte cède / La porte c'est de la musique."[34] Thirteen years later, "Toutes les écolières ensemble" (All the schoolgirls together) ends with the homophonic lines "Après une dictée où *Le coeur m'en dit* / S'écrivait peut-être *Le coeur mendie*." (After a dictation in which *the heart takes* / Was perhaps written *the heart aches*).[35] The poem is formally more traditional than his early work, however, using repetition, insistent hyperbole, and a single narrative thread:

> Tu dis Toute la mer et tout le ciel pour une seule
> Victoire d'enfance . . .
> Et quand tu dis cela toute la mer et tout le ciel
> S'éparpillent comme une nuée de petites filles dans la cour d'un
>   pensionnat sévère

> (You say The whole sea and the whole sky for a single
> Victory of childhood . . .
> And when you say it the whole sea and the whole sky
> Settle like a cloud of little girls in the yard of a strict boarding school)

This later poem has greater thematic and linguistic unity and a clearer emotional center than "Clé de sol," whose scattered effect is more nearly that of automatic texts.

What Breton wrote during the political or "analytical" phase of surrealism supports the argument that his poetry was much less susceptible to outside influence or even to changing group goals than was the poetry of Auden or Spender. Breton the poet was separate from Breton the chameleonic polemicist. Published in *Ralentir travaux* (Slow works) (1930), "Façade" (Facade) is consistent with Breton's work of several years earlier. The speaker reaches from a waking state into the dream world to locate a love as powerful as poison:

> Je donne sur le coeur
> Partout où ton ombre a pu rejoindre la mienne
> Le sang est à la pointe de la vue comme d'une épée
> Et la rosée vient t'éveiller aux songes uniques
> Qui demandent raison à l'amour d'être l'amour
> Ainsi qu'à la belladone d'être le poison
>   (Breton 1988, 764)

> (I give on the heart
> Everywhere where your shadow has been able to rejoin mine
> The blood is on the tip of the gaze like that of a sword
> And the dew comes to wake you to singular dreams
> Which ask the right for love to be love
> As well as for belladonna to be poison)

The cluster of nouns evoked in a handful of lines—shadow, blood, sword, dew, dreams, poison, heart, love, gaze—illustrates the unique surrealist mixture of medieval and Romantic topos with a systematic deformation of these motifs through the use of surprising images such as "blood on the tip of the gaze." Poison and love form a traditional topos, but the demand that each have a right to exist, independent of specific context, lends a surrealist twist to an old motif. What separates this poem from Breton's earlier work is a greater attention to formal concerns: the last five lines are of approximately equal length, the imagery is more developed, and the meaning is clearer than in earlier poems designed to jolt the reader out of his or her complacency.

Over time, Breton's poetic themes change little. The early poem "Plutôt la vie" (Rather life) represents well his philosophy of choosing raw experience over a life deadened by habit and the avoidance of pain:

> Plutôt la vie que ces prismes sans épaisseur même si les couleurs sont
>   plus pures
> Plutôt que cette heure toujours couverte que ces terribles voitures de
>   flammes froides
> Que ces pierres blettes
> Plutôt ce coeur à cran d'arrêt
> Que cette mare aux murmures.[36]

> (Rather life than those prisms without depth even if the colors are
>   purer
> Rather than that always clouded hour those terrible wagons of cold
>   flame
> Than those soft stones
> Rather this triggered heart
> than that murmuring mere.)

Rather life than "ses cicatrices d'évasions" (its escape scars), writes Breton, who embraces the uncertainty of not knowing what the next moment will bring. He advances a philosophy of free will by portraying life as radically contingent and essentially lonely: "La vie de la présence rien que de la présence / Où une voix dit Es-tu là où une autre répond Es-tu là" (The life of presence nothing but presence / Where a voice says Are you there where another answers Are you there.) In a rare gesture, Breton concludes by making language less important than experience: "Et comme tout s'est déjà dit / Plutôt la vie" (And since words have become over-rife / Rather life). "Les attitudes spectrales" (Spectral attitudes), published nine years later in 1932, seems to suggest a reversal of this view, but is actually a celebration of life during a moment of distress. Breton opens with the line, "Je n'attache aucune importance à la vie" (I attach no importance to life) and confesses that "Je n'importe pas à la vie" (I am of no importance to life), only to begin a litanic contradiction of this thesis. In the end, "la voiture lancée au grand galop / Emporte jusqu'à ma dernière hésitation" (the carriage hurling forward at full gallop / Carries away even my last hesitation).[37] Across a decade, Breton's poetic voice does not change substantially, though—his morale worse—he takes another path to the same poetic end.

"Hôtel des étincelles" (Hotel of the sparks) (1932) is very similar in its stream of tenuously related images to Breton's poems of the early 1920s. Its insistence on the present moment is likewise characteristic of the early Breton; the reader is repeatedly forced to confront new images with the reminder that something is happening *now:* "On n'aperçoit plus qu'une main très blanche le pouls est figuré par deux minuscules ailes" ("All you can see now is a very white hand its pulse marked by two tiny wings") (Breton 1969b, 52–55). The concluding lines also echo early surrealism's fascination with objects and language as codified forms of reality:

A portée d'un petit livre griffé de ces mots *Pas de lendemain*
Dont l'auteur porte un nom bizarre
Dans l'obscure signalisation terrestre

(Close to a little book scrawled with these words *No Tomorrow*
Whose author bears a curious name
In the obscure codes of the earth)

In poems of the 1930s, such as "Au beau demi-jour" (To the lovely half-light), Breton tends to develop his images more fully than he did in earlier poems. As a consequence, he uses fewer of them:

Quand les deux pans du bois qui s'étaient brusquementécartés s'abattirent
Sans bruit
Comme les deux feuilles centrales d'un muguet immense
D'une fleur capable de contenir toute la nuit

(When the two ends of the wood that had suddenly moved apart closed in again

Noiselessly
Like the two central leaves of an immense lily of the valley
A flower capable of holding all the night)

While this is less a change of kind than of degree, it illustrates the fact that over time Breton becomes formally somewhat more traditional. His ability to create a memorable fusion of two very different things—kissing and drinking, a woman's body and a glass—has not changed in more than a decade, however: "J'eus le temps pour poser mes lèvres / Sur tes cuisses de verre" (I had time to place my lips / On your thighs of glass).[38]

Breton's famous "L'union libre" (Free union) is a beautiful litany of possible linkages between the feminine body and the natural and human worlds:

Ma femme à la chevelure de feu de bois
Aux pensées d'éclairs de chaleurs
A la taille de sablier
Ma femme à la taille de loutre entre les dents du tigre
Ma femme à la bouche de cocarde et de bouquet d'étoiles de dernière
    grandeur

(My wife with the woodfire hair
With the heat lightning thoughts
And the hourglass waist
My wife with the waist of an otter in the tiger's jaws
My wife with the mouth of cockade and clustering maximal stars)

Though the woman's body is described piece by piece, the sense of dismemberment is outweighed for many readers by the diverse images of nature Breton chooses here. The woman is a sort of Whitmanesque figure who transcends human boundaries to become like "buée aux vitres" and "foin coupé" ("steam on windows" and "new-mown hay") (1969b, 30–31). The infinite possibilities of a woman whose body is the site of animal life are framed by a poem whose most frequent gesture is one of alliance and ownership: "ma femme" (1969b, 32–33). Though the poem's title attests to the richness of such a union, the insistence that it is "free" is compromised by a proprietary voice obsessively reinforcing the male speaker's relationship to the sexuality of this female body.

That Breton's poetry is so consistent over time is quite unusual for the poetic avant-garde in general and presents a strong contrast to the Auden group's political poetry and to that group's poetic diversity. What appears to be an exceptionally volatile avant-garde movement (especially compared with the Argentine or Auden poets) is in important respects poetically the most stable of the three. This can be attributed to the surrealist decision to keep politics out of the poetry, a commitment to avoid social realism, and Breton's ability to seek novelty in the familiar:

> . . . à me pencher sur le précipice
> De la fusion sans espoir de ta présence et de ton absence
> J'ai trouvé le secret
> De t'aimer
> Toujours pour la première fois
>
> > (Breton 1982, 110; my translation)
>
> (. . . leaning over the precipice
> Of the hopeless fusion of your presence and your absence
> I found the secret
> Of loving you
> Always for the very first time)

In the conclusion of "Toujours pour la première fois" (Always for the first time), Breton illustrates his belief that the secret of perpetual renewal is found in the act of collapsing the binary division between presence and absence. Even in 1934, he is true in poetry to his original vision of dismantling the dualisms that alienate people from their dream life and the power of the imaginary.

Though Eluard has frequently been described by critics as having traditional lyric tendencies that make him only partially suited to surrealist poetics, it would be incorrect to imagine that he is less than a full-blown surrealist during his many years with the group. His poems of the late 1920s to mid-1930s are characteristically surrealist in their use of imagery; they resemble Breton's poems of the same period in their tendency to develop a thematic or imagistic thread. Classic surrealist images such as "La terre est bleue comme une orange" (The earth is blue like an orange) and "La verdure caresse les épaules de la rue" (Greenery strokes the shoulders of the street) dominate the poems, and even the evocations of women are musical and imaginative: "Tu glisses dans le lit / De lait glacé tes soeurs les fleurs" (You slide in the bed / Of frozen milk your sisters the flowers). (Eluard 1968, 507)

Eluard's early attachment to punctuation, especially periods, pastoral subject matter, and poetic form identify him as a more traditional poet than Breton. Occasionally his early poems seem to stand at least partially outside the surrealist movement. Though "L'égalité des sexes" (The equality of the sexes) is surrealist in its imagery, it has strong rhythm and regular rhyme and stanza formation:

> Tes yeux sont revenus d'un pays arbitraire
> Où nul n'a jamais su ce que c'est qu'un regard
> Ni connu la beauté des yeux, beauté des pierres,
> Celle des gouttes d'eau, des perles en placards
>
> (Your eyes have returned from an arbitrary country
> Where no one ever knew what a gaze is
> Nor ever knew the beauty of eyes, beauty of stones,
> That of drops of water, pearls in cupboards)
> (1968, 137)

Formally traditional poems, however, are not the rule in Eluard's poetry. Among other things, his poems reflect surrealism's habitual representation of woman as poetic muse. "Celle de toujours, toute" (She of always, everything) (1926) uses words like "candeur," "innocence," "mystère," and "pure" to describe the woman who liberates the poet to "sing" his text: a traditional woman-as-muse topos. The inspiring "otherness" evoked here, as in other surrealist poems, ultimately becomes sameness as the poet signals ownership of his creation. Two of Eluard's early "proverbs" reflect surrealism's obsession with women and the poet's own self-absorption: "Qui n'entend que moi entend tout" and "Une femme nue est bientôt amoureuse" (1968, 157) ("Who understands only me understands everything" and "A naked woman is soon amorous").

In *Les mains libres* (The free hands), a 1937 collaboration with Man Ray, Eluard sounds like Borges in the classic simplicity of his images and like Breton in his imaginative journey. "Objets" (Objects) consists of four lines:

> Dans cette chambre que j'habite
> J'assemble tous les paysages
> J'entre au bois diamant
> Le ciel est un aveu
> (1968, 575)
>
> (In this bedroom where I live
> I gather together all landscape

I enter the diamond woods
The sky is a vow)

Recall, for example, the last line of Borges' "Singladura" (Day's run): "En la cubierta, quietamente, yo comparto la tarde con mi hermana, como un trozo de pan." (On deck, peacefully, I share the afternoon with my sister like a piece of bread.) Though the movement in these two poems is different—Eluard expands outward from a bedroom to a spiritualized world, and Borges shrinks the infinite ocean and the innumerable instants in an afternoon to a single piece of bread—they are much the same in their basic impulse. As ultraist and surrealist aesthetics are based on creative use of the metaphor, a marginally more conservative surrealist—Eluard—sometimes sounds like an ultraist.

Rhetorically similar poems are produced by groups that have very different philosophies and goals. That the ultraists are less concerned with spiritual and personal transcendence than the surrealists is reflected in their poetry. Aragon's "J'ai abandonné l'espoir à côté d'un mécanisme d'horlogerie / Comme la hache tranchait la dernière minute" (I abandoned hope next to a piece of clockwork / As the axe chopped off the last minute) (qtd. in Caws 1970, 44) resembles metaphorically ultraist Leopoldo Marechal's "El ómnibus es el vermouth de la muerte; es una coctelera, de cuyo zarandeo nace un copetín democrático."[39] (The [public] bus is the vermouth of death; it is a cocktail shaker, from whose shaking is born a democratic little drink.) Aragon's image is clearly less elaborate and less clever than Marechal's. Its subject is universal human experience, as opposed to Marechal's commentary on socioeconomic class. Breton would have enjoyed Marechal's punning: "coctelera" means both a cocktail shaker and a mixture of different sorts of people. But by drawing too heavily on his conscious mind to work out the image, Marechal loses the beauty that comes of fresher, more surprising, juxtapositions. Aragon (1945) objects to such conventional associations as "blond comme les blés" (blond as wheat), preferring instead, "blond comme l'hystérie, blond comme le ciel, blond comme la fatigue, blond comme le baiser" (blond as hysteria, blond as the sky, blond as fatigue, blond as a kiss). As in ultraism, the trigger "comme" dulls the surprise of these images (49). We may recall here William Empson's comment about tropes that are *trop voulu*: "My pleasure in the simile thins."

Though Aragon's poetry evolves formally more than that of Breton during the period between the early 1920s and the beginning of World War II, his work is characteristically surrealist for the better part of two decades. The very early "Pour demain" (For tomorrow), written before Aragon was an active surrealist, has regular stanzas and a fixed rhyme scheme, and his early poetic experiments are occasionally openly derivative. "Soifs de l'ouest" (Western thirsts), in *Feu de joie* (Bonfire) (1920), is a generic attempt at Americana resembling, for example, Juan Marín's "Shimmy" and "Yankilandia," published in *Proa* in Buenos Aires in 1925. Both poets try to create atmosphere by bandying about such terms as banjo, bar, chewing gum, rifle, black groom, and skyscraper. Aragon's poetry of the mid- and late 1920s, however, is fairly consistent with surrealist norms. In *Le mouvement perpétuel* (Perpetual movement), whether as a product of mimicry or innovation, Aragon chooses rhymed misogyny: "La face de cette fille que j'ai tant aimée / Pour ses mains ses yeux faits et sa stupidité" (The face of this girl I have so loved / for her hands her set eyes and her stupidity). "Pierrette" contains the following crude passage, whose homophonic wordplay reveals the dependence of surrealist imagery on manipulating the different meanings of a single word:

Elle court dans l'enceinte
Elle n'est pas enceinte
Est-ce une revendeuse à la toilette
Ou une toilette à revendre[40]

(She runs in the enclosure
She isn't pregnant
Is she a second-hand saleslady
Or a used toilet for sale)

Aragon (1970) also shares the surrealist love of playing with sound: "Jamais la boule en buis ne pourra retomber / Sur le bout de bois blanc du bilboquet" (44).

Like Breton, Aragon is most concerned with themes of personal identity. At the end of "Sommeil de plomb" (Deep sleep), his mythically metamorphic speaker acknowledges language's imperfect capacity for expressing experience:

Mon corps je t'appelle du nom que les bouches ont perdu depuis la création du monde
Mon corps mon corps c'est une danse rouge c'est un mausolée un tir aux pigeons un geyser

Plus jamais je ne tirerai ce jeune homme des bras des forêts

(1970, 66)

(My body I call you from the name that mouths have lost since the
   creation of the world
My body my body it is a red dance it is a mausoleum a pigeon shoot
   a geyser
Never again will I pull this young man from the arms of the forests)

Because Aragon is a nominalist who believes that thought is expressed only
in words, he depends heavily on linguistic experiments to represent various states of consciousness.[41] Switching from first to third person midline
in "Sommeil de plomb" is Aragon's personal grammar of alienation: he is
so many things in language that eventually—in a surfeit of naming—he is
no longer himself.

Though he changes less than Borges, who repudiated his poetics and
then gave up poetry for prose, and Auden, who in the late 1930s discarded
a belief system based on free will, Aragon shows himself to be a linguistic chameleon. In *Le mouvement perpétuel* (1925), he experiments with the
appearance of words on the page. One poem consists of the word "persiennes" arranged twenty times, eight times capitalized, the final word
followed by a question mark (1970, 82–83). During his years as a surrealist,
his work is not altogether different from Breton's. Later poems, however,
display a change of heart. "Les lilas et les roses" (Lilacs and roses), written
during World War II, consists of three octaves framed by quatrains, *rime
croisée,* and a series of allusions that reflects a quite un-surrealist evocation
of prewar France. The lines "je ne sais pourquoi ce tourbillon d'images /
Me ramène toujours au même point d'arrêt" (I don't know why this whirl-
wind of images / Always brings me back to the same stopping point)
are personally and poetically self-conscious in a way uncharacteristic of
Aragon and of surrealism (1944, 36). His evolution as a writer, however, is
neither linear nor consistent. Because he did not publish a book of poetry
between *Persécuté-persécuteur* (Persecuted-persecutor) (1931) and *Le crève-
coeur* (Heartbreak) (1941), it is difficult to map his poetic development
through the 1930s. Though Aragon and Breton parted ways fairly early on,
it is noteworthy that many poems of his later decades are surrealist in their
imagery, syntactic inversion, and especially their sometimes pained examination of how the human subject ages through language.

Desnos's experiments with a wide variety of forms of repetition make
Aragon his closest peer. His "Le Bonbon" (1930), for example, resembles

Aragon's "Persiennes" (1925), the poem that consists of a single word repeated over and over. In the 1930s, Desnos's poetry—like Eluard's—becomes formally simpler (though both poets go on to write in traditional forms) and he does not give up his quest to plumb the human psyche's inner workings. In "J'ai tant rêvé de toi" (I dreamed so much of you), his fantasy world proves more powerful than reality:

> J'ai tant rêvé de toi que tu perds ta réalité . . .
> J'ai tant rêvé de toi que mes bras habitués en étreignant ton ombre . . .
>   ne se plieraient pas au contour de ton corps, peut-être.[42]

> (I have dreamed so much of you that you lose your reality . . .
> I have dreamed so much of you that my arms accustomed to
>   embracing your shadow . . . may not bend to fit the shape of
>   your body.)

Caws identifies Desnos as the most difficult of the surrealist poets; he is also Aragon's match in terms of poetic range achieved in the course of their lives. Like Aragon, Desnos ventures into a brief experiment with political poetry.[43] Both poets experiment to the fullest with the transformative power of simile and metaphor: "Comme, je dis comme et tout se métamorphose, le marbre en eau, le ciel en orange, le vin en plaine, le fil en six, le coeur en peine, la peur en seine" (Like, I say like and everything is metamorphosed, marble into water, the sky into an orange, wine into plains, thread into six, the heart into pain, fear into a net).[44]

For Desnos, dreams, like women, are a vehicle linking the potential self and the ideal world. In "La destinée arbitraire" (Arbitrary destiny), he writes:

> Voici venir le temps des croisades.
> Par la fenêtre fermée les oiseaux s'obstinent à parler
> comme les poissons d'aquarium. . . .
> ô mon rêve quand je vous caresse!
> Demain on enterrera gratuitement
> on ne s'enrhumera plus
> on parlera le langage des fleurs
> on s'éclairera de lumières inconnues à ce jour.
>
> (1926, n.p.)

> (The time of the crusades is coming.
> Through the closed window the birds insist on talking

like aquarium fish. . . .
o my dream when I caress you!
Tomorrow we will bury for free
we will no longer catch cold
we will speak the language of flowers
we will brighten with lights unknown up to now.)

Like his fellow surrealists, Desnos makes a specialty of images that yoke objects from different worlds. The dream makes absent things present and works against the deadening forces of habit and banality. But in many of his poems, the images are ambivalent. Woven through a language of liberation ("on s'éclairera de lumières inconnues à ce jour") are ominous, perhaps historically conditioned premonitions of slaughter ("le temps des croisades" and "on enterrera gratuitement").

Soupault, who was ousted during the crisis of 1929, displays a higher degree of poetic consistency during the 1920s and 1930s than Aragon. Even poems written in the 1930s, when he was no longer a surrealist, are largely surrealist in nature. Soupault's early poems link the poet, language, and the natural world:

j'ai écris [*sic*] des poèmes près d'une anémone sylvie
en cueillant les mots qui pendaient aux branches
le petit chemin de fer me faisait penser au transcanadien
et ce soir je souris parce que je suis ici devant ce verre tremblant
où je vois l'univers [45]

(I have written poems next to a wood-anemone
reaping the words which hung from the branches
the little train made me think of the transcanadian
and this evening I smile because I am here in front of this trembling
    glass
where I see the universe)

Like the young Breton, Soupault the poet is quick on his feet, shifting rapidly from one set of images to another, focusing now on images of railway travel and now on a cosmic ability to see the universe in, and as, trembling glass. The images are tenuously but clearly joined by the movement of train and glass and the motif of seeing long, perhaps impossible, distances.

"Fleuve" (River) (1926) exemplifies Soupault's habit of combining a series of metaphors to create a master image conflating the human and the natural. Here the moon is river, human, and fish:

> ô lune affreuse qui court comme une grande lueur fleuve
> les sillages des bateaux sont tes cheveux
> la nuit est ton manteau
> les reflets qui dorment sur toi sont tes écailles[46]

> (o hideous moon which runs like a great gleaming river
> the wakes of the boats are your hair
> the night your overcoat
> the reflections which sleep on you are your scales)

The key to the metaphor is the metamorphic power of light, which distorts the world into alien shapes while itself taking a human form. In the line "Fleuve sinueux comme des lèvres" (River sinuous as lips), Soupault warns that language too is a distorting, though infinitely creative, medium. He proves this by creating a symbiotic relationship between the river of light and the poet's stream of language in which each creates the other. In the early 1930s, Soupault continues to explore these themes, identifying himself as making and being made by the forces of light and water:

> la mer est autour de moi
> insolente imbécile éternelle
> Je voudrais une lueur faible comme le pardon
> un point à l'horizon . . .
> Je marche sur l'océan
> à grandes enjambées[47]

> (the sea surrounds me
> insolent eternal imbecile
> I would like a dim shimmering light like forgiveness
> a point on the horizon . . .
> I walk on the ocean
> taking huge strides)

Still later in the decade, his metaphors have changed little, though he is more willing to put aside metaphoric density for wordplay and rhyme: "Car tu es l'eau qui rêve / et qui persévère / l'eau qui creuse et qui éclaire" (Because you are the water which dreams / and perseveres / the water which empties and illuminates).[48] There is tension here between water, air, and glass; the object of Soupault's love is (like) water which "persévère" (or which perhaps can "percer" a "verre"). Like most surrealist representations of women, the woman here is two-edged, half-destructive. She cuts through things and illuminates their insides.

In spite of the comparative stability of its poetics and the internal consistency of its members' poetic oeuvres—a consistency that endures in a number of cases until the beginning of World War II—surrealism in the 1930s has a changed face. Its fourth journal, *Minotaure* (Minotaur) (1934–39), is fancy, eclectic, and traditional; it publishes essays focusing on mythology, architecture, and psychology. Plates of major works of art from previous centuries are given a prominent place in the journal and there are few signs of resistance to the notion of a traditional canon or its influence on contemporary art. *Minotaure*'s statement of purpose is both interdisciplinary and intergenerational, calling for "un terrain de collaboration entre les éléments les plus aigus et les plus importants" (a ground for collaboration among the sharpest and most important elements) of art, poetry, and science.[49] Though not edited or financed by the surrealists, *Minotaure* nevertheless is soon dominated by them. Unusually vague statements such as "cette revue ne s'est pas formée selon un esprit préconçu. Elle est dégagée de toute doctrine"[50] ("this journal didn't form itself along preconceived lines. It is independent of all doctrines) suggest a marked, if temporary, weakening of the movement's platform of rebellion. Essays on art history, such as Salvador Dali's "Le surréalisme spectral de l'éternel féminin préraphaélite" (The ghostly surrealism of the Pre-Raphaelite eternal feminine),[51] do little to alter this picture.

In 1939, after Breton has become a Trotskyite, *Minotaure* conflates communism and fascism, bringing the age of political binarisms to a close, and rejects out of hand the subordination of art to politics: "En Allemagne, en Italie, en URSS les pinceaux et les porte-plumes obéissent aux consignes imposées par les chefs politiques, ils servent à la propagande. . . . A ce régime, l'art est mort instantanément dans ces pays." (In Germany, in Italy, in the USSR, paintbrushes and pens obey the orders of the political leaders, they serve propaganda. . . . Under this kind of regime, art is instantly dead in these countries.)[52] If this is any index, surrealism has in important ways come full circle back to its original stance of privileging aesthetic concerns over political exigencies. There is irony in this warning about obeying "the orders" of political leaders, given Breton's behavior over the years. For the Auden poets, too, the political is a phase that comes to a close even more definitively than the communist phase of the surrealists. The political involvement of the surrealists continued long after World War II, though its allegiances shifted. They denounced the Soviet Union in 1956 for its massacre of insurgent Hungarian workers and continued to work for what they saw as their most important goal, human liberation (see Breton 1978, 344–45).

During the 1930s and in later years, Breton's role as leader remained remarkably stable, and he continued to exercise his right to expel members from the group and old loyalties from his heart. One detects little change from one of his first dramatic gestures—selling his correspondence with Paul Valéry on the day in 1916 when Valéry entered the Académie Française (Browder 1967, 8)—to thirty-five years later when he expelled his friend Michel Carrouges for speaking about surrealism to the Cercle des Intellectuels Catholiques de France (Carrouges 1974, translator's preface). In 1954, he expelled Max Ernst for accepting the Grand Prize for Painting at the Venice Biennale (Browder 1967, 43). As Soupault (1967) said of Breton: "Ce qui me surprenait et qui provoquait mon admiration c'est qu'il voulait, envers et contre tous, rester fidèle à lui-même. André Breton à dix-huit ans et à soixante-huit ans, n'était pas tellement *différent*" (671). (What surprised me and provoked my admiration is that he wanted, above all, to remain faithful to himself. André Breton at age eighteen and at age sixty-eight was not so very *different*.)

Surrealism represented itself as a cohesive movement, yet one person— who favored the first-person singular pronoun—wrote most of its important doctrinal statements. Among others, Breton wrote *Légitime défense*, *Manifeste du surréalisme*, *Second manifeste du surréalisme*, *Misère de la poésie*, *L'Affaire Aragon devant l'opinion publique*, *Qu'est-ce que le surréalisme?*, and *Position politique du surréalisme*. Sometimes he collected signatures as a post facto sign of group solidarity. Breton achieves a considerable degree of freedom in his personal quest for liberation, though at the same time as he successfully curtails the freedom of the other surrealists. Breton has two faces: he is a polemicist and a poet. His poems act like poems; his polemical texts, however, turn in two directions at once: inward toward members of the group and outward as statements to the public. As for surrealism's quest to achieve independence and authenticity, the best that can be achieved is a compromise: surrealism does not allow any external ideology—such as communism—to dominate it, yet it is inevitably the product of the particular circumstances of its makers and their historical time and place. Similarly, although the surrealists try to resist the commodification of art so common in bourgeois society, they manage significantly less well than the Dadaists to escape it. That they publish prolifically—

Breton published many more major texts or books during the 1920s and 1930s than Borges or Auden—is an important sign of the degree to which printed language is deemed the most effective, and inevitable, means of communicating the surrealist message.

The surrealist quest was most successful on the idealist plain of language where the collapsing of binary oppositions was possible and the politics of totalitarianism barely intruded. To his credit, Breton ultimately rejects tools that strike him as unsuited to a task. Though in the name of the surrealists he states that "we hold the liberation of man to be the *sine qua non* of the *liberation of the mind,* and we can expect this liberation of man to result only from the proletarian revolution," he also strongly resists allowing propaganda a place in poetry on the grounds that "*control* exercised by reason" destroys the fundaments of surrealism (Breton 1978, 128). For many readers, what remains after the purges and the politics is a legacy of poetry as a provocative vehicle for personal exploration and liberation. On the messy human level of the group itself, such idealism was unsuccessfully enforced with strategies borrowed from the civilization the poets set out to reject. Though the goal of freeing poetry from its status as commodity was not viable, the surrealists created a poetry that resisted rapid co-optation and that remains a distinctive body of work more than half a century later. To their credit, they achieved in poetry what they failed to accomplish in life.

Ex-members and competent critics cannot agree even whether the movement was essentially pessimistic or optimistic in the face of decaying values; whether it represented a brilliantly planned fraud designed to promote the interests of its leaders or a courageous attempt to reach a higher level of sincerity on which to start living all over again.

—Roger Shattuck

9. Surrealism's Divided Critics

The single most important goal of surrealism was human liberation through the freeing of the imagination and the unconscious. While Breton and his followers were largely successful in their experiments with trance states and automatism, the vast majority of people they hoped to include in their revolution were never affected. Breton's rigorous demands on the group's membership resulted in the erection of a barrier between members and nonmembers, and between current and former members. This "inside-outside" dichotomy extended to critics, the majority of whom have divided into two camps, those who view surrealism through the lens of the movement's own philosophy and those who stand on the outside and tend to evaluate it from a historically relative perspective. Not surprisingly, the "inside" critics—among them Mary Ann Caws and Michel Carrouges—tend to see the movement as successful in its aims, while those "outside"—including Shattuck—point out its shortcomings and failures. A third group presents surrealist ideas with little evaluation or advocacy, but its members function more as "translators" for the uninitiated than as critics.

Avant-garde theorist Renato Poggioli (1968) argues that it is only in "rare moments" that the avant-garde "seeks to justify itself by the authority or arbitration of history, in any one of the partial and infrequent fits of humanism or traditionalism that now and again afflict it" (70). Literary criticism, in contrast, is by nature "afflicted" with a historical perspective, humane values, and a strong loyalty to the literary tradition in which it participates. Surrealism soundly rejects interpretation and evaluation of its oeuvre, causing critics interested in the surrealist project extra troubles, chief among them the problem of how to talk about surrealism. An early Dada manifesto states categorically: "DADA, ne reconnaissant que l'instinct, condamne *a priori* l'explication" (Breton 1988, 230). (DADA, recognizing only instinct, condemns *a priori* explanation.) Surrealism presents itself as a path of liberation, not as a set of ideas. A careful reading of Breton's polemical texts, however, shows it to be both. The split among critics reflects surrealism's unusual, mystical nature and is in part a product of its unusual methodologies. The split, however, goes against the grain of the movement's binarism-collapsing goals. Nor is surrealism well served by a polarization that reflects the tendency of critics of the avant-garde to echo, perhaps unconsciously, the habits of the movements they study.

I argue that surrealism is, as the insiders claim, a spiritual path in its own right and that those who have never experienced its methods as personal practice cannot fully understand it. In this sense, it is possible to argue that early surrealism, the surrealism of automatism and dreams, is a religion of sorts and its members are part of a cult. Because most critics do not engage in surrealist practice, they are forced instead to evaluate its products, which were never the manifestation of surrealism most highly valued by the poets themselves. These critics tend to judge the movement from the vantage point of the traditionalism the poets themselves despised. "Inside" critics ought perhaps to be less unremittingly enthusiastic about the movement's achievements, which, after all, never lived up to its goals. "Outside" critics, who vastly outnumber their counterparts, ought to begin with the premise that surrealism cannot be judged, nor its works interpreted, by the usual standards and methods of literary criticism. A middle ground seems both desirable and possible, and an examination of the inside-outside problem is an appropriate first step in laying the groundwork for a more synthetic criticism.

Clifford Browder (1967) exemplifies the traditional inside critic. Writing in the 1960s, he downplays Breton's authoritarianism and makes the group dynamic sound impossibly natural and spontaneous. His description defies laws of nature, however, reflecting instead a version of the movement's idealized self-image:

> Thus it was not rigid adherence to a literary dogma that characterized the Surrealists of the mid-1920s, but rather a spontaneous attraction, the participation in a common quest presupposing similar modes of thought and feeling. One could not be a Surrealist without sharing

certain attitudes [including] an absolute devotion to the Surrealist conception of poetry, uncompromised by any social, material, or literary concerns. (18)

It is well that Browder (1967) modifies this description by limiting it to the more harmonious days of the mid-1920s. Nevertheless, he acknowledges that Breton "dominated these meetings" and that Breton was referred to as both the "priest" and "pope" of surrealism (19). Discussing the surrealist crisis of 1929, Browder uses an authoritarian and fascistic vocabulary, perhaps intending to reflect Breton's point of view. The "violent" crisis, he argues, was an attempt to "purify" the movement by eliminating two types of "deviations." They were, "on the one hand, undue preoccupation with the speculative side of the movement, leading to a purely literary and artistic activity; on the other hand, interest in political action to the point of compromising the group's autonomy" (27). The middle ground guarded by Breton was dangerously narrow, especially as its boundaries changed regularly and as deviation from it became the equivalent of moral failure. The group functioned increasingly like an army; even Browder refers to new members as "recruits." Similarly, Audoin (1973) attributes the acquisition of "de vastes territoires dans l'empire culturel" (vast territories in the cultural empire) to their "barbarism" (79). In contrasting the two *Manifestes,* Browder exhibits another view typical of the inside critic, which is to value the *Manifeste du surréalisme,* with its high hopes for an aesthetic revolution, and to discount the *Second manifeste,* which he describes as being idealistic but flawed by "slanderous personal satire," "a savage intransigence," and "a passionate scorn" for conceptual or human opponents of surrealism. That he then cites Breton's 1946 apology for the *Second manifeste* suggests that Browder not only thinks the manifesto a mistake, but believes that Breton may have dismissed it as one (Browder 1967, 167–69). In fact, Breton's apology refers to his harsh judgments of fellow and former surrealists, not to the body of his thought in 1929.

Helena Lewis (1988), who chronicles fairly dispassionately surrealism's relationship to politics, is typical of many critics who remain on the outside but subscribe occasionally to an "inside" view. Unsympathetic to the surrealists' treatment of women, she (like many others) is Breton-centered in her perspective, calling Aragon's waffling between the Communist Party and the surrealists "treachery." She finds Breton's disciplinary choices inevitable. "In such a closely knit group," Lewis comments, "disagreements were intolerable, and *had to be dealt with by means of the most violent per-*

sonal attacks" (64; my emphasis). Most critics would agree with her, especially in such an egregious case as Aragon's disloyalty, but the tendency by inside critics to accept uncritically the behavior of the surrealists is alarming in its fulfillment of Breton's demand that everyone agree with him. According to Aragon, Breton was willing to suppress opinions that differed from his, including in the early days of Dadaism when Maurice Barrès was subjected to a mock trial for "Crimes Against the Security of the Human Spirit." Aragon claims he was so successful in defending Barrès from the charges that Breton, who took the trial seriously, prevented the transcript from being published, claiming to have lost it (Wallard 1979, 123; see also Lewis 1988, 15). Aragon's account, interestingly, is not found in most histories of Dadaism and surrealism. Aragon also claims that he wrote the equivalent of a surrealist manifesto and published it in *Une vague de rêves* (A wave of dreams) before Breton's manifesto appeared, but that it was ignored (Arban 1968, 45).

Anna Balakian (1971) argues that the surrealists "look[ed] with contempt upon the exterior world." As early as 1925, however, an event in the exterior world—the war in Morocco—caused the group to commit itself to a political cause. Because "disorder becomes the real god" (10–11) of the surrealists, according to Balakian, critics sensitive to surrealist values find it hard to judge the movement by the values of the hated "exterior world." Inside critics tend not to question the surrealists' inability to live up to their own goals. Aragon reported for instance that during the 1920s, he, Breton, and Eluard went "au café écrire des sonnets . . . avec la technique de la rapidité abolissant la conscience" (Arban 1968, 64). (to a café to write sonnets . . . with the technique of speed erasing consciousness). An outside critic would likely ask how what Aragon reports were formally correct sonnets could be created without the intervention of the conscious mind, but it is likely that inside critics would not. Aragon would also have us believe that "la main qui écrit invente ainsi plus vite que l'esprit ne pense" (Arban 1968, 44, 65) (the hand that writes invents faster than the mind thinks), but that when it comes to sonnets, "on imagine mal . . . l'extrême habilité de Breton à ce jeu" (one little imagines . . . Breton's extreme competence at this game). Surrealist "talent," we are asked to believe, transcends the conscious mind even where sophisticated linguistic skills are involved.

Michel Carrouges, a critic who had the unusual good fortune to participate actively in the movement, offers a striking comment on the inside-outside dichotomy: "For the man who looks at it from the outside, surrealism is an absurd monstrosity. But for anyone who has penetrated within, it is the most extraordinary of human revelations." This makes the movement sound like a source of spiritual revelation and like something of a secret cult. Carrouges (1974) naturalizes his assertion by adding: "Understanding surrealism is nothing more than understanding one's self" (introduction). He is a loyal surrealist of the 1920s, agreeing with the views espoused in the *Manifeste du surréalisme*. About poetry, he writes, "[T]he subconscious is the sole supplier of poetic images and of their organic shape" (103–5). He dates surrealism to "the discovery of the natural link existing between the automatism of dreams and the manifestations of poetry" (7). The surrealist questioning of concepts such as normalcy and mental health leads inside critics to put aside normative standards, just as it leads outside critics such as Shattuck to view surrealist values and behavior as willful and pleasurable social rebellion.

Because the surrealists shifted their emphasis a number of times, even critics such as Carrouges find it difficult, if not impossible, to embrace simultaneously the conflicting goals of the movement's various phases. Most inside critics focus on the early doctrine, a sort of pure aestheticism with grand claims for dissolving the world's basic conceptual binarisms. The choice to embrace the early period only was made credible by Breton's periodic reiteration of its principles. In 1937's *Limites non frontières du surréalisme* (Limits not borders of surrealism), he pleads his Trotsky-era case for collapsing binary oppositions by 1924 methods: "It is by calling upon automatism and automatism alone . . . that one can hope to resolve, other than on an economic basis, *all* those antimonies which, because they existed prior to the social regime under which we live, may well outlast it" (Carrouges 1974, 13). Carrouges (1974) writes, "Surrealism has wrought the boldest doctrine of our era . . . for it assigns to humanity the task of reaching a goal that encompasses all the others" (275). The tone here certainly differs from Breton's and Aragon's, but Carrouges's hope for the movement in the 1970s is not different from theirs in the early 1920s. In contrast, critics such as Albert Leonard, publishing the same year as Carrouges, offer a view from the other end of the spectrum. Even the titles of their books reflect this difference. Carrouges's *André Breton and the Basic Concepts of Surrealism* eulogizes the movement's leader and praises its conceptual framework, while Leonard's *La crise du concept de littérature en France au XXe siècle* (The crisis of the concept of literature in twentieth-century France) lays the blame for much of the perceived literary "crisis" at the surrealists' doorstep. Leonard's (1974) critique of surrealism's failure to live up to its own values provides a good composite of the "outside" critic's view:

Un lecteur attentif des *Manifestes* arrive à conclure que les textes théo-riques, de Breton, loin d'être des témoignages de transgression et de subversion, sont fondés sur une utilisation mensongère du langage, sur une théologie du sujet et une rhétorique de l'expression alors que le marxisme orthodoxe exige de s'attacher d'abord au problème de la pro-duction du discours. . . . Breton s'évertue à utiliser un langage destructif et antirationaliste pour asseoir une philosophie qui, en fin de compte, reste profondément spiritualiste et fort respectueuse de la métaphysique idéaliste. (48)

(An attentive reader of the *Manifestes* comes to the conclusion that Breton's theoretical texts, far from being evidence of transgression and subversion, are based on a mendacious use of language, on a theology of the subject, and on a rhetoric of expression where orthodox Marx-ism demands an alliance with the problem of producing discourse. . . . Breton does his utmost to use destructive and antirationalist language to establish a philosophy which, in the end, remains profoundly spiri-tual and very respectful of idealist metaphysics.)

In mentioning Marxism, Leonard emphasizes the *Second manifeste,* a choice frequently made by outside critics, who tend to be more interested in politics than aesthetics. He exaggerates in arguing that Breton uses de-structive, antirationalist language to advance what he correctly identifies as a spiritual end. More often than not, Breton uses rational argument to ex-plain an unusual method for reaching a constructive, though unorthodox end. By arguing that a destructive means cannot produce a constructive end, Leonard fails to acknowledge that modernism functioned well with just such a mechanism. Period critic Marcel Raymond (1970) agrees with Leonard that surrealism's agenda is ultimately Romantic, but finds that both the political aims and the poetry were unsuccessful by the standards of surrealism. Raymond questions whether the poets were able to produce a single image "of spontaneous dreamlike thought," and adds: "We may go farther: some of the surrealist poems manufactured on the assembly line during the last few years strike the reader as capricious games, less enter-taining than monotonous; their authors flout logic for the fun of it or from weariness, all the while taking a secret pride in the freedom of their frolics" (265).

Another common perception of outside critics is that the surrealists were more product- than process-oriented. Henri Lemaître (1984) argues that the poets were most concerned with creating "oeuvres," which in his opinion were so similar they might as well have been signed "Anonymous" (101). Many of the early automatic texts were quite similar, but the poetic oeuvres of the various poets are, as we have seen, different from one another. Lemaître also hints that surrealism was a somewhat anomalous phase in the careers of lyric poets, citing Desnos's early use of rhymed alexandrines and Eluard's traditionalism (124–25). He illustrates the argument that Eluard, Desnos, and Aragon aspired to membership in the French canon with a statement from Aragon's *Yeux d'Elsa* (Elsa's eyes), 1942: "Il fallait au-delà de l'affreux peigne à dents cassées du vers libre, les mille et un arts poétiques d'un demi-siècle, des *Illuminations* aux surréalistes" (152). (It is necessary to have—beyond the horrible broken-toothed comb of free verse—the thousand and one poetic arts of a half century, from *Illuminations* to the surrealists.) By the late 1930s, of course, surrealism had incorporated lyrical and Romantic elements into its poetics. Critics of Aragon acknowledge that he consistently exhibited signs of individualism, Romanticism, and lyricism (see, for example, Juin 1960, 68, and Raillard 1964, 9–10). One proof is that the traditional publisher NRF (Gallimard) published seven—nearly all—of the books Aragon wrote in the 1920s.

In 1938, Henri Peyre (1938) sizes up the surrealists: "L'oeuvre de ces jeunes gens, dont beaucoup revenaient des tranchées, a voulu, par un surprenant paradoxe, ignorer, et le sacrifice de soi, et la souffrance des hommes" (67). (The work of these young people, many of whom returned from the trenches, is, by a surprising paradox, unaware of both self-sacrifice and the suffering of men.) Though surrealist poetry in the 1930s is substantially less public in theme and purpose than that of the Auden poets, the surrealists nevertheless suffered many hardships for the sake of their project. They were financially less well off than either the Auden poets or the Argentine avant-garde and were the only group which, by historical accident, was unlucky enough to serve in both world wars. Their rejection of traditional means of earning a living caused them substantial hardship and their surrealist practices caused them periods of marginalization by publishers and newspapers, as well as serious problems with the police and the French government. Their Marxism, though it involved minimal personal sacrifice and maximum ambivalence, appears to have been genuine while it lasted. Peyre is unfair in his assertion that surrealist poetry fails to treat the problem of human suffering. Many poems take as themes the individual's quest to become free of the deadening weight of habit and fear. Eluard's (1975) "Sans âge" (Ageless) balances future transcendence against past imprisonment:

Nous aborderons tous une mémoire nouvelle
Nous parlerons ensemble un langage sensible.

O mes frères contraires . . .
Où vous ai-je laissés
Avec vos lourdes mains dans l'huile paresseuse
De vos actes anciens
Avec si peu d'espoir que la mort a raison
O mes frères perdus.

(34)

(We will all approach a new memory
We will speak together an accessible language.

O my contrary brothers . . .
Where did I leave you
With your heavy hands in the sluggish oil
Of your former acts
With so little hope that death is right
O my lost brothers.)

The existential suffering the surrealists seek to alleviate is certainly different from the Auden poets' more materialist humanitarianism, which is based on eliminating poverty and preventing war. Surrealist poetry is more subtle than the Auden group's poetry and its celebrations of life are easily overlooked because they are personal and philosophical in nature and their messages are often metaphorically veiled.

The experience of living with a high level of awareness and vulnerability to suffering, achieved through a poetics that brought the surrealists into contact with their most basic psychic experiences, is both painful and joyous. The converse of the pain of living is perpetual rediscovery of the natural world and beloved things. In Breton's words, "J'ai trouvé le secret / De t'aimer / Toujours pour la première fois." (I discovered the secret / Of loving you / Always for the very first time.) In 1934, Breton celebrates the Marquis de Sade's creation of "une brèche dans la nuit morale" (a break in the moral night) that dissolves the traditional barriers to the fusion of eros and agape. Sade's "ordres mystérieux" (mysterious orders) permit Breton a primordial love:

Comme le premier homme aima la première femme
En toute liberté

Cette liberté
Pour laquelle le feu même s'est fait homme[1]

(As the first man loved the first woman
In total liberty
This liberty
For which even fire became man).

The poetic subtlety of surrealism and its members' awareness of human suffering are perhaps most obvious in the war poetry, which is considerably less didactic and narrative than that of the Auden poets. Eluard's "Finir" (To end), written in 1940, uses many of Auden's themes of decade's end: the failure of poets to alter the course of history and the failures of love, diplomacy, and the human spirit:

La charrue des mots est rouillée
Aucun sillon d'amour n'aborde plus la chair
Un lugubre travail est jeté en pâture
A la misère dévorante
A bas les murs couverts des armes émouvantes
Qui voyaient clair dans l'homme
Des hommes noircissent de honte
D'autres célèbrent leur ordure
Les yeux les meilleurs s'abandonnent

Mêmes les chiens sont malheureux.

(1975, 56)

(The word plow is rusty
Not a single loveseat still accosts the flesh
A funereal labor is thrown into pasture
To the devouring unhappiness
Down with walls covered with emotionally stirring arms
Which saw clear into man
Men blacken with shame
Others celebrate their filth
The best eyes abandon themselves

Even the dogs are unhappy.)

Instead of attributing blame to human dishonesty and hypocrisy, as Auden does in "September 1, 1939," Eluard speaks more directly to the grief felt in the face of these many human failures. Where Auden is a diagnostician, Eluard reaches for elemental metaphors of loss: black shame, the excrement of human civilization (weapons and war), the animals who cannot be unaffected by such a world.

Most critics agree that Dadaism and to a lesser degree surrealism grew out of the cultural shock of World War I. But what Peyre specifically objects to is the "strangeness" and difficulty of the surrealists, especially "leur poursuite acharnée de coincidences souvent puériles, des incohérences les plus baroques" (their furious pursuit of often infantile coincidences, of the most baroque incoherences). The strangeness of surrealist art and poetry is clearly influenced by the psychological and physical trauma of personally witnessing the human cost of the war. It is also linked to the poets' belief in chance ("le hasard") as a determining aspect of life. It is not surprising, Peyre argues (1938), that surrealist strangeness causes "un divorce entre le gros du public raisonnable et les auteurs" (30) (a divorce between the majority of the reasonable public and the authors). But such advocacy of *clarté* is precisely what the surrealists objected to and the "divorce" between conventional reason and their brand of unreason points to just how far poets who wanted public recognition were willing to go in the name of an isolating and unusual quest. They took seriously Rimbaud's problematic imperative, "Changer la vie" (Change life).

For many outside critics, the test of surrealist mettle is political. "The simple truth," Rosemont (1978) argues, "is that in 1927 the overthrow of bourgeois society (a prerequisite for the full fruition of surrealism) seemed possible *only* through the agency of the Communist Party" (38). Assuming that the surrealists believed this, as his argument implies, one can conclude that their ambivalence about the Party meant that they were bourgeois first, surrealists second. While he claims that the surrealists were dedicated "to the cause of the proletariat," Rosemont calls Aragon a "Stalinist hack." The proletariat's cause, however, was less important to surrealist politics than the outcome of the "crisis of '29," which determined what Rosemont calls "the necessarily autonomous position of surrealism within the revolutionary framework" (Rosemont 1978, 30, 36, 42).

Shattuck goes further to suggest that the surrealists' political waffling was perhaps a product of malicious forethought. His essay "Having Congress: The Shame of the Thirties," on the First International Congress of Writers for the Defence of Culture, held in Paris in June 1935, attacks everyone associated with the congress, from its hypocritical organizers to the marginalized surrealists. The congress was intended to address the role of the writer in an era of spreading fascism. Its grossest flaw, according to Shattuck, was the squelching of dissent and a failure to take any meaningful action. It was neither democratic nor productive and the organizing committee systematically excluded "undesirable" speakers, among them Breton, who was banned for hitting Ilya Ehrenbourg, the head of the Soviet delegation, who earlier had accused the surrealists of sexual deviance. The congress was, Shattuck concludes, "one of the most thoroughly rigged and steamrollered assemblages ever perpetrated on the face of Western literature in the name of culture and freedom." Its conservatism in the face of a possible revolution in France and political chaos in Europe illustrates how paralyzed bourgeois culture was at this time. The final declaration could hardly have been more bourgeois, calling as it did "for more translations, more travel opportunities for writers, and an international literary prize" (Shattuck 1960, 24–25). The surrealists were divided: Eluard read Breton's speech arguing against propagandistic poetry, while Aragon took the opposite position, arguing in favor of Soviet-style realism.

Shattuck's reading of the surrealists' relationship to communism is unsympathetic to the movement's original goals. Citing Breton's faith in Freud, his refusal "to give automatic obedience to directives from Moscow," and his defense of Trotsky, Shattuck (1960) asserts that "from 1927 to 1933 the Surrealists carried on a steady guerrilla war with the Party while insisting on their right to participate in events and organizations designed to give some shape and direction to artists on the left" (16).

We have seen that the surrealists struggled with the conflict between politics and aesthetic-spiritual ends, that they came to blows over it in 1929, and that the French Communist Party was quite frustrated by their stand. The *Second manifeste* and other documents clearly display ambivalence about which kind of revolution—social or of the unconscious—should receive the most immediate attention. Breton waffled frequently on the question, but the charge of waging "guerrilla war" on the Party suggests a willful hypocrisy for which Shattuck provides no convincing evidence (Shattuck 1960, 16). Shattuck elsewhere argues that Breton "argued himself into" taking on communism, whereupon he realized it was a mistake and "scrambled out as fast as he could." This is hardly accurate in light of Breton's long affiliation with the Party. "Aragon," Shattuck continues, "I cannot fully understand—whether he became Communist out of opportunism, in an attempt to mock all his friends and enemies, or under the spell of Elsa Triolet." Eluard "slithered about in many directions and allowed himself to be used, but politics rarely tainted the inspiration of his poetry," he adds, raising the question of whether Shattuck believes that politics have any place in poetry.[2]

Breton's relationship with the Party was inarguably adversarial, because of the conflict between surrealist practice and Party goals and Breton's stubborn refusal to pledge obedience to anyone. In this sense, Shattuck (1960) is right that the surrealists were "plus royaliste que le roi," for Breton did refuse to yield to any other authority (9). What one might also assert is that in significant measure Breton's interest in communism was linked to his sense that poetry wasn't so powerful a vehicle as he had earlier imagined; he was exploring new tools for accomplishing surrealist goals. English surrealist David Gasgoyne (1970) provides the insider's rebuttal to Shattuck's argument:

> Again and again the surrealists have been forced to point out that a consciousness of the class-struggle does not necessarily express itself in terms of "socialist realism," that the need for writing of the propaganda type does not in itself condemn research along other lines and that Communism has nothing to gain by suppressing the liberty of thought and expression of declared revolutionaries. (80)

This sounds reasonable enough in hindsight, but it was no more acceptable in the age of binarism than in the eyes of critics schooled in that age's polarized choices. Nevertheless, surrealist philosophy demanded that member poets collapse binary oppositions wherever possible. Accepting this premise, which by 1930 forced the surrealists to attempt the difficult task of fusing communism and surrealism, makes it problematic to charge the poets with deceit.

Aragon's behavior offers a noteworthy exception. In the Affaire Aragon, he is often criticized for pledging loyalty first to Soviet-style proletarian literature and to poetry as propaganda, then reneging and pledging loyalty to the surrealists, and finally, offering his primary loyalty to the communists once again. His abdication, in Shattuck's (1960) view, was preceded by "a lengthy period of despicable, two-faced maneuvers" (16). Since Aragon knew well the type of loyalty required by Breton, these choices were indeed a betrayal of his commitment to the movement and its leader. Whether he had malicious intent or behaved as he did because he couldn't decide between two very different imperatives is unclear. Shattuck (1960) reproaches him for his Stalinist bent, which lasted until the Soviet invasion of Czechoslovakia in 1968: "[Aragon's] wrigglings to explain the thunderbolt of the Hitler-Stalin pact were despicable. The Occupation forced him to retire to patriotic poetry, underground publishing, and a new literary career after the war" (28). But Aragon published books with Gallimard in 1941 and 1942, and Juin (1960) claims Aragon objected so vigorously to the German-Soviet pact that he was at one point threatened by fascists and forced to take refuge in the Chilean embassy (34). Shattuck is right about Aragon's tendency to wriggle, however: when the communist went into the military after World War II broke out, he asked for a transfer from the workers' regiment to which he had been assigned. He was reassigned to a more suitably bourgeois role, the command of a group of medical students (see Juin 1960, 34).

Aragon's poem "Front rouge," which calls for the murder of specific political enemies, provides an interesting test of surrealists' commitment to fellow members. The group stood by Aragon when he was charged with incitement to murder and it circulated a petition, signed by more than three hundred intellectuals, asserting that poetic discourse is simply that: poetic, that is, not to be taken as performative language or even as literal imperative. Such an argument about the status of poetic discourse necessarily undermined the power of poetry to influence the social revolution. André Gide and Romain Rolland, among others, refused to sign the petition for just this reason. The journal *L'humanité* accused the surrealists of advocating special protection for poets. That the surrealists' stand was uncharacteristically conservative and aesthetics-oriented caused Aragon's subsequent rejection of the movement to be all the more bitterly received. For Caws (1970), the French government's alarmed reaction to and literal reading of "Front rouge" is a sign of the power of poetry. She does not comment, however, on how the surrealists' statement of anti-literalism made this a Pyrrhic victory and undermined the group's position on social revolution (12).

The contrast between Shattuck's (1960) view of surrealism's moral failures and its inability to create "a revised version of mind" or "a surpassing of individuality" (44) and Caws's vision of surrealism as a profoundly successful moral pursuit is a striking illustration of the inside-outside division. Surrealism, one infers from Caws (1970), is moral, sincere, and sensitive; its poetic practice is a vehicle of spiritual transcendence and revolution (12). Her approach is the opposite of Shattuck's in its rejection of historical context and any other context outside the movement:

> Dada and surrealism . . . cannot be (or should not be) theorized about, exemplified, and handled at an efficient arm's length . . . [as] they are, by

their nature, present and possible only *within* their manifestations. . . . To dwell on the factual circumstances of the surrealist movement, no matter how important they may have been in the formulation of the texts, is necessarily to remain outside those texts. (1970, 5)

Caws's premise is interesting for a number of reasons, not least of which is that she proposes a criticism based almost entirely on poetic texts, a choice that excludes the social context and puts limits on the interpretation of poems. Though appealing in light of surrealism's values, this view leaves us with the question of how to get inside these texts without becoming surrealists ourselves. As Caws points out, the surrealist emphasis on process and on what she calls a surrealist motive makes such texts different from all others and, one might infer, uninterpretable. "The fact that no exterior categorization is possible," she concludes, "leaves the text open."[3]

Caws's textual criticism illustrates this critical openness that verges on eulogistic praise for all possible interpretations. Eluard's "majestic" poem "Sans âge" (Ageless) is a "poetic vision of liberation." Her interpretation of it overgeneralizes the positive emotion of the poem, whose power comes from the contrast between the difficult and painful realities of the past and a hopeful vision of personal transcendence. Caws's (1970) critical synopsis elides this contrast and embraces an unusually high degree of interpretive "openness":

Entirely constructed about the themes of creation, fraternity, childlike innocence and freshness, and around the parallel images of purity and light, joy, warmth, and language, "Sans âge" can be read either as a poem about surrealism or about Communist fraternity, or about the fraternity of poets, or better still as an example of the similarity between all three. (146)

Eluard does not identify the fraternal group in the poem except to hint that it is composed of fellow poets: "Nous aborderons tous une mémoire nouvelle / Nous parlerons ensemble un langage sensible." (We will all begin a new memory / Together we will speak an accessible language.) But the poem is rife with discontent about the past:

> Nous en avions assez
> D'habiter dans les ruines du sommeil
> Dans l'ombre basse du repos
> De la fatigue de l'abandon

(We were tired
Of living in the ruins of sleep
In the lowly shadows of rest
Of fatigue of abandon)

It is not until the poem's end that the liberating dawn comes. In the meantime, the speaker warns "O mes frères contraires gardant dans vos prunelles / La nuit infuse et son horreur" (O my contrary brothers holding in your eyes / The night infused with horror) (Caws 1970, 147–49; Caws's translation). And despite the group references, the main thrust of the poem is the speaker's quest to overcome personal isolation. The vehicle of this transcendence is, ironically, the self. A sense of community follows:

Moi je vais vers la vie j'ai l'apparence d'homme
Pour prouver que le monde est fait à ma mesure

Et je ne suis pas seul
Mille images de moi multiplient ma lumière
Mille regards pareils égalisent la chair

(I move toward life I have the look of man
To prove that the world is made to my measure

And I am not alone
A thousand of my images multiply my light
A thousand similar gazes equalize the flesh)

Caws correctly points out that the movement of the poem is from self to fraternity, but her *explication* is more celebratory than critical. Describing "Sans âge," she uses the following language: innocent revolution, positive integration, liberty, clarity, purity, expansion, unique revelation, perfect vision (1970, 147–51; Caws's translation). Ironically, she describes Eluard's poem as being formally litanic, a description that perhaps more accurately reflects her own criticism.

While Shattuck does not include textual criticism of poems in his essay on the Dadaist-surrealist "experiment," Caws focuses on it. Because she is little concerned with biography and historical context, the world of the poem stands in for those elements in her critical practice. I argue that this choice creates a tendency toward overdetermining the poems themselves. Of this excerpt from Eluard's *Défense de savoir* (Forbidden to know),

Ma présence n'est pas ici.
Je suis habillé de moi-même. . . .
La clarté existe sans moi.

Née de ma main sur mes yeux
Et me détournant de ma voie
L'ombre m'empêche de marcher
Sur ma couronne d'univers,
Dans le grand miroir habitable,
Miroir brisé, mouvant, inverse
Où l'habitude et la surprise
Créent l'ennui à tour de rôle.

(My presence is not here.
I am dressed in myself. . . .
Brightness exists without me.

Born of my hand over my eyes
And turning me aside from my path
The shadow keeps me from walking
On the crown of my universe.
In the great liveable mirror,
Broken mirror, moving, inverted
Where habit and surprise
Alternately create tedium.)

Caws (1970) writes:

When the poet loses his sense of immediacy and necessity in the world ("La clarté existe sans moi"), the bright surface of the mirror which reflected his genuine image is replaced by the artificial and empty appearance of an image ("habillé de moi-même") and the misleading obscurity for which the poet realizes he is somehow responsible ("née de ma main"). (156–57; Caws's translation)

Caws imputes a hubris to the speaker in her explanation of "La clarté existe sans moi" that is not necessarily warranted and which, if true, suggests a rather messianic relationship of poet to world much like that of Borges's Berkeleyan poems, where the speaker saves his world by remaining awake when all others are asleep. But Borges's hubris is based on metaphysics and his power is transferable, while Caws here seems to impute to the speaker a need to be the *source* of all "clarté." She tends also to assume that the speaker's assertions of personal power are signs of public power, citing other parts of *Défense de savoir* where "the poet has sufficient strength to deny all knowledge ('carcasses of the known'), all 'illusions of memory,' and all experience in order to assert his own present power over the world." She offers in illustration, however, two unmistakably personal lines: "Et je soumets le monde dans un miroir noir. . . / Je suis au coeur du temps et je cerne l'espace." (And I dominate the world in a black mirror . . . / I am at the center of time and I surround space.)

Caws (1970) claims that the images of Eluard's poem are "contemporary with and absolutely inseparable from the poet's feeling. . . . The image of a broken mirror in Eluard is itself the basis of a whole poem" (157; Caws's translation). Modernist poetry by nature demands that the reader not make too many assumptions about the degree of autobiography present in a work. Caws, however, suggests that the speakers in surrealist poetry are inextricably and consistently linked to the poets' personal experience. While much of the surrealist oeuvre is in the first person and much of it is personal, it is too great a leap to suggest that the liberated unconscious speaks only in the voice of the conscious poet, that there is only one voice freed by automatist practice, or that poet and speaker are the same. Certainly Caws's view is consistent with surrealist philosophy, which holds that the unconscious liberated by surrealist poetry is our purest, most honest self, but to imagine a single, unified voice issuing from the unconscious is to diminish our expectations of what the surrealists did in fact accomplish.

Writing in 1970, Caws does not address the objectification and appropriation of women in surrealist poems. Her synopsis of Desnos's "Si tu savais" (If you knew), from *A la mystérieuse* (To the mysterious woman), addresses the binary tensions of the poem as "desire and distance . . . knowledge and ignorance, submission and freedom, reality and illusion, actual absence and emotional presence." Desnos, referring to the woman in his poem as a "volontaire et matériel mirage" (voluntary and material mirage), has a fantasy based on the tension between dominance and submission. The roots of this tension can be found in the *fin amors* tradition of the troubadours and certainly in much subsequent poetry that constructs a "love" based on erotic domination. While true to the tradition of French poetry written by men, in the context of the surrealist commitment to freedom for all, Desnos's choice has an especially coercive flavor, one with which Caws subtly colludes. We recall here that she has labeled the opposite of submission "freedom," which it certainly is from the speaker's point of view, though hardly from that of the female figure he addresses. Desnos writes:

> Si tu savais comme le monde m'est soumis.
> Et toi, belle insoumise aussi, comme tu es ma prisonnière.
> O toi, loin-de-moi à qui je suis soumis.
> Si tu savais.

> (If you knew how the world submits to me.
> And you, beautiful unsubmissive one, how you are my prisoner.
> You, far from me, to whom I submit.
> If you knew.)

Caws (1970) comments about the female figure in the poem:

> She cannot know, but if she knew—the unfinished statement once more produces the inexplicably sad undertone characteristic of the love poems of Desnos. . . . She is the prisoner of the poet's imagination, of the mirage that he voluntarily pictures, but he is subject to the same mirage in its silence and unrelenting implication of cruelty. (187–88; Caws's translation)

Written before the coming of age of feminist criticism, Caws's comment sounds today like an apology for the poet's misogyny: suggesting that the dominating speaker suffers from the same cruelty as the fantasized woman is problematic. If we read the poem literally—as Caws elsewhere seems to recommend—the speaker suffers from the inaccessibility of an imaginary love object and the love object in turn, being imaginary, can't suffer. Even in fantasy, Desnos's speaker controls his poetic object in a manner that is difficult to call loving. Caws (1970) avoids ideological commentary on gender dynamics, explaining the line "Les ongles des femmes seront des cygnes étranglés" (The womens' nails will be strangled swans) by contrasting the "unnatural whiteness of the women's nails" with the "natural whiteness of the swan."[4] The violent strangulation is referred to simply as "unnatural," which indeed it is (189; Caws's translation). That parts of women's bodies are made to carry the burden of this violence is not examined.

Caws's approach exemplifies how inside critics tend to focus most closely on early surrealism and textual commentary, especially explicating poems, and tend to exclude historical information. In contrast, Shattuck's approach illustrates the tendency of outside critics to evaluate the movement historically, choosing not to ignore its political phase, and to emphasize how infrequently the movement makes good on its grand promises. Nadeau inhabits the uneasy middle ground between Caws and Shattuck; he is primarily an outside critic, but he acknowledges the limitations of his own perspective. He makes the disclaimer that he hasn't "lived the surrealist life *from within*," but asserts that his perspective affords him greater objectivity. In the 1944 foreword to *The History of Surrealism,* he pokes the obvious holes in surrealism's failed myth of itself: "For this antiliterary, antipoetic, antiartistic movement leads only to a new literature, a new poetry, a new painting, infinitely valuable of course, but a poor excuse for what we had been promised. . . . This is a long way from the *total transformation of life* proposed as a goal" (1989, 36).

Nadeau's voice is hard to pin down. He speaks often as though from within surrealism's myth, referring to the surrealist poet as prophet and magician, claiming that the "miracle he achieves can be achieved by all. Everyone is among the elect." He refers to surrealism as "a true revolution" (49–50). And though Nadeau slips in a number of direct quotations from Breton, much of his early text is a paraphrase or a projection of surrealism's idealistic goals. Like many other historical critics, Nadeau weaves his own view into the surrealist ideology, forcing the reader to try to separate the two. He describes Breton's "trial of *talent*," for example, as never more "than a booby trap" for surrealists (64), and he alternates between two voices, his own and one clearly borrowed from Breton.

Nadeau's tendency to oscillate between inside and outside views goes a long way toward a desirable integration of them. At times, however, it is difficult to tell who is speaking, as when Nadeau comments, "Poetry does not ask for knights-errant, it demands lovers who can, if necessary, violate her" (72). As he is referring here to Jarry, Rimbaud, Ducasse, and Lautréamont, the comment seems to be his. But it partakes of the misogynistic language characteristic of the surrealists and raises the question of influence: To what degree is Nadeau's critical language taken over by his experiment with assuming Breton's voice? And for critics of the avant-garde in general, how is it possible to avoid assimilating a radicalized vocabulary when discussing radical and not so radical groups? Nadeau's response is to remain primarily on the "outside" of the surrealist experience. But to do that experience justice requires attempting to understand it on its own terms. Discussing *Traité du style* (Treatise on style), Nadeau tries to present Aragon's point of view: "He does not want surrealism to pass for what it is not, a liberation from the literary rules, when it has actually taken a place outside of literature. . . . He sees quite clearly where the critics are ready to pigeonhole it in their little collections" (149).

On the next page, however, Nadeau retreats to his own voice: "All these revolts in which the surrealists indulge, this desire for omnipotence which they proclaim, this insistence on the radical destruction of the world and the mind . . . is this not still literature?" (150). Nadeau's approach has the advantage of avoiding Shattuck's excessive moralizing and Caws's tendency toward idolatry. In supporting the critical consensus that considers Breton a success and Aragon a failure, however, he is too charitable about Breton's behavior as group leader: "Breton's role was one of conciliation and arbitration, though he remained the only man capable of achieving the fusion [of the political revolution and the exploration of the unconscious]" (175). The fact is that Breton was a poor conciliator and he achieved the synthesis of revolutions poorly, as his relationship to the Communist Party proves. In the 1932 tract "The Poverty of Poetry: The Aragon Affair Before Public Opinion," Breton divides the problem into social and poetic "faces," a choice that can hardly be labeled "fusion." Nadeau uses a strange euphemism to describe the slapping of Ilya Ehrenbourg. Breton, he suggests, merely "corrected" Ehrenbourg for his charge of surrealist pederasty (194). Does this make him an apologist for Breton?

Nadeau concludes that surrealism failed in its aims, his proof being that "the world continued to live as if the surrealists had not existed" (220). This is too high a standard to hold any aesthetic movement to, and though Nadeau admits that surrealism is "quite different" from other literary schools, he does not examine the poetry in any depth. He focuses on products (which he finds lacking) rather than process, and in doing so he fails to consider fully what is unique about the movement. Nadeau sees surrealism as having "values" but no "doctrine" in 1924. It is "not written or painted," he argues (in the voice of the surrealists), but rather "lived." Whether he finds this business of living surrealism meaningful or important, however, is unclear, as he seems here to be echoing surrealism's myth of itself. In a similar way, he calls the surrealists "so many apostles of a new religion celebrated in cafés" (97) and argues that the surrealists found all "pragmatism, all concrete material activity" to be "shameful" (101). "It has been noted that art ultimately found a place within surrealism. This was not entirely the fault of the surrealists. The movement was envisaged by its founders not as a new artistic school, but as a means of knowledge" (80). Surrealism's movement from the anti-literary journal *Littérature* to the traditional *Minotaure* is rooted at least partly in the nature of the literary institution itself. How were the surrealists to gather a public for their revolution without participating in widespread publishing or without appealing to the literary market? There is no canonized avant-garde movement that does not share in this particular "failure."

Outside critics are correct that the surrealists had impossible expectations of themselves. The surrealists raise the Foucauldian question of how to reach beyond existing linguistic, mental, and institutional structures. Their failure to provide a quick or easy solution is certainly to be expected, and their experiment is the more valuable for its attempt to achieve the nearly impossible. The movement provides an unusual challenge for critics: to do justice to the movement's unique qualities without judging it exclusively on its own terms or by traditional criteria. It is through the struggle to find our own synthesis of these radically different choices that we learn more about surrealism's special nature and about the difficulties inherent in the practice of criticism.

Man is a history-making creature who can neither repeat his past nor leave it behind; at every moment he adds to and thereby modifies everything that has previously happened to him.

—W. H. Auden

It is absurd to believe that art is a department of politics.

—Jorge Luis Borges

10. "Lights becomings darks, boys, waiting for the end": Comparing the Fates of the Groups of Borges, Auden, and Breton

The avant-garde groups of Borges, Auden, and Breton followed similar trajectories. Though their rebellions took very different forms, all three rebelled against the literary establishment and at the same time sought conventional sorts of recognition and assistance from that establishment. Constituted by poets and then by critics, these groups engaged in polemics and in aesthetic projects, though they often kept the two separate. Each had troubles of audience, internal dissent, and historical circumstance; eventually they either gave up (Auden and Borges) or adopted new strategies and tried to keep going (Breton). Their shared quest for greater amounts of power for writers developed partly out of anxiety and fear. The Auden group feared the loss of certain humane values; the Argentines had to face the failure of their elitist vision of a budding national literary tradition; and for the surrealists, there was the cultural bankruptcy of the status quo and the prospect of a communist future.

The three groups present a spectrum of openness to social and literary change: the Argentines sought it least, the ambivalent Auden poets vacillated wildly, and the surrealists wanted it but did not know how to achieve it. In addition to being the product of fear or anxiety, the quest shared by the groups was fueled by desires ranging from renovating the linguistic and thematic nature of poetry to giving poets a starring role in political and social history. To varying degrees and in varying forms, the groups were committed to changing (or, in the case of the Argentine vanguardia, protecting) the writer's situation in society. In Auden's and Breton's cases, there was an attempt to empower the writer sociopolitically; in Borges's case, an attempt to save the status quo from the impact of massive immigration. Ironically, becoming leftists amounted to a marketing strategy for the Auden poets, whereas what would now be considered a right-wing call for ethnic and linguistic purity played the same role for the Argentine vanguardia. In spite of how different their aims and values were, all three groups were attracted to traditional literary establishments: only the surrealists could honestly claim that they did not want to *be* that establishment.

The Argentine vanguardia feared it stood to lose access to the privileges accorded poets of high culture and at the same time hoped to play a major role in building a national literature that would be internationally respected. By itself, the vanguardia did not substantially influence the course of Argentine literary history, though the group carved out for itself a modest but enduring niche. In its prose writings, the Argentine vanguardia made the sounds revolutionaries make, but the writers had few extrapoetic goals beyond wanting to enter the upper echelon of Argentine literary society and keep certain others from following. No one has argued that their aesthetic—*metaforismo*—was morally inadequate or misguided. Unlike the Auden poets, the vanguardia did not have to worry that they were practicing propaganda and thus tainting their poetic tradition. Like the surrealists, they kept their aesthetics-oriented poems separate from their strident polemics. The result is a somewhat schizophrenic body of work, though it is arguable that little has been lost: the ultraist poems have not transcended the decade of their composition and are thus considered primarily of historical interest. As an avant-garde group, the poets were long on form and short on content. Their circumstances—the building of a national literature in a time of national prosperity and relative stability—did not permit any greater agitation than their extreme position as a kind of cultural cabal. As it is, the next generation of poets indicated that it wanted to avoid their "excesses." In a manner reminiscent of the vanguardia's own habit of exaggeration, it identified these excesses as the "aggressive" use of language and "the abolition of all external norms."

The Auden poets drew on a stable and continuous literary tradition of more than five hundred years. Their attempts at revolutionary rhetoric rang false in the context of that history and even in the context of what was brewing in Europe in the 1930s. While the Argentine vanguardia's project was almost exclusively constructive, the Auden poets were divided between trying to preserve their privileged status in the English literary world and trying to absorb the fact that that world appeared to be disintegrating before their eyes. Caught between two conflicting imperatives—preserving the old and finding a morally viable alternative to it—they ultimately chose the conservative and the familiar. The Auden poets were diagnosticians, recognizing and describing an endemic illness, but they were not prepared to perform what they perceived to be the necessary surgery. In the end, their instincts proved to be right: English high culture was not disintegrating, but things were shifting nonetheless. Modernism gave way to postmodernism as T. S. Eliot gave way to Samuel Beckett and the political Auden gave way to the religious Auden. Their world had changed, and the English poet had arguably even less power than before.

The Auden group stands between the French surrealists and the Argentine vanguardia both in terms of its level of radicalism—we can call it a moderate case—and in its desire for change within the context of the status quo. More than either of the other groups, it had trouble making up its mind. The preface to *New Signatures* shows that in 1932 the poets—and especially Michael Roberts—had begun to combine conservative values and revolutionary rhetoric in a search for a compelling cause. Keeping in mind the Argentine poets' situation in 1924, we can infer that the Auden poets might have turned out to be a lot like their Argentine counterparts had the political situation in Europe been less dire. As has often been remarked, Spender and Day Lewis were romantics at heart, as were a number of the vanguardia poets.

The surrealists came from a tradition of revolutionary violence, and they shared their English and Argentine counterparts' romantic penchant for exaggeration. They had to be extreme in word and deed in order to stand out in the French cultural landscape. Their philosophical platform was radical, but their methods for retraining the mind were inadequate to the task of changing the world order and its deeply entrenched conceptual framework and institutions. It goes almost without saying that the surrealists were a product of the thing they loathed. Their sense of personal oppression can be guessed at by examining the ways they objectified women in their poetry and, in some cases, in their lives.

The surrealists' central conflict was over the wielding of power, though the power struggle was more an in-house affair than a battle between the group and the world. The surrealists' methods, however, were inadequate and their revolutionary impulse became inbred and localized. By the late 1920s, their "revolution" had largely taken the form of an internal civil war. The conflicts within the movement hint that in an era of totalitarian ideologies, many writers thought it essential not to yield ground to outside ideologies without careful consideration of the consequences, a circumspection that contributed to intolerance of dissent within the ranks. Ironically, though Breton argued intelligently—and ultimately rationally—for surrealism's independence from all other -isms of his era, he succumbed in spite of himself to the temptation to borrow from political ideologies he disdained and, later, found too narrow in their behavioral prescriptions. In the end, however, perhaps because of the group's insular nature and Breton's devotion, surrealism maintained a greater distance from the literary establishment than did the Argentine vanguardia or the Auden poets. Arguably, it had the greatest involvement with communism.

The surrealists shared the Auden poets' feeling that the world as they knew it had been destroyed, though they had less to lose than these English elite if their society underwent further change. They were more inclined toward forging a new mode of perceiving human experience. Even in the midst of their internal civil war, the surrealists struggled with the things middle-class writers have long struggled with: achieving an acceptable standard of living and finding an audience. Along the way, they managed to amplify the French poet's right to participate in politics and to make everything in capitalist society a legitimate subject for the creative writer.

The surrealist journals were the most radical of the magazines of the three groups. As surrealism changed, so its journals were created and discarded one after another. The Auden group's formative "journals"—*New Signatures* and *New Country*—were peripheral to the poets' success and lacked the coherence of purpose of the surrealists' journals. The Auden poets, by virtue of being well-connected products of Oxford (and, more peripherally, Cambridge), had access to excellent publishing opportunities. They did not really need their own journals. For the Argentine vanguardia, in contrast, journals were the essential means of presenting themselves. Paradoxically, however, the Argentine poets undermined their movement in the very pages they created to promulgate it. Borges rejected ultraism in the first issue of *Proa,* and in a later issue Guillermo de Torre dismissed surrealism, from which the vanguardia borrowed a number of strategies, as destructive of "normal intellectual interaction." It soon became clear that even having all the right signatures would not sustain a weakly conceived movement. French surrealism was truer to the spirit of the avant-garde than was the Argentine vanguardia; for it, the content of a text was more important than the signature attached to it. And though surrealist poets are now read and evaluated individually, it is the group that has left the most indelible mark on modern culture.

The poetics of surrealism was far more innovative than that of the Argentine vanguardia. Both relied heavily on metaphor, even though for the surrealists metaphor was instrumental, a vehicle to a radically new world, whereas for the Argentines it was more nearly decorative, a "new" aesthetic. The Auden poets, in contrast, did not pursue a program of formal innovation. Their contribution (which was not necessarily their goal in 1932) was to expand the range of subjects considered appropriate to English poetry. If they had been surrealists, the Auden poets would not have cared whether their impulse was *appropriate*. In fact, if they had been surrealists, they would have been dismayed to find that it was. Being who they were, however, the Auden poets argued energetically about how to define propaganda and that propaganda can have a place in poetry. They won the battle in England, but they also learned that propaganda—insofar as it is topical or strident—gives a poem a short shelf life. Even many of Auden's poems, which are hardly what one would call propaganda, have taken on a topical resonance. Auden of the 1930s is now read as the "social Auden," the "early Auden," or the "English Auden."

If as an exercise one puts these poets on a continuum running from conservative to radical, the coherence of the various groups dissolves somewhat. A "conservative" surrealist—Eluard—might be placed among the Argentine ultraists, while the radical Girondo finds his nearest of kin among the surrealists. The three group leaders share certain traits, chief among them a measure of charismatic authority. Comparing their poems, however, presents a more complex problem. Breton's poems are much more ambitious than those of Borges. Breton, in his hope of changing the conceptual landscape of Western civilization, sought to collapse dualisms and create world-altering images, whereas Borges's goals were more purely poetic and linguistic: to create novel, memorable metaphors and images and to evoke argentinidad in the process. However, when analyzed rhetorically—especially in regard to their very similar attachment to metaphor and simile—the poems of Borges and Breton can seem remarkably alike. We therefore cannot simply say that ultraist poems are conservative and surrealist poems are not. In the ideologies behind the poems, this is true; formally, however, the two poetics share important common ground. Auden's poems belong in a category of their own. They speak in a sometimes cagey and ironic, sometimes bluntly honest voice; to Auden's credit, it is often difficult to know exactly how best to read them. His is a poetry of great range both in the formal dexterity reflected in the poems and in the choice of subject matter.

Each group had internal limits demarcated by the roles meted out to or withheld from group members. Girondo's track record, for example, strongly suggests that had he been the leader of the Argentine vanguardia, he would have been openly critical of its weak ideology and would have pushed it toward acts of radicalism and perhaps even toward self-extinction. The irony of this, of course, is that if he had been given a larger role, the vanguardia would have had more vitality and might have survived longer. Girondo had real discontents and would have stirred something memorable into the Argentine literary brew. As it is, he lacked this power until the 1940s, when he was no longer young. It is worth asking whether, if Girondo had not been wealthy, able to help finance his publications, and well connected in Europe, his voice would even have been heard in the Argentina of the 1920s. Analogously, Louis MacNeice, who understood the pitfalls of the frenetic search for values and right action in a decade filled with cultural malaise, was not altogether wanted at the center of his group. Nor were his observations welcomed by critics who admired the Auden poets' commitment to social change. In a decade of extremes, MacNeice was too moderate. In the context of the 1930s, however, he wasn't moderate at all; insofar as he came to be seen as an outcast of the group, it was because he chose a form of neutrality at a time when it was unacceptable to make such a choice. As for surrealism's misfits, they either stepped aside or were pushed out. Surrealism's elastic ideology proved surprisingly brittle when it came to personnel. The frequent comings and goings of surrealists and former surrealists had the effect of making the public focus more on the group than on individual personalities.

The surrealists and the Argentine vanguardia cared about disrupting art's role as a commodity in bourgeois culture, but they cared for very different reasons. Whereas the surrealists sought to de-commodify art because they felt that a work of art's authenticity was compromised when it became a commodity, the vanguardia was quietly nostalgic for the days of patronage and of the upper-class gentleman writer. The Argentine poets largely resisted the popularization of art, whereas the surrealists were attracted to the idea of circumventing traditional means of self-promotion and hoped to reach a large audience. Girondo's strategies of self-promotion suggest both Dada/surrealism's unorthodox, hostile, and self-mocking overtures toward the market and the Auden group's unapologetic attraction to that market. Like the surrealists, Girondo was not averse to patronage from the state, but he scorned government interference in the arts. In many ways, he was a surrealist in spirit who found himself in the wrong group.

Although the avant-garde is often thought to be fundamentally anarchic, these groups presented themselves to varying degrees as models of order that arose to deal with social and cultural chaos or the real or imaginary threat of such chaos. All three of the groups participated in the civilization-versus-barbarism dichotomy that dominated during the interwar period. The vanguardia and the Auden poets located barbarism out in the world, while the surrealists ultimately found it in their own ranks. This difference in orientation—the surrealist pride in its own barbarism versus the English and Argentine self-identification with "civilization" (and thus the status quo)—is an extremely important distinction that shows how different avant-garde movements can be. Surrealism was much more inclined to what Terry Eagleton calls the "negative" avant-garde, whereas the vanguardia and the Auden poets—in spite of their sometimes negative rhetoric—were almost wholly "positive" in impulse. In a sense, surrealism was a microcosm, an insular society struggling to achieve a new order based on inverting many of the old assumptions and modes of thought. That Breton in his leadership style borrowed so heavily from fascism and communism illustrates the impossibility of escaping pervasive cultural influences. It is hard to imagine Breton leading either the vanguardia or the Auden poets, largely because member poets would never have allowed him such control over them.

Why were the Argentine goals so modest and the Auden and surrealist groups' goals so ambitious? The answer is partly linked to what was at stake at the time: the vanguardia came into being at a time of general stability and prosperity, while the Auden poets felt that the private life and the upper classes were threatened with extinction, and the surrealists believed that hastening that extinction might be the best way to free human beings from an unfortunate history. The vanguardia was very politically conservative partly because there was no need to be otherwise. It is important to recall in this context that Borges took more political risks under Perón's regime, when there was much more for him and his nation to lose.

He was rewarded in 1946 by the government, which "promoted" him to inspector of poultry and rabbits at the municipal market. A police officer was assigned to take notes when he gave public lectures.

England, true to its insular nature, had chosen to try to appease Hitler and to try to continue with business as usual. The poems of the Auden group reflect the degree to which this was impossible, but they also map the line dividing what was really happening from an inflated rhetoric spawned in part by a romantic attraction to disaster. Like the vanguardia, the Auden poets wanted to keep the proletariat from dominating the cultural landscape. Unlike the vanguardia, however, they were morally troubled by their attitude. They nevertheless confessed to it and acknowledged their suspicion—shared by their counterparts in Argentina—that the masses were capable only of mediocrity. On paper, the surrealists were less worried by the proletariat's potential incursions into their discursive domain. However, in spite of their stated commitment to a socialist revolution, their ranks were dominated by disaffected members of the middle class. Either their door was not so open as they claimed it to be or their revolution held little appeal for the prerevolutionary proletariat, or both.

All three groups displayed a high degree of elasticity in their willingness to discard old and to adopt new strategies from one year to the next. The interwar period was also a time of unusual elasticity in the meanings and usages of words. What the Argentines called "ethics," the Auden poets called "politics." And whereas politics were anathema to the vanguardia, it was the private life (with its attendant subjectivity) that came to be considered wrongheaded by the Auden poets. The three groups used the word "revolutionary" to mean many different things, and what a group meant by the word one year might not be what it meant the next. Over time, values and the meanings of words changed substantially. Whereas "political" was an eminently acceptable word (and personal orientation) for the Auden group of the mid-1930s, two decades later "moral" was the term of choice to describe personal concern with social issues. Conversely, it was all right to express "moral" and "ethical" (but not "political") concerns in Argentine high culture in the 1920s and 1930s. By the 1950s, however, it was generally held that writers should be political. In both countries, "politics" were associated with the public realm and "morality" with the private. In Auden's 1930s, to be fixated on the private life was to be selfish and atavistic. In interwar Argentina, in contrast, focusing on the private was the most appropriate stance a writer could take. John Cornford aptly observed that there is a fundamental separation of politics and literature in the English literary tradition. Auden's 1930s were indisputably anomalous. In France and Argentina, in contrast, especially the Argentina of recent decades, the writer was more likely to be expected to be politically involved.

One test of the avant-garde's mettle is what it will do in moments of cultural insecurity or crisis. These three groups provide a spectrum of reactions: the Argentine vanguardia—and *Sur* after it—turned to the outside, to Europe, for reassurance and authority even as they rejected foreign ideologies such as surrealism. The Auden poets vacillated over whether their chief goal was to protect the old or create the new. Unlike the Argentines, however, theirs was primarily an insular reaction; with the exception of pleasure trips to Germany and other countries in the early 1930s and their support for Republican Spain, the Auden poets did not often look beyond their borders for answers. The surrealists, who were the most vociferously antinational of all, were in a sense even more insular than the Auden poets. They invented and reinvented the wheel but, with the exception of the surrealists' experiment with communism, their efforts were a largely in-house affair.

Both the surrealists and the Auden group revealed the limits of the writer's power to effect social change. Both introduced new aesthetics, changing the course of their national poetries forever, but neither made a revolution. The surrealists arguably didn't even try to achieve the global revolution called for in the *Manifeste du surréalisme*. Social and aesthetic impulses converged in surrealist poetry as language became the trigger of personal psychic liberation. The problem was that individual liberation did not create social revolution. In the end, the surrealists' choices revealed that they were more concerned with themselves than with what went on outside their group. Those on the outside, for that matter, were of necessity an enemy. Their experience offers the lesson that one cannot stage a revolution without inviting the masses. While the Auden poets and the Argentine vanguardia borrowed the rhetoric of politics, the surrealists borrowed the *tools* of politics: inquisitions, pressure to achieve "consensus" (as if the poets were members of a communist cell), internal purges. This application of tools of oppression to an agenda of liberation had predictable results.

On the whole, these groups of poets reacted intelligently to their historical moments and found (though did not always test) the limits of the possible given their circumstances. If each group is an outgrowth of the culture that gave rise to it, one can also argue that a given talent plucked from its roots and replanted elsewhere (a Stephen Spender in Argentina, for example) would have behaved differently. The vanguardia's extreme conservatism must be considered in context; the proof of its relative "radicalism" is that both *Sur* and the "novísima generación" (newest generation) of poets that followed on its heels were more conservative, the latter as a public and direct reaction to its predecessor.

All three of the groups explored the limits of the poet's power. For the surrealists to have come closer to accomplishing their mission, they would probably have needed to abandon poetry, their attachment to patriarchy, their ambivalence about alternative political systems, and their messianic leader. Even so, we can say with the confidence of historical hindsight, they would have failed because they wanted something nearly impossible to achieve. But there were also internal limitations; their choices show that many of them were poets first, surrealists second. In an important way, they were traditionalists. The Auden group was bolder than the surrealists in its attempt to give politically important roles to poets. And its messianic complex was in some ways stronger than that of Breton, who wanted fidelity from fellow surrealists more than a role as leader of the general public. The Auden group's failure to achieve its social goals was more public and more humiliating than the surrealists' "failure," largely because the poets were so outspoken, tried so hard to make rational arguments, spoke to the intelligentsia, and had marginally more viable—though still unattainable—goals. Most of all, the Auden poets were capable of a personal humiliation that Breton would have scorned. The experience of the surrealists illustrates what became painfully clear during the course of the cold war: group consensus on an agenda for "liberation" does not freedom make. Though their dream of freedom eluded them, the surrealists had ample energy to make inroads on other goals. They and the Auden poets struggled over the conflicting imperatives of the aesthetic and sociopolitical platforms for change, providing themselves—thanks to the rising chaos in Europe—with ample internal tensions to keep their groups going.

The Argentine vanguardia's problem was different. Its social agenda was too weak to sustain it and there was little tension to its aesthetic agenda; no amount of rhetoric could make up for the fact that the group lacked a sustaining dialectic. The Auden poets came down on the side of social reality and the surrealists moved from a predominantly aesthetic agenda to one more concerned with social experience. If one measures their failures in the coin of the avant-garde's ideology, all three of the groups discussed in these pages fell short of their stated goals, and the most radical—the surrealists—fell the hardest, followed by the Auden poets. The avant-garde's successes are not always mentioned by the avant-garde itself; this is partly because the avant-garde understands the irony of even having mainstream successes. Insofar as a group is strict in its antiestablishment ideology, such "successes" should, within the movements themselves, be considered failures.

The Auden poets, and their critics after them, struggled over the creation and control of literary and cultural value. By the late 1930s, the limits on how much power a poet could have in English society had become so clear that irony unmistakably crept into Auden's "Voltaire at Ferney," written in February 1939:

> Soon he would be dead,
> And still all over Europe stood the horrible nurses
> Itching to boil their children. Only his verses
> Perhaps could stop them: He must go on working.
> Overhead
> The uncomplaining stars composed their lucid song.
> (Auden 1977, 240)

That same month, in "In Memory of W. B. Yeats," Auden (1977) baldly admitted, "For poetry makes nothing happen" (242). Even before that, in a sonnet sequence written in 1938, he confessed his disappointment:

> The life of man is never quite completed;
> The daring and the chatter will go on:
> But, as an artist feels his power gone,
> These walk the earth and know themselves defeated.
> (1977, 259)

The Auden group's struggles and failures to empower the English poet raised the question: Whose responsibility is it to create humane values and literary value? The debate continues, largely because writers and critics are inherently in conflict over these issues.

The Argentine vanguardia poets, with the exception of Borges and Girondo, are often still considered and read as a group. The Auden poets, in contrast, have achieved something grander: as individual writers, they have achieved a measure of enduring fame, and as a group, they are still the subject of vigorous debate. Because they stuck to poetry, which does not translate so well as prose, and because they were quintessentially English in orientation (as was Auden even after he became a United States citizen), they have not achieved anything close to the more cosmopolitan Borges's fame. Ironically, the most conservative avant-garde produced the most startlingly memorable writer—Borges—and the most radical group is remembered more for its vision than for what it managed to accomplish. Turning away from what he came to view as his mistakes of the 1920s helped Borges become the universalist fiction writer who went on to achieve international fame. As Borges's training ground, the vanguardia played a major (if largely unrecognized) role in putting Argentine literature on the world stage.

Borges became an internationally respected writer of the first order. He did this by changing genres—from poetry to fiction—and by turning his attention to timeless, universal themes. He also began to publish frequently in *Sur,* a journal designed to be read in Europe. He published essays in *Sur* from its debut in late 1931 until 1939, and they did not bring him fame. Though he was recognized in Argentina as an important writer by the late 1920s, it was not until the 1940s, when he was regularly publishing short fiction and had the good fortune to be translated into French, that he began to achieve a measure of international recognition. His greater fame began when he shared the Formentor Prize with Samuel Beckett in 1961 and the Latin American literary "boom" of the years that followed brought him and other writers international acclaim. His politics were mild during the era of the vanguardia, but when Argentina was becoming increasingly enamored of fascism, he came down on the side of Western liberalism: opposing the Nazis, decrying anti-Semitism, supporting the Republicans in the Spanish civil war, and daring to criticize Juan Perón. Later in life, he was an archconservative, supporting Argentina's military government and the institutionalized repression and killing of the Argentine Dirty War. He kept his politics out of his fiction and his late poetry, though he sometimes wrote stories that have fascinating political subtexts. The choice has been good for his international reputation.

While Borges successfully crossed the genre line, Auden never really attempted to. His early dramas were not very successful and he soon abandoned them; his essays were written mainly in the service of poetry. He remains a key figure in modern English poetry, but his poetry relies so heavily on the English tradition—from Anglo-Saxon alliteration to intertextual allusions—that it does not survive translation very well. Auden remains a well-respected poet of his tradition, but he has not—unlike Borges and Breton—become an important figure in other parts of the world.

André Breton is now read as a polemicist and a poet. For those most attracted to his philosophy, he is a polemicist. For a much smaller group, he is a poet of enduring value. He did not try to rehistoricize himself by editing his personal canon the way Auden and Borges did, and therefore did not disrupt the unwritten contract among poet, critic, and public domain as his counterparts did. And, unlike Borges, he did not try to transcend his moment, or even for that matter fully to transcend surrealism's obvious limitations. Instead, he tried to make the surrealist moment last for decades, clinging doggedly to what he believed in and making himself a lasting niche as a thinker (though he hated rationalism) and as a leader.

That surrealist philosophical writings are still of considerable interest is illustrated by the fact that their strategies have been appropriated again and again by admiring young groups of artists in many parts of the world. As an avant-garde, the surrealists have preserved the strongest reputation of the three groups discussed here. As poets, their individual reputations have shaken loose somewhat from the group, though their work is also offered in surrealist collections. Their leader achieved an unusual kind of fame. Breton is best known for his statements about surrealism itself; his poetry is these days probably less admired than that of Desnos and Eluard. The leaders of the other two groups, however, are more famous than Breton for their individual creative work. Breton will always be synonymous with surrealism, whereas Auden and Borges have shed many of the associations of their formative decades.

In French literary history, Breton heads one of several generations of radical postrevolutionary French writers. Beyond the borders of France, he has a different cachet. His dogmatism seems more radical, his idealism more alluring in its exported form. It is certainly noteworthy that his movement figures as *the* model for the theory of the avant-garde, including for many scholars from other countries. On the whole, surrealist poems are difficult poems written during a century whose genre of choice is fiction. The surrealists made no attempt to write an accessible, let alone popular, poetry. Their poems speak to people who share the sensitivities and inclinations of the surrealists; they are less vehicles of personal conversion than offerings to the already converted.

Of the three groups, the Argentine vanguardia remains most limited to its historical moment. Conservative in its goals, it nevertheless succeeded at what it most wanted: to enter the Argentine canon and achieve modest but lasting recognition within that tradition. For a number of reasons, it has not achieved much fame outside of Latin America. It experienced failure on a couple of fronts: Borges repudiated ultraism soon after he introduced it, and the journals of the vanguardia were short-lived. The vanguardia wanted a role offering radicalism, novelty, and excitement at a time of stability, retrenchment, and tradition-building. In a sense, the movement never left the Buenos Aires of the 1920s because it created little of enduring aesthetic or polemical interest, though some of Borges's early poems deserve more attention than they have received.

Critical reception of these poets and their groups followed a changeable course: whereas Borges has been severely criticized for his failure to be sociopolitical, Auden and his gang have been attacked for their excess of sociopolitical fervor. The current trend perhaps is to be more tolerant of both sets of choices. As we have seen, MacNeice and Empson have been evaluated by different standards, as have the *Sur* group and the vanguardia. The reasons for a shifting politics of reception are not hard to deduce; critics, like literature itself, are a product of their tradition. Within each critical tradition, there are schools and generations of critics, each as much a product of its time and place as the avant-garde poets were of theirs. Proponents of the Argentine literary tradition as it existed when the vanguardia began to publish, represented in later decades by conservative (that is, nonleftist) critics, arguably chose not to examine the socially regressive motives of the vanguardia poets because to do so would have been to expose their institutional ideology to unwanted scrutiny.

The official history of the Argentine vanguardia—an account that has remained remarkably stable for decades—contrasts markedly with the shifting receptions of Borges and *Sur,* which have resulted in part from the changed political agenda of the post–World War II era. The reappraisal of *Sur* is particularly interesting for what it reveals about critics, who came to see socioeconomic elitism and apathy toward social responsibility where earlier critics had seen either cultural elitism or nothing objectionable at all. Whereas for Borges and *Sur* a friendly reception was replaced in Argentina by a politically hostile one, the Auden poets were the subject of a struggle over value, including whether they had been evaluated correctly as poets. There is a fundamental difference of orientation here: Latin American critics were often concerned with whether the writer or the journal had fulfilled an important social responsibility, whereas Auden group critics argued over the question of taking responsibility as arbiters of culture. Where the Argentines have argued over the duties of the writer, the English and Americans have argued over the duties of the critic as well. The critics of surrealism, in their division into insiders and outsiders, are more akin to the writer-oriented Argentines; "inside" critics exalt the writers that "outside" critics find lacking.

In his theory of the avant-garde, Poggioli (1968) warns that it is important to distinguish between "the history of taste and the history of art. The inability to distinguish between these two disciplines is exactly what impedes us from realizing how novelty in an artistic accomplishment is something quite different from novelty in the artist's attitude vis-à-vis his own work, and vis-à-vis the aesthetic task imposed upon him by his own era" (13).

Here Poggioli enters social territory, hinting at something Bürger formulates more explicitly: that the true avant-garde involves attempting to change the relationships among art, artist, and society. In this sense, the surrealists were the most successful avant-garde group studied here. Their project was the most innovative, their attitude one that suggests a great willingness to pursue change. The Auden poets did not seek a fundamental restructuring of the relationship between art and society. They claimed to want one, but they did not take the necessary steps. Instead, they sought more power for poets without losing the poet's status in English society. Like the Argentine vanguardia, they were averse to many kinds of risk. However, their poems are in ways the most personally revealing of the three groups studied here. They arguably took the greatest emotional risks.

Bürger (1984) maintains that the avant-garde is most effective in its global critique of the "art institution" when it focuses on aesthetics rather than social issues: "The self-criticism of the social subsystem that is art can become possible only when the contents also lose their political character, and art wants to be nothing other than art. This stage is reached at the end of the nineteenth century, in Aestheticism" (26–27). Bürger's view underestimates the effectiveness of the political strategies of modernism and the innovative ways writers such as T. S. Eliot and Auden expressed social discontent. But as the surrealists show, he is right to argue that aestheticism can sometimes be the most effective strategy available to a group, though it also, like political commitment, can in extreme cases resemble a fundamentalist religion. By breaking with traditional forms, modes such as realism and naturalism,[1] and conventional vocabularies and social behaviors, the avant-garde draws attention to its discontents and its diagnosis of society's ailments.

Bürger (1984) is right to define the European avant-garde as "an attack on the status of art in bourgeois society" (49). Unfortunately, if the regime of power in question remains fundamentally unchanged, even strategic amorality loses its power. The Dadaists learned this bitter lesson when the bourgeoisie began to enjoy its antics and to write favorably about them. On 1 August 1920, Jacques Rivière published an article in the *Nouvelle Revue Française* that showed a respectful interest in Dada's projects. Bürger (1984) argues that the avant-garde collapses the dichotomy of pure art versus political art (91). The Argentine avant-garde actually reinforced this dichotomy, however, while surrealist theory went furthest in the direction of collapsing it. Surrealist poetry was nearly apolitical and the gap between the poetry and the theory spread to the poets' lives as they became increasingly divided over political issues. Aragon acquiesced too completely to the propaganda needs and ideological requirements of the Soviet Communist Party, causing his expulsion from the poetic group. A commitment to personal success as a writer and a privileging of aesthetics were equally risky choices for surrealists.

It is difficult to define failure in the context of the avant-garde. A group can, for example, fail to live up to its stated goals (say, revolutionary change) or it can fail to achieve what may be unspoken goals (a desire for fame, for example). In the interwar period in general, in spite of a litany of calls for the "new," the avant-garde was quite preoccupied with the fate of the old, the "truth" of the past. This is nowhere clearer than with the Auden poets, whose call for a new world order coexists with a desperate effort to entrench the power of Oxford-educated poets. The price of failure was not the absence of a communist revolution in England, but rather the poet-critic's lack of power at a time when geopolitical issues were overshadowing other sorts of cultural concerns. By 1939, the Auden poets learned that they had little power to influence historical events; their hopes for the influence of poets and poetry shrank correspondingly. After World War II, English poets continued to be arbiters of the aesthetic, but did not again attempt to claim the role of legislators of the world order.

Insofar as it is possible to theorize the avant-garde, I have presented evidence that the body of theory needs to take into account less "orthodox" (that is, non-Continental) groups. Myths of the avant-garde need to be acknowledged for what they are. The reasons for their existence, whether a group's publicly disseminated self-image or a critic's romantic attraction to this self-image, need to be identified and their implications understood. Poggioli (1968), for example, refers to "that predestined unpopularity which avant-garde followers, light-heartedly and proudly, accept" (39). Or do they? It depends on what is meant by unpopular. The Argentine vanguardia did not mind being unpopular if it meant not appealing to the lower classes; it comes closest to fitting Poggioli's description. The Auden poets claimed to want to speak to all socioeconomic classes but were not willing to make the sort of effort even they realized would be required. They did, however, mind the fact that they spoke to a comparatively small, elite audience. The surrealists were arguably more sincere in their stated desire to reach all people with their ideological message: How then could they really welcome unpopularity? In the sense that all of these groups were elitist and participated in a kind of intellectual snobbery, however, they accepted "that predestined unpopularity." All three succumbed to the coterie spirit that characterizes the avant-garde even when its goal is to transform an entire society or world order. What they worried about more than being democratic was sustaining their revolutionary zeal, the life force that was the foundation of their existence as a group. This commitment was not always evenly distributed, however; Spender and Day Lewis were attached to the idea of the "Auden group" in a way that Auden himself was not.

Discussing the radical avant-garde, Poggioli (1968) argues that the "immolation of the self to the art of the future must be understood not only as an anonymous and collective sacrifice, but also as the self-immolation of the isolated creative personality" (67–68). This is another instance of the theoretical ideal of the avant-garde exaggerating its reality. The vast majority of choices made by the groups promoted their reputation, power, and survival. The groups kept a suicide watch, making sure that things did not get out of hand. Though Dadaism stands out for its enthusiastic attraction to self-destruction, even Dadaist leader Tristan Tzara squabbled with Breton after Dada's collapse over who deserved more credit for Dadaism. Breton realized that conservatism lurks near radicalism when he wrote during the Dada years: "The dadaists from the start have taken care to state that they want nothing. In other words, there's nothing to worry about; the instinct of self-preservation always wins out." [2]

Poggioli (1968), in contrast, sees avant-garde writers and artists as disposed "to make dung heaps of themselves for the fertilization of conquered lands, or mountains of corpses over which a new generation may in its turn scale the besieged fortress" (68). Insofar as avant-garde movements inevitably lay groundwork on which future generations will build, this is true. But the implication that self-destruction was something avant-garde groups did with a generous eye to the future is wrong, at least in the case of the historical avant-garde, which did not expend much energy conceiving of a future in which it had no place. As we have seen, the avant-garde may take pleasure in a rhetoric of destruction, but it rarely plots its own demise. In spite of their rhetoric, the poets discussed in these pages did not make a practice of leaving creative work unsigned. The notion of a poem as private property is extremely strong in the modern era, and the historical avant-garde's work is no exception.

The lesson of these three groups is that the avant-garde is above all goal-oriented and strategic in its choices. While it often takes pleasure in some degree of mayhem, it does not lose sight of the bare necessities of survival. Poggioli argues that the avant-garde's more anarchic impulses "are capable of producing a morbid condition of mystical ecstasy, which prevents the avant-garde artist from realizing that he would have neither the reason nor the chance to exist in a communist society" (100). A romantic and very common conception of the avant-garde holds that it is irrational, even childlike. But behaviors by avant-garde groups that appear to be this way, when examined with care, usually reveal themselves to be strategic, sometimes even methodically planned. The Auden group was forced by its hubris to consider carefully its fate in a communist society—and the idea made the poets so nervous they admitted these feelings in print. Breton had to decide what sort of relationship the surrealists were going to have with the French Communist Party. Given the fact that a Popular Front government came to power in France during the 1930s, this was no abstract question. Despite his political sympathies, Breton held back from turning surrealism over to the demands of the Party. It is highly unlikely, given his close and unpleasant encounters with the Party, that he did not understand that under communism surrealism's freedom would wither.

These three groups also teach us to avoid confusing a group's blueprint for action with its actual behavior. The gap between word and deed reveals the inevitable gulf separating the avant-garde's idealized new world and the realities of its historical time and place. Each of these groups exhibited some degree of hypocrisy, if we define hypocrisy as a fairly consistent disparity between stated intent and actual performance. Although each group had moments of offering itself as a pinnacle of poetic achievement, only the surrealists viewed themselves—if briefly—as the apogee of avant-gardism, the avatars of a philosophy to end all philosophies. The Argentine vanguardia and the Auden poets were much more aware of themselves as products of literary lineages. They wanted to have prominent roles, but they believed in the necessity of history and sometimes even in the inevitability of their own passing.

Again and again, Poggioli's model reveals an idealized view of the Continental avant-garde, one that not even the surrealists lived up to. Bürger's theory, while more transferrable to non-Continental cases, emphasizes the notion that the avant-garde rebels against a long tradition and the firmly entrenched institutions upon which art depends. He, too, takes as his focus the Continental example, especially the surrealists. Institutions need not be firmly entrenched to be the focus of rebellion; avant-garde artists are often ambivalent about institutions imported from colonial powers to their newly independent states. Their rebellion may be against social and racial injustice (the case of César Vallejo) or it may oppose the popularization of literary culture (the case of the Argentine vanguardia). Poggioli (1968) views the Latin American avant-garde impulse as wholly derivative. Hispano-American ultraism, he argues, is a hybrid arising "from the crossing of imagism and cubism . . . [and] modernism and futurism" (228). He does not inquire into the specific circumstances of the Latin American avant-garde, seeing in its literary modernism "an incipient vulgarization of artistic novelty and the literary modernity of French coinage" (228). The subject does not appear to interest him much.

It is important to look beyond the initial act by foreign literatures of borrowing from Europe to see what kinds of movements arise in non-European countries. What distinguishes the Argentine from the Continental avant-garde is that its project is more constructive; some of the sources of its authority are imported; and it is the product of a plethora of influences, both local and foreign. The choices of the vanguardia show that foreign authority was limited and strategic, and it never dominated local imperative. In the 1930s, the *Sur* core writers displayed their independence from Europe by rejecting fascism and communism so they could cling to liberalism, the very model considered bankrupt by the Auden poets. But liberalism was not bankrupt for them, and they did not become so imitative of European models as to try to alter the course of their own political history. Although the Auden poets also borrowed from the Continental model, their tradition was so strong that they had no need to import foreign authority. Their tradition was so strong, in fact, that the borrowing of foreign rhetoric rang embarrassingly false in England.

As for the crucial question raised by Eagleton—Do these artists and their art acknowledge the degree to which they were compromised by the conditions under which writers worked in their time and place?—the answer is a qualified yes. Earlier I argued that the avant-garde makes public its confusion and rage and that in its ambivalence and ambition it lays bare the complex relations among art, artist, and the institutions supporting them. It is not exaggerating to say that the raison d'être of these groups is fueled in large measure by a sense of threat (an important reason why the avant-garde defines itself in relation to its enemies) and by ambivalence about the high cultural status quo. Whether it wants to preserve or destroy that status quo, its polemical texts and sometimes its poetry as well reflect the avant-garde's obsession with what Bürger calls the "art institution."

The irony of the avant-garde, of course, and of art in general, is that it tends to reproduce what it resists, compromising itself and betraying its internal contradictions in its effort to create something new. Surrealism's choice, in spite of its call for global revolution, was to withdraw into itself. The poetry—an island within an island—remained largely immune to the effects of political strife. The vanguardia largely rejected the Continental models from which it borrowed its name, its rhetoric, and some of its strategies. Borges publicly repudiated ultraism soon after presenting it, leaving a movement that identified itself as aesthetics-based officially without a poetics. This sort of abrupt about-face was common during these years. The Auden poets went full circle, from the apolitical to the apolitical, in an embarrassingly short span of years. The surrealists, who made a point of avoiding embarrassment and apology, did much the same as they moved from an aesthetic platform to an aesthetic-political hybrid and back to an aesthetic platform in little more than a decade.

These groups show that while it is not possible for the products of bourgeois culture to employ language or aesthetics that are nonbourgeois, it is possible to resist aspects of mainstream culture. In their struggle to change the relationship between art and society, they teach us that poetry is vitally interested in its own fate. In its grandest conception, the historical avant-garde can be a path of liberation. In its more moderate form, it offers a blueprint for a revision of art's relationship to society. In its conservative form, it illustrates the lengths to which art will go to lodge something quasi-new in the throat of the old. For all of their efforts to stand outside the institutional structures that helped give rise to them, these groups show that there was no escaping the institutional dynamics of what the surrealists disdainfully called "literature."

Notes

Chapter 1. Elite "Fellowships of Discourse"

1. Vicente Huidobro, self-proclaimed founder of the avant-garde movement *creacionismo* (Creationism), was a prominent figure in Paris, Madrid, and his native Chile. Though Huidobro's rebellious impulse and many of his ideas were clearly his own, his highly imagistic and apparently spontaneous poems of the early 1920s were strikingly Dada-like. He spent many of his formative years—from 1916 to 1925—in Europe and was not even in Chile during the short-lived Creationism movement. Critics differ on what dates to assign to Creationism, but it is clear that Huidobro's development was quintessentially European. Some critics date Creationism from 1916 and others limit it to 1921–24. For the latter point of view, see de Costa (1984), 21.

Huidobro claimed to have begun to theorize Creationism in 1912 and announced, with perhaps a trace of self-satisfaction, that Dada leader Tristan Tzara's best poems adhered to a strict creationist conception (Verani 1990, 218, 220). He went to Paris in 1916, where he collaborated with Guillaume Apollinaire and Pierre Reverdy on the journal *Nord-Sud*. Although he was heavily influenced by the surrealists, by 1925 he had taken to excoriating Breton. Reverdy suggested that Huidobro borrowed his "invention" of Creationism from him, but Huidobro's 1914 manifesto *Non serviam* (I shall not serve), while clearly influenced by Europe, predates Dadaism; see Carter (1986), 99–100.

2. The aesthetically innovative and socially radical Peruvian poet César Vallejo was another candidate for this study. However, he left Peru for good in 1923 after his second book, *Trilce*, attracted the bewilderment and scorn of local critics. He was imprisoned in 1920 for what the Peruvian government believed was his criminal involvement in the *indigenista* movement, a native peoples' civil rights movement focused on social justice and colonial abuses. As the eleventh child in a family of mixed Indian and Spanish heritage, Vallejo identified with this cause.

In self-imposed exile in France, he became well connected to both the Continental and Latin American avant-gardes. He did not, however, fit my criterion of being a member of a group, for he was not part of a group in Peru beyond a brief early association with the Trujillo poets. He was fundamentally a loner. In addition, his last work, *Poemas humanos* (Human poems), published in 1939, with its apocalyptic evocations of an industrial society in moral and social crisis, is unmistakably European. In fact, it sounds somewhat like what the Auden poets were writing in the mid-1930s.

3. The quest of indigenismo, which attempted to eschew European and North American influences, was to find a means to portray and express native experi-

ence. Indigenismo was in some instances associated with Marxist ideology and the international workers' movement. While in Europe, Vallejo participated in the Latin American avant-garde through the journal *Amauta,* established by the founder of the Peruvian Communist Party, José Carlos Mariátegui. The movement raises the interesting question of whether it is appropriate to apply the avant-garde label to a movement whose focus is deeply anticolonialist. The answer depends in part on whether the term has shaken loose enough from its Continental roots and become, including in the eyes of critics, truly international. Another important question concerns how we choose to talk about a movement that opposed all forms of postcolonial co-optation. The indigenista writers, who were mainly from countries with sizable indigenous populations such as Peru, Ecuador, Bolivia, and Mexico, preferred realism to aestheticism, and were, in contrast to avant-garde writers, not confined to the middle and upper classes. Vallejo's *Trilce* (1922) has been considered by some to be the first expression of the "indigenous-avant-garde form" (see, for example Morales 1967, 2:220).

Argentina had the predicament of having very little indigenous culture left in the early twentieth century. Most of the descendants of the indigenous peoples had died or been driven to remote parts of the country. Cultural influences, especially in cosmopolitan Buenos Aires, were almost exclusively European. Moreover, most of these Europeans had arrived relatively recently. Early in the twentieth century, when Italian families decided to emigrate to the Americas, Argentina and the United States were believed to offer equally good economic prospects. When Borges began looking for a literary expression of argentinidad, the Argentine national essence, it is revealing that he looked to local discourse—to phonetic spelling and "Argentine" vocabulary—and not to human experience. In Buenos Aires, easily the most European city of the Americas, indigenismo was hard to locate.

Whether or not one can consider the most innovative expressions of indigenismo avant-garde in nature is problematic. I would say yes, especially in light of the confluence of its aesthetic and social impulses. It is certainly possible to function as an avant-garde, with social concerns very different from those of Continental models. Of course, there are political implications inherent in the act of naming: either the label "avant-garde" needs to expand to encompass non-European models or, as in the case of indigenismo, it perhaps ought to be avoided altogether.

4. Beatriz Sarlo, "Sobre la vanguardia, Borges y el criollismo," in Barrenechea, Jitrik, Rest, et al. (1981), 1:73–74.

5. Spender (1935), 236; "Spender and Auden," *New Republic* 80 (26 September 1934): 189.

6. Matthew Hodgart, in "The Age of the Audenesque," qtd. in Haffenden (1983), 57.

7. W. H. Auden, "In Memory of W. B. Yeats" (1939), in Auden (1977), 242.

8. See Bürger (1984), 80–81, for a discussion of how the avant-garde uses shock tactics to change the public's habits of literary reception.

9. See, for example, "La nadería de la personalidad," *Proa*, 1st ser., 1, no. 1 (1922): 1.

10. Jorge L. Borges, "Entretiens avec James E. Irby," in *Jorge Luis Borges* (1964), 392.

11. For a discussion of the avant-garde's denial of individual production and reception, see Bürger (1984), 53.

12. See Foucault (1972), 224–25, for a discussion of the principles of rarefaction, which deny access to discourse to those not following certain rules. Foucault addresses the question of speaking truth versus being *dans le vrai* of a given discursive tradition, pointing out that scientists have often spoken truth in a context that contradicts it. For this reason, their truths were for a time discarded.

13. See, for example, Helio Piñon's prologue in Bürger (1987), 22–23, and the discussion of Dadaism in Bürger (1984), 22–23.

14. The angst that gave rise to Dadaism predates the war, however. In 1914, Simmel (1968) wrote, "Unlike men in all these earlier epochs, we have been for some time now living without any shared ideal, even perhaps without any ideals at all" (15).

15. As Adorno (1991) writes, "Poetic subjectivity is itself indebted to privilege: the pressures of the struggle for survival allow only a few human beings to grasp the universal through immersion in the self or to develop as autonomous subjects capable of freely expressing themselves" (1:45).

16. Benjamin (1978), 229. In a famous statement, Adorno (1967) makes a related complaint later in the century: "Even the most extreme consciousness of doom threatens to degenerate into idle chatter. Cultural criticism finds itself faced with the final state of the dialectic of civilization and barbarism. To write poetry after Auschwitz is barbaric" (34).

17. For the first view, where surrealism is the "negation of negation; a new affirmation," see Gasgoyne (1970), 45. For the second, see Poggioli (1968), 63, and Alexandrian (1971), 24.

18. Hugh Kenner, in an essay aptly titled "Whose Yeats Is It, Anyway?" (*New York Times Book Review* [27 May 1990], 10), expresses frustration at the proliferation of "definitive" versions of Yeats's work, which, by his count, numbered seven in 1990. Yeats was to marketing what Auden was to line editing; he knew how to do it well and he enjoyed it. Both resisted letting their work pass into the public domain or even the private domain of critics and publishers ready to cater to their own values and taste. Of Yeats, Kenner writes: "By the time William Butler Yeats died . . . he'd seen to it that anyone desirous of possessing all his published volumes would have to buy some 200 items, many of them handset limited editions; and 30 of these came from the Cuala Press, which by no coincidence was a Yeats

family enterprise. . . . The collectors' market he understood. . . . In 1908 he published his 'works' in eight volumes, limited to 1060 sets. Your 'works' are published when you're dead." But Yeats, of course, wasn't to die for another fourteen years.

19. Jarrell (1941), 39. Perhaps this marks the New Critical transition from a focus on value creation to a focus on meaning and interpretation.

20. Said (1983) has listed the components of "the power of culture" as follows: "to authorize, to dominate, to legitimate, demote, interdict, and validate" (9).

21. Borges (1962) points out beautifully that no two books are the same even if they contain the same words. In "Pierre Menard, Author of the *Quixote*," one of his favorite explorations of apocrypha, Borges claims that an early twentieth-century writer by the name of Menard wrote word for word the text of Cervantes's *Quixote*, though to very different effect. Where Cervantes's statement about "truth" is labeled by the narrator "mere rhetorical praise of history," Menard's version is interpreted as a belief in the relativity and constructed nature of historical truth (43).

22. See Michel Foucault, "What Is an Author?" in Rabinow (1984), 104.

23. Bové (1986), 194. As Dreyfus and Rabinow (1982) point out, "Interpretation and the modern subject imply each other. The interpretive sciences proceed from the assumption that there is a deep truth which is both known and hidden" (180).

Chapter 2. The Radical Conservatism of the Journals

1. This was variously referred to as argentinidad or a new criollismo or authentic nativism.

2. "Ultra manifesto," in Ilie (1969), 106; qtd. in Running (1981), 1.

3. Victoria Ocampo, "Vision de Jorge Luis Borges," in *Jorge Luis Borges* (1964), 21.

4. All quotations from the March 1922 issue of *Prisma* can be found in a facsimile reprint in de Torre (1965), n.p., insert between 560 and 561.

5. "Pour la préhistoire ultraiste de Borges," in *Jorge Luis Borges* (1964), 164; Bastos (1974), 18; Iturburu (1962), 28.

6. César Vallejo, "Autopsia del superrealismo"; repr. Ulla (1969), 449–56.

7. Roberto F. Giusti, "Sobre la 'nueva sensibilidad,' " *El Día* (Montevideo) (10 January 1923); qtd. in Bastos (1974), 18–19.

8. All material quoted here can be found in Borges (1921b), 466–71.

9. See José Miguel Oviedo, "Borges: The Poet According to His Prologues," in Cortínez (1986), 124.

10. *Revista Martín Fierro* (1969); see, for example, Sabajanes's prologue, 7–8.

11. Rock's (1987) description of pre–World War I Argentine traditionalism is ironically evocative of the martinfierristas. The traditionalists, he argues, "often

made a virtue of apoliticism" and were interested in a materialism-free "national identity."

12. Evar Méndez, "Rubén Darío, poeta plebeyo," *Martín Fierro* 1, no. 1 (1924); repr. *Revista Martín Fierro* (1969), 18–19.

13. Héctor Castillo, "Elegía del Aue's Keller," *Martín Fierro* 1, nos. 5–6 (1924); repr. *Revista Martín Fierro* (1969), 35.

14. "Manifesto de 'Martín Fierro,'" *Martín Fierro* 1, no. 4 (1924); repr. *Revista Martín Fierro* (1969), 26.

15. "Suplemento explicativo de nuestro 'Manifesto,'" *Martín Fierro* 1, nos. 8–9 (1924); repr. *Revista Martín Fierro* (1969), 55. See also Sarlo in Barrenechea, Jitrik, Rest, et al. (1981), 78.

16. See the "Suplemento explicativo" (note 15), and "Martín Fierro y yo," *Martín Fierro* 1, no. 7 (1924); repr. *Revista Martín Fierro* (1969), 53–54, 47.

17. See Santiago Ganduglia, "Párrafos sobre la literatura de Boedo," *Martín Fierro* 2, no. 26 (1925); repr. *Revista Martín Fierro* (1969), 129.

18. Roberto Mariani, "Ellos y nosotros," *Claridad* 131 (March 1927): 16; qtd. in Bastos (1974), 65.

19. "Extrema izquierda," *Martín Fierro* 1, nos. 8–9 (1924); repr. *Revista Martín Fierro* (1969), 57.

20. See, for example, *Martín Fierro* 1, no. 16 (1924). See also *Martín Fierro* 3, nos. 30–31 (1926): 5; repr. *Revista Martín Fierro* (1969), 137–38.

21. *Martín Fierro* 1, nos. 8–9 (1924); repr. *Revista Martín Fierro* (1969), 54.

22. *Los Pensadores* III (2 June 1925): 3–4; qtd. in Bastos (1974), 51.

23. See Borges, "Página sobre la lírica de hoy," *Nosotros* 57, nos. 219–20 (1927): 75–77.

24. *Martín Fierro* 1, nos. 12–13 (1924); repr. *Revista Martín Fierro* (1969), 73.

25. "Asunto fundamental," *Martín Fierro* 4, nos. 44–45 (1927); repr. *Martín Fierro* (1969), 180.

26. *Nosotros* 136 (1920); repr. Ulla (1969), 23.

27. "Aclaración," *Martín Fierro* 4, nos. 44–45 (1927); repr. *Revista Martín Fierro* (1969), 180–81, 185–86.

28. "Nuestra encuesta sobre la nueva generación literaria," *Nosotros* 168–71 (1923); see Ulla (1969), 241ff.

29. *Proa* 1, no. 1 (1924): 3; repr. *Proa* (1983), 3.

30. Leland (1986), 33. Brandán Caraffa, *Inicial* 1:3–6.

31. *Proa* 1, no. 1 (1924): 3.

32. Ibid., 4.

33. "Editoriales Proa y Martín Fierro," *Martín Fierro* 3, no. 34 (1926); repr. *Revista Martín Fierro* (1969), 154.

34. Boedans published fewer books than Floridians, but in no way were they excluded from the book market.

35. "Asociación amigos del arte," *Proa* 1, no. 1 (1924): 28.

36. Jorge L. Borges, "Acotaciones," *Proa* 1, no. 1 (1924): 30–31.

37. Valéry Larbaud, "Carta a dos amigos," *Proa* 2, no. 8 (1925): 5.

38. Jorge L. Borges, "El Ulises de Joyce," *Proa* 2, no. 6 (1925): 3.

39. Qtd. in Running (1981), 72, from *Prisma* (1923): 22.

40. Qtd. in Masiello (1986), 143. The poem is "Hombre de mar" (Seaman).

41. Masiello's (1986) insightful discussion of his work (136–43) offers one of the few critical treatments. See also Senkman (1987), 163–75.

42. Borges, "Montevideo," *Martín Fierro* 1, nos. 8–9 (1924); repr. *Revista Martín Fierro* (1969), 60. Lugones, *Los fuegos artificiales*, qtd. in Torres et al. (1964), 19. Gónzalez Lanuza, "Apócalipsis," *Revista Martín Fierro* (1969), 56. Darío "Sinfonía en gris mayor," in Darío (1979), 97. Gustavo Angel Riccio "Claudio G. Amoroso," in Aguirre (1979), 1:268.

43. Altamirano and Sarlo (1980) argue that the avant-garde is always acting *against* something, be it institutions, society, or aesthetic norms. Rhetorically, this is nearly always true, except in odd cases like *Proa*, about which there is little that is avant-garde.

Chapter 3. Borges and Girondo

1. See, for example, the references to Borges and Girondo as the most important poets of the decade and as participants in the vogue of the Grand Tour of Europe (Masiello 1986, 23, 126).

2. Introduction to *Revista Martín Fierro* (1969), 11–12. See also Sarlo's "Síntesis y tensiones," in Altamirano and Sarlo (1980), 168–69.

3. As Bürger (1984), 51–52, points out, the art market privileges the signature over the work itself. Foucault's author-function, then, is in a sense more important than the literary or artistic work. Paradoxically, avant-garde movements tend to undermine somewhat the notion of individual artistic production, erasing differences among their members in order to present a united front.

4. Sylvia Molloy points this out in *"Flâneries* textuales: Borges, Benjamin y Baudelaire," in Lerner and Lerner (1984), 495.

5. "Nuestra encuesta sobre la nueva generación literaria," *Nosotros* 44, no. 168 (123): 16–17; repr. Ulla (1969), 254.

6. For the transition between "Georgie" and "Borges," see Rodríguez Monegal (1978), 232–33.

7. See, for example, Graciela Palau de Nemes, "Modernismo and Borges," in Cortínez (1986), 221.

8. This essay can be found in Flores (1984), 30ff.

9. The vanguardia was not in fact consistent about its condemnation of rhymed verse. Although no poet wrote an essay justifying the use of rhyme, some

of the lesser vanguardia poets used it and *Martín Fierro* did not shy away from publishing rhymed poems, especially satirical ones.

10. Borges, "Al margen de la moderna lírica," *Grecia* (Sevilla) 39 (31 January 1920); qtd. in Pezzoni (1986), 70.

11. Meneses (1978), 71; from *Tableros* (Madrid) 1 (15 November 1921).

12. Unless otherwise noted, translations of poems from the Spanish are mine, sometimes in consultation with Ana Rosa Rapaport de Genijovich. Any errors, of course, are mine.

13. From *Luna de enfrente*; qtd. in Ibarra (1930), 43.

14. *Proa* 1, no. 1 (1924): 49.

15. Oliverio Girondo, "Membretes," *Martín Fierro* 3, no. 34 (1926); repr. *Revista Martín Fierro* (1969), 150.

16. "Contestaciones a la encuesta de 'Martín Fierro,'" *Martín Fierro* 1, nos. 5–6 (1924); repr. *Revista Martín Fierro* (1969), 42.

17. *Martín Fierro* 1, no. 2 (1924); repr. *Revista Martín Fierro* (1969), 21.

18. Borges (1974), 17. "Entraña" can be defined as heart, insides, entrails, disposition. Here it means the deeply personal and essential.

19. From *Nosotros* 39, no. 151 (1921); 471.

20. Pezzoni (1986), 91. Masiello (1986), 87, argues that the mature Borges has "personalized" literary history as a "precondition" of artistic excellence.

21. Borges, "La nadería de la personalidad," in Borges (1925), 93, 84; Borges (1926b), 152.

22. *Proa* 1, no. 1 (August 1924): 49–50.

23. "Examen de metáforas," in Borges (1925), 65–75.

24. The 1921 and 1943 excerpts from the poem are quoted in Pezzoni (1986), 79. I am grateful to Pezzoni for his analysis of the two versions. He calls the early version of the poem "formalist" and the late version a product of "lived experience."

25. Girondo (1987), 27. Many of the city poems of *Veinte poemas,* such as "Verona," "Sevillano," "Biarritz," "Venecia," and "Rio de Janeiro," were written in the cities they took as their subjects.

26. Jorge L. Borges, "Calcomanías," *Martín Fierro* 11, no. 18 (1925); repr. *Revista Martín Fierro* (1969), 91.

27. Delfina Muschietti uses these terms in her prologue to Girondo (1987).

28. The first of these descriptions is by Ramón Gómez de la Serna, "La vida en el tranvía," review of *Veinte poemas para ser leídos en el tranvía, El Sol* (Madrid) (4 May 1923). The second is by Jules Supervieille, "*Veinte poemas* para Oliverio Girondo," *Revue de l'Amérique Latine* (Paris) (March 1924). Both critics were friends of Girondo's. The reviews were reprinted in *La Nación* and may also be found in J. Schwartz (1987), 326–29.

29. This is the story told by Norah Lange, who married Girondo some years later. See J. Schwartz (1987), 216, for her account.

30. See Running (1981), 129. Four years later, in 1936, the average edition was only 3,500 copies. Rivera (1985a), 582.

31. This refusal is reminiscent of the major French newspapers' refusal to write about surrealist *spectacles* in Paris in the aftermath of the Saint-Pol-Roux banquet. In early 1920s France, Girondo's display would have been considered an artistic act in its own right.

32. This account is from "Nahuelpan: Diez minutos con Oliverio Girondo, fuerte mentalidad agridulce," *Columba* 1, no. 3 (2 June 1925): n.p. It can be found in J. Schwartz (1987), 43.

33. Muschietti points to the central contradiction of Girondo's behavior: "Su rechazo del burgués como *celui qui ne comprend pas* más un aparente desdén por el mercado literario se contredicen con su intento por generar un nuevo público que, además de masivo, tuviero acceso a los criterios de ruptura estético-ideológicos y a una competencia especializada." (His rejection of the bourgeois as *celui qui ne comprend pas* plus an apparent disdain for the literary market contradict his intention to generate a new public that, in addition to being massive, would have access to [understanding] the criteria of an aesthetic-ideologic rupture and to a specialized competence.) Muschietti (1985), 162.

34. For one of Girondo's statements of opposition to the state's role in professionalizing the writer, see "Girondo no cree que en el exterior interese la literatura argentina," *Crítica* (15 May 1960), in J. Schwartz (1987), 48.

35. The description of Borges paraphrases a comment by Evar Méndez (1927), 26.

36. J. Schwartz's (1979) useful comparison is one of few that portrays Borges and Girondo as opposites (151).

37. As its publicist, his role was analogous to those played by Michael Roberts and John Lehmann of the *New Signatures* group in England.

38. *Martín Fierro* took much of the credit for its agent's successful mission. See "Oliverio Girondo en misión intelectual," *Martín Fierro* 1, no. 7 (July 1924); repr. J. Schwartz (1987), 173. Though avant-garde movements distribute power and roles in the way that best suits their needs and goals, they are rarely credited with such rational behavior. For example, Roberts and Lehmann, whose poetry was never so good as that of the core group of Auden poets, had important roles as editors and publicists.

39. In the 1940s and 1950s, as Girondo became more surrealist in practice, his philosophies were in some ways as revolutionary as those of the French surrealists. Girondo's later work has often been compared to the early poetry of Peru's César Vallejo, author of *Trilce* (1922), as a map of the discursive limits of poetry in Spanish.

40. Enrique Molina, "Hacia el fuego central o la poesía de Oliverio Girondo," in Girondo (1968), 12. Molina was a disciple of Girondo in the 1940s during the heyday of Argentine surrealism.

Chapter 4. Borges and *Sur*

1. Juan José Sebreli, as qtd. in Matamoro (1971), 11.

2. King (1986), 42. King's book is an excellent source of cultural and historical context, in addition to being the most thorough treatment of the journal available. I am indebted to it for my account of how the journal was established.

3. Alfonso Reyes, "Un paso de América," *Sur* 1 (Summer 1931): 152. This article takes its inspiration from Reyes's 1926 lunch with Jules Romains in Paris.

4. See King (1986), 72–84, for information on foreign contributors to *Sur* during the late 1930s and 1940s. See Meyer (1981), 190, for several of *Sur*'s first translations into Spanish.

5. *Sur* 56 (May 1939): 103.

6. Qtd. in Meyer (1981), 190. From Fierro (1975), 19.

7. Borges "L'éléctricité des mots," trans. J. R. Outin, in *Jorge Luis Borges* (1964), 413.

8. From *Sur* 30 (March 1937): 98–99, here qtd. in King (1968), 63.

9. Qtd. in King (1986), 56. From "Notícula," *Sur* 8 (1933): 158.

10. *Sur* 2 (Autumn 1931): 8.

11. Victoria Ocampo, "Visión de Jorge Luis Borges," in *Jorge Luis Borges* (1964), 19.

12. Borges, "Entretiens avec Napoléon Murat," in *Jorge Luis Borges* (1964), 379.

13. Adolfo Bioy Casares, "Lettres et Amitiés," in *Jorge Luis Borges* (1964), 13–15.

14. Borges, "Pornographie et censure," in *Jorge Luis Borges* (1964), 96ff.

15. Borges, "Entretiens avec Napoléon Murat," in *Jorge Luis Borges* (1964), 377–78.

16. Borges (1932), 12–14. First published in *Sur* 4:131ff. This essay was later suppressed by Borges.

17. Ocampo, "Despues de 40 años," published in *Sur* in 1971; repr. Ocampo (1975), 205.

18. This particular sample is derived from definitions in *Webster's New Collegiate Dictionary,* 8th ed. (1980).

Chapter 5. The Mutable Myth of Auden's 1930s

1. Auden (1977), 317. From a May 1933 article in *Twentieth Century.*

2. Stephen Spender, *Twentieth Century* 3 (July 1932): 13–15.

3. Unsigned review of "Georgian Poetry, 1913–1915," *The Nation* (11 December 1915): 394, 396, 398; qtd. in Rogers (1977), 129. Arthur Waugh, "The New Poetry," *Quarterly Review* (October 1916): 365–86; qtd. in Rogers (1977), 143.

4. "E. M. of the Anthologies," unsigned, *New Verse,* 2d ser., 1, no. 2 (May 1939): 52.

5. Stephen Spender, "It Began at Oxford," *New York Times Book Review* (13 March 1953): 5; qtd. in Replogle (1964), 136.

6. From "Modern Poetry and Modern Society," unsigned, *The Athenaeum* (16 May 1919): 325–36; qtd. in Rogers (1977), 218.

7. James Burnham, *The Nation* 139 (8 August 1934): 164–65; qtd. in Haffenden (1983), 160.

8. From B. Rajan, "Georgian Poetry: A Retrospect," *The Critic* (Autumn 1948): 7–14; qtd. in Rogers (1977), 363.

9. Hynes's (1972) *The Auden Generation,* whose organizing principle is the calendar year, offers a valuable look at the literary and political events of each year and how quickly things changed.

10. Italo Calvino (1986) points out the cyclical nature of this phenomenon. Referring to the radical politics of Italian university students in 1968, he writes: "Literature was accused . . . of being a waste of time in comparison with the one thing that mattered: action. That the cult of action was first and foremost an old literary myth was understood—or is being understood—very slowly" (93).

11. W. H. Auden, "August for the people and their favourite islands," in Auden (1977), 157; my emphasis.

12. W. H. Auden and C. Day Lewis, preface to *Oxford Poetry* (1927/1929); qtd. in Hynes (1972), 31.

13. "Pick a quarrel, go to war," (1929–30), in Auden (1977), 50.

14. "In Memory of W. B. Yeats," in Auden (1977), 243.

15. "September 1, 1939," in Auden (1977), 245.

16. Ernst Fischer (1963) argues that the act of naming is also an act of marking and appropriating an object or concept. If literary texts have an "unchanging truth," as Fischer puts it, it is perhaps that they tell the story of meaning-making (31).

17. See Auden's "How Not to Be a Genius," *New Republic* (26 April 1939): 348. See also Kermode (1988), 25.

18. *New Verse* 1, no. 2 (March 1933): 15.

19. Roberts (1971), 27, 34. See Crossman's (1950), *The God That Failed,* an anthology of essays on the failure of communism. Spender's essay in the anthology draws a number of parallels between his religious and political impulses.

20. *New Verse* 1, no. 1 (1933): 1.

21. Ibid., 2.

22. *New Verse* 1, no. 2 (1933): 1.

23. Ibid., 17.

24. *New Verse* 3, no. 15 (1935): 17.

25. *New Verse* 1, no. 1 (1933): 4–5.

26. See, for example, *New Writing* 1 (Spring 1936), in Lehman (1936), ix–xi.

27. Critics have noticed this dynamic; Riddel (1971) identifies as a "recurrent

schizophrenia" of the period "the incompatible argument that the poet must be socially and politically engaged but that his first loyalties must be to his craft" (76).

28. Connolly (1973), 425. See 414 for his distinction between short-lived "dynamic" journals and anthological "eclectic" journals.

29. C. H. Madge, "Poetry and Politics," *New Verse* 1, no. 3 (1933): 1.

30. *New Verse* 2, no. 12 (1934): 14.

31. *New Verse* 4, no. 23 (1936): 24.

32. For example, Roberts places Spender's ambivalent and conservative "Poetry and Revolution" third in the *New Country* prose lineup and Day Lewis's more passionate "Letter to a Young Revolutionary" first.

33. Kermode (1988), 41. He quotes Edmund Wilson's 1932 "manifesto": "The present crisis of the world . . . [is] something more than a mere crisis of politics and economics; and it will not pass with the depression. It is a crisis of human culture" (Wilson 1977, 222).

34. Walter Benjamin, "The Work of Art in the Age of Mechanical Reproduction," in Benjamin (1969), 242.

35. Auden and Isherwood (1937). These two stanzas are from pages 16 and 46, respectively.

36. C. Day Lewis (1977), 115. This poem and the following are from *Overtures to Death* (1938).

37. "In Memory of W. B. Yeats," in Auden (1977), 242.

38. Julian Bell, *New Statesman and Nation* (9 December 1933): 731–32; qtd. in Stansky and Abrahams (1966), 109.

39. From *Student Vanguard* (January 1934); qtd. in Stansky and Abrahams (1966), 221.

Chapter 6. The Struggle Over Value and Belief

1. Auden (1941), 140. This moral reading of *The Waste Land* and the statement of the problem of the lack of belief are supported by nearly all of Auden's choices during the 1930s.

2. T. S. Eliot, *The Enemy* (January 1927); qtd. in Leavis (1960), 118.

3. Letter of 6 October 1932; qtd. in S. Day-Lewis (1980), 72; my emphasis.

4. From "The Creative Imagination in the World Today," in *Folios of New Writing* (London, 1940), 157; qtd. in Riddel (1971), 98.

5. "Poetry, Poets, and Taste," *The Highway* (December 1936), in Auden (1977), 359.

6. Introduction to *The Poet's Tongue* (1935), in Auden (1977), 329.

7. *I Believe,* ed. Clifton Fadiman, in Auden (1977), 379.

8. From Spender's "Five Notes on W. H. Auden's Writing," *Twentieth Century* 3 (July 1932): 13–15; repr. Haffenden (1983), 105.

9. D. M. T., review of *Vienna,* in *New Verse* 2, no. 12 (1934): 20.

10. From *The Use of Poetry;* qtd. in Gillie (1975), 85.

11. Benjamin, "Theses on the Philosophy of History," in Benjamin (1969), 257.

12. Edward Callan, *"Disenchantment with Yeats:* From Singing-Master to Ogre," in Bloom (1986), 163.

13. George Orwell, letter, in *Time and Tide* 19, no. 6 (5 February 1938): 165; qtd. in Hoskins (1969), 101.

14. W. H. Auden, "How Not to Be a Genius," review of *Enemies of Promise* by Cyril Connolly, *New Republic* 98, no. 1273 (26 April 1939): 348.

15. "XXVIII" (1929), in Auden (1977), 45.

16. "XXX" (1930), in Auden (1977), 47.

17. Inside quotes are from Auden's *Letter to Lord Byron.* From Replogle's "The Pattern of Personae," in Bloom (1986), 22–23.

18. *New Verse* 1, no. 4 (1933): 5.

19. *New Verse* 1, no. 5 (1933): 14–15.

20. For the text of the poem, see Hynes (1972), 286–87. For an explanation of its method, see Symons (1960), 114–15.

21. Internal quote by Neal Wood, *Communism and the British Intellectuals,* 64. The explanation of Mass Observation is from Hoskins (1969), 187.

22. *New Verse* 5, no. 24 (1937): 3.

23. Historians point out that propaganda is a periodic phenomenon that arises when there is strong need for belief. During World War I, for example, the propaganda that "seems shoddy in retrospect" was "felt to have great virtue at the time" (Thomson 1965, 59).

24. Spender (1951), 236. MacNeice (1965) reports that the London newspapers had distorted views of the Spanish civil war (166).

Chapter 7. MacNeice, Empson, and Auden

1. Hobsbaum (1965) concurs, referring to Empson as the most interesting of "a number of poets of the Thirties who [have] been unjustly neglected" (100–101).

2. Empson (1931), 61. For a fuller discussion of this review, see Hynes (1972), 54–55.

3. *New Verse* 2, no. 12 (1934): 15.

4. MacNeice, "Modern Poetry Should Be Subtle and Tough," *New York Times,* sect. 7 (9 August 1953): 7; qtd. in E. E. Smith (1970), 42.

5. See also "An Eclogue for Christmas" (1933) for illustrations of MacNeice's tendency—borrowed perhaps from Auden—to diagnose the ills of an effete society.

6. "Homage to Clichés" (1935), in MacNeice (1967), 59.

7. MacNeice, *I Crossed the Minch,* 125–29; qtd. in E. E. Smith (1970), 53–54.

8. From a letter to T. S. Eliot, dated 22 November 1938; qtd. in Marsack (1982), 43.

9. *Autumn Journal,* "XVIII," in MacNeice (1949), 158–60.

10. "An Enquiry," *New Verse* 2, no. 11 (October 1934): 7.

11. MacNeice, "A Statement," *New Verse* 6, nos. 31–32 (1938): 7.

12. From MacNeice's "Poetry To-day," *The Arts To-Day* (1935), ed. Geoffrey Grigson; repr. MacNeice (1987), 35.

13. MacNeice, "Modern Writers and Beliefs," review of *The Destructive Element* by Stephen Spender, *Listener* 330 (8 May 1935); repr. MacNeice (1987), 6–7.

14. MacNeice, "Poetry To-Day"; repr. MacNeice (1987), 25.

15. MacNeice, "The Poet in England To-day: A Reassessment," *New Republic* 102, no. 13 (1940): 412–13; repr. MacNeice (1987), 111.

16. See, for example, "The Tower that Once," *Folios of New Writing* 3 (Spring 1941): 37–41; repr. MacNeice (1987), 119–24.

17. Stephen Spender, "Mr. MacNeice's Poems," *New Verse* 3, no. 17 (1935): 17.

18. Qtd. in the introduction to Empson (1988), 46.

19. MacNeice, "Eclogue by a Five-Barred Gate," in MacNeice (1949), 24.

20. MacNeice, "An Eclogue for Christmas," in MacNeice (1949), 21.

21. MacNeice, "Mr. Empson as a Poet," *New Verse* 3, no. 16 (1935): 18.

22. Empson published more frequently in university journals during the 1920s than he did in national journals during the 1930s. On this point, see Gardner (1978), 23.

23. Kathleen Raine, "Extracts from Unpublished Memoirs," in Gill (1974), 17; my emphasis.

24. M. C. Bradbrook, "The Ambiguity of William Empson," in Gill (1974), 6.

25. George Fraser, "The Man Within the Name: William Empson as Poet, Critic, and Friend," in Gill (1974), 69.

26. Empson, "A London Letter," *Poetry* 49 (January 1937): 218–22; qtd. in Gardner (1978), 34.

27. Hugh Kenner, "The Sons of Spiders," review of *Collected Poems* by William Empson, *Poetry* 76 (April–September 1950): 155; qtd. in Day (1984), xxii; my emphasis.

28. Finch (1935), 121; my emphasis. Similarly Flint (1938) begins his "New Leaders in English Poetry" with a statement that values most highly the Auden poets most valued by English critics (502).

29. As Bauman (1987), 4–5, writes, the "typically modern strategy of intellectual work" often relies on "procedural rules which assure the attainment of truth, the arrival at valid moral judgement, and the selection of proper artistic taste." I. A. Richards illustrates this role.

30. Richard Goodman, *Daily Worker* (2 June 1937): 7; qtd. in Haffenden (1983), 238.

31. Malcolm Cowley, *New Republic* (7 April 1941): 473–74; qtd. in Haffenden (1983), 310.

32. Auden, "Authority in America," *The Griffen* (1955); qtd. in Davison (1970), 29.

33. Edward Mendelson, "Auden's Revision of Modernism," in Bloom (1986), 117.

34. Ibid.

Chapter 8. The Surrealists' Search for Authenticity

1. *La révolution surréaliste* 5 (15 October 1925): 31–32.

2. André Breton, "Patinage Dada," *Littérature* 13 (May 1920): 9; qtd. in Lewis (1988), 6.

3. Arban (1968), 43. *Littérature*, 2d ser., 6 (November 1922).

4. Breton (1988), 623–24. From "Les 'enfers artificiels.' "

5. *Littérature* 18 (March 1921): 1–7.

6. "Deux manifestes dada," in Breton (1988), 230.

7. Breton, *Littérature*, new ser., 1, no. 2 (April 1922): 10.

8. See *Littérature* 10 (December 1919): 24–26.

9. Breton, "Le bouquet sans fleurs"; repr. Breton (1988), 897.

10. Qtd. in Alexandrian (1971), 101–2; my emphasis. From Breton, "La dernière grève," *La révolution surréaliste* 3 (15 April 1925).

11. "Communiqué sur le bureau de recherches surréalistes," in Breton (1988), 481–82.

12. Breton (1988), 311. Dadaism was also a male-dominated movement. *Littérature*'s "Pourquoi écrivez-vous?" survey evoked responses from 104 men and 9 women.

13. Anna Balakian, "From Mallarmé to Breton: Continuity and Discontinuity in the Poetics of Ambiguity," in Caws (1984), 118.

14. *Littérature* 17 (December 1920): 2–3.

15. See *Littérature* 18 (March 1921): 1–7.

16. Ibid., 18.

17. The surrealists had themselves photographed much more often than other avant-garde groups. Though attributable in part to their scopic fantasies, this choice is also a sign of their impulse toward self-historicization.

18. *La révolution surréaliste* 1 (1 December 1924): 17.

19. See *La révolution surréaliste* 11 (15 March 1928): 32–40.

20. *Les pas perdus;* qtd. in Leonard (1974), 41.

21. See, for example, *La révolution surréaliste* 2 (15 January 1925).

22. *Manifestoes of Surrealism* (Breton 1969a, 125, 128). Pierre Naville aptly notes in 1926, however, that surrealism's public scandals "n'empêchent pas de conserver

la tête de la hiérarchie intellectuelle dans la république bourgeoise" (do not interfere with the retention of the top of the intellectual hierarchy in a bourgeois
republic). From *La révolution et les intellectuels* (Paris: Gallimard Idées, 1926), 88;
qtd. in Guiol-Benassaya (1982), 8.

23. Desnos is expelled for "journalistic activities" in 1929. Caws (1970), 10–11.

24. Rejected in the *Second manifeste* are Antonin Artaud, Jean Carrive, Joseph
Delteil, Francis Gérard, Georges Limbour, André Masson, Philippe Soupault, and
Roger Vitrac.

25. The manifesto was published in October 1935. Qtd. in Breton (1978), 50.

26. For a fuller account of these decisions, see Lewis (1988), 113, 115, 150.

27. Compare *La révolution surréaliste* 5 (15 October 1925): 31 with 11 (15 March
1928): 22.

28. *La révolution surréaliste* 3 (15 April 1925): 16–17.

29. Cf. the following numbers of *Le surréalisme au service de la révolution:* 2
(October 1930): 17; 3 (December 1931): 34; and 4 (December 1931).

30. Louis Aragon, "Ecritures automatiques," in Aragon (1970), 145. Later automatic texts were often punctuated.

31. Qtd. in Lewis (1988), 28. See also "Communiqué sur le Bureau de Recherches Surréalistes," in Breton (1988), 481–82.

32. As Michel-André Bossy has reminded me, colonialists are often in love with
the groups they seek to subjugate. This brings up the complex question of the
nature of human love in the French tradition. For the reader who considers the
love portrayed in surrealist poetry to be subjugating, it may have little redemptive value.

33. *Littérature* 1 (March 1919): 17.

34. Ibid., 21.

35. From *Le revolver à cheveux blancs* in Breton (1982), 60. The translations of
all excerpts from this work, including the translation of "Toutes les écolières ensemble" (All the schoolgirls together), are those of Cauvin and Caws.

36. Breton (1969b), 18–21. From *Claire de terre* (1923). The translations of all
excerpts from this work are White's.

37. Breton (1969b), 46–47, 50–51. From *Le revolver à cheveux blancs*.

38. Breton (1969b), 76–79. From "au beau demi-jour," in *L'air de l'eau* (1934).

39. *Martín Fierro* 2, no. 20 (1925); repr. *Revista Martín Fierro*, 101.

40. Aragon, *Feu de joie*, in Aragon (1970), 119.

41. As Aragon wrote in "Le discours à la première personne," in *Le roman in-
achevé* (1956):

> Jamais je ne perdrai cet émerveillement
> Du langage
> Jamais je ne me réveillerai d'entre les mots
> (qtd. in Caws 1970, 57)

(I shall never lose this astonishment
Of language
I shall never awaken from among words.)

42. From *Corps et biens* (1930); qtd. in Buchole (1956), 90.

43. Cf. Aragon's "Front rouge" with Desnos's "Camarades," in *Fortunes,* published in 1942, but containing poems Desnos began writing in 1928.

44. Desnos, "Comme," *Fortunes;* qtd. in Buchole (1956), 164.

45. Soupault (1937), 62. From *Westwego* (1917–22).

46. Soupault (1937), 84. From *Georgia* (1926).

47. Soupault (1937), 212. From *Etapes de l'enfer* (1932–34).

48. Soupault (1937), 229. From *Sang joie tempête* (1934–37).

49. *Minotaure* 6 (1935).

50. *Minotaure* 5 (1934): 1.

51. See *Minotaure* 8 (1935).

52. "Le nationalisme dans l'art," *Minotaure* 12–13 (1939): 70.

Chapter 9. Surrealism's Divided Critics

1. Breton (1982), 98. "Le marquis de Sade a regagné l'intérieur du volcan en éruption, from *L'air de l'eau.*

2. From Shattuck's introduction to Nadeau (1989), 26.

3. In another essay, Caws cites Breton's "Nothing is inadmissible, in my opinion," from *Point du jour,* before stating her critical stance: "A plural meaning and a serious matter; these are indeed the basic tenets of an open surrealism as I view it now." From "The Meaning of Surrealism, and Why It Matters," in Caws (1984), 147.

4. From "Au petit jour" (Dawn), in *Les ténèbres* (The darkness).

Chapter 10. "Lights becoming darks"

1. See Bürger (1984), 72, for a discussion of how the avant-garde sometimes emphasizes its artifice in a reaction against naturalism and realism.

2. "For Dada," in Breton (1978), 6.

Selected Bibliography

Abdala, Raúl Oscar. 1981. "Sobre el 'extranjerismo' de la generación del 80." *Letras de Buenos Aires* 1, no. 2:39–47.

Adorno, Theodor W. 1967. *Prisms*. Translated by Samuel and Shierry Weber. Cambridge: MIT Press.

———. 1991. *Notes to Literature*. Vol. 1. Edited by Rolf Tiedemann. Translated by Shierry Weber Nicholsen. New York: Columbia University Press.

Aguirre, Raúl Gustavo, ed. 1979. *Antología de la poesía argentina*. Vol. 1. Buenos Aires: Ediciones Librerías Fausto.

Ahearn, Edward J. 1989. *Marx and Modern Fiction*. New Haven: Yale University Press.

Alazraki, Jaime, ed. 1976. *Jorge Luis Borges*. Madrid: Taurus Ediciones.

———. 1987. *Critical Essays on Jorge Luis Borges*. Boston: G. K. Hall.

Alexandrian, Sarane. 1971. *André Breton par lui-même*. Paris: Seuil.

Altamirano, Carlos, and Beatriz Sarlo. 1980. "La Argentina del centenario: Campo intelectual, vida literaria y temas ideológicas." *Hispamérica* 9, nos. 25–26:33–59.

———. 1983a. *Ensayos argentinos: De Sarmiento a la vanguardia*. Buenos Aires: Centro Editor de América Latina.

———. 1983b. *Literatura/Sociedad*. Buenos Aires: Hachette.

Andrews, Wayne. 1988. *The Surrealist Parade*. New York: New Directions.

Aney, Edith T. 1954. *Modern British Poetry of Social Protest in the 1930s: The Problem of Belief in the Poetry of W. H. Auden, C. Day Lewis, "Hugh MacDiarmid," Louis MacNeice, and Stephen Spender*. Ann Arbor: University Microfilms International.

Ansermet, Ernest. 1931. "Los problemas del compositor americano." *Sur* 1 (Summer):124.

Antle, Martine. 1987. "Le statut de l'image dans l'écriture et la peinture surréaliste." *Perspectives on Contemporary Literature* 13:3–10.

Aragon, Louis. 1931. "Le surréalisme et le devenir révolutionnaire." *Le surréalisme au service de la révolution* 3 (December):3.

———. 1944. *Le crève-coeur et les yeux d'Elsa*. London: Edition "La France Libre."

———. [1926] 1945. *Le paysan de Paris*. Paris: Gallimard.

———. [1925] 1970. *Le mouvement perpétuel*. Paris: Gallimard.

Arban, Dominique. 1968. *Aragon parle avec Dominique Arban*. Paris: Editions Seghers.

Auden, W. H. 1931. "Speech for a Prize Day." *Criterion* 11, no. 42:60–64.

———. 1935. "Everyman's Freedom." *New Statesman and Nation*, 23 March:422–23.

———. 1937. "Impressions of Valencia." *New Statesman and Nation,*
30 January:159.

———. 1939. "How Not to Be a Genius." Review of *Enemies of Promise* by Cyril
Connolly. *New Republic,* 26 April:348, 350.

———. 1941. "Criticism in a Mass Society." In *The Intent of the Critic,* edited by
Donald A. Stauffer, 125–47. Princeton: Princeton University Press.

———. 1963. "Louis MacNeice." *Encounter* 21, no. 5:48–49.

———. [1956] 1964. *Selected Essays.* London: Faber and Faber.

———. [1932] 1967. *The Orators: An English Study.* New York: Random House.

———. 1977. *The English Auden: Poems, Essays and Dramatic Writings,*
1927–1939. Edited by Edward Mendelson. London: Faber and Faber.

———. 1979. *Selected Poems.* Edited by Edward Mendelson. New York: Vintage.

Auden, W. H., and Christopher Isherwood. 1937. *The Ascent of F6.* New York:
Random House.

Audoin, Philippe. 1973. *Les surréalistes.* Paris: Seuil.

Avellaneda, Andrés. 1983. *El habla de la ideología.* Buenos Aires: Editorial
Sudamericana.

Ayarragaray, Lucas. 1926. *Cuestiones y problemas argentinos contemporáneos.*
Buenos Aires: J. Lajouane.

Balakian, Anna. 1947. *Literary Origins of Surrealism.* New York: New York
University Press.

———. 1971. *André Breton: Magus of Surrealism.* New York: Oxford University
Press.

———. 1976. "Where is the 'Garde' of the Avant-Garde?" *Actes du VIIIe Congrès*
de l'Association Internationale de Littérature Comparée 8:907–10.

Barletta, Leónidas. 1967. *Boedo y Florida: Una versión distinta.* Buenos Aires:
Ediciones Metrópolis.

Barnstone, Willis, ed. 1982. *Borges at Eighty.* Bloomington: Indiana University
Press.

Barrenechea, Ana María. 1957. *La expresión de la irrealidad en la obra de Borges.*
Mexico: El Colegio de México.

Barrenechea, A., N. Jitrik, J. Rest, et al. 1981. *La crítica literaria contemporanea.*
Vol. 1. Buenos Aires: Centro Editor de América Latina.

Barrenechea, Ana María, and Emma Speratti Piñero. 1957. *La literatura fantástica*
en Argentina. Mexico: Imprenta Universitaria.

Barthes, Roland. 1966. *Critique et vérité.* Paris: Seuil.

Bastos, María Luisa. 1974. *Borges ante la crítica argentina, 1923–1960.* Buenos
Aires: Ediciones Hispamérica.

———. 1980. "Escrituras ajenas, expresión propia: *Sur* y los *Testimonios* de
Victoria Ocampo." *Revista Iberoamericana* 110–11:123–37.

Bauman, Zygmunt. 1987. *Legislators and Interpreters: On Modernity,*
Post-Modernity and Intellectuals. Cambridge: Polity.

Beach, Joseph Warren. 1957. *The Making of the Auden Canon*. Minneapolis: University of Minnesota Press.

Benda, Julien. 1969. *The Treason of the Intellectuals*. Translated by Richard Aldington. New York: Norton.

———. [1927] 1975. *La trahison des clercs*. Paris: Bernard Grasset.

Benjamin, Walter. 1969. *Illuminations*. Edited by Hannah Arendt. Translated by Harry Zohn. New York: Schocken.

———. 1978. *Reflections: Essays, Aphorisms, Autobiographical Writings*. Edited by Peter Demetz. Translated by Edmund Jephcott. New York: Harcourt Brace Jovanovich.

Bloom, Harold. 1973. *The Anxiety of Influence: A Theory of Poetry*. London: Oxford University Press.

———, ed. 1986. *W. H. Auden*. New York: Chelsea House.

Bloom, Robert. 1968. "The Humanization of Auden's Early Style." *PMLA* 83, no. 5:443–54.

Borda, J. G. Cobo. 1981. "Las memorias de Victoria Ocampo." *Letras de Buenos Aires* 1, no. 2:149–63.

Borges, Jorge L. 1921a. "Anatomía de mi ultra." *Ultra* 11 (20 May):41.

———. 1921b. "Ultraísmo." *Nosotros* 151:466–71.

———. 1923a. *Fervor de Buenos Aires*. Buenos Aires: n.p.

———. 1925. *Inquisiciones*. Buenos Aires: Editorial Proa.

———. 1926a. "Leopoldo Lugones, romancero." *Inicial* 2, no. 9:207–8.

———. 1926b. *El tamaño de mi esperanza*. Buenos Aires: Editorial Proa.

———. 1928. *El idioma de los argentinos*. Buenos Aires: M. Gleizer.

———. 1932. *Discusión*. Buenos Aires: M. Gleizer.

———. 1962. *Labyrinths*. New York: New Directions.

———. 1974. *Obras completas, 1923–1972*. Buenos Aires: Emecé.

———. 1979. *El "Martín Fierro."* Buenos Aires: Emecé.

———. 1985. *Selected Poems, 1923–1967*. Edited by Norman Thomas di Giovanni. London: Penguin Books.

Borges, Jorge L., Silvina Ocampo, and Adolfo Bioy Casares, eds. 1941. *Antología poética argentina*. Buenos Aires: Editorial Sudamericana.

Bové, Paul A. 1980. "The End of Humanism: Michel Foucault and the Power of Disciplines." *Humanities in Society* 3, no. 1:23–40.

———. 1986. *Intellectuals in Power: A Genealogy of Critical Humanism*. New York: Columbia University Press.

Breton, André. 1969a. *Manifestoes of Surrealism*. Translated by Richard Seaver and Helen R. Lane. Ann Arbor: University of Michigan Press.

———. 1978. *What Is Surrealism?* Edited by Franklin Rosemont. New York: Pathfinder.

———. 1969b. *Selected Poems*. Translated by Kenneth White. London: Jonathan Cape.

———. 1982. *Poems of André Breton.* Translated and edited by Jean-Pierre Cauvin and Mary Ann Caws. Austin: University of Texas Press.

———. 1988. *Oeuvres complètes.* Vol. 1. Paris: Gallimard.

Bridel, Yves. 1988. *Miroirs du surréalisme.* Lausanne: Editions l'Age d'Homme.

Briosi, Sandro, and Henk Hillenaar, eds. 1988. *Vitalité et contradictions de l'avant-garde: Italie-France, 1909–1924.* Paris: José Corti.

Brooks, Cleanth. 1964. "W. H. Auden as a Critic." *Kenyon Review* 26 (Winter):173–89.

Browder, Clifford. 1967. *André Breton: Arbiter of Surrealism.* Geneva: Droz.

Brown, Terence. 1975. *Louis MacNeice: Sceptical Vision.* New York: Barnes and Noble.

Buchole, Rosa. 1956. *L'évolution poétique de Robert Desnos.* Brussels: Palais des Académies.

Buell, Frederick. 1973. *Auden as a Social Poet.* Ithaca: Cornell University Press.

Bürger, Peter. 1984. *Theory of the Avant-Garde.* Translated by Michael Shaw. Minneapolis: University of Minnesota Press.

———. 1987. *Teoría de la vanguardia.* Translated by Jorge García. Barcelona: Ediciones Península.

Calinescu, Matei. 1987. *Five Faces of Modernity.* Durham: Duke University Press.

Calvino, Italo. 1986. *The Uses of Literature.* Translated by Patrick Creagh. San Diego: Harcourt Brace Jovanovich.

Carpenter, Humphrey. 1981. *W. H. Auden: A Biography.* Boston: Houghton Mifflin.

Carrouges, Michel. 1974. *André Breton and the Basic Concepts of Surrealism.* Translated by Maura Prendergast. University: University of Alabama Press.

Carter, Boyd G. 1968. *Historia de la literatura hispanoamericana.* Mexico: Ediciones de Andrea.

Caws, Mary Ann. 1970. *The Poetry of Dada and Surrealism.* Princeton: Princeton University Press.

———. 1982. "Maximization with No Margins: Reading the Commonplace." *L'Esprit créateur* 22, no. 3:82–85.

———, ed. 1984. *Writing in a Modern Temper: Essays on French Literature and Thought in Honor of Henri Peyre.* Saratoga, Calif.: ANMA Libri.

———, Rudolph Juenzli, and Gwen Raaberg, eds. 1991. *Surrealism and Women.* Cambridge: MIT Press.

Chadwick, Charles. 1971. *Symbolism.* London: Methuen.

Coates, Willson H., and Hayden V. White. 1970. *The Ordeal of Liberal Humanism: An Intellectual History of Western Europe.* Vol. 2. New York: McGraw-Hill.

Connolly, Cyril. 1973. *The Evening Colonnade.* London: David Bruce and Watson.

Corro, Gaspar Pío del. 1976. *Oliverio Girondo: Los límites del signo*. Buenos Aires: Fernando García Cambeiro.

Cortínez, Carlos, ed. 1986. *Borges, the Poet*. Fayetteville: University of Arkansas Press.

Cowley, Malcolm. 1934. "Spender and Auden." *New Republic* 80 (26 September):189–90.

Craig, Gordon A. 1961. *Europe Since 1914*. 3d ed. New York: Holt, Rinehart and Winston.

Crossman, Richard, ed. 1950. *The God That Failed*. New York: Bantam.

Daiches, David. 1940. *Poetry and the Modern World: A Study of Poetry in England Between 1900 and 1939*. Chicago: University of Chicago Press.

Darío, Rubén. 1956. *Antología de Rubén Darío*. Edited by Raúl Silva Castro. Santiago: Empresa Editora Zig-Zag.

———. 1979. *Prosas profanas*. Madrid: Colección Austral.

Davison, Dennis. 1970. *W. H. Auden*. London: Evans Brothers.

Day, Frank. 1984. *Sir William Empson: An Annotated Bibliography*. New York: Garland.

Day Lewis, C. [1934] 1942. *A Hope for Poetry*. Oxford: Basil Blackwell.

———. 1960. *The Buried Day*. New York: Harper and Bros.

———. 1977. *Poems of C. Day Lewis, 1925–1972*. Edited by Ian Parsons. London: Jonathan Cape and the Hogarth Press.

Day-Lewis, Sean. 1980. *C. Day-Lewis; An English Literary Life*. London: Weidenfeld and Nicolson.

de Costa, René. 1984. *Huidobro*. Translated by Guillermo Sheridan. Mexico: Fondo de Cultura Económica.

de Torre, Guillermo. 1925. "Oliverio Girondo." *Proa* 2, no. 12:18–27.

———. 1965. *Historia de las literaturas de vanguardia*. Madrid: Ediciones Guadarramas.

Desnos, Robert. 1924. *Deuil pour deuil*. Paris: Editions de Saggitaire.

———. 1926. *C'est les bottes de sept lieues cette phrase "Je me vois."* Paris: Editions de la Galérie Simon.

Dreyfus, Hubert L., and Paul Rabinow. 1982. *Michel Foucault: Beyond Structuralism and Hermeneutics*. 2d ed. Chicago: University of Chicago Press.

Drieu la Rochelle, Pierre. 1931. "Carta a unos deconocidos." *Sur* 1:53–63.

Eagleton, Terry. 1984. *The Function of Criticism: From The Spectator to Post-Structuralism*. London: Verso.

———. 1990. *The Ideology of the Aesthetic*. Oxford: Basil Blackwell.

Eco, Umberto. [1973] 1986. *Travels in Hyper Reality*. Translated by William Weaver. San Diego: Harcourt Brace Jovanovich.

———. 1987. "La abducción en Uqbar." *La Papirola* 1 (September):3–9.

Ellmann, Richard, and Charles Feidelson Jr., eds. 1965. *The Modern Tradition: Backgrounds of Modern Literature*. New York: Oxford University Press.

Eluard, Paul. 1968. *Oeuvres complètes.* Vol. 1. Paris: Gallimard.

———. 1975. *Uninterrupted Poetry: Selected Writings.* Translated by Lloyd Alexander. Westport, Conn.: Greenwood.

Empson, William. 1931. "A Note on W. H. Auden's 'Paid on Both Sides.' " *Experiment* 7 (Spring):61.

———. [1930] 1953. *Seven Types of Ambiguity.* 3d ed. London: Chatto and Windus.

———. 1955. *Collected Poems.* London: Chatto and Windus.

———. 1963. "Early Auden." *The Review* 5, no. 5:32–34.

———. [1935] 1974. *Some Versions of Pastoral.* New York: New Directions.

———. 1988. *The Royal Beasts and Other Works.* Edited by John Haffenden. Iowa City: University of Iowa Press.

Fernández, Teodosio. 1987. *La poesía hispanoamericana en el siglo XX.* Madrid: Taurus Ediciones.

Ferrari, Osvaldo. 1985. *Borges en diálogo: conversaciones de Jorge Luis Borges con Osvaldo Ferrari.* Buenos Aires: Ediciones Grijalbo.

Fierro, Danubio Torres. 1975. "Entrevista a Victoria Ocampo." *Plural* 51 (December):18–25.

Finch, John. 1935. "Spender and Auden." *Sewanee Review* 43 (January–March):121–24.

Fischer, Ernst. [1959] 1963. *The Necessity of Art: A Marxist Approach.* Translated by Anna Bostock. Baltimore: Penguin.

Flint, F. Cudworth. 1938. "New Leaders in English Poetry." *Virginia Quarterly Review* 14 (October):502–518.

Flores, Angel, ed. 1984. *Expliquemos a Borges como poeta.* Mexico: Siglo Veintiuno Editores.

Foucault, Michel. 1972. *The Archaeology of Knowledge and the Discourse on Language.* New York: Pantheon.

———. 1973. *The Order of Things: An Archaeology of Human Sciences.* New York: Vintage.

———. 1977. *Language, Counter-memory, Practice.* Ithaca: Cornell University Press.

———. 1979. *Michel Foucault: Power, Truth, Strategy.* Edited by Meaghan Morris and Paul Patton. Sydney: Feral Publications.

———. 1986. *Power/Knowledge.* New York: Pantheon.

Frank, Waldo. 1931. "La selva." *Sur* 1 (Summer):25.

———. 1932. *América hispana: Un retrato y una perspectiva.* Madrid: Espasa-Calpe.

———. 1975. *Memorias.* Buenos Aires: Ediciones Sur.

Frye, Northrop. 1971. *The Critical Path.* Bloomington: Indiana University Press.

Fussell, Paul. 1975. *The Great War and Modern Memory.* London: Oxford University Press.

Gardner, Philip, and Averil Gardner. 1978. *The God Approached: A Commentary on the Poems of William Empson*. London: Chatto and Windus.

Gascoyne, David. [1935] 1970. *A Short Survey of Surrealism*. London: Frank Cass.

Gill, Roma, ed. 1974. *William Empson: The Man and His Work*. London: Routledge and Kegan Paul.

Gillie, Christopher. 1975. *Movements in English Literature, 1900–1940*. Cambridge: Cambridge University Press.

Girondo, Oliverio. 1987. *Espantapájaros y otros poemas*. Buenos Aires: Centro Editor de América Latina.

———. 1968. *Obras completas*. Buenos Aires: Editorial Losada.

———. 1987. *Veinte poemas para ser leídos en le tranvía, Calcomanías, Espantapájaros*. Buenos Aires: Centro Editor de América Latina.

Goodheart, Eugene. 1978. *The Failure of Criticism*. Cambridge: Harvard University Press.

Gramuglio, María Teresa. 1986. " 'Sur' en la década del treinta: Una revista política." *Punto de Vista* 28 (November):32–39.

Griffin, Howard. 1981. *Conversations with Auden*. Edited by Donald Allen. San Francisco: Grey Fox.

Grigson, Geoffrey, ed. 1939. *New Verse: An Anthology*. Compiled by Geoffrey Grigson. London: Faber and Faber.

"La guerra civil española: cinquenta años después de una lucha que también dividió a la Argentina." 1986. *La Nación,* Sunday magazine (20 July).

Guiol-Benassaya, Elyette. 1982. *La presse face au surréalisme de 1925 à 1938*. Paris: Editions du Centre National de la Recherche Scientifique.

Güiraldes, Ricardo. 1962. *Obras completas*. Buenos Aires: Emecé.

Habermas, Jürgen. 1987. *The Philosophical Discourse of Modernity*. Translated by Frederick G. Lawrence. Cambridge: MIT Press.

Haffenden, John, ed. 1983. *W. H. Auden: The Critical Heritage*. London: Routledge and Kegan Paul.

Harper, Robert D. 1940. "Back to the Personal." *Poetry* 57 (October):46–49.

Harris, Wendell V. 1991. "Canonicity." *PMLA* 106, no. 1:110–21.

Hobsbaum, Philip. 1965. "The Growth of English Modernism." *Wisconsin Studies in Contemporary Literature* 6:97–105.

Hollier, Denis, ed. 1988. *The College of Sociology, 1937–39*. 1979. Reprint, Minneapolis: University of Minnesota Press.

Hoskins, Katharine Bail. 1969. *Today the Struggle: Literature and Politics in England During the Spanish Civil War*. Austin: University of Texas Press.

Hyman, Stanley E. 1955. "William Empson and Categorical Criticism." In *The Armed Vision: A Study in the Methods of Modern Literary Criticism*. Edited by Stanley Hyman. New York: Vintage.

Hynes, Samuel. 1972. *The Auden Generation: Literature and Politics in England in the 1930s*. Princeton: Princeton University Press.

Ibarra, Nestor. 1930. *La nueva poesía argentina: Ensayo crítico sobre el ultraísmo, 1921–1929*. Buenos Aires: Molinari e Hijos.

Ilie, Paul, ed. 1969. *Documents of the Spanish Vanguard*. Chapel Hill: University of North Carolina Press.

Iturburu, Córdova. 1962. *La revolución martinfierrista*. Buenos Aires: Ediciones Culturales Argentinas.

Janover, Louis. 1980. *Surréalisme, art et politique*. Paris: Editions Galilée.

Jarrell, Randall. 1941. "Changes of Attitude and Rhetoric in Auden's Poetry." *Southern Review* 7 (Autumn):326–49.

Jitrik, Noé. 1970. *Ensayos y estudios de literatura argentina*. Buenos Aires: Editorial Galerna.

———. 1980/1985. "El modernismo." *Capítulo, cuadernos de literatura argentina*. Buenos Aires: Centro Editor de América Latina.

Jorge Luis Borges. 1964. Paris: Editions de l'Herne.

Josephson, Matthew. 1962. *Life among the Surrealists*. New York: Holt, Rinehart and Winston.

Juin, Hubert. 1960. *Aragon*. Paris: Gallimard.

Karl, Frederick R. 1985. *Modern and Modernism: The Sovereignty of the Artist 1885–1925*. New York: Atheneum.

Kermode, Frank. 1985. *Forms of Attention*. Chicago: University of Chicago Press.

———. 1988. *History and Value*. Oxford: Clarendon Press.

King, John. 1984. "Civilization and Barbarism: The Impact of Europe on Argentina." *History Today* 34 (August):16–21.

———. 1986. *Sur: A Study of the Argentine Literary Journal and Its Role in the Development of a Culture, 1931–1970*. Cambridge: Cambridge University Press.

Larra, Raúl. 1978. *Leónidas Barletta: El hombre de la campaña*. Buenos Aires: Ediciones Conducta.

Leavis, F. R. 1943. "The Liberation of Poetry." Review of *Auden and After* by Francis Scarfe. *Scrutiny* 11:212–15.

———. [1932] 1960. *New Bearings in English Poetry*. Ann Arbor: University of Michigan Press.

Lehman, John, ed. 1936. *New Writing*. London: Bodley Head.

Lehmann, John. 1940. *New Writing in Europe*. Harmondsworth: Allen Lane.

———. 1955. *The Whispering Gallery*. London: Longmans.

Leland, Christopher Towne. 1986. *The Last Happy Men: The Generation of 1922, Fiction, and the Argentine Reality*. Syracuse: Syracuse University Press.

Lemaître, Henri. 1984. *L'aventure littéraire du XXe siècle: 1920–1960*. Paris: Pierre Bordas et fils.

Leonard, Albert. 1974. *La crise du concept de littérature en France au XXe siècle*. Paris: José Corti.

Lerner, Lía Schwartz, and Isaías Lerner, eds. 1984. *Homenaje a Ana María Barrenechea*. Madrid: Editorial Castalia.

Lewis, Helena. 1988. *The Politics of Surrealism*. New York: Paragon House.

Littérature. 1919–24.

Llagostera, María Raquel. 1987. *Boedo y Florida*. Buenos Aires: Centro Editor de América Latina.

Loprete, Carlos Alberto. 1976. *La literatura modernista en la argentina*. Buenos Aires: Editorial Plus Ultra.

Lourau, René. 1967. "André Breton et la *N.R.F.*" *Nouvelle Revue Française* (April):909–17.

Lugones, Leopoldo. [1909] 1961. *Lunario sentimental*. Buenos Aires: Editorial Centurion.

MacNeice, Louis. 1937. "Subject in Modern Poetry." In *Essays and Studies by Members of the English Association*, 22:144–58. Oxford: Clarendon Press.

———. 1948. "English Poetry To-day." *The Listener* 40 (2 September).

———. 1949. *Collected Poems, 1925–1948*. London: Faber and Faber.

———. 1959. *Eighty-Five Poems*. New York: Oxford University Press.

———. 1965. *The Strings Are False: An Unfinished Autobiography*. London: Faber and Faber.

———. 1967. *The Collected Poems of Louis MacNeice*. Edited by E. R. Dodds. New York: Oxford University Press.

———. [1938] 1968. *Modern Poetry*. 2d ed. Oxford: Clarendon Press.

———. 1987. *The Selected Literary Criticism of Louis MacNeice*. Edited by Alan Heuser. Oxford: Clarendon Press.

Mallea, Eduardo. 1935. "El escritor de hoy frente a su tiempo." *Sur* 12 (September). Reprint, *Sur* 354 (January–June 1984).

———. 1945. *Historia de una pasión argentina*. 4th ed. Buenos Aires: Espasa-Calpe Argentina.

Marsack, Robyn. 1982. *The Cave of Making: The Poetry of Louis MacNeice*. Oxford: Clarendon Press.

Martín Fierro. 1924–27.

Martínez Estrada, Ezequiel. 1933. *Radiografía de la pampa*. Buenos Aires: Babel.

Masiello, Francine. 1986. *Lenguaje e ideología: las escuelas argentinas de vanguardia*. Buenos Aires: Hachette.

Mastronardi, Carlos. 1980/1986. "El movimiento de 'Martín Fierro.'" *Historia de la literatura argentina: Los proyectos de la vanguardia*. Buenos Aires: Centro Editor de América Latina.

Matamoro, Blas. 1971. *Jorge Luis Borges o el juego trascendente*. Buenos Aires: A. Peña Lillo.

———. 1975. *Oligarquía y literatura*. Buenos Aires: Ediciones del Sol.

———. 1986. *Genio y figura de Victoria Ocampo*. Buenos Aires: Editorial Universitaria de Buenos Aires.

Matthews, J. H. 1967. *André Breton*. New York: Columbia University Press.

Maxwell, D. E. S. 1969. *The Poets of the Thirties*. London: Routledge and Kegan Paul.

McDiarmid, Lucy. 1984. *Saving Civilization: Yeats, Eliot, and Auden Between the Wars*. Cambridge: Cambridge University Press.

McFarland, Thomas. 1987. *Shapes of Culture*. Iowa City: University of Iowa Press.

Mendelson, Edward. 1983. *Early Auden*. Cambridge: Harvard University Press.

Méndez, Evar. 1927. "Doce poetas nuevas." *Síntesis* 1, no. 4 (September):15–33.

Méndez, Jesus. 1981. "The Origins of *Sur*, Argentina's Elite Cultural Review." *Revista Interamericana de Bibliografía* 31, no. 1:3–15.

Meneses, Carlos. 1978. *Poesía juvenil de J. L. Borges*. Barcelona: José Olañeta.

Meyer, Doris. 1981. *Victoria Ocampo: Contra viento y marea*. Buenos Aires: Editorial Sudamericana.

Minotaure. 1933–36.

Moore, D. B. 1972. *The Poetry of Louis MacNeice*. Leicester: Leicester University Press.

Morales, Angel Luis. 1967. *Literatura Hispanoamericana*. Vol. 2. Puerto Rico: Editorial del Departamento de Instrucción Pública.

Mulhern, Francis. 1979. *The Moment of "Scrutiny."* London: NLB.

Munoz, Maryse Bertrand de. 1972. *La guerre civile espagnole et la littérature française*. Ottawa: Didier.

Muschietti, Delfina. 1985. "La fractura ideológica en los primeros textos de Oliverio Girondo." *Filología* 20, no. 1:153–69.

Nadeau, Maurice. [1944] 1989. *The History of Surrealism*. New York: Macmillan.

New Verse. 1933–39.

New Writing. 1936. Edited by John Lehmann. London: John Lane/The Bodley Head.

Noé, Julio. 1927. "La poesía argentina moderna." *Nosotros* 219–20:69–74.

Norris, Christopher. 1978. *William Empson and the Philosophy of Literary Criticism*. London: Athlone.

Nugent, Robert. 1974. *Paul Eluard*. New York: Twayne.

Ocampo, Victoria. 1946. *Testimonios*. 3d ser. Buenos Aires: Editorial Sudamericana.

———. 1975. *Testimonios*. 9th ser., 1971–74. Buenos Aires: Ediciones Sur.

———. 1981. *Testimonios*. 2d ser., 1937–40. Buenos Aires: Ediciones Sur.

———. 1984. *Autobiografía VI: Sur y cía*. Buenos Aires: Ediciones Revista Sur.

Ortega y Gasset, José. 1985. *La rebelión de las masas*. Barcelona: Editorial Planeta-De Agostini.

Orwell, George. 1952. *Homage to Catalonia*. San Diego: Harcourt Brace Jovanovich.

———. 1961. *The Road to Wigan Pier*. New York: Berkley.

———. 1968. *An Age Like This, 1920–1940*. Edited by Sonia Orwell and Ian Angus. Vol. 1. New York: Harcourt Brace Jovanovich.

Oxford Poetry. 1927/1929. London: Basil Blackwell.

Panesi, Jorge. 1985. "Cultura, crítica y pedagogía en la Argentina: *Sur/Contorno.*" *Espacios de crítica y producción* 2 (July–August):13–17.

Partridge, A. C. 1976. *The Language of Modern Poetry: Yeats, Eliot, Auden.* London: André Deutsch.

Pérez, Alberto Julián. 1986. *Poética de la prosa de J. L. Borges.* Madrid: Editorial Gredos.

Perkins, David. 1976. *A History of Modern Poetry: From the 1890s to Pound, Eliot, and Yeats.* Cambridge: The Belknap Press of Harvard University Press.

———. 1987. *A History of Modern Poetry: Modernism and After.* Cambridge: The Belknap Press of Harvard University Press.

Peyre, Henri. 1938. *Hommes et oeuvres du XXe siècle.* Paris: Editions R.-A. Corrêa.

Pezzoni, Enrique. 1952. "Aproximación al último libro de Borges." *Sur* 217–18 (November–December):101–23.

———. 1986. *El texto y sus voces.* Buenos Aires: Editorial Sudamericana.

Pierre, Jose. 1986. "Du surréalisme agi." *Etudes littéraires* 19, no. 2:35–44.

"Poemas ultraístas." 1922. *Nosotros* 160:55–62.

Poggioli, Renato. 1968. *The Theory of the Avant-Garde.* Translated by Gerald Fitzgerald. Cambridge: The Belknap Press of Harvard University Press.

Prieto, Adolfo. 1954. *Borges y la nueva generación.* Buenos Aires: Letras Universitarias.

———. 1968. *Literatura y subdesarrollo.* Rosario, Argentina: Editorial Biblioteca.

Prisma. 1921–22.

Pritchard, William H. 1988. "'Auden and Co.' The Balance Sheet." Review of *History and Value* by Frank Kermode. *New York Times Book Review* (17 July):14–15.

Proa. 1924–25.

———. 1983. (1924–25), Edición facsimilar de los números 1, 6, 8, 14. Buenos Aires: Centro Editor de América Latina.

Rabinow, Paul, ed. 1984. *The Foucault Reader.* New York: Pantheon.

Racevskis, Karlis. 1980. "The Discourse of Michel Foucault: A Case of an Absent and Forgettable Subject." *Humanities in Society* 3:41–53.

———. 1983. *Michel Foucault and the Subversion of Intellect.* Ithaca: Cornell University Press.

Raillard, Georges. 1964. *Aragon.* Paris: Editions Universitaires.

Raymond, Marcel. [1933] 1970. *From Baudelaire to Surrealism.* London: Methuen.

Replogle, Justin. 1964. "The Auden Group." *Wisconsin Studies in Contemporary Literature* 5:133–50.

———. 1965. "Auden's Marxism." *PMLA* 80, no. 12:584–95.

———. 1969. *Auden's Poetry.* Seattle: University of Washington Press.

———. 1986. "The Pattern of Personae." In Bloom (1986), 22–38.

Revista Martín Fierro. 1969. (1924–1927). Edited by Beatriz Sarlo Sabajanes. Buenos Aires: Carlos Pérez.

La révolution surréaliste. 1924–29.

Reynaud, Louis. 1929. *La crise de notre littérature.* Paris: Librairie Hachette.

Richards, I. A. [1925] n.d. *Principles of Literary Criticism.* New York: Harcourt Brace Jovanovich.

Riddel, Joseph N. 1971. *C. Day Lewis.* New York: Twayne.

Riding, Laura, and Robert Graves. 1927. *A Survey of Modernist Poetry.* London: Heinemann.

Rivera, Jorge B. 1985a. "El auge de la industria cultural (1930–1955)." *Capítulo 3: Cuadernos de la literature argentina.* Buenos Aires: Centro Editor de América Latina.

———. 1985b. "El escritor y la industria cultural." *Capítulo 3: Cuadernos de la literatura argentina.* Buenos Aires: Centro Editor de América Latina.

Roberts, Michael, ed. 1932. *New Signatures: Poems by Several Hands.* London: Hogarth.

———. 1934. *Critique of Poetry.* London: Jonathan Cape.

———. [1933] 1971. *New Country: Poems and Poetry by the Authors of New Signatures.* Reprint, Freeport, N.Y.: Books for Libraries.

———. ed. [1936] 1982. *The Faber Book of Modern Verse.* London: Faber and Faber.

———. 1980. *Selected Poems and Prose.* Edited by Frederick Grubb. Manchester: Carcanet.

Rock, David. 1987. "Intellectual Precursors of Conservative Nationalism in Argentina, 1900–1927." *Hispanic American Historical Review* 67, no. 2:271–300.

Rodríguez Monegal, Emir. 1978. *Jorge Luis Borges: A Literary Biography.* New York: Dutton.

———. 1973. "Symbols in Borges' Work." *Modern Fiction Studies* 19 (Autumn):325–40.

Rodway, Allan. 1984. *A Preface to Auden.* London: Longman.

Rogers, Timothy, ed. 1977. *Georgian Poetry, 1911–1922: The Critical Heritage.* London: Routledge and Kegan Paul.

Romano, Eduardo. 1980. "Julio Cortázar frente a Borges y el grupo de la revista 'Sur.'" *Cuadernos Hispanoamericanos* 364–66 (October–December):106–38.

Rosa, Nicolás. 1971. "*Sur*, o el espíritu y la letra." *Los Libros* 2, nos. 15–16:4–6.

Rosemont, Franklin. 1978. *André Breton and the First Principles of Surrealism.* London: Pluto.

Ross, Robert H. 1965. *The Georgian Revolt, 1910–1922: Rise and Fall of a Poetic Ideal.* Carbondale: Southern Illinois University Press.

Rowse, A. L. 1987. *The Poet Auden: A Personal Memoir.* New York: Weidenfeld and Nicolson.

Running, Thorpe. 1981. *Borges' Ultraist Movement*. Lathrup Village, Mich.: International Book Publishers.

Said, Edward W. 1983. *The World, the Text, and the Critic*. Cambridge: Harvard University Press.

Sarlo, Beatriz. 1980/1985. "La poesía postmodernista." *Capítulo, cuadernos de literatura argentina: el modernismo*, 97–120. Buenos Aires: Centro Editor de América Latina.

———. 1981. "Sobre la vanguardia, Borges y el criollismo." In A. Barrenechea, N. Jitrik, J. Rest, et al. (1981), 1:73–74.

Scarfe, Francis. 1942. *Auden and After: The Liberation of Poetry, 1930–1941*. London: Routledge.

Scholes, Robert, 1985. *Textual Power: Literary Theory and the Teaching of English*. New Haven: Yale University Press.

———. 1989. *Protocols of Reading*. New Haven: Yale University Press.

Schwartz, Delmore. 1939. "The Two Audens." *Kenyon Review* 1 (Winter):34–45.

Schwartz, Jorge. 1979. *Vanguardia y cosmopolitismo en la década del veinte: Oliverio Girondo y Oswald de Andrade*. Ph.D. diss., Universidade de São Paulo, Brazil. Ann Arbor: University Microfilms International.

———, ed. 1987. *Homenaje a Girondo*. Buenos Aires: Ediciones Corregidor.

Schwartz, Sanford. 1985. *The Matrix of Modernism: Pound, Eliot and Early Twentieth-Century Thought*. Princeton: Princeton University Press.

Seif, Morton. 1954. "The Impact of T. S. Eliot on Auden and Spender." *South Atlantic Quarterly* 53:61–69.

Senkman, Leonardo. 1987. *Etnicidad y literatura en los años 20: Jacobo Fijman en las letras argentinas*. Vols. 4–6. Río de la Plata: Culturas.

Shattuck, Roger. 1961. *The Banquet Years: The Arts in France 1885–1918*. New York: Anchor.

———. 1960. *The Innocent Eye*. New York: Farrar, Straus and Giroux.

Simmel, Georg. 1968. *The Conflict in Modern Culture and Other Essays*. Translated by K. Peter Etzkorn. New York: Teachers College Press.

———. 1971. *On Individuality and Social Forms*. Edited by Donald N. Levine. Chicago: University of Chicago Press.

Skelton, Robin. 1964. *Poetry of the Thirties*. Middlesex, England: Penguin.

Smith, Barbara Herrnstein. 1988. *Contingencies of Value: Alternative Perspectives for Critical Theory*. Cambridge: Harvard University Press.

Smith, Edward Elton. 1970. *Louis MacNeice*. New York: Twayne.

Smith, Stan. 1985. *W. H. Auden*. Oxford: Basil Blackwell.

Sola, Graciela de. 1967. *Proyecciones del surrealismo en la literatura argentina*. Buenos Aires: Ediciones culturales argentinas.

Somville, Léon. 1971. *Devanciers du surréalisme: Les groupes d'avant-garde et le mouvement poétique, 1912–1925*. Geneva: Droz.

Soupault, Philippe. 1937. *Poésies complètes, 1917–1937*. Paris: GLM.

————. 1967. "Souvenirs." *Nouvelle Revue Française* (April):660–71.

Spender, Stephen. [1933] 1934a. *Poems*. New York: Random House.

————. 1934b. *Vienna*. London: Faber and Faber.

————. 1935. *The Destructive Element*. London: Jonathan Cape.

————. 1937. *Forward from Liberalism*. New York: Random House.

————. 1953a. *The Creative Element: A Study of Vision, Despair and Orthodoxy Among Some Modern Writers*. London: Hamish Hamilton.

————. 1953b. *World Within World*. London: Readers Union.

————. 1964. "An English Writer's Experience of the 1930's." *New Hungarian Quarterly* 5 (Winter):87–92.

————. 1966. "Remembering Eliot." *Sewanee Review* 74 (Winter).

————. 1978. *The Thirties and After*. London: Macmillan.

————. 1980. *Letters to Christopher*. Edited by Lee Bartlett. Santa Barbara, Calif.: Black Sparrow.

————. 1986. *Collected Poems, 1928–1985*. New York: Oxford University Press.

Spender, Stephen, and John Lehmann, eds. 1939. *Poems for Spain*. London: Hogarth Press.

Sprinker, Michael. 1980. "The Use and Abuse of Foucault." *Humanities in Society* 3:1–21.

Stansky, Peter, and William Abrahams. 1966. *Journey to the Frontier: Two Roads to the Spanish Civil War*. Chicago: University of Chicago Press.

Suleiman, Susan Rubin. 1990. *Subversive Intent: Gender, Politics, and the Avant-Garde*. Cambridge: Harvard University Press.

Sur. 1931–70.

Le surréalisme au service de la révolution, 1930–33.

Symons, Julian. 1960. *The Thirties: A Dream Resolved*. London: Cresset.

Thomson, David. 1965. *England in the Twentieth Century, 1914–1963*. Baltimore: Penguin.

Tison-Braun, Micheline. 1983. "*Traité du style* et style du traité." *L'Esprit créateur* 23, no. 4:51–61.

Tolley, A. T. 1968. "The Thirties Poets at Oxford." *University of Toronto Quarterly* 37:338–58.

Torres, Juan B. Aguilar, et al. 1964. *Lugones: cuaderno de homenaje*. Buenos Aires: Grupo Editor Argentina.

Ulla, Noemí, ed. 1969. *La revista Nosotros*. Buenos Aires: Editorial Galerna.

Vázquez, María Esther. 1980. "Victoria Ocampo, una argentina universalista." *Revista Iberoamericana* 110–11 (January–June):167–75.

————, ed. 1984. *Borges: Sus días y su tiempo*. Buenos Aires: Javier Vergara.

Verani, Hugo J. 1990. *Las vanguardias literarias en hispanoamérica*. Mexico: Fondo de Cultura Económico.

Villordo, Oscar Hermes. 1983. *Genio y figura de Adolfo Bioy Casares*. Buenos Aires: Editorial Universitaria de Buenos Aires.

Viñas, David. 1965. *Del apogeo de la oligarquía a la crisis de la ciudad liberal: La ferrère*. Buenos Aires: Editorial Jorge Alvarez.

————. 1971. *Literatura argentina y realidad política: De Sarmiento a Cortázar*. Buenos Aires: Ediciones Siglo Veinte.

Wallard, Daniel. 1979. *Aragon: un portrait*. Paris: Editions Cercle d'Art.

Ward, A. C. n.d. *Twentieth-Century English Literature, 1901–1960*. New York: Barnes and Noble. (First published in 1928 as *Twentieth-Century Literature, 1901–1925*.)

Warley, Jorge A. 1985. *Vida cultural e intelectuales en la década de 1930*. Buenos Aires: Centro Editor de América Latina.

Watson, George. 1977. *Politics and Literature in Modern Britain*. Totowa, N.J.: Rowman and Littlefield.

Weatherhead, A. Kingsley. 1975. *Stephen Spender and the Thirties*. London: Associated University Presses.

White, Hayden. 1978. *Tropics of Discourse: Essays in Cultural Criticism*. Baltimore: Johns Hopkins University Press.

Whitehead, John. 1965. "Auden: An Early Poetical Notebook." *London Magazine*, n.s., 5, no. 2:85–93.

Wilson, Edmund. 1977. *Letters on Literature and Politics, 1912–1972*. Edited by Elena Wilson. Introduction by Daniel Aaron. Foreword by Leon Edel. New York: Farrar, Straus and Giroux.

Wright, George T. 1969. *W. H. Auden*. New York: Twayne.

Index

Bell, Julian, 139, 143, 161
Benda, Julien, 25–26, 55, 98
Benjamin, Walter, 29, 153–54, 176, 195
Berkeley, George, 79, 85, 271
binarisms/binary logic, 10, 30–32, 55,
    57, 158, 164, 194, 203, 213, 215, 225,
    245, 256, 257, 260, 267, 281, 283
Bioy Casares, Adolfo, 113
Bloom, Harold, 23, 126
Bloom, Robert, 207
Bloomsbury, 128–29
Boedo vs. Florida, 10, 16, 33, 52, 55–60,
    58, 70, 72–74, 80–83, 85–90, 102,
    104, 112–14, 127, 176, 234
Borges, Jorge Luis, 6, 7, 16, 43, 44, 47,
    58–59, 64, 65, 71–91, 96, 98–99, 112–
    19, 138, 157, 210, 246, 271–72, 288,
    290
    fiction, 112–14
    poetry, 10, 80–83, 85–90
    Fervor de Buenos Aires, 16, 74, 78,
        79, 85–87, 91
    El idioma de los argentinos, 78
    Inquisiciones, 78, 89
    Leopoldo Lugones, 79
    Luna de enfrente, 85
    Los naipes del tahúr, 78
    Obras completas, 86, 89
    Otras inquisiciones, 76, 85
    El tamaño de mi esperanza, 75, 78
Borges, Jorge Luis, and Adolfo Bioy
    Casares, *Seis relatos para don Isidro
    Parodi*, 113
Bové, Paul, 36, 38, 130, 207–8
Breton, André, 24, 33, 63, 77, 138, 216,
    221–40, 253–54, 258, 283, 266, 267,
    289
    poetry, 221–22, 240–45, 263–64
    Les champs magnétiques, 240
    Claire de terre, 218
    Entretiens, 234

Nadja, 230
Les pas perdus, 218
Ralentir travaux, 241
bourgeois art, 24, 27, 215–16, 291
bourgeoisie, 29, 61, 142, 149–50, 195,
    209, 235, 265, 291
Brooks, Cleanth, 206
Browder, Clifford, 227, 237, 257–58
Brown, Terence, 193–94, 200
Bürger, Peter, 3, 18, 19, 21, 24, 25, 213,
    291, 296

Caillois, Roger, 104
canon and canonization, 2, 35, 119, 184,
    252
capitalism, 13, 30, 151, 280
Caraffa, Brandán, 62
careerism, 130, 139, 233, 239–40, 262
Castillo, Hector, 53
Caws, Mary Ann, 213, 239–40, 250,
    256, 268–75
Carrouges, Michel, 256, 259–60
Cendrars, Blaise, 240
civilization and barbarism, 30–32, 107,
    118, 283
Coates, Willson H., 37
colonialism, 5, 6, 237
commodity, poetry as, 213, 255, 282
communism, 25, 26, 30, 133, 148, 156,
    161, 188, 201, 204, 231, 253, 267, 294,
    295
Communist Party, 108, 144, 146, 147,
    165, 168, 191, 215, 216, 231, 235,
    265–67, 292, 294
Connolly, Cyril, 151–52, 193
conservatism, literary, 3, 6, 95, 130, 281,
    293
Contorno, 111–12
Cornford, John, 139, 161, 182, 284–85
Cortázar, Julio, 115–17
Cowley, Malcolm, 157, 205

Vargas Llosa, Mario, 115
Viñas, David, 51, 53, 58, 104

Warley, Jorge, 104–5, 115
White, Hayden V., 37
Whitman, Walt, 81, 83
women, 66, 107, 229–30, 233, 240, 244, 247–48, 252, 258, 272–73, 279

Woolf, Virginia, 126, 128, 195
World War I, 27, 30, 50, 63, 163, 217, 225, 265
World War II, 12, 15–16, 110–11, 151, 292

Yeats, William Butler, 125, 128, 166